Exploring the
Southern Sierra

Salmon Creek Falls

Exploring the Southern Sierra: East Side

J. C. Jenkins
and
Ruby Johnson Jenkins

Wilderness Press
Berkeley

Jim

Jim was born in Pasadena, California in 1952. He graduated from Beverly Hills High School and received his degree in English from California State University at Northridge. While in college he began his many years of fieldwork in the Southern Sierra backcountry. In 1973 Jim co-authored *The Pacific Crest Trail, Volume 1: California*. He was responsible for the section of trail from the town of Mojave to Mount Whitney. The following year he co-authored the *High Sierra Hiking Guide to Kern Peak-Olancha*.

After five years of gathering material and scouting trails, he completed *Self-Propelled in the Southern Sierra, Volume 1: The Sierra Crest and the Kern Plateau*. The first guidebook to the area, this book received high praise from prestigious sources including the Sierra Club, the *Los Angeles Times, Sunset* magazine and the American Library Association.

The next year, 1979, Jim completed the field and desk work for Volume 2. During these years of book work, university study and conservation activities, he also held summer jobs with the National Park Service and Forest Service. While the second volume of *Self-Propelled in the Southern Sierra* was being printed, Jim, returning to his job as ranger in the Golden Trout Wilderness, was fatally struck by a car driven erratically by an elderly man whose vision and driving ability had greatly diminished.

In 1984 Mount Jenkins, on the Sierra crest where the Pacific Crest Trail winds, was named to honor Jim for his contribution to the Southern Sierra.

James Charles Jenkins
"Jim"
1952–1979

This book is based on the research and writing of J. C. Jenkins' *Self-Propelled in the Southern Sierra, Volume 1: The Sierra Crest and the Kern Plateau,* 1978. All the trails and most of the mountains described in Volume 1 were hiked and climbed several times for this revision, and more trails and mountains have been added. Although much has changed on the Southern Sierra's east side—new wilderness, new trails, new policies, new trips—the original script is retained where possible.

Photo Credits
Pictures by Ruby Johnson Jenkins except for the following:
Robert Luthey: II
Abe Siemens: VIII
Ernest DeGraff (USFS): 2
Beverly Steveson: 4, 6, 26, 27, 84, 104, 107, 115, 178
Lyn Haber: 8, 13, 33 right, 205 top, 221
Bill Jones (NPS): 10
J.C. Jenkins: 29, 56, 72, 79, 80, 86, 101, 105, 109, 113, 120, 125, 147, 152, 192, 206, 224
U.S. Forest Service: 42
Tim Salt (BLM): 61
Jim Osmundsen: 99
Claus Engelhardt: 119
John W. Robinson: 145
W. Harland Boyd Collection: 207

FIRST EDITION May 1978 (entitled *Self-Propelled in the Southern Sierra, Vol. 1: The Sierra Crest and The Kern Plateau*)
SECOND EDITION May 1982
Second printing May 1984
Third printing September 1986
REVISED THIRD EDITION (entitled *Exploring the Southern Sierra: East Side*) January 1992

Cover photo by Ruby Johnson Jenkins *First Light* South Fork Kern National Wild and Scenic River near Strawberry Meadows
Cover design and page production by Michael Batelaan, Lake Design
Book design by Ruby Johnson Jenkins
Printed in the United States of America
A Frontier Trail Book
P.O. Box 1544
Kernville, CA 93238

International Standard Book Number 0-89997-128-8
Library of Congress card number 91-38517

Library of Congress Cataloging-in-Publication Data

Jenkins, J.C. (Jim C.), 1952-1979
   Exploring the Southern Sierra, east side / J.C. Jenkins and Ruby Johnson Jenkins. — Rev. 3rd ed.
     p.   cm.
   Rev. ed. of: Self-propelled in the Southern Sierra. Vol. 1. c1978.
   Includes bibliographical references (p.) and index.
   ISBN 0-89997-128-8
    1. Hiking—Sierra Nevada (Calif. and Nev.)—Guide-books.
   2. Outdoor recreation—Sierra Nevada (Calif. and Nev.)—Guide-books.
   3. Sierra Nevada (Calif. and Nev.)—Description and travel— Guide-books. I. Jenkins, Ruby Johnson. II. Jenkins, J.C. (Jim C.), 1952-1979. Self-propelled in the Southern Sierra. III. Title.
GV199.42.S55J46   1991
917.94'4—dc20   91-38517
                                          CIP

Acknowledgements

Mount Jenkins

My husband Bill, our daughter Jan and I are grateful to the many people who gave their time in support of naming a mountain to honor our Jim. Tom Winnett, publisher of Wilderness Press, suggested the project and accomplished the preliminary work. Steve Smith recommended the mountain that was selected, which is on Bureau of Land Management (BLM) governed land. Tim Salt and Steve, both with BLM, secured that agency's approval. Paul Lipsohn ably coordinated the effort and the late Gayle and Ardis Walker organized the letter-writing campaign. The U.S. Board on Geographic Names saw the merit of the project and approved the name "Mount Jenkins" for a Southern Sierra mountain in December, 1984.

Exploring the Southern Sierra: East Side

I am thankful to those who encouraged me to continue Jim's effort to introduce people to the beautiful Southern Sierra and to inform them of its history, both geological and human, and of its flora, fauna and preservation. While doing fieldwork for this book, I appreciated the companionship of friends who accompanied me on several backpack trips: Pat Clark, Ellen Halpin, Mae Osmundsen, Bonnie Strand, Bob Tollefson and my husband Bill, who referred to himself as my "Sherpa." On day hikes, my thanks for the company of the Kern River Valley Hiking Club members. When I needed expert advice on trails, policies and backcountry conditions, I received unstinting help from Jim Jennings of BLM, Mike Mendoza of Sequoia National Forest and Bob Olin of Inyo National Forest. In the process of producing this book, Tom Winnett graciously advised me along each step of the way; Lyn Haber skillfully edited the text and her suggestions improved my writing; Jeff Schaffer taught me the art of map overlays and designed the basic Southern Sierra map; Bob Tollefson loaned me numerous books and maps from his extensive library; and Bill mastered microwave cooking.

My family and I and the people who helped all dedicate this book in memory of Jim to those who use it on their odysseys in the Southern Sierra.

Ruby Johnson Jenkins

Olancha Peak beyond Monache Meadow from Smith Mountain

Contents

Part 1   Presenting the Southern Sierra: East Side

Part 2   Adventures in the Southern Sierra: East Side
Section 1   Highway 58 to Highway 178

Section 2 Highway 178 to Nine Mile Canyon/Kennedy Meadows/Sherman Pass Road

Section 3 Nine Mile Canyon/Kennedy Meadows/Sherman Pass Road to Horseshoe Meadow Road and Golden Trout Wilderness North Border

Part 3   Appendix

Part 1
Presenting the Southern Sierra: East Side

Chicken Spring Lake

Chapter 1: Attributes

Geographers disagree on the southern terminus of the Sierra Nevada Range: some include the Tehachapi Mountains, while others contend they are two separate land forms divided by Tehachapi Pass and delineated by State Highway 58.

This book's coverage includes the Sierra Nevada north of Highway 58 and west of highways 14 and 395, plus a few side trips into the desert. The Pacific Crest Trail, the east slopes of the Piute Mountains, and the North Fork Kern River comprise the west boundary. The north boundary, around 7.0 air miles south of Mount Whitney, coincides with the north border of Golden Trout Wilderness. This defines the Southern Sierra's east side.

The trips in this book invite you to explore unusual desert features, high desert terrain and mountain wilderness; to walk along paths traveled by Native Americans and poke around mines excavated by gold rush men of yore. Car and bicycle tours and day hikes touch a myriad of mountain meadows; wind through oak and pine forests; skirt slender streams, meandering and tumultuous rivers; and cross scenic mountain passes. Mountain climbs offer rugged cross-country routes to numerous peaks for experienced hikers and climbers, while backpack and equestrian trips probe the wilderness interiors for the enjoyment of robust outdoor enthusiasts. Nordic ski tours are not excluded as many of the trips described for summer activity can easily be converted to wintertime cross-country journeys. These various trips take place on or around the east side of the vast Southern Sierra, a lightly traveled, hospitable country with many special attractions.

Kern Plateau   *Before the Sierra*
Nevada tumbles to its Southern
terminus, it has one final fling of
high-country splendor known as
the Kern Plateau.
      Sunset magazine, June 1980
The majority of the trips in this book are located on this high plateau, which stretches north of Highway 178 to the far border of

Golden Trout Wilderness, between Highway 395 and the North Fork Kern River. This block of vast tableland, about 900 square miles of lush meadows, conifer-clad mountains, and craggy peaks, was left untouched by the carving actions of ice-age glaciers. Within this country are three federally designated wildernesses: Dome Land, South Sierra and Golden Trout. To the east, the Owens Peak, Sacatar Meadows and Little Lake Canyon Study Areas, all on or near the sharp ridges of the Sierra crest, were recommended by the Bureau of Land Management for wilderness, approved by President Bush in 1991, and now await approval by Congress.

Dome Land Wilderness   This 94,695-acre wilderness, the oldest of the three, occupies the center of the southern end of the plateau. As the name implies, the numerous granite domes, obelisks and other monoliths—a rockclimber's heaven—dominate the gentle streams, pines and meadows of this wilderness. As you journey east from Manter Meadow (7020') to Rockhouse Basin (5540'), the wilderness becomes increasingly arid. But even in the hot, dry basin there are streams and the curvaceous South Fork Kern River—watercourses favored by fly-fishermen.

To the south, still in Dome Land Wilderness, the river plunges through the "Roughs," a stretch of wild, precipitous cliffs and massive boulders between Rockhouse Basin and South Fork Valley—rumored to be a stronghold of rattlesnakes. This section is visited only by the most daring adventurer. The antithesis of the "Roughs" is the well-watered valley of virgin pines in the pocket between the Sirretta-Sherman peaks ridge and the northwest border of Dome Land Wilderness. This valley was not included in the wilderness because of its harvestable timber, but it deserves protection and inclusion. The ridge above the valley would mark a better defined boundary line than does the existing border.

South Sierra Wilderness   North of Sher-

man Pass/Kennedy Meadows Road, sandwiched between Dome Land and Golden
Trout wildernesses, this newest (1984) and
smallest (63,000 acres) wilderness filled a
missing link in a chain of federally protected
land along the Sierra. Ranging in elevation
from 6100 feet to 12,123 feet, this pristine
land boasts the stateliest aspen grove on the
Kern Plateau, the grove at Hooker Meadow,
and shares with Golden Trout Wilderness the
highest mountain, Olancha Peak. Meadows,
springs, and pine forests of predominately
pinyon pine, are abundant in this wilderness.
Here, too, flows the sensuous South Fork
Kern River.

Bordered on three sides by wilderness, but
excluded from protection is Monache
Meadow, the largest meadow in the Sierra.
Sagebrush and its ilk are gradually replacing
the meadow grasses, and OHV tracks scar
the land. With work this meadow can be
returned to its former grassy expanse, but it
needs special care and should be included in
South Sierra Wilderness.

Golden Trout Wilderness   Before the late
1940s, the only way you could reach the

gentle Kern Plateau was on foot, on animal,
on the rudimentary Nine Mile Canyon Road,
or on a breathtaking flight in a small aircraft.
Then logging began in the southern part,
slowly pushing northward. The loggers'
roads opened the land to jeeps and their
cousins, motorcycles. All these intrusions
resulted in slope erosion, damaged meadows,
and silted streams. Led and inspired by the
late Ardis and Gayle Walker, environmentalists successfully campaigned to protect the remaining land: in 1978 President
Carter signed into law the 306,916-acre
Golden Trout Wilderness, the ancestral
home of the golden trout—California's state
fish.

Over half of this wilderness is located on
the Kern Plateau, comprising all the plateau
land north of Sequoia/Inyo National Forest
and South Sierra Wilderness borders. In this
spacious open country, hikers and equestrians can travel for days and see nary a
person. Among the mountains this land hosts
are the rugged twin peaks of Olancha and
Kern, which anchor the east and west sides of
the plateau, and Cirque Peak, which anchors

Removal of nonnative fish by electroshock

the north Wilderness border. Numerous creeks tumble down the pine-clad slopes of the mountains to thread the velvety meadows below. In these clear waters live the beautiful golden trout.

The plateau golden trout, blending with the colorful volcanic and granitic rocks that line creek and river beds, has a brilliant red to orange belly that extends up its sides and glitters like a gold nugget in the dappled light of cold, pure streams. For thousands of years this trout thrived in its habitat on the Kern Plateau, while its sister species, Little Kern golden trout, lived successfully west of Kern Canyon in the Little Kern River watershed. But in the 1930s, man stocked the streams, where golden trout lived, with nonnative trout to increase fishing opportunities. The more aggressive introduced fish nearly wiped out the goldens.

Three important steps have been taken to restore both golden trout species. In the 1970s, an extensive program began to remove nonnative and hybrid fish by electroshock and chemicals. Simultaneously, propagation of pure golden trout strains began in fish hatcheries. When the fish matured, they were placed in their natural habitats. In 1977 the Little Kern golden was listed as a federally endangered species. The program of restoration continues for both golden trout species.

Wild and Scenic Kern Rivers In 1968 the Wild and Scenic Rivers Act became a federal law. It was established to preserve the natural settings of rivers which possessed remarkable characteristics. In 1987 Congress approved the inclusion of the North and South Forks of the Kern River in this prestigious system.

The North Fork Kern River begins as droplets from snowfields high above timberline on glaciated, craggy slopes of the Kings-Kern Divide. The snowmelt merges to become slender rills, then rivulets, then gathers neighboring creeks to become a river, then rushes south for 83 miles from 12,800 feet to Lake Isabella at 2600 feet. It is one of the steepest and swiftest rivers in North America. Of this magnificent river, named

for General Fremont's cartographer Edward M. Kern, 78.5 miles, embracing some of the most spectacular scenery in the Sierra, came under the aegis of the Rivers Act.

The Act protects 72.5 miles of the South Fork, whose headwaters begin on the slopes of Trail Peak in the Golden Trout Wilderness. From there the South Fork glides hither and yon across the Kern Plateau, missing little along its unhurried way, more a creek than a river. This placid stream takes on a different character during snowmelt when it swells to overflow its confining banks and hurries to a roaring plunge off the southern rim of the Kern Plateau. Then the river leaves its protective status, turns abruptly west where a web of ditches tap much of the water to irrigate the South Fork Valley. What remains of the South Fork Kern River enters the reservoir of Lake Isabella.

Whitewater Rafting, Kayaking and Canoeing These Kern River activities are the fastest growing sports in the Southern Sierra. Commercial rafting began in earnest in 1980, and has tripled since then. River rapids with incongruous names such as "Joe's Diner" and "Betty's Bakery" to brazen tags such as "Bombs Away" and "Sock-em-Dog" are rated from Class I, few riffles, small waves, to Class V, long violent rapids, dangerous drops and unstable eddies. Outfitters in Kern River Valley offer one-hour trips on a 3.0 mile run to four-day trips on the Forks of the Kern run, and all combinations of trips in between. The hour trip introduces participants from six years old on, to the thrill of running Class I & II rapids, and to the excitement of paddling and navigating the rafts. The four day trip on the Forks of the Kern's 21-mile journey is perhaps the most demanding stretch of whitewater commercially run in California. The wildly scenic section of river south of the Forks drops 60 feet per second, offering a continuous adventure of Class IV & V rapids.

Kayaking and canoeing on the Kern River have become world renowned. Teams from Great Britain, Italy and Canada have trained on the Kern. Each spring since the late 1960s competitive slalom races have been run on

Kayaker on North Fork Kern River

the river in the Kernville area. Members of the U.S. Slalom team honed their skills for the 1972 Olympics on the Kern River; and many Olympic team members will take experience gained here to the 1992 Games in Spain. Besides these world-class kayakers and canoeists, numerous noncompetitors enjoy the sport here. Classes are offered by outfitters so that private rafters as well as kayakers and canoeists can ply these waters safely.

Swimming and Tubing The Kern River can be dangerous to people who enjoy these sports. Its deceptive currents, eddies and underwater snags, especially on the lower Kern, are not understood by visitors. The Forest Service can recommend safe areas and safe times for swimming and tubing in the Kern River.

Rubber Ducky Regatta And, yes, there is the Annual Rubber Ducky Race each summer on the North Fork Kern River!!

Fishing Years ago the Kern River was known for its large, native Kern River rain-bow trout, a subspecies of rainbow trout. One fisherman indicated they used to talk pounds, not inches in those days. In those earlier days, the Kern River rainbow, so favored by anglers, was transplanted to trout waters around the world. In New Zealand today, this fish flourishes, while in its native Kern River it flounders—but there is hope. Because of habitat alterations, overharvesting and intro-duction of nonnative trout, the pure strain was thought to be extinct here. However, through genetic analysis methods developed in the 1970s, it was discovered that Kern River rainbow trout still exist above the Forks of the Kern.

A program to restore Kern River rainbow trout for fly-fishing above Johnsondale Bridge, 19.6 miles north of Kernville, and to return the Kern River north of that point to a prime wild trout fishery, was begun in 1990 by the California Department of the Fish and Game (CFG). This requires special regula-tions and will take a number of years to accomplish.

Surveys taken by CFG since 1984 indicate that nearly all anglers questioned support a wild trout program above Johnsondale Bridge, and the majority of them would like to see it extended to the Edison diversion dam.

If this program is extended to the dam, CFG will increase fish planting (put and take) below the dam for bait anglers, probably with brown trout which thrive in less than cold water, and introduce a method to reduce squawfish predation there. This will make fishing on the entire North Fork Kern River a quality experience for fly and bait fishermen alike.

On the Kern Plateau, according to a few long time local residents, formerly you could camp each night at a stream with bountiful native trout while traveling the length and breadth of the plateau. This experience diminished with the disruption of habitat by logging and grazing, and overharvesting by anglers, but here, too, restoration programs have begun.

National Trails A study indicated that, next to driving, walking was American's most pleasurable sport. Noting that, Congress passed the National Trails System Act in 1968. As a twofold act it included National Recreation Trails for short to medium length trails, often near metropolitan areas, and National Scenic Trails for long, back-country trails.

Cannell Trail, 33E32, which climbs the mountains east of Kernville off Sierra Way, is a National Recreation Trail. This multiuse trail crosses a variety of fascinating terrain, and offers eye-catching vistas of Kern River Valley and Big Meadow basin. But logging roads have segmented the trail, and intense trailside logging has marred its scenic beauty. Now just the first 8.5 miles qualify as a National Recreation Trail.

The Pacific Crest Trail (PCT) and its eastern sister, the Appalachian Trail, were the first two National Scenic Trails. Constructing these scenic trails was a major accomplishment and an example of far-sighted planning, which will be enjoyed by generations to come. The 2700-mile PCT extends from Mexico to Canada. This hiking and riding path stays under a 15% grade so that most everyone can enjoy at least a part of it. Motorized vehicles are forbidden on it. Trips in this book describe the 180-mile section of the PCT from Mojave to Sequoia National Park.

Cross-Country Skiing Cross-country skiing is permitted throughout Sequoia and Inyo national forests, but there are no easy accesses to skiable snow on these forests in the eastern Southern Sierra. Lengthy hikes on patchy snow are often required after you leave your car at snowline. This may change on Sequoia National Forest. In 1990 Cannell Meadow Ranger District began developing a plan for improving winter sports on the plateau.

Current wintertime road accessibility to the Kern Plateau is as follows: On the east side, Nine Mile Canyon Road is kept open to Kennedy Meadows. The road gate 2.3 miles beyond the South Fork Kern River bridge is closed. Horseshoe Meadow Road, west of Lone Pine, is open to snowline, but potential avalanche hazards exist. On the south side, unpaved Canebrake Road is open to snowline. On the west side, Sherman Pass Road is open to snowline. Cherry Hill Road to Big Meadow is closed.

Accessibility to the Piute Mountains: all access roads are open to snowline, but they are unpaved and often rutted.

Once you reach skiable snow, after parking your car at snowline, you can ski on the numerous logging roads, identified on the Forest Service map, or follow the trails in the area described in this book. At present there are no marked cross-country ski routes. On the central Kern Plateau, the east slopes of Sherman Peak provide good telemark skiing if the snow is 5- to 6-feet deep. Overall, the terrain between and around Sherman Pass to Fish Creek Campground provides excellent opportunities for cross-country skiing.

Farther north, an exhausting 5.6-mile climb up Cottonwood Creek Canyon from TH82 (T111, in reverse) offers ski mountaineers access to deep, untouched snow on the ranges around and beyond Horseshoe Meadow.

The Kern River Preserve In 1980 The Nature Conservancy, a private, non-profit conservation organization whose mission is to protect biological diversity by buying ecologically significant land, purchased 1127 acres along the South Fork Kern River. The acquisition included a 100-yard swath of a Fremont cottonwood/red willow riparian area, a section of the largest contiguous cottonwood/willow forest left in California.

Although attentive to all flora and fauna on the preserve, the Conservancy's overriding interest is to restore the breeding habitat of the state endangered Yellow-billed Cuckoo, once a common summer resident, now on the edge of extinction. The Nature Conservancy established an ambitious program to reforest willows, where the birds nest, and cottonwoods, where they feed. Most of the work is done by volunteers who work with the preserve manager.

Other activities at the preserve include educational programs, research study, bird and butterfly counts and documentaries. Visitors are welcome to explore and walk the trails, but groups are asked to make advance arrangements.

Human History In historic times, two separate and distinct groups of Native Americans lived on the east side of the Southern Sierra. The Kawaiisu (Ka-why-a-su) Indians lived, hunted and gathered nuts and seeds on the land from the Tehachapi range north to Kelso Valley and its surrounding mountains. The Tubatulabal (Too-bot-a-labble) Indians lived and sought food from the South Fork Kern River Valley north to the Mount Whitney area. In the 1850s, discovery of gold hereabouts brought in hordes of prospectors, but their tenure was short and they were replaced by cattle and sheep ranchers. However, some nominal gold, tungsten and barite mining continues. Today recreation-bound visitors and retirees have found the Kern River Valley and surrounding country to their liking and provide the dominant economic base.

The Kern River Valley Historical Society's museum in Kernville has a beautifully selected and described assemblage of local artifacts and offers numerous relevant books and articles for sale. The society also conducts group tours to historic places by appointment.

Plant study

Chapter 2: Precautions

Outings A few general safety rules apply to all trips in the mountains: drive a reliable vehicle; understand your physical ability; and give someone your itinerary and the phone number of a person or agency to contact if you do not return when indicated.

When planning a car trip in the mountains, especially on seldom traveled dirt roads, take extra water, blankets, warm clothing, and a saw and shovel as well as regular car tools. Keep in mind that a fairly smooth dirt road can become deeply gutted by heavy rain, blocked by fallen trees, truncated by flash floods and iced by sudden winter storms.

You require extra skill and vigilance when driving on narrow, winding mountain roads: a vehicle or animal may be around a blind curve or invisible in a dip ahead. Also, sections of these mountains are logged, and roads in these sections carry trucks careening with heavy timber. For safety, try to pull off the road, if possible, to give wide berth to oncoming logging trucks.

If bicycling, you need to take extra precautions on mountain roads, too. Quickly pull off the road when a car or truck approaches from either direction.

For hikes, climbs or backpacks in the Southern Sierra, wear long-sleeved shirts and long pants. This clothing protects your skin from sunburn, insect bites, and scratches from thorny bushes. A first-aid kit, reflector, flash light, matches, warm wrap, rain gear, extra food and a space blanket should be included in your pack. (Metallic space blankets prevent body heat from escaping, but do not wrap yourself in one during a lightning storm.) For multiday trips, include a tent for cover during soaking, though infrequent showers. For guidance, take this guidebook, map and a compass. And always carry water—a minimum of two quarts a day per person is recommended even though that water weight means you are carrying four extra pounds. Most people will require more than that minimum on a demanding hike or in the heat of summer.

Water courses indicated on maps are not always reliable. The USGS 7.5 minute provisional edition maps north of Highway 178 do not differentiate between seasonal and year-round water courses. In addition, they were surveyed during exceedingly wet years in the Southern Sierra. If you count on the systems shown on these maps to draw your water, you may be in trouble. Also remember that in drought years many springs and streams dry up.

Conversely, during snowmelt too much

Drive a reliable vehicle

water may create a problem; crossing swollen rivers and creeks may become difficult. A few tips: do not cross above rapids or logs; unbuckle your waist strap when crossing a stream for a quick exit from your backpack should you fall; and use a walking stick for stability. Moreover, logs and boulders used for crossings may be slippery and unstable underfoot any time of year.

Bears "Lions and Tigers and Bears, Oh my!" Well, maybe not tigers. Substitute deer. A fleeting deer lightly touching ground as it dashes through the forest; a plodding bear adroitly scrambling up granitic boulders—these sights are privileged moments for you while strolling along a Southern Sierra path. Unlike those in national parks or heavily used wildernesses, animals here are not accustomed to people—they are truly wild. You may see a doe and yearlings, rarely a buck. You will see bear tracks and droppings, but not the bear if it can help it. The stealthy mountain lion has been seen by very few; only an occasional footprint on a path suggests its presence.

A hungry bear (unlike a deer or mountain lion) will quickly lose its fear of people if it associates food with people. To prevent this, maintain a clean camp, keep food packed away but never in a tent, and bearbag your food, toothpaste, garbage, etc., especially if you are camping along the North Fork Kern River or at popular campsites in the back country. Bearbagging instructions can be obtained with wilderness and campfire permits. An unprovoked brown bear will not attack you, but you should give a sow and her cubs plenty of space and do not try to retrieve your food if Bruin has discovered it.

Bears, Oh my!

Rattlesnakes All rattlesnakes are potentially poisonous. Non-venomous gopher snakes, sometimes mistaken for rattlesnakes, have similar markings, but they do not have the triangular-shaped head, the thin neck, nor the rattles. Both snakes, important to the environment where they live, should be left unharmed. Of the many rattlesnake species, three inhabit the eastern Southern Sierra or adjacent desert. The *Speckled Panamint,* 25–50 inches, appears sandy and speckled like gravel with muted crossbar to diamond-shaped blotches. Ranging in elevation to 8000 feet, it is usually seen around boulders and chaparral. The greenish tinged *Mojave,* 25–50 inches, has black bands alternating with wider white bands encircling its tail next to the rattles. It lives in the desert and up to 8000 feet on arid slopes. The *Sidewinder,* 20–30 inches, has horn-like projections over each eye. This snake inhabits the desert and ranges up to 5000 feet. The track it leaves in the sand resembles a series of parallel "J" marks. Injection of venom (envenomation) by any of the species effects the circulatory system, but envenomation by the Mojave rattlesnake affects the nervous system as well—considerably more dangerous.

A snake never chases you; it only strikes (⅓ of its body length) when it feels threatened; and it does not always inject venom. Swelling at the bite site and numbness and tingling around the mouth are symptoms of venom injection. According to the latest medical advice, you should try to stay calm, rest the affected part if possible, and get to the hospital—immediately if you suspect you were bitten by the Mojave rattlesnake. The hospital in Ridgecrest has Mojave antivenom. Do not cut the fang marks, immerse the bitten area in icy water, or apply a tourniquet. Most people survive a snake bite; small children are at greater risk. Not one envenomation of a hiker in the Southern Sierra has been reported—cases other than hikers have: trail builders, fire fighters, people who taunt snakes or handle "dead" snakes.

A snake's searching tongue aids its sense of smell. It cannot hear. A snake lacks internal means of controlling its body temperature; therefore, it sun bathes when the day is cool, sometimes on the trail; and seeks shade under bushes, by rocks and logs or in burrows as the temperature rises. You are most apt to see a rattlesnake in the spring when it emerges from its den and mates; then you will seldom see one the rest of the hiking season. In the pitch of summer, this rodent-eating reptile becomes nocturnal. Nevertheless, always be careful: watch where you step and place your hands, and wear boots and long pants. Your body heat, odor, and tremor of the ground as you hike alert the snake of your presence, and it will usually be gone before you arrive.

Ticks This insect climbs to the tips of grass or low brush such as sagebrush, then transfers to an animal or your pant leg, should you pass by. It then climbs up to exposed skin where it attaches itself for a meal. Ticks vary in size from a dot (slightly larger than a period on this page) to ¼ inch. Adults have eight legs; they cannot jump or fly.

In 1976 inflammatory Lyme disease was linked to tick bites. Early signs of this disease are a rash at the bite site and flu-like symptoms. If not treated with antibiotics, the disease can progress to arthritis and other involvements. No cases of Lyme disease have been attributed to ticks in the Southern Sierra. Still it is wise to wear long pants and tuck them into your sock tops, wear long-sleeved shirts, buttoned up and tucked in, and check your clothes frequently when brushing by low vegetation. Ticks seem to be most abundant in late winter and spring.

To remove ticks grasp the insect with tweezers as close to your skin as possible then gently pull up. Try not to crush them.

Yellow Jackets These yellow- and black-banded wasps attack if their paper-comb nests under ground, under logs or in trees are disturbed. Their sting is painful, but serious only if you are sensitized to the venom. If so, ask your doctor about a bee-sting kit. Yellow Jackets buzz around bright, colorful clothing and perfumed products, and are also attracted to meat, sweets and water. They become inactive at dusk. Colonies of these wasps increase to large populations by fall. All but the new queens die over winter.

Poison Oak This three-leafed shrub or vine is rare on the east side of the Southern Sierra, but it does occur in roadside patches along the North Fork Kern River and in a few spots along the River Trail. The oil from this plant produces a seeping, itching skin rash. Check with your pharmacist for treatment.

Giardiasis Gone are the days when you can drink deeply from a cold, clear Sierra stream without questioning its purity. Now you must be aware of the microorganism *Giardia lamblia* lurking in some streams. Man's careless hygiene introduced the organism, then it spread by animals. This gastrointestinal disease, giardiasis (jee-ar-dye-a-sis), is extremely debilitating (diarrhea, bloating, nausea) but treatable. You can prevent giardiasis by treating all water in the wilderness before you drink it. The best method is to boil water at a rolling boil for five minutes, longer at high elevations. Commercial filter systems obtained at mountain supply stores also seem to be effective. Less trustworthy are chemical disinfectants such as four drops of household bleach per quart of water or 10 drops of 2% tincture of iodine. These chemicals need time to act in water.

Hypothermia Uncontrolled shivering is the first sign that your body temperature is dropping below normal, which is hypothermia. Slurred speech, sluggish gait and inappropriate thinking follow. It can happen when it is cold (30°–50°F) and windy and you are wet and tired, or any combination of theses factors. Make camp immediately, get out of your wet clothes, get into your sleeping bag, and drink warm fluids. (The bag and you will warm up faster if another person gets in it with you, and both of your are mostly stripped.) Do not delay: your life depends on returning your body temperature to normal. Prevent hypothermia by having proper clothes and equipment—wool and some synthetics provide warmth even when wet.

Chapter 3: Back-Country Etiquette

An abundance of written material on back-country ethics has bombarded mountain travelers of late with good results. People are taking better care of their wild country than ever before. They spend a great deal of effort hiking or riding into the backcountry to become one with unspoiled nature, and they see to it that the next person has that same esthetic experience. So the following do's and do nots are for the benefit of newcomers, and serve only as reminders to others.

Do

Stay on the trails

Stand quietly, down slope if possible, to let stock pass

Use existing campsites and fire rings. If none are available, remove all indications of your new campsite (no trace camping)

Use camp stoves for cooking

Keep social campfires small, or have none at all

Use only dead and down wood for your campfires

Extinguish campfires with water—dead out

Bury feces and toilet paper at least 6 inches deep and 100 feet away from lakes, streams and washes. Cover with soil, stamp down and top with large rocks.

Carry out all trash, yours and a little more

Tie or hobble horses at least 100 feet from camp or water

Scatter horse manure away from possible campsites

Limit group size (check land agency for maximum size)

If you observe inappropriate back-country use by people or agencies, report it to the agency governing the area. Join conservation organizations, which have numerous campaigns to eliminate abuse. To express your gratitude for the pleasure you have derived from your mountain treks, do volunteer work on trails, etc., and write a letter of thanks to the governing agency if their work and policies added to your enjoyment.

Do Not

Make multiple, parallel trails, especially in meadows

Shortcut switchbacks

Smoke on trails

Pick wildflowers, trample meadows unnecessarily, remove artifacts, etc.

Strip trees of twigs and branches, even dead ones

Camp in meadows or on private land

Cover hot coals of a campfire with dirt

Wash in streams and lakes even with biodegradable soap

Group hike in the Southern Sierra

Chapter 4: Resources & Regulations

Agencies

U.S. Department of the Interior
Bureau of Land Management
Bakersfield District
Hours 7:30–4:30 weekdays
Information, maps, fire permits

Headquarters
800 Truxtun Ave.
Federal Bldg, Room 311
Bakersfield, CA 93301
(805) 861-4191

Ridgecrest Resource Area—For areas east of
the Sierra crest
300 So. Richmond Road
Ridgecrest, CA 93555
(619) 375-7125

Caliente Resource Area—For the Pacific
Crest Trail and areas west of the Sierra crest
4301 Rosedale Highway
Bakersfield, CA 93308
(805) 861-4236

U.S. Department of Agriculture
Forest Service
Sequoia National Forest
Hours 8:00–4:30 weekdays
Information, books, maps, fire permits,
Golden Trout Wilderness permits

Headquarters
900 West Grand Ave.
Porterville, CA 93257
(209) 784-1500

Cannell Meadow Ranger District—For Kern
Plateau and North Fork Kern River
105 Whitney Road
P.O. Box 6
Kernville, CA 93238
(619) 376-3781
Summer hours 8:00–5:00 daily

Blackrock Station on the Kern Plateau
Sherman Pass Road at Blackrock Road
No phone
Hours 8:00–4:30 Thursday to Sunday
8:00–2:30 Monday
Closed Tuesday, Wednesday and winters

Greenhorn Ranger District—For Piute
Mountains
15701 Highway 178
P.O. Box 6129
Bakersfield, CA 93306
(805) 871-2223
Summer hours 8:00–5:00 daily

Inyo National Forest
Hours 8:00–4:30 weekdays
Information, books, maps, fire permits,
Golden Trout Wilderness permits

Headquarters
873 North Main St.
Bishop, CA 93514
(619) 873-5841

Mount Whitney Ranger District
640 So. Main St.
P.O. Box 8
Lone Pine, CA 93545
(619) 876-5542
Summer hours 6:00–4:30 daily

Hospitals

Ridgecrest Community Hospital
1081 North China Lake Blvd.
Ridgecrest, CA 93555
(619) 446-3551

Kern Valley Hospital
6412 Laurel Ave.
Mountain Mesa, CA 93240
(619) 379-2681

For emergencies dial 911

Community

Desert Tortoise Preserve
Committee, Inc.
P.O. Box 453
Ridgecrest, CA 93556

Kern River Preserve
18747 Highway 178
P.O. Box 1662
Weldon, CA 93283
(619) 378-2531
(Call for hours)

Kern Valley Museum
49 Big Blue Road
Kernville, CA 93238
(619) 376-6683
Hours 10:00–4:00 Thursday through Sunday

Packers

Kennedy Meadows
Pack Trains
P.O. Box 1300
Weldon, CA 93283
(619) 378-2232

Cottonwood Pack Station
Star Rt. Box 81-A
Independence, CA 93526
(619) 878-2015

Campgrounds, Campsites & Fire Safe Areas

Developed Campgrounds   Campgrounds referred to as "developed" have individual sites and offer some or all of the following: tables, fire rings, faucet water (off in winter), rest rooms and trash removal. No reservations. Limited number of days at a site. Campgrounds are free of charge and are closed in winter, unless otherwise noted. Further regulations are posted in each campground.

Bureau of Land Management Campgrounds

Walker Pass Area
Highway 178

Walker Pass Trailhead
Walk-In Campground
Open all year   Corrals

Chimney Peak Recreation Area
North of Highway 178

Chimney Creek Campground
Open all year

Long Valley Campground   Open all year

Alabama Hills Recreation Area, Lone Pine
Horseshoe Meadow Road

Tuttle Creek Campground

Sequoia National Forest Campgrounds

Lake Isabella
Sierra Way

Eastside Campground 9 and Launch Ramp

North Fork Kern River, South to North
Sierra Way/ TC Road MTN 99

Headquarters Campground   Fee
Open all year

Camp 3 Campground   Fee

Hospital Flat Campground   Fee

Gold Ledge Campground   Fee

Fairview Campground
Open all year   Fee
No water, no fee in winter

Limestone Campground

Central Kern Plateau, East to West
Kennedy Meadows/Sherman Pass Road

Kennedy Meadows Campground
Open all year

Fish Creek Campground

Troy Meadow Campground

Blackrock Over-Night
Walk-In Campground
(End of Blackrock Road)   Corrals

Horse Meadow Campground
(Off Cherry Hill Road)

Inyo National Forest Campground

Horseshoe Meadow Area
End of Horseshoe Meadow Road

Horseshoe Meadow Over-Night
Walk-In Campground
Corrals   Fee

Campsites   Any suitable place in the Sierra can serve as a campsite. See the chapter on "Back Country Etiquette."

Fire Safe Areas   These areas for camping are scattered throughout the Sequoia National Forest, except in wildernesses, and very often are places shorn of vegetation where logs were stacked and loaded onto trucks. Campfires and gas stove use are permitted in Fire Safe Areas even during periods of restricted fire use.

Permits

Campfire A permit is needed for campfires and camp stove use outside developed campgrounds. The permits can be obtained for the Sierra from the Bureau of Land Management and the Forest Service, and are good for a calendar year. A wilderness permit also serves as a campfire permit.

In addition to fire prevention suggestions mentioned in the etiquette chapter, during extreme hazardous conditions further regulations are imposed upon certain areas. *Stage I* restrictions prohibit campfires or stove fire, except portable stoves using gas, jellied petroleum or pressurized liquid fuel, outside a developed campground or a Fire Safe Area. *Stage II* restrictions prohibit all stove use outside developed campgrounds or Fire Safe Areas. All OHVs are restricted to roads only. Dome Land Wilderness and a few other areas are exempt. Check with the Forest Service for current conditions and restrictions.

Wilderness Golden Trout Wilderness campers need to obtain a wilderness permit

for each trip; day hikers need not. Permits are not required for South Sierra or Dome Land wildernesses. Permits for Golden Trout Wilderness may be obtained at no charge from any Forest Service district office. A quota system, in effect from the last Friday in June to September 15, limits the number of people entering the wilderness each day on popular trails. The only trail in this book under the quota system is Cottonwood Trail out of Horseshoe Meadow. There is a charge for a reservation. Call Mount Whitney Ranger District for information.

Mechanized equipment including motorcycles, bicycles and chainsaws are not allowed in a wilderness. Unnatural to the wilderness ethic, but still allowed, are cattle grazing, hunting and fishing.

River Use Commercial and private rafters, kayakers and canoeists need to obtain a permit at the Kernville Ranger Station before floating the North Fork Kern River.

Fishing A mix of regulations apply in the Southern Sierra. Contact the governing agency for current information on your area of interest.

Mule deer

Chapter 5: Trip Format

The Kern Plateau is sometimes referred to as "The Gentle Wilderness" because it was not sculptured and sliced by glaciers, as was the High Sierra to the north. The plateau's rolling, mountainous land, where most of the trips in this book are located, lends itself well to travel by foot or hoof. But without the glacial carving, the terrain often lacks sharp features, and the inexperienced hiker some- times finds it difficult to identify guiding land- marks. Furthermore, not all trails are signed or well-defined, and some paths, easily mis- takable for hiking trails, are off-highway vehicle tracks and cow paths. These condi- tions exist in the area surrounding the plateau as well.

It is important, therefore, to use this detailed guidebook in the field as well as for preparation at home. If you would rather not tote the book on your trip, duplicate the pages needed and tuck them in your pocket or pack for quick reference. The following explana- tion of the book's format should help you plan your trips as well as use the book most effectively.

Car Tours   Although high-clearance cars are preferable on dirt roads, conventional cars can be driven unless otherwise indi- cated. These car tours offer sightseeing, guidance and information about the country in and around the mountains. The tours also include directions to trailheads, thus doubl- ing as guidance and information resources to those heading for trips described in this book.

Each of the car tours connects with another tour to link the roads along side of, or in the mountains from Mojave to Lone Pine. En route you can refer to all the connecting tours or just the closest one to your destina- tion. It is important to note the mileages to locales given in the tours and to check your odometer as you drive. Occasionally the mileage reading will be the only clue that you have reached the destination you seek. Each car tour includes brackets with two or three figures (5360/0.6/7.1), which are elevation, mileage from point to point and cumulative mileage. Elevations are given at the begin-

ning and end of trips, at low and high points of grades and at departure points for other car tours. All trips on major roads are described from south to north and from east to west. Cumulative mileages are given in one direc- tion only. When traveling in the opposite direction, simply subtract your point of inter- est from the total mileage.

Paved roads are signed at junctions while dirt roads are seldom signed. County, Forest Service and Bureau of Land Management roads are coded and the code numbers are mentioned in the text if these numbers appear on signs, road paddles and/or on maps.

Bicycle Tours   Most car tours serve as bicycle tours as well: multigeared bikes for paved roads, all-terrain bikes for dirt roads. Many day hikes and backpack trips are equally accommodating to all-terrain bike trips and are identified in the Tripfinder Table.

Day Hikes   With few exceptions, day hikes are under 10 miles in length and usually take place on main, well-defined trails.

Peak Climbs   Most peak ascents follow cross-country routes. Often a trail develops to the peak by hikers using the same route ("use" trail) and placing stacks of rocks ("ducks") to mark the way. The term "peak- bagger" refers to a person whose interest is climbing peaks.

Backpacks   These trips of two or more days in the backcountry, with provisions carried in a backpack, take advantage of all kinds of trails and terrain.

Excursions   When an optional day hike or peak climb appears within a trip, it is referred to as an "Excursion." It always requires a hike to get to the excursion's point of departure.

Equestrians   All hikes equally accommo- date equestrians except where otherwise indicated, based on Forest Service trail classifications. Horse travel is not recom- mended on cross-country peak climbs. The trips are written for hikers in order to simplify the description; the writing is not intended to slight equestrians.

Format Headings By scanning the headings, you can quickly tell whether the trip is the kind of outing you desire. Most self-propelled trips in this book, with the exception of day hikes, are too subjective to rate. To determine the difficulty of a trip, consider the distance, steep ascents, elevation gain and skills involved, then factor in your capability and your time limitations. To approximate the duration of a trip, decide on the average number of miles you can comfortably hike in one day and divide that into the total mileage of the trip. Within this average number of miles per day, each day will differ. The accepted generalizations of hikers' speed are: 1.0 mile per hour on uphill trails; 2.0 miles per hour on level, smooth paths; 3.0 miles per hour on downhill treks if the grade is not extreme. Allow extra time for cross-country hiking; for rough trails; for carrying a heavy or unfamiliar pack; for observing the flowers, listening to the birds, picnicking.

Distance This indicates the total distance of the trip. Field surveys with a measuring wheel yielded most of the readings; distances on terrain impassable for a wheel were taken from topographic maps. A *round trip* means that you follow the same route to your destination and back. A *loop trip* infers just that, a loop, sometimes with a very small round trip segment; whereas a *semiloop trip* combines a loop and a significant round trip portion. A *shuttle trip* indicates a one-way journey: either you need to be met at your trip's end, or to leave a car at the end of the route, then arrange transportation to the beginning point. You need to allow time for the extra driving involved on shuttle trips. A *one-way trip* appears on car/bicycle tours only.

Steep Ascents Here you have an approximate figure that indicates the sum total of grades around 21%—that is 21 feet elevation gain in 100 feet.

Elevation Gain This is the trip's total gain, ignoring minor trail undulations.

Skills: Day Hikes To assist novices, day hikes receive ratings. In this catagory, an *easy* rating promises a hike of few miles on fairly level terrain; *moderate* means a longer dura-

tion and includes some elevation gain; *moderate to strenuous* includes significant elevation gain, perhaps some rough terrain, and may require some pathfinding skills.

Skills: Route Finding *Easy route finding* means well-defined trails or roads along the way, and cross-country routes, if any, are short and/or obvious. Hikes on main trails and car/bicycle tours are in this catagory.

Duck: a low stack of rocks

Intermediate route finding includes trails with obscure sections (when scouted), and/or cross-country routes where the destination cannot be seen at departure. When the trail becomes obscure, look for these clues to guide you: blazes on trees, either in the form of a vertical rectangle with a square above carved in the tree trunk, or a metal diamond nailed to the trunk; orange plastic ribbons tied to protruding objects; or low stacks of rocks, known as ducks. Usually there is a series of like clues. More subtle trail guides are: remains of downslope retaining walls; smooth cuts on branches of trees and shrubs, cut during trail construction or maintenance; or dark grass in a trail through a meadow. Tall stacks of rocks, known as cairns, sometimes mark junctions and summits; and this guidebook describes landmark features. For cross-country trips such as peakbagging, your aids are compass, topographic maps, type of terrain and guidebook descriptions.

Advanced route finding, few trips in the

contents of this book, indicates extended cross-country hikes with skill in map and compass orientation and keen awareness of topographical features.

Skills: Climbing This book describes Class 1–3 climbing routes, one Class 4 route, and identifies a large number of interesting, more difficult route possibilities. *Class 1* terrain requires no particular expertise, and ordinary, comfortable, supportive walking or running shoes are adequate. *Class 2* requires good balance and shoes or boots that afford good traction on boulders. Rock climbing falls into this category when the degree of difficulty assures a challenge, but good hand and foot holds assist your ascent and a precipitous drop is not present. *Class 3,* sheer cliffs, exposure, arêtes, narrow hand and footholds and precipitous drops await you. You may wish to use a rope. *Class 4* refers to steep, exposed rock with narrow holds; you will need to use a rope as well as your climbing skill. *Class 5* routes refer to technical climbs.

Seasons This indicates the time of the year for the trips most temperate climate and minimal snowpack.

Maps In the 1980s, the U.S. Geological Survey published photographic revisions and new provisional editions of topographic maps of the Southern Sierra in the large, easy-to-read 7.5 minute series. These maps are listed next to the heading in each trip in order of use as additions to the map included with this book. There are several ways you can obtain these inexpensive yet invaluable maps. You can buy them at your mountain supply store or your local map store; or order them from:

Western Distribution Branch
U.S. Geological Survey
Box 25286, Federal Center, Bldg 41
Denver, CO 80225

In 1991 the cost was $2.50 per map; prepayment is required; allow four weeks.

The offices of the Bureau of Land Management sell maps of areas under their jurisdiction. The maps include points of interest and some have road and trail numbers, as well. Offices of Sequoia National Forest have maps for a nominal price which include road and trail numbers in their area. The Tourist Center in Lone Pine offers at little cost an Inyo National Forest, USGS 15 minute topographic map of Golden Trout and South Sierra wildernesses. Their map differentiates between main and secondary trails on the forest.

Trailhead and Tourhead To avoid repetition and to increase interest while driving, trailhead directions are included in the car tour descriptions. If a trailhead serves only one trip, its concluding spur road directions, if any, will appear in the trip's format. Check the odometer while driving to trailheads— mileage is often the best guide. If parking space is limited to fewer than five cars, that is noted. Tourheads serve car and bicycle tours.

Description A detailed account of each trip is given so that a traveler, unfamiliar and inexperienced, can journey safely and confidently. The account includes information about campsites, water sources and viewpoints. To enhance the adventure, cameos of natural and human history, geology and geography, flora and fauna appear as part of the text. Salient features of the flowers are described, so you can readily identify them.

Trail signs occur at the trailheads and junctions; signs are inexplicably destroyed by people and sometimes chewed by bears. To assure a successful trip, do not depend on signs, but follow the maps and book descriptions, and note the landmarks as you hike. Sequoia National Forest uses codes for trails and roads; sometimes only code numbers appear on signs. These numbers are mentioned in the text. In contrast, Inyo National Forest signs indicate destinations.

A few of the trails described in this book are also open to motorcycles. Cyclists tend to drive on the weekends, and are prohibited from all trail travel during Stage II fire restrictions. Trails open to motorcyclists are identified as *M'cyclepaths.*

Trip logs are used in the description where two or more trips overlap while heading in the same direction. The point to point elevations and mileages given in the logs help you identify corresponding text and locate your position in the field.

Part 2
Adventures in the Southern Sierra: East Side

Section 1
Highway 58 to Highway 178

Yucca blooms

T1   Mojave Desert Car Tour on Highway 14: Highway 58 to Highway 178
(With Directions to Trailheads 1–7)

Spring and autumn present the ideal setting for this journey: for then the sun in the distant south accents the nearby furrowed slopes and craggy outcrops with long, shadowy strokes; and then the terrain of summer's flat light and wavy heat illusions transforms into deeply-etched engravings. The drama of long desert shadows is additionally enhanced in early spring when an overlay of snow softens distant mountain peaks, and a spread of wildflowers covers rocky, sloping lands.

Distance   41.2 miles, one way
Steep Ascents   None
Elevation Gain   1100 feet
Skills   Easy route finding; paved road
Seasons   All year
Map   Kern County road map
Tourhead   1. The forked junction of highways 14 and 58, north of the town of Mojave, is **TH1**. PCT backpackers seeking **TH2** of T2 take the Highway 58 fork.
Description   Your ride begins on **State Highway 14** (2850/0.0/0.0) along the west edge of the Mojave Desert north of the railroad town of Mojave. This desert town, known mostly as a fast-food stop for skiers bent on conquering the slopes of Mammoth Mountain, burst into international fame when a tiny aircraft built here, the Voyager, became the first plane to fly around the world without refueling. In 1986 travelers on this highway observed the "flying fuel tank" on its test flights.

The route parallels that of the two Los Angeles aqueducts buried at the foot of the Sierra Nevada range. The original aqueduct, built between 1908 and 1913, tapped water from Owens River, which is fed by eastern Sierra snowfields. It was later extended northward to tap the streams that feed Mono Lake, 338 miles in all, and a second aqueduct was added. This water delivered to Los Angeles is directly responsible for the city's growth explosion: a blessing some say; a curse say others. A foul act, say the citizens of Owens Valley, who claim that the water, no matter how "legally" obtained is stolen from them. The Mojave Yard of the Los Angeles Department of Water and Power Aqueduct Division, Southern District Headquarters, is to your left. This station's employees are responsible for the operation and maintenance of 160 miles of the system between Los Angeles and the Haiwee Reservoirs.

Running under the aqueducts here is the Garlock fault zone, a structural break between the Sierra Nevada block and the Mojave block. It is an active fault which intersects the famous San Andreas Fault to the south near Frazier Mountain. From there it slashes along the southeast slopes of the Tehachapi Mountains, and then follows the irregular border of the Sierra Nevada's east slopes. Parts of the fault, a left-lateral slip, are locked and scientists expect a great quake will rupture those sections in the not too distant future.

You next arrive at paved California City Boulevard (4.9/4.9), where a right turn (east) reaches the Desert Tortoise Natural Area, **TH3** of T3. This large preserve was set aside for the protection of the lumbering, benign desert tortoise, which, after surviving through natural upheavals since the age of the dinosaurs, is now on the verge of extinction.

Among other cohabitants sharing this vast desert with the tortoise, California's state reptile, is another reptile, but this one slithers and is only benign when left alone: the extremely venomous Mojave green rattlesnake. Other creatures are the comical roadrunner, which forgets it has wings and scurries about on its sturdy legs, and the Burrowing Owl, which uses its wings in silent flight, but also hops along the ground in pursuit of prey. Owl castings, regurgitations of bone, hair, fur and feathers that are not digested, are found around posts and other perches.

In contrast to these native creatures, the space shuttles, creatures of man, also share the desert. Thousands of people gather to watch the spacecraft glide on swept-back wings from supersonic space travel to landings on the dry lake bed at Edwards Air Force Base. The base was the home of the X-1 aircraft that broke the sound barrier, and the X-15 that explored the edge of space. Its achievements are ongoing.

The Mojave Desert has beauty, too. If you arrive during early spring, it is awash with blooming bushes and wildflowers. The ubiquitous creosote bush (4–6 feet) sports its windmill-vanelike flowers of yellow; the cheese bush (2–3 feet) presents its waxy, cupped, creamy blooms. The leaves of this bush smell like cheese when crushed. And in a favorable year, the fragile, ground hugging desert primrose, clustered along roadsides and sandy flats, displays its showy, heart-shaped petals of white flowers, which wilt to a pink with age.

While contemplating these things, if you intend to climb Chuckwalla and Cross mountains, T4 at **TH4**, watch for a dirt road to the left (west) (8.6/13.5). To help identify it, look for a road that dips under a highly visible white aqueduct bridging a canyon.

Beyond the turnoff, you quickly pass the charred remains of a restaurant, all there is to the burg of Cinco, then the Cantil post office, small store and gas pumps, and then reach Jawbone Canyon junction (2135/5.5/19.0). This is **TH5** of T5 for car and bicycle tours to Kelso Valley and the Piute Mountains. This is also the forked junction of the Sierra Nevada and Garlock fault zones: the Garlock Fault ventures southeast of the El Paso Mountains; the Sierra Nevada follows the eastern slopes of the Sierra. You next cross painterly Red Rock Canyon State Park at the southwest flank of the El Paso Mountains, T7, and the road to **TH6** (5.1/24.1). This colorful country runs the gamut from prehistoric fossils to television productions; it is one of California's most interesting state parks.

Traveling north in the arid Mojave Desert, your route passes unpaved roads to the west with multiple branches to enticing place names such as Dove Spring, Bird Spring, Horse Canyon Well and Cow Heaven Spring before reaching Freeman Canyon and Highway 178 West at **TH7** (3186/17.1/41.2). The west route on Highway 178 to the Kern River Valley is described in T8, while the north route, continuing the ride along the eastern escarpment, is described in T46.

PCT next to Highway 58

T2   PCT Backpack on the Southernmost Sierra Nevada Mountains: Highway 58 to Jawbone Canyon Road

This trip in a rugged mountainous area little known to hikers, takes you along the southern Sierra crest from Joshua/juniper to pine/fir plant zones. Some of the trip's beauty lies in the unobstructed views of rows of sharp ridges and deep valleys, and in distant vistas of historic landforms and populated enclaves. This is also the southern-most trip in this book of the Mexico to Canada Pacific Crest National Scenic Trail.

Distance   34.6 miles, shuttle trip
Steep Ascents   None
Elevation Gain   6600 feet
Skills   Easy route finding
Seasons   Spring, fall
Maps   USGS 7.5 min *Monolith, Teha-chapi NE, Cache Pk, Cross Mtn, Emerald Mtn, Claraville* (The PCT trail is not on these maps at this writing.)
Trailheads   2 & 25. This trip requires two cars. Highway 14 approach: see car tour T5. Highway 178 approach: see car tour T24. Leave the first car at **TH25**, the end of the trip in the Piute Mountains. Drive the second car east on Jawbone Canyon Road to a right turn on Highway 14, then south to Highway 58 in Mojave (car tours T5 and T1, in reverse). From the junction of highways 14 & 58 in Mojave (0.0/0.0), drive north on **Highway 58**. Take the Cameron off ramp across Highway 58. Park where safe on the south side of the overpass at **TH2** (9.6/9.6). This is 55.0 miles from the first car.
Description   The BLM plans to establish a trailhead campground for PCT hikers on the south side of Cameron Overpass. The facilities are to include much needed water. Presently, the only water source on the trail is 16.1 miles ahead, about half way. Hydrate yourself well before starting this trip and carry at the very minimum two quarts of water per day. The trail passes through a crazy quilt of private and BLM lands. Because of private lands, users are asked not to stray from the trail, even for peakbagging.

Begin your *PCT* trek at the south end of Cameron Overpass (3800/00) and cross busy Highway 58 on the overpass to the trail on the north side of the highway. You parallel the highway east-northeast along a fenced corridor and through a gate (3780/1.2) opposite the *Cameron Road Exit 1 Mile* sign. You dip through a large wash soon after and turn northeast to ascend to the right of a flood control berm by the wash. Leaving the berm, you progress east, passing en route groves of juniper trees interspersed with yuccas. As you cross over the northeast-southwest Garlock fault zone, the second largest fault zone in California, you encounter a mishmash of granitics and metamorphics. Geologists identify these as mafic and ultramafic Plutonic rocks and associated amphibolite, gneiss and granulite. Climbing north via switchbacks and curves, you arrive on a broad slope 3.0 miles into your trip, an ideal first spot for a first night camp.

From below you hear the distant chug of locomotives pulling their long chain of freight cars to and from the famous loop at Walong, just west of Tehachapi. Built in 1875–76, this is one of the most photographed railroad sites in the world. The loop is comprised of a spiral of curves and tunnels that gains 80 feet elevation and puts the locomotives over the caboose if the train is more than 4000 feet long.

Clustered on ridges about you are forests of metal windmills activated by prevailing winds that race through Tehachapi Pass. Electricity generated by the turbines is purchased by Southern California Edison. Wind farms were developed as an alternative to energy generated by air polluting fossil fuels, but the windmills, some claim, are esthetically polluting. The turbines—two blades, three blades and egg beater types—are com-

Campsite 3 miles north of Highway 58

puterized to turn toward the wind, which must be blowing at 20 to 40 mph for their maximum efficiency.

Moving on, you climb a long, tight series of switchbacks that on the map resemble a recorded earthquake on a seismograph. At length you reach gentler slopes along a broad ridge where camping is possible. Viewing clockwise from the ridge: the Mojave Desert to the east reveals a grid of roads with California City at the hub; the town of Mojave sits just below the Sierra to the southeast; and the isolated features of Soledad Mountain and Elephant Butte rise south of town. Contacts between rhyolite and granite rocks in these low volcanic mountains produced millions of dollars worth of gold and silver extracted from veins along 100 miles of tunnel. Farther southeast sprawls the barren expanse of Edwards Air Force Base with Rogers Dry Lake air strips, which is home base for space shuttles and experimental aircraft. To the south of you loom the Tehachapi Mountains, and west along the pass spreads their namesake town. The large scar of disturbed earth on the north side of Tehachapi Pass resulted from excavations by Monolith Cement Company. Their product was used in the construction of the LA aqueduct.

The PCT descends to straddle a narrow ridge between steep canyons, and shortly crosses from east-facing to traverse west-facing slopes. Here you encounter pinyon pine trees. In days of yore, the Kawaiisu Indians gathered pinyon nuts and acorns and hunted from the Tehachapi Mountains north through this area to the South Fork Kern River Valley.

Now the trail ascends a broad slope, tops a knoll, and descends abruptly. Colorful Waterfall Canyon dominates west views. Your trail next crosses a jeep road that leads to a prospect, crosses a spur road, then climbs a ridge via a few switchbacks, and passes a chalky white hill of tuff protruding from an east-facing canyon. Soon the PCT parallels the jeep road, crosses it a second time, and curves around the head of Waterfall Canyon and beyond. Abruptly, the trail ends and you join the jeep road (6120/7.1).

On the seldom used jeep road, your course heads generally north, descends to the east, then heads north again. At the bottom of the descent, 2.0 miles along the road, the PCT curves around a huge digger pine tree on a flat offering several sites for camping. Pine Tree (Lone Tree) Canyon falls away to the east— the same canyon in which climbers drive from Highway 14 to Chuckwalla Mountain. Still on the road, the trail again climbs a ridge, perhaps serenaded by a Mountain Chickadee's clear three-note "How-are you"—the "How" a whole note with the "are you" eighth notes at a lower pitch.

Ahead, as the route descends into a swale, you see the first of many towers perched on peaks and ridges. Instruments on these towers gather wind data. If the information is favorable, the towers will be replaced by ridges of wind turbines twirling their blades like giant pinwheels: then future PCTers will hear chickadee serenades through a mechanical hum. In this hollow the course crosses a dirt road, passes a road returning to nature, and forks right where the sign on the gated road to the left declares *Sky River Ranch—No Trespassing*. In 0.2 mile from the gated road, the PCT branches right, leaving the jeep road (6000/4.3) before it descends abruptly and curves west.

The PCT, a trail now, zigzags, crosses a tower road, turns sharply left and crosses the jeep road you just left. Here you see your first view of Olancha Peak far to the north over waves of ridges. Mount Langley and Mount Whitney barely reach above the waves. Southeast of Olancha rises pointy-shaped Owens Peak, with Mount Jenkins next to it. The PCT eventually passes near all of these peaks—but not on this trip—and long distance hikers on the trail are given many opportunities to view this scene as they progress.

Your path now begins a long traverse around the east side of Sweet Ridge, cut on very steep slopes, then around the flanks of Cache Peak, the highest peak in the southernmost Sierra. The ridge and peak comprise weathered volcanic rocks of the Tertiary period. The trail crosses a jeep road and arrives at a stone and cement trough catching a piped-in, year-round trickle from Golden Oaks Spring (5480/3.5). The BLM hopes to develop this important water source so that it is protected from possible cattle contaminants for trail users, but will still serve the needs of domestic and wild animals. The agency also hopes to develop a campsite

above the spring. The potential site is on private land, part of the Sky River Ranch owned by Zond Systems Inc.

Springs are important to wildlife, of course, as well as hikers. The area's mule deer, bobcats, mountain lions and black bears will shy away from this water source while people are near. Bighorn sheep frequented this spring as well as other springs in these mountains as recently as the early 1900s. At that time domestic sheep infected with scabies were released in the area. The scabies spread to the native bighorns, resulting in their demise. In 1978 tule elk were transplanted here from Owens Valley, but most of the elk migrated to lower elevations and found their way to the alfalfa fields in Fremont Valley.

With full water containers to last 18.5 miles, you head generally northwest, passing more roads to wind testing towers, and traversing steep slopes to round prominent Point 5683. You take a pair of switchbacks on a descending route below a jeep road. The descent eases and camping is possible: the first sites, other than on dirt roads, since the spring, 3.7 miles back. You then cross a ravine, climb up its west side and arc west around the drainage of Indian Creek, providing good views of Cache Peak to the south and of Emerald Mountain, a point on an extended ridge from Cache Peak. You soon reach an east-west ridge, which you cross via a green gate (5102/6.5) in a cattle fence.

Beyond the gate, the route heads generally west then curves north following the crest, a watershed divide between Caliente Creek to the west and Jawbone Canyon drainage to the east. From the crest are comprehensive views of Jawbone Canyon, and to the northeast, of Kelso Valley. The trail undulates near or on the crest, then descends a north-facing ridge to a blue oak savannah with camping potential, crossed by an east-west road (5010/3.0). This road extends from Highway 14 east to Highway 58 west, but it is a private gated and locked road.

Traveling north, you ascend easily up a ridge, curve around a minor east extension and then hike along a narrow saddle. The trail ahead looks steep but manages to stay within a 15% grade, the maximum allowed by PCT standards. The curious upslope swath cut through scrub oak followed the original trail design, which must have exceeded the maximum grade and was replaced. You ascend north through a scrub oak aisle. Scrub oak resembles its tree relatives in miniature: its growth is dense; its branches are ridged; its forest is impenetrable without the help of cutting tools. Upon turning northwest, you leave the chaparral oak for the domain of lofty Jeffrey pines and spreading black oaks, the first appearance of the pines on this journey. A shaded flat off the path at the northern limits of the forest offers campsites. Descend just beyond the flat to traverse below Hamp Williams Pass (5530/3.3).

The PCT climbs four steep switchbacks up another scrub oak aisle. Then a traverse, a zig zag, a crossing over a saddle to west-facing slopes, and you are again among welcome Jeffrey pines.

Just where the Piute Mountains begin in the south is not clearly indicated on the topographic map, but it shows that you are on the Piutes now. Way below to the west snippets of the country villages of Twin Oaks and Loraine appear, a bit to the north sprawls the ranching community of Walker Basin. A brown, polluted haze—the smog from the San Joaquin Valley slops over the far west

passes. Your trail descends gently on a traverse around two peaks and part way around Weldon Peak, then more sharply down a west-facing ridge, then gently as it turns northeast to enter a cluster of privately owned small parcels. No camping allowed. The path ends on a curve of a private dirt road (5620/3.2) onto which you turn right. (A parcel owner allows hikers the use of his spring ¼ mile left on this road. This is a wonderful gift, especially for long distance PCTers who have several miles before the next water.)

You now proceed up the main private road, permitted for PCT use. Keep left of the first fork at 0.1 mile, continue past several spurs, past a triangle left fork at 0.8 mile, then turn onto the PCT path, which resumes on the left side of the road (6160/1.2). The road meets Jawbone Canyon Road 0.2 mile later.

Walking north on the path below and parallel to Jawbone Canyon Road, you enter Forest Service land in 0.2 mile, pass a campsite with a fire ring to the left, and pass a use trail to the right. In 1.0 mile from the trail junction, you angle across a dirt road, and shortly thereafter, climb up the slope to your car on Jawbone Canyon Road, where this shuttle trip ends (6620/1.3). T20 takes backpackers on the next PCT section through these Piute Mountains, a subrange of the Sierra.

Deciduous oak arches over PCT

T3   Desert Tortoise Natural Area Side Trip

With a face like E.T. (an extraterrestrial creature), with skin like an elephant, with a shell that, pound for pound, would make a backpacker groan, this unique and lovable species of antiquity, the desert tortoise (Gopherus agassizii), captures the affection of all who know it.

Distance   Optional
Steep Upgrade   None
Elevation Gain   None
Skills   Easy route finding; easy hiking
Seasons   Winter, spring
Map   Kern County road map
Trailhead   3. See car tour T1. From the Highway 14 junction (0.0/0.0), drive east on *California City Blvd.* to Ransburg Mojave Road (9.6/9.6). Turn left, drive northeast on *Ransburg Mojave Road* past a fork with 20 Mule Team Road (1.7/11.3). Still on the same road, now unpaved, drive to a left turn indicated by DTNA directional sign (3.8/15.1). Drive on the *spur road* to the Interpretive Center (1.2/16.3) at **TH3**.

Description   To be comfortable in the desert, you need to dress in layers, wear a hat and sunglasses, and bring water. After a visit to the kiosk where displays are designed to expand your knowledge of the desert tortoise, its neighbors and its land, begin your explorations at the self-guided *Main Loop Trail*. Plant, animal and discovery trails branch off from this short loop. Interpretive material is available at the start of each trail, except for the Discovery Trail, where you are on your own. Please return the brochures to the boxes after completing each trail.

Your best chance to see a tortoise outside its burrow is in the morning or late afternoon when the temperature is most agreeable for it—and for you. During drought years when its food supply of annuals and perennials is diminished, you may not see a tortoise at all. But if one rambles by, be very careful not to frighten it—you may cause it to lose precious fluid.

In contrast to the studied pace of the tortoise, many varieties of lizards dash about the Desert Tortoise Natural Area (DTNA) like court jesters. The somber sidewinder and Mojave green rattlesnakes live here, too, and are just as important to the desert ecology. They doze in the shade of bushes or curl in abandoned burrows and are harmless to people if not disturbed. Remember that this is a protected area: do not touch or tease the animals, pick the flowers, move or remove anything that is natural to the area.

The desert tortoise, the California state reptile, has survived the effects of drought, extreme temperatures and predators for two million years, but it is having a difficult time surviving the onslaught of man. For years people have taken desert tortoises home to have as pets. Wildlife biologists have suggested that there may be more of them in backyards than in the wild. In 1961 California legislators made it illegal to remove this reptile from its natural habitat. For further protection, this particular area known to have the highest density of tortoises per square mile in their geographic range, was set aside in 1972 by BLM for a tortoise preserve. A group of concerned people formed the Desert Tortoise Preserve Committee to work with BLM for the good of the tortoise and its cohabitants. Within six years the entire DTNA, encompassing over 16,000 acres, was completely fenced. Now the tortoise was protected from the destructive force of OHVs that left crushed shells and collapsed burrows in its wake, and from the unfortunate effects of sheep and cattle, which competed with them for food. Accomplishments in the preserve have been remarkable, but the tortoise is still in trouble.

In addition to destruction by OHVs, unsuccessful competition with domestic grazing animals and removal from its natural home, the desert tortoise faces extinction from additional enemies: a virus introduced by "pet" tortoises, which have been returned to the desert; voracious ravens, rapidly increasing in numbers, which have thrived on

Tortoise

man's garbage and young tortoises; and the effects of an ever shrinking habitat. The committee along with BLM is working to solve each of these problems.

An important boost was given this tortoise in April 1990 when it was listed in the Federal Register by the U.S. Fish and Wildlife Service as a threatened species under the Federal Endangered Species Act. Under this listing the tortoise is protected from all physical and habitat harm. It is uncertain how this will eventually effect the public's entree into the preserve. For current information and for docent guided tours, contact the Desert Tortoise Preserve Committee or BLM Ridgecrest—both listed in Part One of this book.

T4   Chuckwalla Mountain Climb
With Excursion A: Cross Mountain

While a heavy snowpack renders most High Sierra mountains inaccessible, hikers can ascend Chuckwalla for a winter workout and a pleasing introduction to high-desert environs. Intrepid peakbaggers often climb this in tandem with Cross Mountain.

Distance   3.2 miles, round trip
Steep Ascents   0.5 mile
Elevation Gain   1390 feet
Skills   Easy route finding; Class 1-2 climbing
Seasons   Fall, winter, spring
Map   USGS 7.5 min *Cinco*
Trailhead   4. See car tour T1. Turn west from Highway 14 onto unpaved, unsigned, *Lone Tree Canyon Road* (0.0/0.0). Drive under, then over, the LA aqueducts to a road fork (2.2/2.2) immediately beyond the second pipe. Take the right fork, *aqueduct service road.* Drive up the tributary canyon, pass a road to the right, switchback up and out of the canyon, turn left at the next junction (1.5/3.7). Drive to a left turn onto a *jeep road* (0.2/3.9) just before the aqueduct road descends steeply from a ridge. Proceed on the jeep road to **TH4** at a fork (0.5/4.4).
Description   Your trip begins where a spur road and a m'cyclepath branch to the right of

the road on which you arrived (3640/0.0). The rounded summit and southern point of Chuckwalla Mountain, named for the large desert lizard, beckon to the north, but you ascend west up the steep *m'cyclepath* atop the minor ridge between your road and the spur road. (The bladed spur road that descends to the right, then climbs to meet your route near the crest of the south-sloping ridge 1.0 mile later, is very steep and not recommended for wheel or foot travel.)

The trail and ridge fade on the rocky terrain which, nevertheless, supports a scattering of high desert shrubs. You will probably not see a chuckwalla on this trip, but you may see hairy-legged tarantulas pad along the path. Continuing to climb, turn northwest on another *bike path* along the crest of a better defined ridge. You cross the aforementioned spur road (4090/0.4), and, after passing a mine's boundary stake and more steep climbing, you join the *spur road* (4540/0.2) to hike north just below, then on top Chuckwalla's southern ridge.

Leave the road where it crosses the crest and descends west. Climbers of Cross Mountain return here from Chuckwalla's summit to descend on that piece of road. You proceed on a *use trail* (4540/0.2) that begins on this fairly level section of the ridge. Now with lower Peak 4964 of the mountain directly north of you, pick your way along this well-defined path, occasionally marked by ducks. After passing a prospector's dig, you ascend on a curve below the lower peak to a saddle with another boundary marker. The final ascent to the treeless summit follows (5029/0.8).

Comprehensive views on a clear day include Telescope Peak of Death Valley to the northeast, El Paso Mountains and Fremont Valley to the east, the extreme Southern Sierra and the San Bernardino, San Gabriel mountains to the south. A canyon and lesser peaks separate you from Cross Mountain to the west.

Excursion A: Cross Mountain

Cross Mountain's rhyolite, a viscous lava that erupted from a crack in the earth's crust along the Jawbone Fault 11-16 million years ago, interests geologists and laymen who find volcanology a fascinating study. The southern ascent of Cross Mountain attracts peakbaggers who enjoy the extra challenge of the route from Chuckwalla Mountain.

Distance   6.8 miles, round trip
Steep Ascents   0.7 mile
Skills   Intermediate route finding; Class 2 climbing
Elevation Gain   2855 feet
Maps   USGS 7.5 min *Cinco, Cross Mtn*
Description   From the level area atop Chuckwalla Mountain's south ridge, midway between your cars and Chuckwalla's summit, you descend west on the *spur road* 4540/0.0) to a fork on a saddle. The right fork leads to a prospect; you take the left fork that ascends southwest to the top of Point 4616

(4616/0.5), a good place to oversee your route. Cross Mountain's round summit appears northwest; and, below its southwest extended ridge, you see a pastel pink splotch backed by several dark spires (300° on the compass). Your final goal is to hike up the canyon to and over that colorful exposed rock and up the southwest ridge to the summit.

But your immediate goal is a dilapidated hut on the sandy flood plains of the canyon below. To reach that hut, turn sharply right, follow the *m'cyclepath* north along and then steeply down the crest of a northwest descending ridge, staying left where the trail forks just below the crest. Your arrival at the wood and corrugated metal hut (3660/0.8) might startle a few resident cows. Now traveling on a *cross-country* route, you hike up the wash, pass a gully to your right, and arrive at a confluence of two canyons, 0.4 mile from the hut. Turn into the canyon to your right where you soon see on the slopes far ahead, the pink of the rounded exposed rock and the guardian spires, and make your way there. Beyond the rock and the spires, you reach the ridgecrest and climb on hard-pan rhyolite, following a *m'cyclepath* to the summit (5203/2.1).

Coyote

Formally, an easy descent to Jawbone Canyon Road and awaiting shuttle cars saved the demanding return trip to Chuckwalla Mountain. But now Cross Mountain's north flank is blocked by a fence with signs that shout *Hard Hat Area, Authorized Personnel Only* and *No Trespassing,* posted by Monarch Quarry and Rudnick Estate personnel.

T5   Car & All-Terrain Bicycle Tour on Jawbone Canyon Road
(With Directions to Trailheads 8, 20–25: Highway 14 approach)

Jawbone Canyon's chalky sediments with hues of magenta to orange to earth browns were laid down several million years ago. They were later elevated by movements along the Sierra Nevada and Garlock faults, then weathered to foothills. This stark, colorful canyon is a patchwork of private and BLM managed public lands, and a playground for OHVs, as the numerous slope slashes attest. The high desert pastures of Kelso Valley are passed en route to cool, forested Piute Mountains—thus this tour travels through three dissimilar land forms.

Distance   26.4 miles, one way
Steep Ascents   None (Long, hard grades for bicyclists)
Elevation Gain   5585 feet
Skills   Easy route finding; unpaved road (Geringer Grade can be rutted)
Seasons   All year (Omit the Piute Mountains segment in winter; bicyclists should omit this trip in summer as well.)
Map   Kern County road map
Tourhead   5. From Highway 14, turn west on Jawbone Canyon Road, **TH5**. This is 19 miles north of Highway 58 and 22.2 miles south of Highway 178 West. This trip departs from car tour T1.
Description   Traveling west on paved *Jawbone Canyon Road* (2135/0.0/0.0), the route follows this sometimes hot, undulating road, crossing a boundary into BLM's Jawbone–Butterbredt Area of Critical Environmental Concern. In 1982 BLM concluded a lengthy study of this area and confirmed that OHVs have caused extensive damage to the terrain, including some Native American sites, and that overgrazing has greatly damaged the flora. Since then, BLM has restricted OHV use to specific "Open" areas and roads. If BLM restricted cattle and sheep grazing, it is not apparent.

The road leads over the second LA aqueduct, then crosses the Sierra Nevada fault zone. It then crosses the original aqueduct just downslope from the tree-shaded caretakers' houses. Beyond the houses, the road dips through the main wash, then parallels it to the south, losing its pavement. The blue-green hue of Blue Point at the mouth of Alphie Canyon stands in contrast to the browns of the surrounding country. The blue-green is an overlay of welded volcanic tuff-breccia deposited 8-12 million years ago. Today this remnant drifts on a sea of granite, convoyed by a swarm of little faults.

A left road fork just beyond Blue Point (2700/6.2/6.2) was previously used to reach Cross Mountain, but it is now closed to public use. Your wide, washboard dirt road swings north, twists, dips and climbs while passing several lesser closed roads and OHV paths as it gains elevation and access to a spur road (4000/5.5/11.7). This spur road is the south approach to car tour T24 and Butterbredt Spring Wildlife Sanctuary, an 0.9 mile descent into Butterbredt Canyon. Beyond here your route crosses a saddle and reaches another (4846/3.2/14.9) where climbs of T6, Butterbredt Peak begin at **TH8**. Arid Kelso Valley spreads before you as the road descends on Pleistocene sediments to meet Kelso Valley Road (3949/3.4/18.3), which bisects the valley. Here people seeking **THs 20–24** turn right, others continue ahead and skip the following description.

Drive north on sandy *Kelso Valley Road* (0.0/0.0) to its summit where the PCT crosses at **TH22** (5.3/5.3). Continue farther, now descending on paved road, to Butterbredt Canyon Road, BLM SC123, (1.2/6.5), where **TH21** is 0.7 mile up-canyon at the offset PCT crossing. Travel on Kelso Valley Road to **TH20** (1.3/7.8), Piute Mountain Road. Now see car tour T17 for Piute Mountain trailheads.

Your route on Jawbone Canyon Road advances through the junction, then curves south where your car and bike rattle over a cattle guard in half a mile and another one a mile later. Soon your course leaves the barren plains to enter an oak savannah, and then dips to cross seasonal Cottonwood Creek (4705/ 4.8/23.1). Low slung cars need to be driven carefully over the next couple miles as the route ascends steep Geringer Grade, a sharply curved road, sometimes deeply rutted. Bicyclists may wish to dismount. A montage of trees flash by: digger, pinyon and Jeffrey pines, mountain juniper, blue oak and white fir. In time your route gains the plateau, passes into Sequoia National Forest (6250/ 2.2/25.3) and travels on to the PCT of trips T2, T19 and T20 at **TH25** (6620/1.1/26.4). This is as far west as this tour goes.

Since Kelso Valley Road, your tour has overlapped car tour T17, in reverse. You can refer to that tour and continue to explore the Piutes. Jawbone Canyon Road swings north to meet Piute Mountain Road. That road crosses the Piutes and, along with its branch, descends on three "corners" of the plateau— all called *Piute Mountain Road* on some maps. Locally the northwest road is called *Saddle Springs Road* or *Ball Mountain Road* and coded SNF Road 27S02. Trips on the Piute Mountains west of here are described in this book's companion edition.

Cross Mountain from Jawbone Canyon Road

T6   Butterbredt Peak Climb

Outdoor enthusiasts looking for a brief wintertime workout offering generous views of bracing, austere terrain will find this trip tailor-made.

Distance   2.2 miles, round trip
Steep Ascents   0.6 mile
Elevation Gain   1155 feet
Skills   Easy route finding; Class 1-2 climbing
Seasons   Fall, winter, spring
Maps   USGS 7.5 min *Cross Mtn (0.2 mile), Pinyon Mtn*
Trailhead   8. Highway 14 approach: see car tour T5. Highway 178 approach: see car tour T24.
Description   This area receives special management under the California Desert Conservation Act. In 1976 a BLM report stated that approximately 343 species of animals live in this stark high desert: two species of amphibians, 46 species of reptiles, 89 species of mammals and 206 species of birds. However, you will be fortunate to see even a lizard on this hike.

In pursuit of that illusive lizard and the expanse of views ahead, you leave Jawbone Canyon Road and ascend the slope north-east on a **Cross-country** route (4846/0.0), attaining the first of several false summits. Then, after spotting a **use trail** on southeast-facing slopes just below the ridgecrest of outcrops and false summits, you ramble along it, soon reaching a saddle and then the true summit (5997/1.1). If all of the animal species evade you, the vegetation cannot: the common Mormon tea is ubiquitous here. This is a high desert plant, yet its foliage is yellow-green, unlike the blue-to-gray green of most xeric plants. Its many-branched and many-jointed slender stems further distinguish it. Pioneers brewed its dried stems for tea; Indians considered the drink to be a tonic.

From the summit, you can identify Pinyon Mountain to the north in bas-relief over Gold Peak. Tracking the Sierra crest to the west, across Kelso Valley, you gaze on Sorrell Peak, a point on the ridge. Then pivot counterclockwise to pick out Cross and Chuckwalla mountains from a foreground of foothills to the south.

Red Cliffs Preserve

T7   Red Rock Canyon State Park Side Trip

*People traveling on Highway 14 along the edge of the Mojave Desert east of the
nascent Southern Sierra are suddenly treated to a colorful display of the rain- and
wind-carved, corrugated cliffs of the El Paso Mountains. Then just as suddenly they
drive beyond that moment of scenic beauty, perhaps promising to return when time
permits. This trip fulfills that promise.*

*The history of Red Rock Canyon is as colorful as the multihued rocks; and the
unique combination of desert and mountain plants and animals are as fascinating as
the intricate cliffs. It is an area that the whole family can enjoy.*

Distance   Optional
Steep Ascents   None
Elevation Gain   Negligible
Skills   Easy route finding; easy hiking
Seasons   All year
Map   Kern County road map
Trailhead   6. See car tour T1. Turn west on
paved ***Abbott Drive*** (0.0/0.0). Drive to the
entry gate, **TH6** (0.8/0.8).
Description   Although the park is open all
year, you should first consider the weather. A
day trip in early winter can be invigorating,
but night temperatures often drop below
freezing. Summer days are sizzling, but an
overnight camp out under a dazzling canopy
of stars is unforgettable. Late winter and
early spring are best, especially if the 5–6
inches of annual rainfall materialize to trans-
form the desert into a carpet of flowers. It is
then, and again in fall, that nature walks and
campfire programs are offered on weekends.

There are two natural preserves within the
park: Hagen Canyon and Red Cliffs. You can
wander on foot at will in the preserves or in
the rest of the park. OHVs are not allowed in
the preserves and must stay on roads in the
park.

Hagen Canyon Natural Preserve, which
includes Hagen Canyon and White House
Cliffs, is the most popular place to explore.
From the parking lot at the south end of
Abbott Drive, hike into Hagen Canyon,
explore all of it, but also skirt the cliffs at your
right to the dry falls at the end.

The canyon was named for Rudolph
Hagen, a German immigrant, who established a store here in 1896 during the gold
rush—a way station for stage coaches. Hagen
was a man with a rich imagination: he gave

the milticolored land forms names from
Greek mythology. Hagen's predecessors on
the land were the Kawaiisu Native Americans; before them prehistoric people inhabited the area and are thought to have
carved some of the petroglyphs in the El Paso
Range.

Another outing both children and adults
enjoy is a hike along the self-guided ***nature
trail***, which is found at the south end of the
main campground. From the top of the trail
hike to the White House Cliffs above the
campground. Adults may tire from climbing
these "sand castles" long before children
do—children with imaginations to match
Hagen's.

A third popular jaunt is exploring the
formations in the ***Red Cliffs Preserve*** across
Highway 14. These deeply etched cliffs have
enriched the background of many movies and
commercials, which were filmed here.

To enhance the interest of these short
trips, it would help to know a little of the
natural history, as well. During Pliocene
times, around 10 million years ago, much of
this area was a fresh water lake receiving
layers of sediment that flowed in from
streams and poured down from volcanoes. It
had a moist climate with an estimated 35
inches of annual rainfall. This produced
plants that supported a mixture of animals,
including camels, sabre-toothed cats, masto-
dons and rhinoceroses. The climate changed,
the lake dried, the land pushed up and tilted
by movements along the Garlock Fault and
its major splay, the El Paso Fault, and the
layers of sediment that had been compressed
into sandstone became exposed. Then, as
now, channels of water that ran off the

caprock of brown basalt and pink tuff-breccia, both volcanic in origin, and sandstone caused the deep pleating of the exposed softer clay below. The rust reds are the oxidation of iron in the rocks.

Now reptiles and small mammals call this home. Barn Owls and Great Horned Owls screech and hoot at night. Hawks and eagles nest in Nightmare Gulch, a popular canyon for OHVs and hikers just outside the park. It is closed from February 1 to July 1 to accommodate these nesting birds. Black Mountain, Last Chance Canyon, Old Dutch Cleanser Mines and Burro Schmidt's Tunnel are additional attractions east of the park, all of which add an extra dimension to your visit.

T8   South Fork Valley Car & Bicycle Tour on Highway 178: Highway 14 to Sierra Way
(With Directions to Trailheads 9–17)

The valley of this trip is steeped in history from the days when Tubatulabal Indians roamed freely, through the days of the trail blazers, the gold seekers, the cattle ranchers to now when chunks of rangeland for sale are attracting former city dwellers to the peace of rural life. Life seems serene in this pastoral valley where bouldery mountains rise abruptly to resemble in their treeless craggy jumble those above timberline in the High Sierra.

Distance   32.4 miles, one way
Steep Ascents   None
Elevation Gain   2060 feet
Skills   Easy route finding; paved road
Seasons   All year (Bicyclists avoid summer)
Map   Kern County road map
Tourhead   7. From Highway 14, turn west on Highway 178 at **TH7**. This is 41.2 miles north of Mojave and 2.7 miles south of its east road to Ridgecrest. This tour heads west from the junction of car tours T1 and T46.
Description   Traveling on *State Highway 178*, west of the Highway 14 junction (3186/0.0/0.0), you quickly arrive at a California Historical Monument. The plaque on the monument recalls the passage of the Death Valley 49ers after their ordeal; recounts a journey of pathfinder Joseph R. Walker; and, strangely, lumps the misdeeds of bandit Tiburcio Vasquez with the feats of the others.

The outcrop of Robbers Roost can be seen to the left as you follow Highway 178 west from the marker. This granitic protrusion, which withstood erosional forces, was believed to be for a time the hideout of Vasquez and his men. The late climber Carl A. Heller reported that several Class 3–5 routes lead up the rocks, and that they require an upper belay for safety. But from January through June, climbers could conflict with local nesting raptors, including the prairie falcon, therefore, BLM declared the site off limits to climbers during those months.

You soon cross the slab-covered original LA Aqueduct (climbers often drive the adjacent aqueduct service road, left, en route to Robbers Roost). Then you cross the second aqueduct and its service road (0.9/0.9). Here drivers to **TH9** turn north for T25, a short but steep climb to the creosote rings. The largest rings are thought to be among the oldest living vegetation. You next enter Freeman Canyon, where an impressive grove of Kern Joshua trees congregate. This Joshua, according to the late botanist Ernest C. Twisselmann, reproduces from underground root stock, unlike other Joshua trees, which require pollination by a small moth to reproduce. The Pacific Crest Trail becomes visible as you gain the Sierra crest at Walker Pass (5246/7.6/8.5). Hikers en route from Mexico cross the highway here on their way to Canada. This is **TH10** for others whose hikes on the PCT are considerably shorter. Much of this area is under consideration for

Century-old tombstones

wilderness preservation.

The National Historic Landmark here honors pioneer pathfinder Joseph R. Walker, for whom the pass was named. In 1834 Walker was believed to have crossed here while returning to the Great Salt Lake from the San Joaquin Valley: a theory some historians dispute. The band he led at that time had seen the wonders of Yosemite Valley and the giant Sierra sequoias. His route-finding expeditions for the army eventually led to United States' forces wresting control of California from Mexico.

Leaving the pass, which remains open most of the winter, your road descends around a hairpin curve and the road to T9 at Walker Pass Trailhead Campground (1.0/9.5), which was built for PCT hikers. The campsites here at **TH11** are nestled among the pinyon pines. Your route soon converges with Canebrake Creek, which was named for Carrizo grass, once abundant but now extinct in this area. Lieutenant R.S. Williamson found it here, and also along Kelso Creek, while surveying potential railroad routes throughout Southern California in 1853. Botanist Twisselmann believed the demise of this sugar-exuding forage may have been the result of overgrazing.

You cross Canebrake Creek just prior to reaching the vine-covered lattice of Walker Pass Lodge. All that remains of the lodge is the restaurant, which is still in operation and still bears the original name. It was built in the

1930s from lumber salvaged from James Station, a store that offered home-grown fruits and vegetables to miners and stage-coach customers. You soon see the lone standing chimney of the store in the brush to the right as you wend your way along the highway. The James family still operate stores in Kern River Valley.

The valley ahead, collectively called the South Fork Valley, has changed little since it was settled over 100 years ago. Feast your eyes upon the pastoral landscape now, as developers are buying land here and the scene will change. To your left, steep flanks of the Scodie Mountains, a subrange of the Sierra Nevada, rise directly from the road-side. You shortly pass the obscure beginning of T10 at **TH12** (2.9/12.4) (check your mileage to find the trailhead), the only convenient route up Pinyon Peak that avoids trespass on private land.

As the road continues to descend beside a diminishing scythe-shaped ridge, watch for a hundred year old black walnut tree to the left of the road. It once shaded a stagecoach station. Shortly after, you pass a jeep road to the right (2.8/15.2), which in 3.9 miles gives access to the PCT below Owens Peak. Soon after the jeep road, if you look carefully you will notice that some of Canebrake Creek's flow disappears under the road to emerge in a ditch along the left and then on to water what it can in the bajada of Canebrake Flat. This is one example of the numerous flumes that

Old Store

were built many years ago in the South Fork Valley to carry water, mostly from the South Fork Kern River, to irrigate the fertile but parched land. They are still in use. You can locate the ditches as well as the river and creeks by the willows and cottonwoods growing along them.

Just 0.2 mile beyond the Canebrake irrigation ditch you pass BLM's unpaved Canebrake Road, **TH13** of car tour T28 (3284/ 2.4/17.6), which leads to Chimney Peak Recreation Area where many trips originate. Next you pass the developments of Rancho Sierra on Canebrake Flat, the settlement of Canebrake, and the lush growth around the Bloomfield Ranch. The South Fork River tumbles down the distant canyon from Dome Land Wilderness north of the road curve and ranch. Beyond the ranch, set back to the left of the road, are buildings that housed a marijuana crop, then other illegal drug manufacturing, then a ranch for animals offered for adoption. The first two enterprises were busted, the third, unfortunately, did not thrive.

In time you pass Cottage Grove Cemetery, dotted with century old tombstones, located on a parcel of Smith Ranch that was set aside in 1862. The ranch is one of the many in the South Fork handed down from generation to generation and still in operation. Soon you reach the small town of Onyx with its rickety, 1861, old store, founded by pioneer storekeeper Scodie. Onyx Store is thought to be the oldest continuously operating store in

California. In the next town, Weldon, named for a cattleman, you pass Kelso Creek Road (11.6/29.2), entry to T11, Onyx Peak climb at **TH14**. In minutes you see the Methodist Church, the hub of the South Fork community since the turn of the century, then Fay Ranch Road (1.2/30.4),which takes backpackers to **TH15** where they leave their shuttle cars for T40.

The next turnoff of note is Kelso Valley Road, **TH16** (0.8/31.2), to the left, described in car tour T12. It takes hikers and climbers to numerous trailheads and trips. To our right are a pair of driveways. The first just prior to Kelso Valley Road, leads to the A. Brown Mill, built in 1877. The members of the Kern River Valley Historical Society restored this historic structure and offer tours on occasion. Entrepreneur A. Brown had, among other enterprises, country stores in the valley and often acquired land in lieu of payment for overdue accounts. He thus became the largest landowner in the Kern River Valley and surrounding mountains. The second driveway goes to the Kern River Valley Nature Conservancy's riparian holding. The non-profit Conservancy purchased this land to preserve it in its natural state. (For further information see Part 1.) Beyond these past and present important sites, you reach Sierra Way, **TH17** (2630/1.2/32.4), the east road to Kernville and the Kern River described in car tour T37. Highway 178 continues along the south side of Lake Isabella. The route is described in this book's companion edition.

Weldon United Methodist Church

T9   Day Hike to Scodie Mountain via the PCT
With Excursion B: Scodie Peak

In wildflower season the slopes along the trail are painted in a flourish of various colors. In all seasons, crumbling granitic rocks dot the cross-country trek to the fractured crown of Scodie Peak, huddled and solitary. When the air is sparkling, the unobstructed panoramic views from the summit are rewarding.

Distance   8.8 miles, round trip
Steep Ascents   None
Elevation Gain   1630 feet
Skills   Easy route finding; moderate hiking
Seasons   Spring, summer, fall (can be hot)
Map   USGS 7.5 min *Walker Pass*
Trailhead   11. See car tour T8 for Walker Pass Trailhead Campground which is **TH11**.
Description   Your hike commences at the east end of the campground on a ***path*** (5050/0.0) to the PCT. Upon reaching the ***PCT*** (5100/0.1), you turn right to gradually ascend southwest along the canyon of intermittent Canebrake Creek, then dip to cross its usually dry bed. Here a sandy path, the PCT skirts the lower slopes of minor Peak 6018, then climbs in a series of switchbacks. During this climb the trail rounds below a ridgecrest, where tucked out of sight over the crest, a substantial quail guzzler catches water for wildlife.

Beyond the switchbacks, the trail crosses over a ridgeline saddle (5860/2.1), passes a use trail to Jacks Creek, and traverses the west side of Peak 6522. Tangles of spring wildflowers bloom profusely on these slopes. A few, foot-high, intensely-blue bouquets of Charlotte's phacelia, *Phacelia nashiana,* are the prized flowers found among them. Phacelias have several flowers on a stem and many silken stamens in the cup of each bloom, which extend beyond the petals. Knowing you should not pick wildflowers, especially ones so rare, you perhaps linger, admire, imprint them on your memory—and move on.

Your trail switchbacks to brief east views and back, and in 0.4 mile from the switchback, it curves sharply around a northwest ravine (6680/2.2). Here you have several choices: leave the trail to climb Scodie Peak; continue to the rolling plateau and maybe 3.0 miles further to McIvers Spring (See T16); or turn back.

A. Brown Mill

Excursion B: Scodie Peak

The elongated stretch of Freeman Canyon dissolving into endless desert below the slopes of Scodie Peak is one of the vistas for peakbaggers. The ideal campsites on the summit's plateau for star gazers is another of this peak's attractions.

Distance   3.0 miles, round trip
Steep Ascents   0.2 mile
Elevation Gain   675 feet
Skills   Intermediate route finding; Class 1–2 climbing
Map   USGS 7.5 min *Walker Pass* (Scodie Peak is not named on the map. It is 35°37'45"N, 118°1'38"W.)
Description   Peak climbers leave the trail (6680/0.0) at the drainage point of a sharp curve around a northwest canyon, which is less than a ½ mile south of a switchback and less than a ½ mile after the trail descends from the plateau to the north. The *cross-country* climb begins on a moderate-to-steep ascent up the southwest slope of the ravine to a narrow saddle, the division between this long canyon to Jacks Creek and the apex of Cow Heaven Canyon to the southeast. Much of this hike wiggles between pinyon pine and live oak trees. You will want to take careful note of the topography here to find this particular canyon on the return trip. (If when returning, you are still uncertain which canyon to descend, continue on a gently descending course west-northwest and you will find the trail. Because of the sharp turn of the PCT in this canyon, you could miss it altogether if you descend too soon.)

From the narrow saddle, you walk along the crest around the rim of Cow Heaven Canyon, first northeast skirting minor Peak 7042, then east-southeast undulating somewhat as you climb over hills along the way to the ascent of Scodie Peak (7294/1.5). (If you stray off-course to the north of the final leg of the climb, you may stumble upon the remains of a lean-to cabin surrounding a cast iron stove.) Just below the summit block on an open flat rests a singular granite rock with a basin 18 inches in diameter and equally as deep. The origin and significance of this bowl are unknown.

T10   Pinyon Peak Climb

For a vigorous last hurrah of the season, try this trip. It will challenge the average hiker's physical endurance and route-finding skills. But in return, besides the satisfaction of accomplishment, it offers progressively expansive views of the Southern Sierra crest and valley below.

Distance   5.6 miles, round trip
Steep Ascents   1.5 miles
Elevation Gain   2985 feet
Skills   Intermediate route finding; Class 1 climbing
Season   Fall
Map   USGS 7.5 min *Walker Pass*
Trailhead   12. See car tour T8. Mileage is the best way to locate this trailhead—park on the southwest shoulder which is **TH12**.
Description   On this *cross-country* route you leave Highway 178 (4300/0.0) and ascend south in BLM land up a steep ridge amid widespread sagebrush and rabbitbrush, both of which harbor ticks in spring.

You scramble 0.2 mile to an outcrop atop a minor hill, the first of several hills you climb on this trip. (Brush and cliffs on the steep flanks of these hills make them easier to climb over than to circle.) After another steep length with clumps of brush, you top a second hill, from which the Sierra crest to the northeast—especially Spanish Needle, Owens Peak and Mount Jenkins—looms impressively. (Six years after co-author Jim first observed the view from this hilltop, the jagged mountain to the south of pointed Owens Peak was named in his memory.)

At this point the course turns right, dips southwest to a saddle, enters Sequoia

National Forest, crosses low Hill 5101, and reaches another saddle, this one overlying the Pinyon Peak Fault. Pause here before tackling the steepest climb of the trip: a 1000-foot gain in ½ mile. The climb follows a slight ridge with welcome live oak and pinyon pine shade. To avoid a mistake on the return trip, note which is your minor ridge and which is the one that imperceptibly merges with yours midway up the slope. The route tops out on a major east-west ridge at a cairn marking Point 6050 (6050/1.1), where you turn right to follow the crest west.

After ascending a moderate grade you reach the rocky summit of Hill 6522, approaching it from its north side. Views of clefts and jagged peaks include Mount Whitney far to the north. To the west, below your route, you can see the stand of Jeffrey pines, through which you soon pass. On an easy descent from Hill 6522, among pinyon pines, you reach the usually dry bed of a meadow draining stream in the Jeffrey pine forest.

Your route follows the stream 0.3 mile to the meadow's east edge where an old, rusted trough straddles the bed. The route turns left here, south-southwest, along a shallow crease, then follows the crease as it becomes better defined and turns southeast into the canyon between the 6700-foot hill to the left and Pinyon Peak to the right. Although the canyon becomes uncomfortably brushy near the saddle, this route avoids the continuous bushwhacking of other choices. Look for woodrats' stick-nest piles among the brush. Some seen here were about 4 feet tall; they can be as high as 6 feet. The final stretch south up Pinyon Peak is best approached through the pines roughly 100 yards east of the saddle, again to avoid dense brush.

When the summit (6805/1.7) is finally attained, the distant San Gabriel Mountains become apparent on the southern horizon, over the flat profile of the Scodie Mountains. The view north to Mount Whitney from here, however, is nearly blocked by trees.

T11   Onyx Peak Climb

Onyx Peak, an outlier of the Scodie Mountains, withstood erosion just a bit better than the ridge it straddles; and so offers a lookout over the South Fork Valley.

Distance   4.8 miles, round trip
Steep Ascents   0.6 mile
Elevation Gain   2405 feet
Skills   Intermediate route finding; Class 2 climbing
Seasons   Fall, winter, spring
Map   USGS 7.5 min *Onyx*
Trailhead   14. See car tour T8. From Highway 178 (0.0/0.0) drive east on paved *Kelso Creek Road,* which curves to meet South Fork Lane, then continues south. Turn left onto a dirt road (2.7/2.7) located about 60 yards past Walker Road among several private driveways and before a row of mail boxes. The junction of Kelso Creek Road and Kelso Valley Road is 1.8 miles past this dirt road. On the *dirt road,* ascend east to a locked gate, **TH 14** (0.2/2.9).
Description   On this trek you begin by

Cholla cactus

heading east with a step over a chain across a cattle guard (2920/0.0), then amble along the **dirt road** to Short Canyon Well and a nearby cattle loading chute (3039/0.4). From the well you hike north on a **cross-country** route that immediately descends into the washes of Short Canyon and climbs beyond to a **jeep road** (3125/0.3), on which you turn right. You skirt below Onyx Peak ridge, but you cannot see the peak.

The deteriorating road, which has two distinct U curves, cuts northeast across high desert terrain where occasional beavertail and cholla cacti poke through the hardpan. Beavertail cactus, a spineless maverick in the cactus family, wins kudos for its stunning magenta flowers. Cholla, on the other hand, is the spiniest of all cacti. The abundance of these spines gives cholla a glow in the backlight of a low sun.

Follow the road to the apex of the second curve (3460/0.8) where it descends east, but you leave it at this point to curve north. Again on a **cross-country** course you climb up a crease, aiming for the lowest dip on the ridge. On occasion this slope is a mass of wildflowers—a pleasant diversion on this steep ascent. Achieving the rolling ridgecrest, you briefly stroll north-northwest along the crest past the first point to Onyx Peak summit (5244/0.9).

South Fork Valley stretches to the east and to the west, and the little community of Onyx nestles by the highway far below. The semiprecious stone, onyx, is not found here. The village and peak received this name because in the late 1800s, storekeeper Scodie liked its sound.

Beavertail cactus

T12   Kelso Creek Valley Car & Bicycle Tour
(With Directions to Trailheads 18–22)

If it is raining where you are, do not let that stop you from taking this trip, for its locale receives no more than 8 inches of rain each year; much of that in summer thundershowers. Native flowers embellish the austere landforms in late winter and spring, and groves of graceful cottonwoods overarch sandy beaches along Kelso Creek for your picnicking pleasure.

Distance   19.7 miles, one way

Steep Ascents   None

Elevation Gain   2500 feet

Skills   Easy route finding; paved road

Seasons   All year (Bicyclists avoid summer)

Map   Kern County road map

Tourhead   16. From Highway 178 in Weldon, turn south on Kelso Valley Road, **TH16**. This is 31.2 miles west of Highway 14 and 1.2 miles east of Sierra Way. It departs from car tour T8.

Description   Your travels begin on **Kelso Valley Road** (2641/0.0/0.0), shaded on either corner by large Fremont cottonwood trees. These trees have roundish triangular leaves that resemble those of quaking aspen, but do not quiver because they lack flat leaf stems. Cottonwoods usually grow by waterways, and here they are near a ditch in which water diverted from the South Fork Kern River curves around this northwest corner of Kelso Creek Valley.

Your road first heads southeast, then, except for occasional short deviations, it runs in a southern direction. It ascends along the valley between the Scodie Mountains and a transitional range to the left, and the Piute Mountains to the right. As you commence, you can identify Onyx Peak, the highest point at this end of the Scodie range; and Nicolls Peak, the highest point at this end of the Piute range.

Now you pass the irrigation ditch, and, immediately thereafter, on the slope to your right, you pass multilevel ruins of a tungsten mill. You soon cross two cattleguards: the unpaved road to the west immediately beyond the second (4.0/4.0) takes climbers to **TH18** for T13 and T14. Nonclimbers continue on and skip the following description.

For Nicolls and Heald peaks, you turn right, drive northwest on the **dirt road** (0.0/0.0), then southwest toward the canyon south of pointed Nicolls Peak to a scissors fork (1.0/1.0). Take the left fork through the stock-fence gate (please close), through a dip, then a lesser dip, and continue up the canyon until the road becomes impassable at **TH18** (0.6/1.6). Parking here is limited.

Beyond the turnoff, your road dips into the usually dry, wide wash of Kelso Creek, then joins paved Kelso Creek Road (1.3/5.3). This valley is unusually broad and deep for a creek as paltry as Kelso to have carved by itself. Some geologists suggest that the South Fork Kern River flowed south through here toward the ancestral Mojave Desert from 10 to 20 million years ago, before the upheaval of the present ranges.

The road now traverses the mouth of Cane Canyon, rounds Rocky Point and there comes close to a clump of willows where Kelso Creek usually sinks underground for the last time in its down-canyon progress. Next, the road deviates from its course to trace the rectilinear boundaries of private property. The access road to Cortez Canyon subdivision descends to your right at a sharp curve, then apple orchards hide a couple of old adobe houses to your left, and Pinyon Creek Canyon gapes just beyond.

You soon pass the fenced Butterbredt family cemetery with three crosses hidden amid sagebrush, then farther down pause to read the signs at Bird Spring Road, BLM SC120, (6.2/11.5). One sign erected by a troop of Boy Scouts, lacks proper punctuation, and reads like the transcribed speech of a breathless young messenger. It tells of John C. Fremont's crossing of Bird Spring Pass in 1854. Another sign, this one placed by BLM, welcomes you to the Jawbone-Butterbredt Area of Critical Environmental Concern (ACEC). This area, the largest ACEC of its kind, is set aside to receive special management for the protection of wildlife and Native American values. Bird Spring Pass is just barely hidden by intervening ridges. Those heading for **TH19** turn left here; the rest continue on and ignore the following description.

To reach **TH19,** turn east on maintained, unpaved ***Bird Spring Road, BLM SC120,*** (0.0/0.0). Drive up-canyon past Pinyon Well (1.6/1.6). The road can be rough as it crosses Pinyon Creek wash. You ascend the steepening road and climb via a switchback to the pass at **TH19** (4.0/5.6), for Ts 15, 16 & 23.

Continuing on Kelso Valley Road, you ride through the usually dry bed of Pinyon Creek 100 yards from the junction, pass a community of small houses and mobile homes and climb to a broad saddle. Bicyclists need to pay special attention, as there are many blind dips and turns ahead. If a car is heard

Datura

coming from either direction, it would be wise to pull off the pavement until it passes.

Beyond the dips and turns, the road resumes its customary barely perceptible upgrade. Kelso Creek, now close at hand in the west, once again flows on the surface in a bed liberally garnished with willows and cottonwoods—a good place to pause and picnic. Soon your course jogs east before straightening out. Here Frog Creek Road, BLM SC47, (3.4/14.9), emerges from a west-facing canyon. A little farther, Willow Spring Road, BLM SC103, (1.3/16.2), leaves the east edge of the pavement. Both roads pass year-round springs and give access to the PCT. Sometimes conventional cars can be driven to the PCT on these roads; but, on occasion, summer cloudbursts send water roaring down the canyons of this sandy transitional range, slicing wide gaps across these dirt roads, and exposing hazardous boulders in the road beds. Most any storm in the area spreads layers of sand across the road you are on. A faded sign just south of Willow Spring wash warns you are near the Yankee Canyon Rod and Gun Club.

The Piute Mountains have four access roads to the plateau, but the best way to reach it is by Piute Mountain Road to the west (4011/1.0/17.2), which you now ride by. Piute Mountains Car and Bicycle Tour T17 begins here at **TH20.** A plaque commemorating the historic site of Sageland is by the T junction. There were about 400 buildings here over a century ago when Sageland thrived on the trade of the area miners. Only one remains and it is on private property.

Continuing south on Kelso Valley Road, you begin a gentle ascent and pass an unused dry, mortared-stone cattle trough. The springs around it provide water for cottonwood and willow trees and datura plants with their large, white, trumpet-shaped flowers. This comely plant is highly toxic. Indians sometimes used its narcotic in their ceremonies. After passing the foothills of Mayan Peak to your left, another road appears: Butterbredt Canyon Road, BLM SC 123, (1.3/18.5). This is the terminus of car tour T24 and leads to **TH21;** the rest continue straight ahead and skip the following description.

> If you seek Ts 21 & 22, turn left, drive southeast up the **dirt road** (0.0/0.0) to the confluence of two canyons at **TH21** (0.7/0.7). The PCT crosses here at an off-set junction. The canyon is wide enough to allow parking, but if rain is threatened, leave the cars on the paved road.

On your road, bicyclists can soon relax as the upgrade reaches its summit just past debris from St. John Mine, above to the left. Here on the Sierra crest (4953/1.2/19.7), the pavement ends, while T23 on the PCT, which crosses here, begins. The Kelso Valley-Butterbredt Canyon Car & All-Terrain Bicycle Loop Tour, T24, also begins here at **TH22.**

T13   Nicolls Peak Climb

Climbers on this short but taxing adventure of tackling Nicolls Peak from the east are rewarded first with a tungsten mine to explore, then with a breathtaking view of South Fork Valley and Lake Isabella.

Distance   3.4 miles, round trip
Steep Ascents   1.4 mile
Elevation Gain   2670 feet
Skills   Intermediate route finding; Class 2–3 climbing
Seasons   Fall, winter, spring
Map   USGS 7.5 min *Woolstalf Creek*
Trailhead   18. See car tour T12.
Description   Hike up the **road** (3400/0.0)

after driving on its deteriorating surface as far as possible. Half way along, a spring muddies the road's surface, a willow vanguard marches across it, and you proceed to its end at Stardust Mine's gaping mouth (4000/0.6). This tungsten mine was productive for only one year, 1943, when about 1000 tons of ore were shipped to the mill in Weldon. The green rocks at the mine are coarse grain garnet-

Road washout

epidote tactite, not copper. Scheelite grains in the tactite fluoresce blue to green, giving the rocks their malachite appearance.

Two canyons converge at the mine—you, on a *cross-country* route, head up the west-northwest drainage to the right. First along the canyon floor, then climbing steeply, you scramble up the exposed slopes to the right of the canyon among typical brush and scattered trees that withstand the heat and drought of this high desert exposure. Your canyon and the one to the north flatten and merge as the route curves north, and you hike just below a saddle on the crest (5130/0.6).

An alternate route from the mine climbs the same drainage but leaves the canyon floor to follow ducks up the boulder-strewn south side of the gulch until it is opposite the foot of a slope barren of shrubs. The route then crosses to this slope, zigzags to the crest and dips north to the saddle.

Contouring now and staying east of the crest all the way, climb through a notch on Nicolls, pull yourself over boulders, and wind along a steep, multi-ducked route up the summit's main chute to the top (6070/0.5). Sweeping views of the South Fork Valley spread out before you, extending both west into Lake Isabella and east behind Onyx Peak. A cliff curtails the north slope of your viewpoint, plunging 400 feet before ending in talus. The peak was named for rancher John Nicoll.

South Fork Valley from Nicolls Peak

T14   Heald Peak Climb

This climb is similar to that of Pinyon Peak in that it too ascends steep slopes to gain a ridgecrest, then follows the crest over lesser hills, which have better views than the named peak. Hikers in top condition climb this peak in tandem with Nicolls Peak.

Distance   5.8 miles, round trip
Steep Ascents   1.5 miles
Elevation Gain   3700 feet
Skills   Intermediate route finding; Class 2 climbing
Seasons   Fall, winter, spring
Map   USGS 7.5 min *Woolstalf Creek*
Trailhead   18. See car tour T12.
Description   The beginning of this climb is

described in T13.

West-Northwestbound Cross-Country Log

T13	roadhead	3400	0.0
	mine	4000	0.6
	crest	5180	0.6

On the Heald Mountain climb you do not veer as far northwest as those climbing Nicolls, but instead head to the crest south of the saddle. Views to the west of the crest are of Lake Isabella rimmed with Piute and Greenhorn mountains, and to the east of Kelso Creek drainage with the flat-topped Scodie Mountains in profile.

Moving on, your ridgecrest route undulates south via hills and short, steep pitches, then turns southwest to climb minor Hill 6203 before dropping to a saddle. Granite juxtaposed with metamorphics nearly ring the Heald Peak plateau with fractured and convoluted cliffs. Amid these challenging cliffs the route leads you southwest on a ducked passage near the narrow ridgecrest,

as you pick your way up steep but nontechnical rock. Beyond this effort, it heads south past an unforested hill to unobtrusive Heald Peak (6901/1.7), on the pinyon pine-clad plateau.

Upon reaching the peak, read the plaque explaining its place-name origin. In 1973 the U.S. Board on Geographic Names accepted the name to honor the memory of Weldon F. Heald. Although his chief bailiwick was the American Southwest, Heald took an active role in the fight to preserve wilderness in the Southern Sierra.

T15   PCT Day Hike to Skinner Peak

The breeze that whips through Bird Spring Pass and the quick elevation gain to the summit, moderate the heat of summer and make this a three-season hike. A well-defined trail, then an easy walk-up takes hikers to the top of Skinner Peak, the highest southern peak on Scodie Mountain.

Distance   7.8 miles, round trip
Steep Ascents   None
Elevation Gain   1765 feet
Skills   Easy route finding; Class 1 climbing; Moderate to strenuous hiking
Seasons   Spring, summer, fall
Map   USGS 7.5 min *Cane Cyn, Horse Cyn*

Trailhead   19. See car tour T12.
Description   Leaving Bird Spring Pass (5355/0.0), you ascend on the *PCT* northeast into a side canyon along a sandy path ornamented with nosegays of blue penstemons—showy tubular flowers with short lobes: two-lobed upper lip, three lobed lower.

Freight wagon used by miners

Ahead you pass a trail-register box and a spur road, then climb south from the canyon's wash. The curious fenced-in square seen below is a quail guzzler constructed by the Forest Service to catch rain water for the local fauna. An occasional Joshua tree and some straggly pinyon pines dot the slopes that abruptly slant away to the vast alluvium of Bird Spring Canyon spreading below.

Southwest across the pass the radio tower, its road and the PCT of T23, slowly recede as you first climb up long-legged switchbacks and then cross over a ridge with a western orientation (6460/2.4). You can find small flats to sleep on here. After a long ascending traverse and several short, steep switchbacks, you hike over a ridge above the Horse Canyon watershed, which also has room for possible waterless camping. To the north, the High Sierra rises above the crests of east-west Scodie Mountain ridges, while around you manzanita and oaks join the scattered pinyon pines and numerous spring wildflowers.

For the easy walk up Skinner Peak, leave the trail between its summit and the first descending switchbacks and climb *cross-country* (6940/1.3) south-southwest to the summit boulders (7120/0.2), where there are good views and a register can.

Mariposa lilies

T16   PCT Backpack on the Scodie Mountains: Bird Spring Pass to Walker Pass

This segment of PCT is anchored by easily climbable peaks at both ends. The trail wanders between them through pinyon pine forests on the mountain plateau and approaches a grassy nook where spring water slips over granite boulders. The Scodie Mountains honor William Scodie, the proprietor of the first store in Onyx, but many refer to them by their Indian name "Kiavah."

Distance   20.6 miles, shuttle trip
Steep Ascents   None
Elevation Gain   2345 feet
Skills   Easy route finding
Seasons   Spring, summer, fall
Map   USGS 7.5 min *Cane Cyn, Horse Cyn, Walker Pass*
Trailheads   19 & 10 or 11. This trip requires two cars. See car tour T8. Leave the first car at **TH10**, Walker Pass, or **TH11**,

Walker Pass Campground, the end of the trip. Then see car tour T12. Drive the second car to Bird Spring Pass **TH19**, the beginning of the trip. This is 39.8 miles from your first car at the pass.
Description   The beginning of this trip is described in T15.

Northbound PCT Log

T15	Bird Spring Pass	5355	0.0
	ridge	6460	2.4

Skinner Peak climb   6940 1.3

After climbing Skinner Peak you return to the trail, drop along the switchback, and descend northwest close to the ridgecrest above a drainage of Cane Canyon. Across the canyon the northern extension of the Piute Mountains, with Heald and Nicolls peaks, borders Kelso Creek Valley. Near at hand, scattered singularly along the trail, the white flowers of Mariposa lilies grace the slopes. The three large, wedge-shaped petals of the flower have a red-brown spot at the base, which helps you identify it.

Following two quick switchbacks, your trail turns east across north-facing slopes, allowing glimpses of the eastern reaches of Lake Isabella. Lower on the path you see a mining scar across the ravine, and a telephone microwave relay station perched on a peak to the northeast. The route's descent east ends at a saddle, then traverses ⅓ mile across the grassy slopes of minor Peak 6455, above sprawling Horse Canyon. Heading north, the PCT cuts across a road (6260/2.3) that reaches the mine you just saw, and seconds later crosses another road, both branching from Horse Canyon Road. The latter road serves the tower and continues north in rutted fashion to McIvers Spring. You will walk on a section of that road later on this trip.

Fair camping possibilities exist here and you can obtain seasonal water 0.7 mile down the second road at a stream from Yellow Jacket Spring, which crosses the road. To reach the spring itself, hike up the drainage 0.6 mile, fork left up the hill another 0.1 mile to a trough with piped-in water, missigned *Willow Spring*. The next water source is McIvers Spring, 7.0 miles farther.

The PCT gradually gains elevation as it weaves in and around scalloped slopes below the tower, and then below the road to McIvers Spring. Look for a football-sized rock dissimilar to other rocks scattered about. In April 1983 a meteor streaked across the sky above Los Angeles. It was estimated that, if it did not burn up completely, it could have landed somewhere on the Scodie Mountains.

At length, you reach and join the road

(6670/4.5) that served the relay tower and threads along the crest. Here an "Ichabod Crane" forest surrounds you as you walk northeast along the road. The naturally denuded lower branches of pinyon pines, gnarled and twisted, reach in contorted figurations to set your imagination soaring; and all about are broken branches, uprooted trees and a tangled forest. This disheveled scene was caused by a combination of the unusually heavy, wet snows of 1982–83, which greatly burdened the pinyons, unused to more than a dusting, and strong winds that toppled these trees, rooted in soft, soggy soil.

Abruptly, the forest flanking your road gives way to a sagebrush-buckbrush meadow. Here you pass a jeep road with forked access peeling off to the northwest; then a road to the northeast; and, after reentering the woods, a roadlike wash that forks to the right and another road that forks to the left. You begin to cross rills that have early-season water and later-season puddles of lavendar-flowered, inch-high "belly" plants; and, 0.3 mile before the road to McIvers Spring, you cross a brook, also with seasonal water.

The PCT leaves the road and resumes as trail (6680/2.2), now heading northeast, but if you need water or a campsite, stay on the road for 0.3 mile to McIvers Spring. The next water is 7.4 miles ahead at Walker Pass Campground. Snuggled among picturesque slabs at the springs is a small batten-board hut with porch and outhouse once owned by McIvers and Weldon. They equipped it with

Prickly poppy

the bare necessities of a 1938 rustic retreat and, although run down, it remains today. Hunters, motorcyclists and 4WDers have used it over the years, as the litter and graffiti attest. Barring a drought, some water issues from these springs year-round, and good campsites abound here in this bright green oasis among the gray-green pinyons.

At the junction where the trail resumes, you hike northeast on the ascending, undulating PCT past a jeep road crossing. Manzanitas appear along with a few stands of Jeffrey pines and black oaks. The declivitous slopes of Boulder Canyon fall away to the southeast from a shallow saddle, and vistas of the Mojave Desert and the ethereal San Gabriel-San Bernardino mountains appear through the haze. Soon you round some three-story boulders, dashed with rust and chartreuse lichen, supporting a pinyon pine tenaciously growing from a slight crack. Leaving the gentle tableland, you descend on north-facing slopes, with views of the Mount Whitney group in the distant north and, in the northeast, the top of Olancha Peak. In the crease of the first major canyon on the descent, Scodie Peak climbers leave the PCT (6680/3.0) (See T9).

In 0.4 mile beyond the climber's exit, the PCT briefly reaches over the ridgetop at a switchback where you catch a fleeting glimpse of the Owens Peak group and the hairpin curve of Highway 178 with Walker Pass Campground at the south end of that curve. Far to the north, the slash of

Canebrake Road cuts across slopes, and to the northeast the PCT rises above Walker Pass. The trail continues on a long descent on west-facing slopes high above Jacks Creek Canyon. In time it passes a use trail angling down the slope to Jacks Creek, crosses a slight ridgeline saddle (5860/2.2), and descends on the mountain's northeast-facing slopes.

After the second switchback down the mountainside, you round just below a ridgetop where, obscured from view but easily reached, the Forest Service has placed a substantial guzzler for small animals. You then skirt along the lower slopes of Peak 6018. Among other plants along this section of the PCT, the narrowleaf goldenbush, with irregular-petaled yellow flowers, flourishes. An occasional tissue paper-thin, large, white-flowered prickly poppy (resembling a fried egg, sunny side up) grows here, too.

Quite soon the trail crosses the snowmelt trickle of Canebrake Creek then crosses the path (5100/2.1) leading 0.1 mile to the comfortable Walker Pass Trailhead Campground, built especially for PCT trekkers. If the camp faucets are turned off, spring water flows from a pipe into a nine-foot square cement-enclosed "cattail garden" cow-trough, 0.1 mile down Highway 178.

The PCT continues to Walker Pass; it winds northeast exiting at the historical marker (5246/0.6). T27 begins north for backpackers combining sections of the PCT.

McIvers cabin

T17   East Piute Mountains Car & All-Terrain Bicycle Tour

(With Directions to Trailheads 23–25)

The Piute Mountains, a Sierran subrange, rise abruptly from desert environs to a rolling, conifer-clad plateau of modest height. Geomorphological questions abound. Were the Piute Mountains once part of the main Sierra body? Were the Piutes' plateau and the Kern Plateau once joined? If so, how did the intervening South Fork Valley come into being? Pondering such questions makes an outing in the Piutes a diverting experience for the budding geologist and adds to an interesting trip for all travelers.

Distance   30.7 miles, loop trip
Steep Ascents   None (Long, hard grades for bicyclists)
Elevation Gain   4440 feet
Skills   Easy route finding; unpaved roads (some rough sections)
Seasons   Spring, summer, fall
Map   Kern County road map
Tourhead   20. From Highway 178 in Weldon, turn south on ***Kelso Valley Road*** (0.0/0.0). This is 31.2 miles west of Highway 14 and 1.2 miles east of Sierra Way. Drive to Piute Mountain Road at **TH20** (17.2/17.2). This trip departs from car tour T12.
Description   The unpaved roads en route, although maintained, are sometimes gutted and rocky. With care, low-slung cars can be driven on them, but cars with high clearance are preferable.

The tour begins west of Kelso Valley Road on unpaved ***Piute Mountain Road*** (4011/ 0.0/0.0). The road immediately dips to cross the flow of up-canyon springs, then ascends Harris Grade on slopes covered with xerophytic brush. Mayan Peak looms east across the canyon, somewhat resembling the pyramids of Yucatan. After entering Sequoia National Forest and much winding, the grade eases, now in a pinyon pine and live oak woodland. Then the road curves around a canyon and again steepens to gain a ridgecrest with the first of four PCT trail crossings on this trip (6620/6.6/6.6). On the plateau where Jeffrey pines dominate the forest, your route reaches SNF Road 29S04 (0.8/7.4). Here Sorrell Peak climbers of T18 depart for **TH23**.

Continuing on your road, rabbitbrush-riddled Landers Meadow, the largest meadow in the Piutes, spreads to your left. The cattle pen and ramp typify grazing allotments on these mountains; however, commercial timber cutting predominates. In years past, men searching for instant riches punched tunnels into the mountain's interior, and some removed sizable amounts of gold. A few latter-day 49ers still nourish these dreams and still file mining claims here.

Midway around Landers Meadow, SNF Road 29S05 (1.0/8.4) forks northeast 0.9 mile to a Fire Safe Area with spring water, once a campground and station for summer rangers. In quick succession your road passes the second road crossing of the PCT at **TH24** (0.7/9.1), the end of day hike T19; passes the culvert through which Landers Creek flows; and passes the dirt road to an old hut at Waterhole Mine with a Fire Safe Area by the creek.

You next enter the historic site of Claraville where *Private Property* and *No Trespassing* signs abound. Claraville, named for the daughter of an early miner, was founded in 1865. It was home to hundreds of miners during that time. Now ony a few scattered summer cabins comprise the town.

In Claraville, turn left onto ***Jawbone Canyon Road*** (0.6/9.7) for a protracted ride south on the plateau. Slender Landers Creek, then Cottonwood Creek, glide in the canyon to the left. The PCT winds along the canyon slopes below. A rusted sawdust burner, the remains of a sawmill, squats in a clearing to the right. During the gold rush, several sawmills in the Piutes supplied timber for the mines, but this burner is from a later period. You pass the buildings of Sciots Camp Blum, then pass a road that deadends deep in the interior beyond Mace and Grouse meadows.

Now your road ascends to its highest elevation, 6980 feet, then descends, gains a small hill, and winds down to meet the PCT where it crosses this road at **TH25** of Ts 2, 19 & 20 (6620/5.1/14.8). Vandals often remove the PCT sign here and the trail is easily missed.

As you leave Sequoia National Forest, the adventure on the Piute Mountains segment finishes with a plunge down the many, often rutted, switchbacks of Geringer Grade. The road, still Jawbone Canyon Road, now surrounded by rolling hills in an oak savannah, crosses the waters of Cottonwood Creek. Soon the oaks yield to treeless, shrubless plains where you bump across two cattle-guards to a junction with *Kelso Valley Road* (3949/8.1/22.9), 539X on road paddles, were your route turns left.

Heading north in sparsely populated Kelso Valley on the last leg of your loop, the sandy road passes Skyline Ranch, dating from the late 1800s. In those days ranch children attended classes at Landers School, a one room schoolhouse that was south of Skyline Ranch. Again you encounter *No Trespassing, Private* signs, here tacked to

Sawdust burner

fences that line the route as it crosses the valley. In time the road climbs over the Sierra crest, gains welcome pavement, and again meets the PCT (4953/5.3/28.2). A short descent to Piute Mountain Road (4011/2.5/30.7) completes your loop trip.

T18   Sorrell Peak Climb

This brief trip is a climb of the highest peak on the Sierra crest between Tehachapi and Walker passes—Sorrell Peak. From the summit, you can survey the breadth of the Piute Mountains, and consider the awesome span of earth history as revealed by local landforms. This climb and a hike along the PCT make pleasant outings for Piute Mountain campers.

Distance   0.8 miles, round trip
Steep Ascents   None
Elevation Gain   405 feet
Skills   Easy route finding; Class 1 climbing
Seasons   Spring, summer, fall
Map   USGS 7.5 min *Claraville*
Trailhead   23. Highway 14 approach: see car tours T5 & T17. Highway 178 approach:

see car tour T17. Drive south on *SNF Road 29S04* (0.0/0.0). Wind to the switchbacks. Drive about ½ mile beyond the switchbacks to a ridge at **TH23** (3.7/3.7). The road is nearly level here, then descends slightly, and in ½ mile beyond the trailhead, descends noticeably.

Description   There are several routes up Sorrell Peak along the next ½ mile of road, but this is the easiest. On a *cross-country* climb (7300/0.0), you hike east up a minor ridge to gain a northwest-trending ridge (ignore the m'cyclepath). There you curve southeast in an open forest of Jeffrey pine, and soon reach the summit block of coarse-grained, yellow- to reddish-brown weathered granitic rocks. Kelso Valley yawns in the foreground; distant desert ranges spread dimly beyond the middle-ground foothills; and you clamber up the east side of the summit's outcrop (7704/0.4), which juts before you.

Among the notable views, the Sierra crest veers 13 miles to the east, before running north again. The Sierra Nevada range, with its Sierra crest, resulted from great uplifts along the Sierra Nevada Fault. The process is ongoing.

Phlox

T19   PCT Day Hike in the Piute Mountains

The route is shaded by coniferous and deciduous trees, sprinkled with seasonal wildflowers, crossed by musical creeks, and dotted with aged shacks and a forgotten mine. This visual pleasure and aural caress are accompanied by an easy walk on a gently undulating trail. This short one-way trip, as with all shuttle trips, can be converted to a round trip and begun at either end.

Distance   5.6 miles, shuttle trip
Steep Ascents   None
Elevation Gain   340 feet
Skills   Easy route finding; easy hiking
Seasons   Spring, summer, fall
Map   USGS 7.5 min *Claraville* (The PCT is not on this map at this writing)
Trailheads   25 & 24. This trip requires two cars. Highway 14 approach: see car tours T5 & T17. Highway 178 approach: see car tour T17. Leave the first car at **TH24,** for the end of the hike. Drive the second car to the beginning of the trip at **TH25.** This is 5.7 miles from the first car.
Description   This *PCT* hike begins at Jawbone Canyon Road (6620/0.0), where the trail descends north among scattered Jeffrey pines and black and live oaks trimmed with mistletoe. It drops down a few switchbacks and winds along east-facing slopes where cascades of white-flowered spreading

phlox perk up the early-season wayside scenery. This dainty flower has slender, pointed leaves and tiny tubular blooms that open into a disc of five petals. In ½ mile the trail passes above a spring hidden by willows. The path gently undulates now as it dips through several snowmelt streamlets, then adds gravel to the dirt tread as boulders surrounded by manzanitas appear.

In a short time the trail passes a campsite, then crosses a willow-lined branch of Cottonwood Creek: a good source of water until late summer. Coming from Mace and Grouse meadows, this may be water cows have enjoyed as well. The trail briefly parallels another willow-hemmed branch of the creek, crosses it on a log footbridge (6480/1.8), then proceeds above it.

The well-defined path continues to wind and dip, generally heading north. Strips of Jawbone Canyon Road appear to the west

Mine shaft

before the PCT turns up a canyon, crosses a logging road (6720/1.0), and climbs over a saddle: the watershed divide of Cottonwood and Landers creeks. Within ½ mile, watch for a spring above the trail, whose water is caught by a crude cement structure. Below the trail squats the roofless remains of a crumbling log cabin with smaller ancillary huts. This area, with its mine shaft tunneled into a creekbed, is worth investigating.

Back on the trail, you walk above, then switchback to, the headwaters of Landers Creek, which trickles through a pocket meadow with nearby camping potential. After an amble alongside Landers Creek, cross it (6300/1.9), and quickly cross back to the east side again. Shortly thereafter, a dirt road along the west bank leads to creekside Waterhole Trail Camp, and if you wish you can easily make your way there. The camp has a table and piped-in spring water, although a sign indicates the water should be treated. As one of the Fire Safe Areas in the Piutes, you can have campfires here even during periods of restricted fire use. The road continues on to another old structure, the Waterhole mine shack, a relic of past gold grubbing years.

You remain in the little canyon until it flares near Landers Meadow, to the east. After stepping across the meadow's outlet stream, you arrive at Piute Mountain Road (6220/0.9). The PCT hike for those on T20 continues, but this concludes the day hike.

T20   PCT Backpack on the Piute Mountains: Jawbone Canyon Road to Kelso Valley Road

After many miles of traversing a land of drought tolerant plants and harsh, sandy terrain, the PCT climbs to this land of pines, firs, meadows and creeks before returning to desert environs. Here those covering longer stretches of this trail exchange treks in the scorching sun for walks in the cool shade along a path with little challenge, but much beauty and historic interest.

Distance   13.8 miles, shuttle trip
Steep Ascents   None
Elevation Gain   860 feet
Skills   Easy route finding
Seasons   Spring, summer, fall
Maps   USGS 7.5 min *Claraville, Pinyon Mtn* (At this writing, the PCT does not appear on these maps.)
Trailheads   25 & 22. This trip requires two cars. Highway 14 approach: see car tour T5. Highway 178 approach: see car tours T12 & T24. Leave the first car at **TH22,** the summit of Kelso Valley Road, the end of this trip (limited parking). Drive the second car to

TH25, the beginning of the trip. This is 13.4 miles from the first car via Kelso Valley.
Description   The beginning of this trip is described in T19.

Northbound PCT Log

T19			
Jawbone Canyon Rd		6620	0.0
footbridge		6480	1.8
logging rd		6720	1.0
Landers Creek		6300	1.9
Piute Mtn Rd		6220	0.9

After crossing Piute Mountain Road, the PCT once again skirts along the east side of Landers Creek. It leaves the creek to begin an arc to the east on a short piece of road, then resumes on trail where it ascends to cross another dirt road.

Shortly the trail reaches a wider road (6300/1.1) where a 0.3 mile walk north down it leads to another Fire Safe Area. Although no longer a campground and summer ranger residence, it remains a fine place to camp. What is left of the campground amenities are a lonely concrete fireplace and a few broken pipes once used for trailer hookups. The spring above the road is captured in a tank and piped to a cattle trough, the last water on this trip. A curious stone shelter sits near the spring.

Along the PCT, bold wallflowers, standing straight and single, display clusters of bright orange blooms in season, and blue-purple lupines add a dash of contrasting color. Pinyon pines signal your approach to drier climes as yet another road crosses your path. Lichen-splashed boulders appear, along with a few dramatic yuccas. These plants grow tough dagger-like leaves a foot or more long, with sharp tips that puncture the unwary. The stalks, with massive creamy-white blooms that seem to explode in spring, reach 8–14 feet tall.

Again you cross Piute Mountain Road (6620/2.3), this time at the summit of Harris Grade, Piute Mountains' best access. Locate the trail where it descends along the grade. In 0.1 mile, as you begin your trek along the north and then east slopes of St. John Ridge, you see far off to the north majestic Olancha Peak, reigning over the Kern Plateau. To the northeast, pointed Owens Peak with curved, serrated Mount Jenkins next to it, divide the desert from the mountains, and all three delineate the Sierra crest. While gradually losing elevation, you fork left where OHV tracks curve right, and you descend by switchbacks before a long traverse around the ridge. (If you miss the fork and hike to the right of a chimney-like outcrop, you are on the wrong trail, but you can continue along the m'cyclepath, which meets the PCT at the paved road.)

In time you spot a post just below the path near a large fremontia bush, which marks the boundary of a mining claim. Fremontias especially attract attention when frocked in large, wax-like yellow flowers. Further below, a jeep road switchbacks up a steep grade. Soon in the east the serpentine sliver of paved Kelso Valley Road appears. Mayan Peak is east, and, to its right, Butterbredt Road winds to the Sierra crest. Your exposed trail descends through colonies of bitterbrush and its companion plants to meet the road at a pass (4950/4.8), the end of your trip. T23 takes backpackers on the next PCT section through a transitional range.

T21   Mayan Peak Climb

This pile of exposed, khaki-colored rocks, Mayan Peak, appears unappealing to peakbaggers in summer. In winter, however, when the air feels crisp and other peaks are inaccessible and mantled with snow, this mountain with its warm, earthy tones and easy access is especially inviting. Then Mayan Peak and other Sierra east rim mountains below 6500 feet attract hikers from all over Southern California. Although each mountain is interesting and each one offers a good workout, some people combine several of these peak climbs for one challenging outing.

Distance   4.8 miles, round trip
Steep Ascents   0.3 mile
Elevation Gain   1570 feet
Skills   Easy route finding; Class 1–2 climbing
Seasons   Fall, winter, spring
Map   USGS 7.5 min *Pinyon Mtn*

Trailhead   21. Highway 14 approach: see car tour T5. Highway 178 approach: see car tour T12.
Description   To begin your hike, climb east on the *PCT* switchbacks up the ridge between Butterbredt Canyon to the right and an east-trending gulch to the left (4540/0.0). A

deep OHV slash cuts from the canyon floor through the switchbacks. These vehicles are not allowed on this trail, but that does not seem to stop them. Proceed along the trail south of the gulch between you and pyramid-shaped Mayan Peak. When this gulch and its ravines flatten enough to avoid elevation losses and canyon plunges, you leave the trail to curve north toward the peak on a *cross-country* route (5100/1.2). Bitterbrush, among the high desert plants on this trek, an important browse plant for deer and cattle, is easily recognized by its tiny trilobed leaves and small creamy-yellow flowers.

As you near the steeper slopes of Mayan Peak, look for a lone pinyon pine high on the mountain, then look right of the pine for a prominent, square-shaped outcrop. Aim for a point between the pine and the outcrop as you ascend steeply northwest among the rocks, then aim beyond those reference points to the broad, nearly level mountain top. After a final pull up the easternmost of twin igneous boulders, you achieve the summit. These summit rocks, uncovered and worn by the elements like the ruins of an ancient Mayan temple, conceal the peak's register can and tablet inscribed with visitors' names (6108/1.2).

The view from the top includes pasture lands of Kelso Valley and Butterbredt Canyon to the south beyond the east-west crossing of the Sierra crest. Far to the north the snow-capped peaks of Olancha and Langly dominate the horizon.

T22   PCT High Desert Day Hike
With Excursion C: Pinyon Mountain

On this off-season hike in the high desert, you enjoy ranging views of the southernmost Sierra en route and expansive views from the San Gabriel Mountains to the High Sierra atop Pinyon Mountain.

Distance   8.2 miles, round trip
Steep Ascents   None
Elevation Gain   805 feet
Skills   Easy route finding; moderate hiking
Seasons   Fall, winter, spring
Map   USGS 7.5 min *Pinyon Mtn* (The PCT is not on the map at this writing.)
Trailhead   21. See car tour T12.
Description   To begin your hike, climb east on the *PCT* switchbacks up the ridge between Butterbredt Canyon to the right and an east-trending gulch to the left (4540/0.0), and remain just south of the gulch. The slopes of the ravine—and of its neighbors—flatten as you trace the valley's elongated curve to the east. On this trip you may have problems sorting out the many m'cyclepaths from the PCT even though BLM tries to keep the trail well-signed.

Mayan Peak to your left, rules out north-westward views of the Piute Mountains, but it cannot block out the face that Sorrell Peak turns on Kelso Valley. Nor can it hide the ribbon of Kelso Valley Road draped on a shoulder of the Sierra crest. A few six-petaled, many-stamened, less than a foot high, cream cups, as well as other blooms of spring, are scattered amid the scraggly bushes that mat trailside slopes, punctuated by junipers and Joshua trees.

The path crosses a south saddle of Point 5402, descends to wind around the heads of two canyons, ascends gently and then contours past many lesser ravines cut in the north slope of Pinyon Mountain. The impounded waters of Willow Spring glisten like a distant mirage below, while around you a moderately dense stand of pinyon pines cloaks the north slopes, the only forest for miles. Long-eared Owls have been seen on the eastern edge of this forest. Look for their pellets under the trees by the trail. They are composed of bones and fur that are regurgitated by the bird.

As you proceed east across north-facing slopes, the ranks of the forest dwindle and are replaced by sagebrush, bitterbrush, rabbitbrush and buckwheat. Still on the slopes of Pinyon Mountain, parallel to a crude access road, you reach a multi-road and m'cyclepath junction on a Sierra crest saddle (5283/4.1). From here you can climb Pinyon Mountain, or you can scan the desert from the shade of nearby Joshua trees. Those on T23 continue along the trail.

Excursion C: Pinyon Mountain

An "eagle's nest" summit—a small campsite surrounded by rocks and trees protect you from cold, seasonal winds. Striking vistas from atop the protecting rocks *become especially memorable when the sun hangs low in the southern skies, and the shadows stretch long on the desert floor.*

Distance 1.6 miles, round trip
Steep Ascents 0.5 mile
Elevation Gain 900 feet
Skills Easy route finding; Class 1 climbing
Description To climb Pinyon Mountain from the multi-road saddle (5283/0.0), find the first of two jeep roads ascending south on the mountain's eastern slopes. (The second road reaches Gold Peak in 1.7 miles.) On this *jeep road* you curve southwest, climb steeply and reach a notch on top of the mountain. After a few steps to the north and a short climb up the rocks, you reach the "eagle's nest" summit (6182/0.8).

T23 PCT High Desert Backpack: Kelso Valley Road to Birdspring Pass

This austere, high desert trip follows the Sierra crest over a transitional range between Piute and Scodie mountains. The waterless, exposed route is most enjoyable when a breeze chills the air and clears the desert haze. A peak to climb and a defunct open-pit mine to explore add to the attractions along the way.

Distance 15.4 miles, shuttle trip
Steep Ascents None
Elevation Gain 1960 feet
Skills Easy route finding
Seasons Fall, winter, spring
Maps USGS 7.5 min *Pinyon Mtn* (The PCT is not on this map at this writing) *Cane Cyn*
Trailheads 22 & 19. This trip requires two cars. See car tour T12. Leave the first car at Bird Spring Pass, **TH19**, the end of the trip. Drive the second car to the end of the pavement on Kelso Valley Road, the beginning of this trip at **TH22** (limited parking). This is 13.8 miles from the first car. Overnight camping is better back 2.5 miles at Piute Mountain Road junction.
Description After making sure you have at least a minimum of two quarts of water per day, begin your hike east of Kelso Valley Road (4950/0.0). The *PCT* winds on a crenulated path across gullied north-facing slopes. Pepper-colored debris, excavated from several claims collectively known as the St. John Mine, is visible downslope in a gully you cross 170 yards from the road. Beginning in 1867, miners extracted gold here for over 70 years. Most of them lived in the now vanished settlement of Sageland, just a few miles north.

The route descends northeast on a prominent ridge mantled with brush and occasional beavertail and cholla cacti, curves across a ravine, traverses north-facing slopes, and eventually meets Butterbredt Canyon Road at the mouth of a ravine (4540/2.1). Here your route coincides with day hike T22.

Eastbound PCT Log

T22	Butterbredt Canyon Rd	4540	0.0
	Multi-road saddle/		
	Pinyon Mtn Ex. C	5283	4.1

At this point you have the option of climbing 0.8 mile to the summit of Pinyon Mountain, where an ample campsite is protected from strong winds by boulders and pinyon pines. Also at this point, if you need more water, you can descend on the road, BLM SC103, northwest down canyon 1.8 miles to Willow Spring, a pond where there are no willows but plenty of cows. The most used road east of this saddle descends 3.3 miles to Dove Spring.

You leave the saddle to wind north around gullied, east-facing slopes, climbing a little at first and then contouring. Along the way the El Paso Mountains, Fremont Valley and Indian Wells Valley fill the eastern horizon. In the first big gully you cross, you encounter blocks of granite, which, rounded by weathering, stand precariously stacked. Presently you arrive at another multi-road and trail junction (5382/1.6) on a saddle. The road west leads past the Sunset Mine Road to connect with the Willow Spring Road just below the spring.

Your path diagonals northwest across the junction saddle, then winds gently upward, staying west of the crest. Glancing back, you see rubble from the Ora Grande Mine scarring a west-projecting ridge, while closer at hand in downslope corners old timbers, rust-spattered auto husks and a shack stand in disarray around Sunset Mine. Again the trail climbs the slopes beside and then across a road before reaching a ridgecrest saddle (5700/1.1). To the left, churned ground and parallel concrete slabs slash the slope, the result of past activity at Danny Boy Gold Mine.

Wyleys Knob, the 6465-foot microwave tower-crowned summit to the north, stands as a gauge of your progress. Now the wide path makes a moderate descent via two switchbacks to meet three jeep roads on a crestline saddle at a junction (5300/0.8) where roads diverge for Frog Spring (northwest), Dove Spring (southeast) and endless sloping plains (east).

Ahead the austere journey takes you generally north over a low hill to another crestline saddle, crosses Frog Canyon Road and tops a low east-west ridge (5365/0.4) with good campsites among the boulders. Next the PCT dips to a brushy gap, climbs north at a moderate grade, paralleling a gully, and then curves along a ridge. Trailside buckwheat and Mormon tea tend to hide lucia, horsebrush and a blue-petaled variety of gilia. The gradient eases and the trail first winds around spur ridges emanating from the Sierra crest, then crosses a gap in the crest itself. The Scodie Mountains and the granitic outcrop of Wylers Knob loom to the north. The trail parallels the crest just west above you, and passes three rounded crestline boulders that form a balanced stack. A switchback below Hill 5940, erosively cut by cyclists, leads down to skirt a hill on the crest, then the PCT reaches a junction (5740/2.8) with m'cyclepaths leading northwest and southeast along the ridge and down canyons to the northeast and the southwest.

Now your route diagonals north across the junction, curves west, and rounds a bevelled spur ridge. The path soon dips from a granite bluff, then rounds a ridge that drops off to the northeast. A gentle-to-moderate downgrade ensues, at first among pinyon pines but later across the sunnier, northeast-facing slopes of Wyleys Knob. The path descends just downslope from the chuckholed Wyleys Knob Road, and quickly reaches a junction (5355/2.5) at Bird Spring Pass and your waiting shuttle car. T16 takes backpackers on the Scodie Mountains PCT section next.

Ore chute

T24   Kelso Valley-Butterbredt Canyon Car & All-Terrain Bicycle Tour

(With Directions to Trailheads 25 & 8)

Little has changed in the high, dry desert country of Kelso Valley since William Landers grazed his cattle there in the late 1800s to early 1900s—cattle still roam the range. Little has changed along the canyon slopes since Fredrick Butterbredt poked holes in them in search of gold—remnants of prospector's hopes still remain. But the cottonwoods have aged around the spring both gentlemen frequented; and the spring has been dammed to create a pond that has been fenced to provide a sanctuary for migrating and native wildfowl.

Distance   21.1 miles, loop trip
Steep Ascents   None
Elevation Gain   2350 feet
Skills   Easy route finding; unpaved roads (sometimes with deep sand)
Seasons   All year (Bicyclists omit summer)
Map   Kern County road map
Tourhead   22. Highway 178 approach: turn south on *Kelso Valley Road* (0.0/0.0). This is 31.2 miles west of Highway 14 and 1.2 miles east of Sierra Way. Drive south to the pavement's end on the road summit, **TH22**, (19.7/19.7). This tour is an extension of car tour T12. Highway 14 approach: see car tour T5 and start this loop trip at the spur road to Butterbredt Spring Wildlife Sanctuary.
Description   This journey begins where T12 ends, at the summit of *Kelso Valley Road* (4953/0.0/0.0). The PCT crosses here on the Sierra crest pass. Descend south on this wide, washboard, unpaved county road into Kelso Valley. The abundant species of rabbitbrush, *Chrysothamnus nauseosus,* hereabout, can grow seven feet high, but usually achieves only half that growth. In autumn, the disc flowers (no petals) of these ill-smelling plants, as the name implies, cover the slopes in a sea of gold. This species is sometimes referred to as "Rubber Rabbit-brush" because of its high content of rubber, which is not commercially used but available if needed.

Along the sandy road lined with fences posted with *Private Property* signs, a few buildings appear far to the west near the foothills as well as Skyline Ranch in the valley's center. This valley, a checkerboard of private and government owned land, has one dominate private land owner, Rudnick Estates Trust. A Texas cattleman, William Landers, first ran cattle here on government land, then over the years purchased many of the choice parcels. Oscar Rudnick, an immigrant from Lithuania, later bought this land and added more parcels during his lifetime. Today the Trust manages 167,000 acres and leases another 153,000 acres. Soon you arrive at Jawbone Canyon Road (3949/5.3/5.3), which winds west from Highway 14 and on to the Piute Mountains. If you are seeking **TH25** for T2 & T20, turn right here; if not turn left and ignore the following description.

To reach **TH25,** drive west from the junction (0.0/0.0) on *Jawbone Canyon Road,* cross the valley and ascend the sometimes rutted switchbacks of Geringer Grade. Pass a gated side road and the sign marking Sequoia National Forest (7.0/7.0). Proceed to the PCT road crossing (1.1/8.1) at **TH25.**

The car tour route turns east on *Jawbone Canyon Road,* ascends past juniper and Joshua trees to the first saddle, Hoffman Summit (4846/3.4/8.7). Here at **TH8** on T6, hikers embark north to climb Butterbredt Peak, the culmination of a range that separates the watershed of Butterbredt Canyon from that of Kelso Valley. The course continues to a *spur road* (4000/3.2/11.9) on which you turn left. Your route leads north, passes over a cattleguard next to a Butterbredt Spring sign, then descends through a gap into Butterbredt Canyon near the spring (3800/0.9/12.8), owned by the Trust.

This fenced oasis of pond, reeds and cottonwoods, which stands in marked contrast to the starkness of the encircling desert, has been set aside as a bird sanctuary. A few dedicated people, financed by contributions from the Santa Monica Bay Chapter of the Audubon Society and with out-of-pocket funds, worked with the landowners to enclose the spring and surrounding area. Over 250 species have been observed at the spring: a mixture of migrants, such as eastern warblers; and nesting birds, such as the tiny Costa's Hummingbird and the Great Horned Owl. You are asked not to camp within the enclosure and, of course, to be quiet and as unobtrusive as possible.

On the last leg of the trip, you follow **Butterbredt Canyon Road, BLM SC123,** northwest, passing the remains of a Lone Star mine structure to the left and a fenced depression to the right, which was once Butterbredt Well. Fredrick Butterbredt, one of the first miners to seek gold here, married a young Coso Indian whom, historians say, he found hiding in willows with her baby after her husband was killed in the Kern River Valley Indian Massacre of 1863. Some Butterbredt descendants still live in the valley.

If you are fortunate enough to be in the canyon during a good year for desert bloom, you will see numerous wildflowers. Among them, Parry's linanthus, patches of eye-catching, five petaled, white flowers, hug the granitic sand and bloom profusely during sunlight.

Beyond the well area, your route ascends to another crossing of the Sierra crest, then descends past the jeep road to Gold Peak and the offset junction of the PCT (7.5/20.3) at the confluence of this canyon and one south of Mayan Peak. A short ride now takes you to the northern terminus of Butterbredt Canyon Road, BLM SC123, at Kelso Valley Road (4358/0.8/21.1), just over a mile below the paved road's summit.

Butterbredt Spring Wildlife Sanctuary

Section 2
Highway 178 to Nine Mile Canyon/ Kennedy Meadows/Sherman Pass Road

Bart, a favorite among Dome Land rockclimbers

T25   Day Hike to Creosote Rings

It was thought that the majestic sequoia trees were the world's oldest living organisms: the General Sherman Tree in Sequoia National Park is about 3500 years old. Then some gnarled bristlecone pines in the White Mountains were found to be over 7000 years old. Now the oldest living thing, perhaps 11,700 years old, is believed to be a creosote ring on the Mojave Desert in San Bernardino County, dubbed "King Clone." The lowly creosote bush has been elevated to a lofty position! This short hike takes you to old creosote rings on a foothill in the Mojave Desert.

Distance   0.5 mile, round trip
Steep Ascents   0.25 mile
Elevation Gain   420 feet
Skills   Easy route finding; moderate hiking
Seasons   All year (can be hot)
Map   USGS 7.5 min *Freeman Jct*
Trailhead 9. See car tour T8. As you drive north from Highway 178 along the **aqueduct road** (0.0/0.0), note the long, grayish slope of the most eastern foothill. Park on the east shoulder of the road where it curves around that slope (0.8/0.8) at **TH9.** The 42 mile water test hole is 0.2 mile beyond.

Description   From the aqueduct road (3430/0.0), begin your exploration of creosote rings on a steep *cross-country* climb north-northwest up the decomposed granitic slope. With each step on this climb you leave deep footprints in the soft soil. Creosote rings in varying stages of development appear as you climb: tight circles, elliptical shapes, open-ended rings. In a short distance you see a nearly perfect elliptical clone (3850/0.25) measuring 58×38 feet, with a small stake at its center. Then find to the north of it another ring, below that a larger and less perfect group of clones.

Most people traveling through the desert view this ubiquitous creosote bush, *Larrea tridentata,* with indifference. It may catch their attention in the spring when its yellow flowers bloom, or after a rain when its resinous odor smells like the product used to preserve wood, but beyond that this drab olive-green bush is too common to be interesting.

Dr. Frank C. Vasek, professor of botany at the University of California at Riverside, thought these bushes mundane, too, until a series of events triggered his interest. He noticed that some creosote bushes were arranged in circles, and found that some decayed material was in the center of one of the circles, which he suspected was the dead stem crown. Vasek had the crown carbon dated and discovered it was quite old. Further, the crown was genetically identical to the circle of bushes, but not to the other creosote bushes nearby. He deduced, after many studies of creosote rings, that the original plant, grown from seed, eventually died at the core, but the growth around the core, the stem crown, spread outward and sprouted. This on-going process results in an ever expending circle of creosote bushes identical to the original center bush—all clones.

To determine the approximate age of a creosote bush ring, measure the average radius of the circle, convert the figure into millimeters (304.8mm=1ft), then divide that number by 0.66 millimeters, which is the average growth of a bush in one year. The elliptical clone here is over 11,000 years old!

T26 PCT Day Hike to Mount Jenkins Plaque
With Excursion D: Morris Peak

On the weekend of May 4–5, 1985, over 200 of Jim Jenkins' friends gathered in Kernville to dedicate Mount Jenkins. Most attendees had worked in support of naming the mountain in his honor.

May 4th dawned sparkling for the BBQ dinner, which was followed by speeches that were both poignant and in celebration of Jim's life. That evening as his friends gathered for a campfire, a full moon rose slowly over the brimming Kern River, bathing the tumbling water in shimmering light—a fitting climax to the day's events. The following day, 75 people walked among an unusually lavish display of wildflowers on the PCT to dedicate the plaque. This trip follows the path of that hike.

Distance   10 miles, round trip

Steep Ascents   None

Elevation Gain   1535 feet

Skills   Easy route finding; moderate to strenuous hiking

Seasons   Fall, winter, spring

Maps   USGS 7.5 min *Walker Pass, Owens Pk*

Trailhead   10, Walker Pass. See car tour T8.

Description   The *PCT* crosses Highway 178 near the historical marker, and your trip begins north on its path (5246/0.0). The trail ascends moderately northeast, making a highly visible line across steep, sandy slopes, and then the grade becomes gentle as it winds above a canyon. A look back reveals pinyon pine-clad Scodie Mountain, from which the PCT arrived. Below your gaze follows Highway 178 east to the distant El Paso Mountains. In early spring the slopes hereabouts are carpeted with blue chia, a sage that has two and sometimes three pom-poms ringing one stem. Native Americans roasted its seeds for food and Spaniards used its seed for medicinal purposes. Lupines and tiny white forget-me-nots perfume the air.

You veer gradually north on the path, upslope from a shack and its associated rubble, then negotiate six switchbacks in the welcome shade of pinyon pine trees. In a short time you cross the crest at a saddle eroded along the Pinyon Peak Fault, one in a series of minor faults perpendicular to the trend of the major Sierra Nevada fault zone. Northwest views from here foreshorten the Southern Sierra, putting Dome Land Wilderness in immediate contrast with the distant High Sierra.

The trail, an easy grade now near the crestline, crosses a south-facing slope, then regains the crest amid forest near a trailside campsite (6390/2.1). The path proceeds on a long traverse across northwest-facing slopes, a crestline gap, and then west- and north-facing slopes to a saddle (6585/1.8) southwest of Morris Peak, another campsite, and the launching site for climbers of this peak. Here you can either climb the peak or skip the excursion description that follows and continue on the trail.

Excursion D: Morris Peak

This peak, the first of the seven peak climbs along the section of PCT from Walker Pass to Canebrake Road, is the easiest and most accessible. Because it stands in the rainshadow of the Greenhorn Mountains and Kern Plateau peaks, Morris Peak receives a mere 8–10 inches of precipitation each year, making it available when other peaks are snow covered.

Distance   1.0 mile, round trip

Steep Ascents   0.2 mile

Elevation Gain   630 feet

Skills   Easy route finding; Class 2 climbing

Map   USGS 7.5 min *Owens Pk*

Description   You leave the PCT where it turns north (6585/0.0), hike to the campsite on the saddle where a use trail leaves to traverse the southeast, then south slopes of Morris Peak. Animal trails also traverse the slopes. If confused by the maze of paths, ascend moderately ***cross-country***, sometimes steeply, across the slopes, but stay below the ridgecrest and its rock outcrops until you identify the summit, the most eastern outcrop. Upon approaching the summit block, round to the east side and climb atop the peak boulders (7215/0.5), where an unobstructed view adds to the enjoyment of this easy climb.

*   *   *   *   *

On the PCT, after rounding Morris Peak you attain the Morris/Jenkins saddle (6500/0.8), where another campsite sits to the south of the small hill on the crest. Beyond the hill you cross the crest to the east side of Mount Jenkins. Ascend slightly to the commemorative plaque (6580/0.3) cemented to a granite boulder, which has a bench formed during trail construction blasting. Here you may rest, reflect and view. Indian Wells Canyon spreads to the desert below where the towns of Inyokern and, farther out, Ridgecrest waver in the desert sun. Vast China Lake Naval Weapons Center, where many sophisticated weapons are conceived and developed, occupies the land north of Ridgecrest.

In December 1984 the United States Board on Geographic Names officially named this mountain "Mount Jenkins." This sprawling, serrated 7921-foot mountain on the Sierra crest commemorates James (Jim) Charles Jenkins, who as a teenager hiked across its steep slopes while helping scout a route for this trail. He had been assigned to write the section of the PCT from the town of Mojave to Mount Whitney for the guidebook, *The Pacific Crest Trail: Vol 1, California.*

Jim soon expanded his interest to include the whole Southern Sierra. In the following years he hiked several times over all the trails no matter how obscure, climbed most of the peaks, covered miles of cross-country, and traveled on every bumpy, rutted ribbon of dirt that passed for a road. He gathered information about plants and animals, geology, weather, and the lore of gold miners, cattle

ranchers, and of the Indians who preceded these people. While doing fieldwork and research, he developed a deep appreciation for these mountains, and his guidebooks reflect that feeling.

He also became greatly involved in promoting conservation and protection for the Southern Sierra. For his contributions to this area Mount Jenkins was named in his honor. The culmination of a five-year, grassroots effort by his friends. The official record in the archives of the United States Department of Interior reads, ". . . named for James Charles Jenkins (1952–1979), noted authority on the flora, fauna and history of the southern Sierra Nevada who wrote guidebooks on the area."

Co-author Ruby with husband Bill

T27   PCT Backpack in Owens Peak Wilderness Study Area: Walker Pass to Chimney Peak Recreation Area

With Excursions E–J: Mount Jenkins, Owens Peak, Lamont Peak, Spanish Needle, Lamont Point and Sawtooth Peak

This section of the PCT travels through an area recommended for Wilderness—and it truly deserves that protection. The area is predominately pinyon pine forest, and because it is located between desert and high mountains, it has a rich diversity of plant and animal life. Along the path you capture broad views of Mojave Desert and Chimney Peak basin. The variety of nontechnical named peaks accessible from this trail makes this an attractive trip for peakbaggers as well.

Distance   28.3 miles, shuttle trip
Steep Ascents   None
Elevation Gain   4755 feet
Skills   Easy route finding
Seasons   Spring, summer, fall (Can be hot)
Maps   USGS 7.5 min *Walker Pass, Owens Pk, Lamont Pk* (The PCT is not complete on these maps at this writing.)
Trailheads   10 & 28. This trip requires two cars. See car tour T28. Leave the first car at **TH28,** the end of the trip where the PCT crosses the road or at the campground. Then see car tour T8. Drive the second car to the beginning of the trip at **TH10,** Walker Pass. This is 19.8 miles from your first car.
Description   There are two water sources en route: the first is 10.2 miles ahead. Both sources could dry up in late season or during drought years. The beginning of this trip is described in T26.

Northbound PCT Log

T26 Walker Pass	5246	0.0
crestline campsite	6390	2.1
Morris Pk Ex	6585	1.8
Morris/Jenkins saddle	6500	0.8
commemorative plaque	6580	0.3

While hiking along the PCT, look for vivid deep-blue Charlotte's phacelia. This exquisite flower, found beside the plaque when the mountain was dedicated, is uncommon and needs to be left to propagate. Also look for *Nolina parryi,* reaching 10 or more feet high. In the Sierra, this plant is indigenous to this small area. Nolina's pliant leaves are sharp-edged but not sharply tipped. Its trunk is broad and its blossoms dry to resemble creamy parchment paper, which linger until late autumn. Nolinas are often mistaken for yuccas.

The path, weaving around the extensions and recesses of Mount Jenkins, undulates slightly, passes a prominent ridge, curves deeply into the mountain scarred with slides of quartz diorite rocks, and then rounds another ridge. At this point (6950/1.3), ducks flanking the path indicate the best route to climb Mount Jenkins. With all peak excursions on the trip, you can either climb the peaks appearing between titles and asterisks, or skip the excursion descriptions, and continue on the PCT.

Excursion E: Mount Jenkins

On September 22, 1985, a group of Sierra Club members, mostly from its L.A. Hundred Peaks Section, placed a plaque on Mount Jenkins peak identical to the one on the trail, and they added the climb to their "100 Peaks" list. The route is challenging but nontechnical, and the views on top make this climb commensurate with the effort.

Distance   1.2 miles, round trip
Steep Ascents   0.4 mile
Elevation Gain   975 feet
Skills   Intermediate route finding; Class 2 climbing
Map   USGS 7.5 min *Owens Pk*; Mount Jenkins' name does not appear on the map. Its location is 35°42′32″N,117°59′30″W
Description   From the PCT (6950/0.0),

your *cross-country* route turns west on a moderate ascent of the major ridge emanating east-northeast from the summit rocks. A ducked trail has developed that climbs the ridge but stays to the south of the crest rocks, then regains the ridgecrest where it nearly levels for a brief stint. Ahead, Mount Jenkins peak projects from a crest arrayed with similar jagged peaks, making the summit difficult to identify. Your route continues up the steepening ridge, following ducks that soon lead you between the shards and over the boulders—the most difficult part of this trip—to the west side for the final climb to the plaque and the summit rocks (7921/0.6).

* * * * *

Striding along the PCT, you hike over chunks of metamorphic rocks, negotiate minor rock slides, observe Jeffrey pines, sugar pines and white firs, uncommon in this high-desert environment, and proceed around another ridge. You then gradually descend while the trail rounds mountain creases. Above the trail, one of these creases

marked by a duck, 2.9 miles from the trail plaque, conceals scattered pieces of a Navy C-45 twin engine Beechcraft. The 1948 crash took the lives of five scientists and two pilots from China Lake Naval Weapons Center who were on their way to a classified symposium on the Manhattan project in Oakland. Moving on, you pass a major slide area then reach the Jenkins/Owens saddle (7020/2.2). A small campsite is tucked under the trees and more space is available on the windy Sierra crest, the jumping-off point for 8453-foot Owens Peak, the highest peak in Kern County.

Excursion F: Owens Peak

Owens Peak, the highest of the seven on this hike, presents panoramic views of Mojave Desert and the Southern Sierra. Its east ridge of sheer spires beckons the fearless climber skilled in Class 4–5.10+ routes.

Distance   2.0 miles, round trip

PCT north of Walker Pass

Steep Ascents   0.5 mile
Elevation Gain   1435 feet
Skills   Intermediate route finding; Class 2 climbing
Maps   USGS 7.5 min *Walker Pass, Owens Pk*
Description   From the saddle on a *cross-country* route (7020/0.0), you ascend slightly as you contour northeast around the ridge that extends south from the peak. You pick your way over granitic soils and minor slides, then locate the yellow-green lichen-splashed outcrop ahead and climb over its lower boulders, thus avoiding the heavy brush below. Following that, traverse more boulders and drop onto a large rock slide in a conspicuous ravine. Here you meet the ducked *use trail* (7100/0.5) from Indian Wells Canyon among the granodiorite talus, and turn north, up-canyon. Zigzag steeply to a slab, which you climb to continue on the winding course north-northwest to the summit (8453/0.5).

The pioneer explorer John C. Fremont honored Richard Owens, a member of his third expedition, by naming Owens Lake for him. Owens Valley, River, Point and Peak were later named, but there is no evidence that Owens ever saw these places.

*   *   *   *   *

The PCT descends west from the Jenkins/Owens saddle by four switchbacks, then contours northwest, skirts a minor knob and reaches a lesser saddle (6300/1.3) east of Peak 6652, traveling across several slides of diorite rock en route. Again it switchbacks down to curve around another watershed, Cow Canyon. In this canyon the path crosses a rough, 3.9-mile jeep road from Highway 178 (5680/1.3). California Conservation Corps work crews, who built much of this section of PCT, used this road for access.

Beyond the road, you reach a ¼ mile spur trail (5410/0.4) to year-round Joshua Tree Spring. At the spring, boughs of golden oak, not arthritic arms of Joshua trees, arch over places for campsites near an elongated cattle trough. A pipe brings clear water from a spring box, affording easy access for hikers. Volunteers from the American Hiking Society helped BLM develop the spur trail and lay the spring box.

The PCT loses more elevation as it tracks a northwest route around a major ridge from Owens Peak. After crossing this ridge at a saddle (5225/1.1), it climbs northeast up a draw before again resuming a northwest direction to still another saddle (5860/1.1). You continue to hike in pinyon forest and its associated understory brush. The wide, smooth trail loses elevation by a series of short switches while below and off to the west the prominent slash of Canebrake Road gains elevation via a lengthy switchback. A summit block of Lamont Peak looms directly north of you, hiding its sheer, jagged north ridge. The trail nearly levels beyond its switchbacks before again descending east along the steep slopes. Within your view below, a private, gated road hugs the path of Spanish Needle Creek. Your path bends north after crossing a canyon with early-season runoff, and its gradient again eases. A half mile later it crosses, on a neatly laid bed of flat rocks, the main branch of Spanish Needle Creek (5160/2.2). A shelf just off the trail before the creek crossing makes an ideal campsite for weary PCTers.

Usually some water trickles along the Spanish Needle Creek drainage, which is shaded with willows and cottonwoods. While in the drainage, look for a recently discovered species—the Spanish Needle onion, *Allium shevockii*—the tipped-back flower petals are bright maroon above and lime green below.

Leaving the trees momentarily, the trail climbs out of the canyon around exposed slopes and again enters a forest, here with a few alders added, well-watered by a spring-fed finger of Spanish Needle Creek (5300/0.7). Because water is so scarce along the crest, the PCT was routed to drop into Spanish Needle Canyon in order to take advantage of this series of springs. Subsequently, the trail's circuitous route added several extra miles of hiking.

There is ample camping 0.1 mile farther ahead in a pinyon pine woodland along a minor ridge. You are likely to startle coveys of mountain quail, seemingly abundant in these mountains. You negotiate a sharp turn in a side canyon which points you generally east where you cross a spring-fed streamlet, this one frocked with wild roses (5560/0.6). Then clamber briefly along a blasted area, cross a seep and again enter a shady canyon adorned with occasional bracken ferns. Here you again cross a finger of Spanish Needle Creek (5620/0.2): the next reliable water is 10.9 miles away at Chimney Creek.

After a brief stretch south, the trail climbs east across the south-facing slopes of Spanish Needle Creek Canyon, then contours around another ridge. Here a white marbleized vein was blasted to carve the path. On this stretch you are treated to open views of jagged peaks bracketing Spanish Needle, which looks like a rounded, protruding thumb on a clenched fist. The trail again turns southeast, climbs a switchback, abruptly turns back, and climbs out of the canyon. A pair of short switchbacks, spaced 0.3 mile apart, help you gain elevation to reach the ridge between the Spanish Needle group and Lamont Peak (6800/3.0). Campsites were developed along the divide, to the left of the trail, to accommodate trail crews and are now used by PCTers, and by those climbing Lamont Peak.

Excursion G: Lamont Peak & East Lamont Peak

The highest point on tri-ridged Lamont Peak is the boulder summit closest to the PCT on the east ridge, not the named peak. This hike takes you to that summit and to the named peak, the pinnacled hub of the three ridges.

Distance   3.6 miles, round trip
Steep Ascents   0.4 mile
Elevation Gain   1375 feet
Skills   Intermediate route finding; Class 2–3 climbing
Map   USGS 7.5 min *Lamont Pk*
Description   (A trail to Lamont Peak, now in the planning stage, may be in place by the time of your arrival.) The east Lamont peak straddles the ridge extending from the sad-

dle. The PCT turns abruptly northeast, but you leave it to descend northwest on the *trail crew's trail* (6800/0.0) to the lowest point on the saddle. From there you traverse *cross-country* along northeast slopes, gaining elevation but staying well below the ridgecrest with its array of rough outcrops. The outcrop you see on your early ascent is not the east peak you are seeking, but soon you can identify its indistinctive broad top through forest-framed portals. You approach this, the highest peak on the mountain, by curving northwest to its easy walk-up side to the top (7475/1.0). The summit block itself, though, presents a challenge for those unskilled in using the narrow hand and toe holds, found on the west-northwest side.

After a perusal of the nearby peaks and valleys, especially the canyon of Spanish Creek to the south with its very visible, meandering PCT from which you came, you descend northwest along the ridge to hike to the named peak. Soon reaching a saddle, climb around the intervening peak on its north slopes to the next saddle, which you cross by a stick and rock marker. The awesome pinnacles on Lamont's north ridge capture attention, but they are for the experienced, equipped rock climber. You squeeze between the most southern pinnacle, the named Lamont Peak, and the brush, contouring close to the rock to approach it from the southwest. Look for ducks marking passage north to the summit. A pull through a notch, a brief climb along a precipitous granodiorite ridge, and you gain the apex (7429/0.8), a perch not designed for acrophobics.

*   *   *   *   *

On the PCT, once again it curves above a canyon, but this eastward leg takes you through another break from pinyons and live/scrub oaks to north-facing slopes of Jeffrey and sugar pines, white firs and black oaks—a mix of trees found in abundance on the west side of the Kern Plateau. Gaining some elevation, the trail then curves north along the Sierra crest where expansive eastern views unfold of Sand Canyon below, Boulder Peak on the canyon's north wall, and the desert beyond. Nearby, a lone tree protects a campsite from the usual ridgetop winds (7000/1.3). While here on the crest, you may wish to test your skills with an ascent of Spanish Needle.

Excursion H: Spanish Needle

This monolith in the group of needles, although not the highest of the seven peak climbs accessible from this section of the PCT, wins the respect of climbers as the most difficult peak of the seven. The summit yields impressive views to those who attain it, but the heady feeling of accomplishment may be reward enough.

Distance   1.6 miles, round trip
Steep Ascents   0.3 miles
Elevation Gain   845 feet
Skills   Intermediate route finding; Class 3 climbing
Map   USGS 7.5 min *Lamont Pk*
Description   The peak you seek is tucked behind the prominent southeast peak closest to the trail. This climb is described in T30: follow the description beginning at the Sierra crest.

Southbound Cross-Country Log
T30	Sierra crest	7000	0.0
	keyhole notch	7740	0.7
	summit	7841	0.1

*   *   *   *   *

Ahead, the PCT cuts a nearly straight swath northwest, just below ridgeline, taking you once again through pinyons, oaks and brush in sunny, dry country, then swings briefly east into a canyon where another small stand of Jeffrey pines and firs flourishes. These few patches of pine and fir occur typically on north slopes where moisture lingers longer in this dry climate. Now the trail traverses to a narrow saddle and then climbs a bit to a broader one (6900/2.0) with camping possibilities, beyond which the climbers' trailhead to Lamont Point begins.

Excursion I: Lamont Point

This peak, sans its off-set summit block, and Morris Peak are the easiest of the

medley of mountain climbs on this journey. The steepness of this short climb to the peak provides an interesting ascent, and the panoply of expansive views rewards the effort.

Distance   1.0 mile, round trip
Steep Ascents   0.2 mile
Elevation Gain   725 feet
Skills   Easy route finding; Class 2–3 climbing
Map   USGS 7.5 min *Lamont Pk*
Description   Begin your ***cross-country*** climb (6900/0.0) where the PCT curves northwest beyond the saddle, just before it descends to a switchback. Climbing west-northwest, you pass to the right of the dominant rock formations seen from the saddle. You approach the rounded apex as the steep upgrade moderates. After a short scramble up the off-center summit rocks you arrive at the benchmark and at the point— almost. Attaining the summit (7621/0.5) of Lamont's block castle, a hunk of granite

Nolina parryi

about 8 feet higher than the benchmark and separated by a precipitous moat about 3 feet wide, requires careful technique by a climber skillful enough to use the hand and foot holds on the right side of the block.

The lower faint-of-heart summit and its register can rests by the benchmark, and it presents an unobstructed panorama, as well. Viewing clockwise, you see: Whitney, Langley, Olancha and Sawtooth to the north on the Sierra crest; Telescope Peak northeast in Death Valley; Indian Wells Valley in the east desert below; Owens and Lamont peaks in the southern foreground with Scodie, Piute, Breckenridge and Tehachapi ranges beyond them, and the distant San Gabriel Mountains in the dim purple cloak; the Dome Land Wilderness in the western foreground with the Kern Plateau and the Greenhorn range beyond the wilderness.

*   *   *   *   *

Now an extended descent on the PCT to Canebrake Road and Chimney Creek Campground begins. A short switchback leads you northwest to a half-mile-long leg along Lamont Point slopes. Then, rounding boulders, the path heads back nearly as far before turning north onto another Sierra crest saddle (6260/1.4) with limited views, the starting point for hikes to Sawtooth Peak to the north.

Excursion J: Sawtooth Peak

Sawtooth Peak, straddling the Sierra crest and the Tulare/Inyo counties boundary, presents the second highest summit in the family of peaks along this section of PCT. The climax of an extended ridge that reaches the Mojave Desert, Sawtooth Peak yields views of that seemingly limitless expanse.

Distance   2.0 miles, round trip
Steep Ascents   0.6 mile
Elevation Gain   1710 feet
Skills   Intermediate route finding; Class 2 climbing
Maps   USGS 7.5 min *Lamont Pk, Ninemile Cyn (0.3 mile)*

Description   Your *cross-country* climb (6260/0.0) takes off where the PCT bends at a crestline saddle in the far reaches of Lamont Meadow's middle finger watershed canyon. Sighting a notch on the hill directly north, you angle toward it, gaining elevation on the precipitous southeast-slopes. Achieving the crest, you follow it northeast to the summit (7970/1.0), passing a rock which looks chiseled like sawteeth, though too obscure to have given the mountain its name. From the desert the peak somewhat resembles a sawtooth. The next named mountain on the Sierra crest described in this book is Round Mountain, roughly 25 air miles north-northeast.

*   *   *   *   *

Heading in a general northwest direction again, the PCT leaves the Sierra crest not to return again until Gomez Meadow. It slowly loses elevation, occasionally making small rises as it heads along lower slopes of the north side of the canyon between Lamont Point and Sawtooth Peak. Digger pine debuts as you stroll along the path of decomposed granite.

Accompanied by its water-loving willows, a seasonal creek whose water tumbles down multi-colored, sheer-sided rock canyons above, crosses the path (5950/0.8). Here and there by the path, in the most insecure places, solitary rust-brown, shreddy-barked, fragrant, scaley-needled western junipers thrive. Soon Lamont Meadow and a private inholding in this BLM-administered public land come into view, then Canebrake Road. Finally you drop, cross a north-south dirt road, and then cross adjacent year-round Chimney Creek. Immediately, you are ushered by a corridor of late-summer-blooming rabbitbrush to Canebrake Road (5555/2.4) and your awaiting car. T32 takes hikers on the next PCT section through east Dome Land Wilderness.

T28   Chimney Peak Recreation Area Car & All-Terrain Bicycle Tour

(With Directions to Trailheads 26–31)

This little known area, a transitional zone between the Mojave Desert and the main body of the Sierra Nevada, offers vistas of pinyon-clad mountains and vignettes of distant Dome Land Wilderness. Two campgrounds, the Pacific Crest National Scenic Trail, numerous hikes and peakbagging opportunities, a riparian area project, and scattered mines and prospects are within easy access of this tour's route.

Distance   44.5 miles, semi-loop trip
Steep Ascents   None (An extended grade for bicyclists)
Elevation Gain   6280 feet
Skills   Easy route finding; unpaved roads
Seasons   Spring, summer, fall (Bicyclists avoid summer)
Maps   Kern and Tulare counties road map
Tourhead   13. From Highway 178, turn north on Canebrake Road, signed *Chimney Peak Recreation Area* at **TH13**. This is 17.6 miles west of Highway 14 and 14.8 miles east of Sierra Way. It departs from car tour T8.
Description   Leaving the highway (3284/0.0/0.0) on **Canebrake Road,** you immediately dip through the sliver of Canebrake Creek where the road sheds its pavement. Now on a wide, washboard dirt surface, you soon pass a private road to the right that leads up Spanish Needle Canyon. Then at the foot of a hairpin curve, bicyclists brace themselves for a stiff climb via this curve and a switchback to a saddle (5500/6.6/6.6), **TH26** for Lamont Peak climbers of T29.

Continuing on, you wind around the western flank of Lamont Peak and cross Chimney Creek, whose soft whispers gently filter through the mountain silence. Then you pass the obscure entrance of a dirt road to the right, **TH27** (2.4/9.0) for Spanish Needle climb of T30 and Lamont's north pinnacles. Then arrive at *Long Valley Loop Road* (0.1/9.1) where you turn left.

If you are seeking **THs 28 & 29,** stay on *Canebrake Road* (0.0/0.0) to the crossing of the PCT at **TH28** (1.6/1.6) or to the campground for the road to **TH29** (0.3/1.9).

The Loop Road sports old patches of chuckholed, thin pavement on its gullied, washboard dirt surface. Nevertheless, it is maintained and most cars can be driven along it; all-terrain bicycles should have no problems either.

Along the entire trip the dominant tree is the pinyon pine. The distinguishing characteristics of the pinyon, which grows in high desert ranges, are the single, gray-green needle, blackish-barked trunks, much branched crown and 2×3-inch cones. You are allowed to gather the nuts of this tree for noncommercial use.

Pinyon nuts are tucked beneath the scales of the pitchy pine cones and ripen in early autumn. To gather pinyon nuts, collect closed cones in a brown paper bag; then, to open them, place the bags in an oven and turn the dial to low heat. After the cones open and the nuts have been loosened, shell them and, if preferred, roast them again in oil and a little salt.

The fall gathering season of protein-rich pinyon nuts was one of reverence and fellowship for Indian families—the Tubatulabal Indians in this area. After a solemn ritual, the men shook the trees or loosened the cones with hooks fashioned on willow poles. Children gathered the cones in woven willow baskets for the women to roast. Some nuts were eaten whole, but most were ground into flour. The grinding action created the many holes (mortars) in boulders scattered about this country. These nuts are still gathered by Tubatulabal descendants as part of their diet, probably as prehistoric tribes did before them. Continuing this gathering binds today's Native Americans to this important aspect of their past.

Because of the pinyon pines, the area abounds with Native American archeological sites. A reminder, however: Congress passed the antiquities legislation some time ago, making it illegal to remove or disturb anything pertaining to our Native Americans' culture—even pocketing an obsidian chip is unlawful.

After 3.0 miles into this leg of your trip, the bright greens of cottonwood and willow leaves promise water nearby. You soon discover a trough by the road and a spring below whose water eventually commingles with that of Chimney Creek. Your road crosses a creek with more willows and tops out at a saddle (6380/7.2/16.3). From here the granites of Dome Land Wilderness appear to the northwest and curious horizontal rock striations cross the mountains fronting the wilderness.

A short descent now and you arrive at Long Valley Campground Road (5571/2.0/18.3), where people hiking to the South Fork Kern Wild and Scenic River depart on T34 at **TH30**. This delightful, yet seldom used campground has 13 units with tables, several pit-type toilets and water hydrants. Long Valley Creek with its zone of riparian vegetation flows parallel to the camp. The creek over the years has been trampled by cattle and gutted by flash floods, causing the water table to drop in surrounding Long Valley Meadow. In 1987 a group of BLM employees installed sediment retention dams in an effort to reclaim the degraded area. These riparian zones supply important habitat for native animals and migrating birds, but essentially the repair work was done to benefit cattle.

On your journey, you begin a steady climb out of Long Valley, passing an apiary site nestled among sagebrush. With visions of sage-flavored honey, you reach a spur road to Dome Land Wilderness (3.9/22.2) where you turn left to reach **TH31**, otherwise skip the following description and continue on the tour route.

Hikers seeking eastern Dome Land trips T35 & T36, turn west on this sometimes rutted *road* (0.0/0.0) and drive to the locked gate at the entrance of the wilderness, **TH31**. No vehicles permitted, but a gate admits foot and hoof travel. Vistas of domes and slabs spread across the mountains to the west make this large, rather barren parking lot an attractive place to camp. Several mines flank this spur road; barite and tungsten mines predominate in this region.

Northeast on the Loop Road, you skirt one of the fingers of Long Valley Creek and just before a hairpin curve, cross the PCT (1.6/23.8) on which hikers and equestrians descend to Rockhouse Basin in the Dome Land Wilderness, then beyond. Still climbing, you pass roads to prospects and open pit mines, then attain the road's summit (7875/1.1/24.9) at a cross road. (The road south—left at each fork—leads to open pit mines that pock 8228 Bear Mountain, and a building housing a seismograph on top the mountain placed there by USGS, Menlo Park Division.)

Your loop road descends near a branch of Chimney Creek, past Reinhardt Spring, a cement basin and trough on the right, and picturesque Chimney Creek Ranch, a pastoral spread on Chimney Meadow. Then abruptly the dirt road ends and you turn right (southeast) on paved *Kennedy Meadows Road* (4.3/29.2). This trans-Sierra road climbs onto the Kern Plateau from Highway 395, 11.0 miles east, and descends to MTN99 by the Kern River, 57.5 miles west.

Enjoy your brief stint on a paved road! Leave it shortly before the BLM Chimney

Bedrock mortars

Peak Fire Station and Heliport to turn right onto **Canebrake Road** again (0.4/29.6). Wending your way southwest through the pinyon forest, you make another hairpin turn, cross a branch of Chimney Creek, and arrive at Chimney Creek Campground (3.9/33.5), a good place to stay for day hikes in the area: large, tree shaded, lightly used. The camp-ground road leads to **TH29** of T33.

You again cross the signed but easily missed PCT, **TH28** (0.3/33.8), which also gives access to many climbable peaks. Then on a short ride along sagebrush-covered Lamont Meadow, you return to the start of the loop (5323/1.6/35.4) and retrace your route to Highway 178 (3284/9.1/44.5).

T29　Lamont Peak Climb

With Excursion K: East Lamont Peak

Lamont Peak stirs the interest of hikers and rock climbers for its sound granodiorite faces and its massive pinnacled north ridge. The summit is not the highest point on this mountain but rather the junction of three ridges. The southwest ridge ascent attracts the most hikers, with the southeast ridge ascent a close second, since the advent of the PCT. The north ridge ascent of soaring pinnacles invites competent, well-equipped rock climbers.

Distance　3.8 miles, round trip
Steep Ascents　1.0 mile
Elevation Gain　2250 feet
Skills　Intermediate route finding; Class 2–3 climbing
Seasons　Spring, summer, fall
Map　USGS 7.5 min *Lamont Pk*
Trailhead　26. See car tour 28.
Description　Starting at the saddle on Canebrake Road (5500/0.0), you climb east over a small hill and up the steadily steepening ridge on a sometime ducked *use trail*. The path became so well-defined that it now appears on the 1986 topographic map. Nearby pinyon trees splotch the wayside with welcome shade and hang their pine cones, concealing tasty nuts, on display in the fall. Knots of bell-shaped, yellow-flowered mule ears grow with stubborn abandon in the loose, dry soil by the trail—the flower appropriately named for its long, wide "mule-ear" leaves. Clumps of live oak, buck brush and sagebrush line your route as well but never thwart your progress.

At length, your route takes you by a brief squeeze between salmon-colored granite and a drop-away terrain. Soon after it turns north-east and climbs steeply another 0.2 mile before it eases to contour slopes below the ridge's craggy crest. The trail passes down slope from the first of two saddles where some Jeffrey pines were felled to clear a helicopter pad for fire fighters, then remains at about the same elevation for 0.3 mile before it plummets to the next saddle, and climbs up the ridge of Lamont Peak. Here the ducks are more frequent to the base of the final assault, then suddenly ducks appear to the right and the left! This is the point to which you return for the East Lamont Peak Excursion.

You continue the ascent, briefly scrambling up boulders in a northwest slot to a notch, then climbing east atop a rock ridge to the bouldery summit: a precarious perch with precipitous drops (7429/1.9). Massive pinnacles fill the north view for nearly half a mile. Some stretch as high as Lamont Peak; at least one is higher. From Class 3 to Class 5+, they present an interesting adventure for intrepid rock climbers.

Excursion K: East Lamont Peak

A short extra trip for peakbaggers who would like to climb the highest peak on Lamont mountain.

Distance   1.6 miles, round trip
Steep Ascents   None
Elevation Gain   655 feet
Skills   Intermediate route finding; Class 2 climbing
Description   From the T intersection of ducks (7300/0.0) at the base of Lamont Peak pinnacle, follow the few ducks *cross-country* northeast, hugging the pinnacle, then ease east to the cairn on the saddle. If this is too tight a squeeze, you may have to engage in a short bushwhack. Make your way around the northeast side, below the summit, of the intervening peak to the next saddle on the east ridge. East from there to the top is an easy walk up. The summit boulder is also easy for some climbers, but not for all. It requires a hoist up tight foot and hand holds on the west-northwest side (7475/0.8). Of special interest from here is a view of the PCT as it makes its way north from a ridge south of Spanish Needle Canyon to the Lamont Point saddle.

T30   Spanish Needle Climb

The Spanish Needle cluster forms a jagged segment of Sierra crest just north of landmark Owens Peak. As viewed from the west, the needle itself, in the center of the cluster, resembles a fist with the thumb, at the south, extended up. This exhilarating climb rewards you with far-reaching views of the Mojave Desert and the South Fork Kern River Valley as well as a satisfying sense of accomplishment.

Distance   10.2 miles, round trip
Steep Ascents   0.7 mile
Elevation Gain   2525 feet
Skills   Intermediate route finding; Class 3 climbing
Seasons   Spring, summer, fall
Map   USGS 7.5 min *Lamont Pk* Spanish Needle is 35°46′18″N, 118°00′W
Trailhead   27. See car tour T28.
Description   There are three ways to reach this classy peak: the easiest is a 6.6 mile hike south on the PCT from its crossing of Canebrake Road to the saddle northwest of the peak, then up; the most difficult is a car-bashing grind up Sand Canyon to Rodecker Flat on the east side of the Sierra, then a 3325-foot ascent to the northernmost summit (the southernmost looks higher); or the following trip, which is an alternative to the PCT hike. It is 2.3 miles shorter, one way, but includes 0.4 mile of steep cross-country climbing.

Boulders pose no problem for 4WDs on the sandy road ahead, but on some narrow stretches of it one track rises 18 inches or more higher than the other, creating a threat of car rollover—so you may prefer to hoof it. En route to the base of Spanish Needle, you descend on this primitive *jeep road* (5320/

0.0), which passes through a cattle gate to a leap-across ford of Chimney Creek. Here lush watercress thrives and willows accommodate a campsite. Aquatic watercress (opposite, ovate leaves, ½–3 inches long; trailing stems) was a good source of fresh vegetable in the mountains, but is no longer considered wise to eat because of polluted water.

Your road follows a tributary southeast bisecting Lamont Meadow. At first it parallels it then runs in its dry bed after passing mushy, grassy areas around a pair of springs. The road progresses from the meadow, with southward views of the dramatic pinnacles along side Lamont Peak, through sparse oak woodland to a conifer forest with no views at all, but welcome shade. In this shaded area appear a few campsites, then a cairn to the right where people wishing to reach the saddle east of Lamont Peak leave the road to climb a cross-country route to it. Your route presses ahead.

Upon reaching road's end (6280/3.5), you turn south to scramble *cross-country* up a ravine in quest of the PCT, which traverses below the crest of the Spanish Needle/ Lamont Peak divide. The ravine soon forks: take either fork up the steep slope. At length you climb onto the PCT (6840/0.4), noting this place on the trail for the return trip. Turn left from here on the **PCT** and stroll east through the mixed forest on this well-constructed trail to the saddle astride the Sierra crest (7000/0.4). A large tree shields a campsite a short way up the trail.

To the south and southeast are two peaks of the Spanish Needle group. The Class 3 ascent of the needle nearest you has a register on its summit; but the highest needle, Spanish Needle, lies southeast of that peak. To reach the highest needle, drop down from the saddle a little to traverse **cross-country** around the first needle, ascending to the notch (keyhole) (7740/0.7) on the ridge north of

Spanish Needle, then follow the ridge to the summit.

(The details of the Class 3 portion were provided by mountaineer Ben Schifrin.) From the first keyhole, you walk 10 yards to the east to pause by a pine sapling, then ascend steeply southwest, first up blocks and then up 10 feet of exposed friction slab. Now on the west end of a large ledge, you walk east, then around a gendarme, for 8 yards. Here at the ridgecrest, climb a crack with a sapling in it, after which you ease down a ramp to a point just below a second keyhole, then climb south up the crest and finally stand atop Spanish Needle (7841/0.1).

Spanish Needle (center on crest) from Canebrake Flat

T31   Sawtooth Peak Climb

A hike along the PCT greatly facilitates the approach to Sawtooth Peak, one of the many view-commanding peaks astride the Sierra crest. A return from the peak through a multicolored, steep-sided canyon to the PCT heightens the adventure of this trip.

Distance   8.1 miles, semiloop trip
Steep Ascents   0.7 mile
Elevation Gain   2415 feet
Skills   Intermediate route finding; Class 2 climbing
Seasons   Spring, summer, fall
Maps   USGS 7.5 min *Lamont Pk, Ninemile Cyn (0.4 mile)*
Trailhead   28. See car tour T28
Description   Leaving Canebrake Road (5555/0.0), the **PCT**, hidden among rabbitbrush, heads southeast. It immediately dips to cross year-round Chimney Creek, then a dirt road, then begins its climb among pinyon pines into a broad canyon above the stretches of Lamont Meadow. Digger pines and western junipers join the pinyons.

The canyon gradually narrows as Lamont Point fills your view to the southeast. Then the trail briefly curves to cross a seasonal stream accompanied by willows (5950/2.4). You return here on your homeward loop. Your trail soon arcs south on a crest of a saddle (6260/0.8), where you leave it to begin your climb up Sawtooth Peak. The peak is visible to the north-northeast, the terminus of a far reaching east ridge, which includes rounded Boulder Peak and borders Sand Canyon.

Now you labor up a *cross-country* route along steep southeast-facing slopes to a notch on the ridgeline. From the notch you follow the crest northeast to climb the summit boulders (7970/1.1). After a rest, a snack, and a visual feast, continue your loop by descending west, where the brush is less dense, then southwest down the slopes of Sawtooth Peak. Ahead are strikingly colorful outcrops in the foreground, Lamont Point in the middle ground and the pinnacled north flank of Lamont Peak in the distance—your course follows this alignment to the outcrops. En route pick your way around the pinyon trees,

oaks and scattered manzanita bushes while zigzagging down to a gently slanting plateau where the gradient briefly eases. Towering, massive spires stand on the edge of the plateau like sentinels guarding the entrance of a narrow canyon, which you enter.

In the canyon, you follow a gully as it plunges northwest between sheer walls of granite sprinkled with flecks of quartz and permeated with pinkish potassium feldspar. Along the way you drop among boulders, descend on gravelly soils and climb around willows watered by a seasonal seep. Bypass a precipitous 60-foot granite fall by carefully lowering yourself along the fractured granite ledges to its right. You hike over slabs as the canyon becomes less steep, then you abruptly jog left, pass a side canyon, pass more willow thickets, and shortly thereafter reach the **PCT** (5950/1.4), completing your loop.

With welcome relief from the concentration and physical demands of the cross-country trek, you turn right, quicken your stride, let your thoughts wander and descend along the easy trail on which you arrived (5555/2.4).

View from PCT, Spanish Needle saddle

T32   PCT Backpack into East Dome Land Wilderness: Chimney Peak Recreation Area to Kennedy Meadows

With Excursion L: Bear Mountain

Like a camera's zoom lens, you see Dome Land Wilderness from afar, then ever nearer until the mountains with granite domes and spires fill your view. In contrast, the sinuous South Fork Kern River, lazily meandering within the wilderness, is not seen clearly until the trail abruptly curves to take you to its banks. There, during heavy snowmelt, you often see more of the river than you wish as it swells to overlap the trail.

Distance   23.3 miles, shuttle trip
Steep Ascents   None
Elevation Gain   2990 feet
Skills   Easy route finding
Seasons   Spring, summer, fall (can be hot)
Maps   USGS 7.5 min *Lamont Pk, Sacatar Cyn, Rockhouse Basin, Crag Pk*
Trailheads   28 & 45. This trip requires two cars. See car tour T52. Leave the first car at **TH45**, Kennedy Meadows Campground, the end of the trip. Then drive the second car east on paved Kennedy Meadows Road 16.0 miles from the campground entrance to the dirt road just west of the BLM fire station (T52, in reverse). Drive south on unsigned Canebrake Road 3.9 miles to Chimney Creek Campground. Leave the second car at the campground and walk 0.3 mile farther on Canebrake Road to the PCT trail, which crosses the road at **TH28**. (Canebrake Road continues 10.7 miles to Highway 178. T28, in reverse.)

Description   Your *PCT* trek begins (5555/ 0.0) west of Canebrake Road in BLM's Chimney Peak Recreation Area, 0.3 miles south of the campground. Your route leaves the rabbitbrush and sagebrush behind for a short while to climb above and parallel the road and campground amid a flurry of spring blooms featuring the daisy-like coreopsis. These flowers have yellow petals and centers and top reddish stems that grow from a tuft of basal leaves. The path, less sandy now, dips to cross a creek and then proceeds up the south-facing slopes of the creek's canyon. It soon tops out of that canyon and enters another above a stream whose chortle echoes

as the precipitous granodiorite walls of the canyon close in.

Beyond the canyon, to the left of the route, the curious trekker will find a scattering of debris to poke through where the multilevel ruins of a barite mill appear. The barite mineral, used in drilling muds, was mined hereabouts until the early 1950s. This clutter overlooks a sagebrush- and willow-choked meadow where the stream mentioned provides the last water, except for seasonal streams, until the South Fork Kern River, 14.4 miles ahead in Rockhouse Basin. Immediately the trail crosses a dirt road (6580/2.2) descending from a flat area used for camping.

The path wends along slopes, passing an eroded dirt track. The gray-greens of the pinyon forest enhance the red-browns of the soil, and an occasional juniper adds to the pleasing palette. Several sagebrush meadows diminish below, while Chimney Peak seems just a stone's throw across the canyon east-northeast. Do not scan the peak for a chimney—it was named for one still standing in Chimney Meadow.

Soon you cross another dirt road, round a nose about ½ mile later, then tramp through sagebrush and cross yet another road. Now begin a northwest trek involving a series of seemingly endless curves around steep ridges and retreats across dry furrows, slowly ascending over metamorphic soils and chunks of rock. To the east, beyond the meadows below and the dirt roads that snake through them, stand the peaks that anchor the eastern Sierra. At last you attain the trail summit (8020/3.6), which crosses a minor ridge suitable for camping. You begin a descent now, bearing west where you cross a road to an excavation, the beginning of the optional mountain excursion (7980/0.2).

Excursion L: Bear Mountain

The easily reached summit presents fine views. Even though the rounded mountain top reaches above 8000 feet, man traveled here over the years and etched his presence: witness the holes, the slices, the roads, and a building with its ancillary equipment.

Distance   1.8 miles, round trip
Steep Ascents   None
Elevation Gain   250 feet
Skills   Easy route finding; Class 1 climbing
Map   USGS 7.5 min *Sacatar Cyn*
Description   The easiest way to Bear summit is to start the excursion at the dirt road just 0.2 miles west of the trail's summit (7980/0.0). Walk southeast on the *road* past a huge gouge into the metamorphic slate of Bear. Soon to the right you pass the bulldozed remains of a squatter's house heaped in unsightly piles. It is an example of BLM's stepped-up effort to rid the areas it governs of illegal dwellings occupied by people who live, usually in unhealthy filth and clutter, rent-free and tax-free on public lands.

Beyond the clutter the road along the mountain's crest forks. Here you leave it to angle *cross-country* southeast up the pinyon-covered slopes to the slightly rounded summit of Bear (8228/0.9). A register can is by the bench mark. Continue your stroll 0.3 mile farther to the next peak south on Bear, nearly equal in elevation, to the locked facility housing a seismograph. This is one instrument in an important network of many placed by USGS, Menlo Park Division, to record earth tremors.

*   *   *   *   *

Resuming the PCT trek, you immediately cross another road leading to an excavation sliced into the earthy-red slate. Several of these gouges attract attention as you progress down the trail. Ahead, the northwest tapestry of Rockhouse Basin appears with the stark granites of Dome Land Wilderness occupying the basin's southwest border. The deep forest greens of Sirretta and other Kern Plateau peaks delineate the northwest curve

Volunteers working on PCT

of the basin where the muted sage greens of Woodpecker Meadow are barely visible. The High Sierra silhouette stretches across the northern horizon encompassing the Great Western Divide and the Mount Whitney group. A bit nearer you glimpse aloof and solitary "Miss" Olancha—the feminine title bestowed by the region's old timers.

The trail, curving northwest, crosses a road and then descends along a canyon. A sun-dappled seasonal creek glitters in the canyon's recess, and a weathered hut squats by the creek's bank. At a bend in this canyon, the path arches over an artfully constructed culvert containing the seasonal stream, next to camping possibilities. In 100 yards the trail crosses Long Valley Loop Road (7220/1.9), climbs over a saddle, and descends along the southwest side of a deeper canyon.

There are better views now of Woodpecker Meadow, an area burned in the Woodpecker Fire of 1947. The trees, unable to reestablish themselves, were replaced by sagebrush and buckbrush. Stegosaurus Fin, Dome Land's resident dinosaur, which sits prominently in the wilderness interior, displays his fin above the intervening ridge. The South Fork Kern River, weaving through the basin below, remains hidden. A flat on a small northeast spur ridge (6600/2.7) offers one last place to camp before the broader lands of Rockhouse Basin. You continue to descend, sometimes clinking over loose, rocky slopes, then slowly plodding through sandy soils near the foot of the descent.

Now in Rockhouse Basin, turn north and cross first a creek (5845/1.8), then immediately cross a closed road. (If water is needed and the creek is dry, follow its bed 1.1 mile to the river.) Once again in national forest, you enter Dome Land Wilderness, near a large campsite. In 1984 a new California wilderness bill became law. It added 32,000 acres to Dome Land Wilderness; you now hike within its expanded boundaries.

Domes, spires and obelisks rise from the semi-arid 94,695 acres of wilderness. Rock climbers find it an excellent place to practice their skills. Surprisingly, beside the granites, there are grassy meadows, forests, and

sizable fishing creeks along with the serpentine South Fork Kern River. A breeze usually moderates the heat of summer in this spacious land.

Your path north roughly follows the South Fork, but the river is about a mile away for the next several miles. However, you do catch vignettes of it occasionally as you scuff along the sandy trail through a forest of pinyon pines. This sandy trail is subject to erosion—if eroded, just follow the corridor through the trees scarred from sawed-off branches.

You soon dip through the sagebrush-lined wash of a waterless basin and then pad across a northeast-southwest-trending closed road, which descends along a gully. In a bit over a mile you cross a willow-lined, seasonal creek (5870/3.2). A large campsite sits at the end of a closed jeep road north of the creek. In late spring, dainty, funnel-like white gilia flowers, fully opened in waning light, cover these sandy grounds. Contouring slightly northwest now, you approach a gateway of resistant metamorphic bedrock through which flows the South Fork Kern River (5760/1.0).

Most of the year the South Fork resembles a placid creek with good fishing holes and refreshing bathing pools, but during snowmelt the river becomes tumultuous, charging wildly through its containing banks. Then it is dangerous to cross. But during snowmelt this river, unspoiled by man, profoundly demonstrates why in 1987 it was included with the North Fork Kern River in the protective custody of the very selective National Wild and Scenic Rivers System.

Turning north again, the path threads passages between the willow and wild rose tangles that edge the river and the boulders composing the cliffs. Sprinklings of flowers add an artist's touch to the captivating scenery, and three-needled, vanilla-scented Jeffrey pines line the water's edge. The trail climbs and dips, generally following the watercourse but allowing the river to leap away now and again.

Shortly you cross spring-fed Pine Creek, and then about ½ mile later join a road (5940/1.3) where 4WDers have left tracks leading to campsites and river views. In time you leave the road at a junction (5950/0.6) where it curves west toward the river; you continue straight ahead, north, following the fence on your right. Soon you pass west of a whimsical, yesteryear comic strip's "Toonerville Trolley" hut with a stovepipe chimney, then cross a stream garnished with sedges and watercress (5916/0.1) and cross a 4WD road next to the stream. A vast outlier of sagebrushy Kennedy Meadows stretches ahead. You begin hiking through it.

Just ¼ mile later the PCT approaches a fence corner, then leaves the fence and angles off to the northeast, away from the river, passing amid the sagebrush, a treeless, grassy area with a fire ring. In the midst of this meadow, the path crosses a 4WD road (5980/0.6) that connects paved Kennedy Meadows Road—about a mile to the east— with other river roads. Not far north of the meadow, the PCT climbs the lower west slope of a hill where you catch your first sight of the paved road, a few buildings along it, and the general store. Pressing near the river again, you pass through three cattle gates (please close). Between the first two gates, you round west of the outcrops where the path is often washed out by high water. You then near a large campsite under a juniper tree, and 0.4 mile later wind up to the road just east of the bridge (6020/1.7).

Across the Forest Service's paved road,

you continue on sandy turf among high-desert flora. Look for apricot mallow, which you can recognize by its brilliant, five-petaled, cupped flowers and silvery, hairy leaves; and for blazing star with its shiny, golden-yellow blooms and narrow, lobed leaves; also for flat-lying sand mats with tiny white flowers touched with purple. Heading north, you dip through washes and cross dirt roads that lead west to riverside campsites, fishing and swimming holes. Occasional junipers offer dots of shade as you pass fences, first on the right and then on the left, then you go through one gate and soon through another. Enticing murmurs of the river increase as you reach and then hike above the musical South Fork. Slowly you leave the sagebrush meadow embraced by the gentle peaks of the semiarid side of the Kern Plateau, and head toward a distant fire-scarred mountain, seen through the river canyon to the north.

Soon the trail crosses the road to the campground (6080/1.8) and proceeds along higher ground. Here it winds for a short time around boulders among pinyon pines and brush. Then it crosses the campground road (6120/0.4), bisects Kennedy Meadows Campground, and takes you to your shuttle car (6150/0.2). T75 takes hikers on the next PCT section to Olancha Pass.

South Fork Kern River at bedrock gateway

T33   Day Hike in Chimney Creek Canyon

This trip offers a stroll up a colorful canyon hidden between towering fractured walls known to Native Americans of yesterday and to cowboys of today, but to very few hikers even though the trail appears on the maps. Conveniently located next to the BLM campground, the trail crisscrosses year-round, slender Chimney Creek, and offers opportunities for rock exploration along the way.

Distance   3.6 miles, round trip
Steep Ascents   None
Elevation Gain   530 feet
Skills   Easy route finding; easy hiking
Seasons   Spring, summer, fall (can be hot)
Map   USGS 7.5 min *Lamont Pk*
Trailhead   29. See car tour T28 to Chimney Creek Campground. Turn right on the **campground road** (0.0/0.0) to a spur road in mid-camp at the left of a cattleguard crossing (0.5/0.5) at **TH29**.
Description   This leisurely trek begins on the **spur road** (5645/0.0), which is several steps from the middle campground sites. You immediately cross willow-hemmed Chimney Creek to stroll northeast along the road, parallel to the creek and the middle and upper sections of the well-designed, lightly used campground. Ahead, unnamed, multicolored, conical Peak 7125 stands serene. Quite soon you pass below a submerged tank, a receptacle for water carried by pipe from the spring in Chimney Meadow. Then after

The chimney of Chimney Meadow

Phenocrysts in canyon boulder

nearly 0.9 mile, you cross the creek and quickly cross back, the second and third of seven crossings on your journey.

Now on a sometimes obscure **path**, you turn north to wend your way in a canyon pinched by thousand-foot-high rock walls, appearing stacked like building blocks, richly salmon colored. In this canyon you may want to explore the overhangs and scramble among the boulders; or perhaps dangle your feet in the cool water or picnic under the shade of willows, live oaks, digger pines or the few but stately Jeffrey pines. You continue to crisscross the creek, where the water often slides over small slabs or drops in miniature falls. Here and there patches of thorny-stemmed, five-petaled, pink-flowered wild roses line the way.

The canyon then opens to lush, grassy, privately-owned Chimney Meadow (6171/1.8). Barbed wire prevents you from investigating the still-standing chimney for which all these nearby features were named and the sparkling pond at the spring. From your distance, the chimney appears like a heap of rocks on the east rim near the south edge of the meadow.

T34   Long Valley Creek Day Hike to a Wild River

Only in Dome Land Wilderness does the Wild and Scenic South Fork Kern River gain this setting: a deep, convoluted canyon with cliffs and domes arrayed along its sides. Where this stretch of river is easiest to reach, cottonwoods arch over swimming and fishing holes, alders hedge sandy shores and smooth granite slabs slant amid potholes where cascades end.

Distance   4.8 miles, round trip
Steep Ascents   None
Elevation Gain   600 feet
Skills   Easy route finding; moderate hiking
Seasons   Spring, fall
Map   USGS 7.5 min *White Dome*
Trailhead   30. See car tour T28. Turn west on *Long Valley Campground Road* (0.0/0.0). Drive to its end at **TH30** (1.7/1.7).
Description   (This canyon becomes a virtual oven in the summer—a time, also, when rattlesnakes like to cool themselves under its bushes and boulders.) Your trip begins on a *trail* at the end of BLM's pine-shaded Long Valley Campground (5240/0.0). You pad west along the abrupt edge of a terrace abutting the willow-accompanied creek. Enter, in 0.25 mile, Dome Land Wilderness and Sequoia National Forest where the trail becomes *Long Valley Trail 36E05*. On it you occasionally dip to creekside, regain the terrace, then return to stay along the creekbed to the river. Although the map shows the trail on the south side of the creek, it is easier in places to cross over for short distances.

The canyon turns southwest, narrows before accepting width-widening side canyons, then narrows again. The creek gurgles through little cascades, slides down slick-

rocks and drops in brief, thready falls. You negotiate granite boulders, cross the slender creek on mossy slabs and make your way among willows, cottonwoods and wild roses, usually finding some kind of trail, and soon reach the creek's confluence with the South Fork Kern River (4640/2.4).

Here the river races by in a sandy trough on its way to the inaccessible country called "The Roughs." A nameless dome rises northwest on the canyonside above the suspended leaves of alder and cottonwood and the needles of Jeffrey pine. A few large campsites lie on both sides of the river here, along with a slab-sided swimming hole a few hundred yards upstream. You may share the river with a Dipper (Water Ouzel); a bird that performs his pliés on water-splashed boulders and under cascades in his own fascinating water ballet.

Farther upstream, near the confluence with Manter Creek, historian Bob Powers reports that you can find traces of Coogan's Cabin, a retreat the parents of child-actor Jackie Coogan built in 1923, just after he co-starred with Charlie Chaplin in the film "The Kid."

Long Valley Creek pools

T35   East Dome Land Wilderness Day Hike to the South Fork Kern River

Looking for an uncrowded place to fish, bathe, picnic, view or just relax? Try this easy trip into vast, open, high desert country where your only companions may be cicadas and perhaps a shy rattlesnake resting in sagebrush shade. You can spend the day fishing or lazing by the river while absorbing the enormity of the country around you.

Distance   2.2 or 3.4 miles, round trip
Steep Ascents   None
Elevation Gain   215 feet or 305 feet
Skills   Easy route finding; easy hiking
Seasons   Spring, fall
Map   USGS 7.5 min *Rockhouse Basin*
Trailhead   31. See car tour T28.
Description   This trip takes you from Chimney Peak Recreation Area to the river in Rockhouse Basin. Before the wilderness was extended in 1984 to include Rockhouse Basin, OHVs drove about the country at will, creating a maze of roads. These roads are now closed or used as foot and hoof trails; this trip takes you on a couple of these trails. Take something to sit on and a wide-brim hat as it can get hot in this basin. But nature's natural air conditioner—a breeze—and nature's body coolant—the river—combine to keep you comfortable.

Pass through the gate at the end of the cul-de-sac (5845/0.0) to begin your trip and hike west along ***Rockhouse Basin Trail 35E16*** in the shade of pinyon pines. Quickly the trail branches (5755/0.2) and you have a choice. The sunny basin trail continues along the right fork and curves north near the river by a campsite (5630/0.9). It then leads on to the northeast corner of Rockhouse Basin. The left fork, ***Manter Creek Trail 35E12***, with more trees for shade, soon crosses the river (5540/1.5). It then circles around a private inholding and climbs steeply up the mountains. This is the only road where you may on occasion see a vehicle legally driven in Dome Land Wilderness. Owners of the private property within the wilderness are allowed access.

On either route you can leave the trail to hike cross-country to the river, or travel beyond the short destinations of this trip—package the outing as you desire.

South Fork Kern River potholes near Long Valley

T36   White Dome Climb in East Dome Land Wilderness

With Excursion M: Rockhouse Peak

This Dome Land trip, commencing from the high desert east border, offers a longer period of accessibility to the domes and peaks than other routes that may be closed by snow. The domes and peaks, emblematic of the Dome Land experience, offer inspiring views of the rugged wilderness.

Distance   13.0 miles, round trip
Steep Ascents   1.3 miles
Elevation Gain   3845 feet
Skills   Intermediate route finding; Class 2-3 climbing (Class 4-5 pitches optional)
Seasons   Spring, summer, fall (can be hot)
Maps   USGS 7.5 min *Rockhouse Basin, White Dome*
Trailhead   31. See car tour T28.
Description   From the gate impeding further vehicle progress, descend a gentle grade on *Rockhouse Basin Trail 35E16* (5845/0.0). You quickly meet a left fork, the end of *Manter Creek Trail 35E12* (5755/0.2), on which you continue, here amid pinyon pines. You take the road/trail west then south through a stock-fence gate and onto a ford of South Fork Kern River (5540/1.5). The river spreads on flood plain here and when full, divides into multichannels. Even so, you may need a good walking stick for balance or a rope belay during the height of spring runoff.

Beyond the river, the route continues on the road/trail south, but soon forks to the right on a path that takes hikers across a tributary and around private Rockhouse Meadow and cow camp to a junction with the old trail west of the inholding. (This detour is only flagged at this writing.) Still on 35E12, the trail begins a serious ascent on steep slopes that gains over 1400 feet in 1.6 miles with no switchbacks, and you understand why it is posted unsafe for stock. At length the trail, somewhat shaded by oaks, reaches the saddle divide (7340/2.7).

The path continues on to Manter Meadow, but you turn left at the saddle, on a *cross-country* route, south, up the ridgecrest. After an initial steep incline you arrive at a prominence where several Class 4 and 5 knobs may be climbed (8040/0.4). With White Dome

visible down the narrowing ridge to the southeast, you descend the crest to a notch (7300/1.4) just north of it. Now you contour past several challenging knobs, cross a Class 3 rib and make an easy traverse upslope to the top (7600/0.3).

The summit offers exciting southward views of the "Roughs" in the South Fork Kern River Canyon. These "Roughs" within the southern extension of Dome Land Wilderness are wildly pinnacled, cliff-jutting slopes of a canyon 4000 feet deep.

After enjoying this view, backtrack to the saddle where you have the choice of either climbing Rockhouse Peak or returning to the car.

Excursion M: Rockhouse Peak

The highest point in east Dome Land Wilderness, this peak allows you to take in a great swath of scenery from its summit.

Distance   2.6 miles, round trip
Steep Ascents   0.3 mile
Elevation Gain   1045 feet
Skills   Intermediate route finding; Class 2-3 climbing (Class 4-5 pitches optional)
Map   USGS 7.5 min *Rockhouse Basin*
Rockhouse Peak is 35°54'4"N, 118°13'40"W
Description   A mild *cross-country* bushwhack north from the pass (7340/0.0) amid mountain mahogany soon leads you up a steep gully just west of the crest. Then you proceed north-northeast, cross a pine flat and later ascend to an apparent saddle (7940/1.0), where you turn and climb briefly west. Upon reaching the summit block, follow the baseline talus around to the north where you scramble to the summit (8383/0.3).

T37   North Fork Valley Car & Bicycle Tour
(With Directions to Trailheads 32–38)

This tour advances from scenes of the wind-spawned white caps on Lake Isabella to the swirling, cascading rush of the North Fork Kern River. The massive exposed rock of the Southern Sierra slopes surrounds these restless waters with a sense of serene stability. However, these mountains, laced with earthquake faults, belie the solidity of their appearance. Movement along these faults influenced the geological and biological diversity and the natural and human history of picturesque Kern River Valley and the North Fork Canyon. The results of this ancient activity unfold as you travel north.

Distance   32.8 miles, one way

Steep Ascents   None

Elevation Gain   1900 feet

Skills   Easy route finding; paved road

Seasons   All year (Bicyclists avoid summer)

Maps   Kern and Tulare counties road maps

Tourhead   17. From Highway 178, turn north on Sierra Way. This is 32.4 miles west of Highway 14 and east of Lake Isabella's high-water line. This tour links with car tours T8 & T52 (described in reverse).

Description   Driving north from the T junction on **Sierra Way** (2630/0.0/0.0), coded on road paddles as 521Z, you bisect pasture on the floor of South Fork Valley, then penetrate willow and cottonwood thickets to bridge South Fork Kern River (1.2/1.2). So much water is siphoned off along South Fork Valley that the river is usually dry here by early summer. You then proceed generally west while skirting both river and thicket at the foot of steep, south-facing slopes. These slopes expose what geologists refer to as the Isabella Pluton. Of particular interest to them is the origin of the irregular shaped mafic enclaves in the granodiorite pluton. These are dark, wart-like protrusions more resistant to weathering than the surrounding rock.

An occasional spring runoff so swells Lake Isabella, a reservoir, that it laps at the road's southern embankment for 1.4 miles past the bridge. Beyond the high-water line, the course curves up a brief, steep incline and tops out in a broad gap on a ridge. Sagebrush and its retinue of drought-tolerant shrubs

hedge the road for a long way to come. The course then swoops down a short moderate grade to cross the entrance road to Hanning Flat Recreation Area (2.7/3.9) near Rabbit Island—sometimes an island, sometimes just a bump on the lake's dry shore. Dead, blackened trees claw the lake's shallow, easternmost waters.

Your road now veers away from the shore to again climb a short, steep grade. Colorfully streaked beds of marble, slate, phyllite and quartzite are exposed in the roadcuts you pass from this ridgecrest to the mouth of Caldwell Creek Canyon. Also of interest in this ridge's road cut are the garnets found along the complex metamorphic/granitic

Winter in Kern Canyon

cantact. The road quickly descends from the crest (notice its limestone ledge) then follows the lakeshore, passing Robinson Cove and Point and Stine Cove and Point en route. The road next turns up 0.7 mile of moderate grade while veering away from adjacent Rocky Point Bay. For the next 24.5 miles the route winds generally northward, entering into the main zone of the Kern Canyon Fault as the road descends past a junction (4.6/8.5) with a westbound entrance to the Eastside Campground 9 and boat-launching ramp, then past Cyrus Flat, which houses the region's dump.

As scarps on the Goat Ranch Fault rise to the east, you once again near the high-water shore of Lake Isabella and pass the Kern Valley Airport—its fluorescent orange windsocks flapping in the wind. The landing strip to the west is inundated on three sides when the reservoir reaches its highest level. The local residents then refer to the strip as the aircraft carrier "USS Kern Valley."

From the airport turnoff (2.1/10.6), your road winds at the base of a west-facing slope that supports a colony of junipers and digger

pines. Such colonies become more prevalent the farther along this trip you progress. Where the slope and its trees recede from the road, hot springs on private property to the east bubble up from the depths of the Goat Ranch Fault. The remains of a community bath house, a bygone meeting ground for young and old, sits forlorn in the canyon. Beyond the springs and Caldwell Creek, your road intertwines with the unmarked boundary of Sequoia National Forest, then enters Kernville.

An engaging achievement of intelligent city planning, this is one town that complements its setting. Kernville residents moved here in 1954 before their original town, four miles down-canyon near the present town of Wofford Heights, was flooded with water backed up behind Isabella Dam. Here you can detour left on Kernville Road (2706/2.5/13.1), a four-lane, divided road, to the commercial district and museum. The log building of SNF's Cannell Meadow Ranger District is at Burlando and Whitney roads, 0.6 mile from Sierra Way.

Back at the junction, the route on Sierra

Way passes octagonal Kernville Elementary School and the eastern Kernville commercial district where a dirt road (0.2/13.3) opposite Buena Vista Drive leads to **TH32** for T38, a hike along the Old Mule Trail. The road ahead narrows. Its shoulders, only intermittently present, are usually unusable by the mounted cyclist. On weekends some reckless drivers exceed the posted 40 MPH speed limit and barrel around the blind curves ahead; thus the cyclist must temper enjoyment of Kern Canyon with caution and the utmost alertness.

Soon you enter Sequoia National Forest (0.4/13.7). While the more water-loving cottonwoods, willows and alders crowd the river banks for the next 19 miles, chaparral, live oaks and gray-green, single-needled digger pines line your route. Digger pines seem to have a way of their own. Some defy gravity by growing perpendicular to the slant of a slope. Even on the flats within a grove, these trees grow asymmetrically in every direction—topography and prevailing wind not withstanding. This tree's unruliness makes it unique—somehow endearing—among the local pines. Interesting to note that around the turn of the century, this canyon from Kernville to Kern Lakes, far to the north, was set afire each year to make forage for sheep and cattle. How much of the forest was lost to his practice will never be known.

Along the river during snowmelt you hear excited howls from those in rafts, kayaks and canoes as their crafts bounce and slide through the crashing white water. Later in the summer, when the waters tame, "tubers" lazily float the currents. Early mornings and late afternoons, fishermen dot the river shores.

The great Kern Canyon Fault bisects the rocks beneath the road beyond the Forest

Kern Slabs

boundary. Roadcuts on this side of the fault show a mishmash of tortured bedrock, mostly slate, phyllite and crystallized limestone. Many of these rocks recur in the roadsides ahead. The road skirts the well-attended grounds of Camp Owens, a rehabilitation camp for juvenile boys. Past the buildings, next to the camp's corral, is **TH33**, Cannell M'cyclepath, (0.9/14.6) for T39 & T40: hikes to Harley Mine and the Southern Kern Plateau.

Shortly you cross penstocks within which water diverted from Kern River drives the generators housed in the concrete structure southwest of the road. Here the road is perched high on a steep southwest-facing slope and commands an inspiring view of Kernville. You quickly reach the SCE road (0.7/15.3) to the aqueduct forebay, **TH34** for aerobic exercisers on T41, then the hamlet of Riverkern. The village is bracketed by a popular swimming beach at its south outskirts and Cannell Creek and Tulare County boundary (1.1/16.4) at its north. The road's code changes to *TC Road MTN 99*. (The county code means "maintained," not "mountain.")

The SCE road to **TH35** for T42, Yellow Jacket climb (0.2/16.6), angles in at the right, and in 0.1 mile more, your road reaches Headquarters Campground. During construction of the aqueduct system from 1915 through 1921, the Southern California Edison Company housed its workmen in eight camps set up between here and the dam north of Road's End. Today, this and the next two SNF campgrounds perpetuate the names of these three vanished SCE camps. In the canyon ahead, your road passes a series of camping areas: some private, some SNF developed campgrounds, some undeveloped. Along the banks of the river on summer holiday weekends, assorted camping gear is spread solidly from Kernville to Johnsondale bridge—campground or not.

In 0.9 mile, the road passes Camp Three Campground. To the east of it rise the Kern Slabs, the granites of locally named "Yellow Jacket Peak" where climbers often scale easily attainable Class 4 and 5 routes. Then 1.6 miles north of the slabs the road skirts

Hospital Flat Campground. Corral Creek claims the next major item on our travel agenda. At this writing it has a picnic area and an unimproved campground. Plans call for a condominium complex with tennis courts, swimming pool and market. The developer has agreed to upgrade the present campground.

You presently pass a junction flanked to the south by the entrance to unimproved Ant Canyon Campground and to the north by a road to **TH36** of T43 & T44, the South Rincon M'cyclepath. Because of the rough surface of the first 0.7 mile of this road, it is better to continue 0.8 mile on MTN 99 to the aqueduct road coded **Salmon 9–12** (8.1/24.7). People seeking the Rincon M'cyclepath turn right here; the rest skip the bracketed information and continue on.

To reach **TH36**, turn southeast on the *aqueduct road* (0.0/0.0), coded *Salmon*. Turn sharply left at an acute angle junction (0.2/0.2) with the road from Ant Canyon. Turn right at the next junction (0.4/0.6). Check odometer. Turn left onto the steep miner's road (0.6/1.2) to the flat at **TH36** (0.1/1.3).

Next on MTN 99 you pierce the woodland of Salmon Creek, cross the creek, then look for its slender falls high to the east. The canyon beyond the creek was burned by illegal fireworks in 1989. In quick time you arrive at McNalley's Fairview Resort. SNF parking lot, **TH37** (3.6/28.3), north of Fairview Campground, accommodates cars parked by people interested in T45, Packsaddle Cave hike. The south lot is for those heading across the suspension bridge for the Whiskey Flat Trail.

North of the Fairview lots, Kern Canyon becomes narrower and more scenic with its metamorphic rock cliffs brushed with chartreuse lichen. Immediately, rusty tailings spilling from Fairview Mine across the river attract attention. In 0.7 mile, Road's End resort is reached. Imported ailanthus trees tempt travelers to linger. The first wagon road up Kern Canyon was forged to this point by

1910, which remained road's end until 1939, when the road was extended to serve the sawmill at Johnsondale.

The road crosses a large zone of crystallized limestone here, which extends east to contain Packsaddle Cave, then arcs northwest to return to the river at Limestone Campground. The route continues to wind up-canyon, very soon passing on a curve a gaping SCE test hole in the roadside cliff, then narrowing where a chain-link fence stands along its west edge. The Edison aqueduct intake structure runs directly behind the fence parallel to the road, and connects with the diversion dam looming ahead. Where the dam meets the opposite bank, concrete fish ladders aid in piscine migrations. The aqueduct pipe dives under the road into the mountain carrying Kern River water 14 miles to the generators.

Beyond this complex the road outflanks a ridge north of Packsaddle and Brin canyons, then bends to skirt the cave-pocked face of a limestone bluff. A one-way paved loop soon splits left from your road at the entrance of Limestone Cliff Campground, 2.7 miles from Road's End. After a few hundred yards MTN 99 curves at the mouth of Brush Creek Canyon and crosses its creek. Brush Creek

hosts much water play. Sunbathers, too, find it entirely congenial.

Now the road curves past a parking lot, which SNF officials classify as an "unimproved campground." Within a few yards the road rejoins the riverbank, then meets paved Sherman Pass Road, ascending at your right (3780/4.3/32.6), the terminus of the Kern Plateau car tour, T52. Your trip continues across Johnsondale Bridge to a parking lot (3800/0.2/32.8), **TH38** for T97 & T99. The elongated steel-girder arch that supports the narrow span gave a classic beauty to the foot bridge when it stood alone; its height still makes the walk to the opposite abutment sensational. This bridge was replaced for vehicle travel in 1983 by the two-lane structure next to it. The River Trail begins at the steps north of the bridges. The road of your tour continues on to Southern Sierra westside attractions and the San Joaquin Valley, described in this book's companion edition.

This scenic view of the Kern River and its colorful canyon concludes this tour. For an extensive trip affording a comprehensive overview of Southern Sierra eastside attractions, combine this trip with car tours T52 & T46 (described in reverse) and T8.

Fish ladder on North Fork Kern River

T38   Old Mule Trail Climb to Harley Mine & Mountain

A brawl between Charles Harley and Big Bill led to gold over a century ago. The altercation terminated in the style of the day: Harley outdrew Bill, shot him, fled to the mountains—and discovered gold. The gold-bearing mountain, which looms over the tiny village of Kernville, is known locally as Harley Mountain. Chinese laborers forged the trail to the top; it was later supplemented with a tram. Then mules carried heavy, unwieldy parts for the tram and mine up this steep path. Now you test your ability to find this path, but take time to enjoy the spectacular views of Kern River Valley.

Distance   5.2 miles, round trip
Steep Ascents   1.6 miles
Elevation Gain   2900 feet
Skills   Intermediate to advanced route finding; Class 2 climbing
Seasons   Fall
Map   USGS 7.5 min *Kernville*, Harley Mountain is 35°46′47″N, 118°24′18″W
Trailhead   32. See car tour T37. Turn right on the bumpy *dirt road* (0.0/0.0) between the commercial center and a small residential area and proceed up-canyon to a broad flat at **TH32** (0.2/0.2).
Description   Begin your trip (2880/0.0) by continuing northeast up the drainage along the *road*, which quickly narrows to *trail*, then climb north to a broad flat on a southwest-facing ridge. The noteworthy view of Kernville and Lake Isabella becomes more impressive as you gain elevation. Follow the ridge 0.1 mile where you near a barbed wire enclosed collection basin (3300/0.5) for a spring several feet above. The pipe you have observed along the way takes this water to the Forest Service work area across Sierra Way.

Leave the basin and continue up the ridge, then curve north across the canyon. Brush often obscures or obliterates the path. Look for clues to locate the trail such as the remains of rock retaining walls built to shore up the path. (This is tick country, especially in late winter and spring. Check for the tiny critters that latch onto you when you brush against bushes.) The gradient steepens considerably. You struggle up zigzags on south-facing slopes near craggy outcrops, to a notch (4390/0.6), the most prominent of the saddles on this ridge.

You curve north after crossing the ridge to a trail fork; descend a tad on the left fork to traverse the bowl of a gaping west-facing canyon. Then, after crossing the canyon's north crease, clamber up the east side of yet another ridge between its crest and the crease on a challenging, sometimes trailless route, then cross the crest where the ridge levels. Hike 0.1 mile beyond and curve back less than 0.1 mile, to a ledge leading to the lower mine shaft (5440/1.2). This ledge supported a makeshift blacksmith shop; the dry masonry platforms served as the tramway landing and way stations. The cable descended south 0.5 mile, then turned at a 45°

Derelict chimney on Harley Mountain

angle southwest to a mill below, near the Kern River next to present day Camp Owens.

Find the path north to the free-standing chimney, all that remains of Harley Mine buildings, then turn south to reach the summit of Harley Mountain (5778/0.3). Record your ascent of the Old Mule Trail in the register pad in the can. For the trip back, return to the derelict chimney, then down the way you came, or, you can return via the Cannell Trail of T39 and cut across the lower slopes to your car.

T39   Day Hike to Harley Mine & Mountain

All who take this trip enjoy the breathtaking views of Kern Canyon and Lake Isabella. Botanists add to their pleasure a scattering of rare Piute cypresses; geologists, an exposed contact of granite and metamorphic rock that lies on the second largest fault in the Sierra: the Kern Canyon Fault; and historians, aficionados of San Francisco, the remains of the Harley Mine cable system.

Distance   10.6 miles, round trip
Steep Ascents   0.5 mile
Elevation Gain   3350 feet
Skills   Intermediate route finding; moderate to strenuous hiking
Seasons   Fall, winter, spring
Map   USGS 7.5 min *Kernville* Harley Mountain is 35°46′47″N, 118°24′18″W
Trailhead   33. See car tour T37.
Description   From the gate next to Sierra Way, north of Camp Owens, walk diagonally northeast across the pasture on ***Cannell M'cyclepath 33E32***, a National Recreation Trail from here to Pine Flat (2790/0.0). Digger pines and blue oaks shade the way as you ascend the canyon's slopes via a pair of switchbacks, then walk through a stock-fence gate (3025/0.4). The grade subsides where you cross a flat. After a SCE dirt road merges with the path, you follow the road north, but leave it twice on paths that shortcut road loops. At the end of the second shortcut, you join the road again, cross through another stock-fence gate, then descend to meet the trail branching to the east (3520/1.1). Now you begin a moderate climb on the trail through a corridor of buck brush. According to the late botanist Ernest Twisselmann, a colony of Piute cypress trees grows on the south slopes of this canyon: a rare remnant of trees that once covered the land extending to and including what is now the Mojave Desert.

The well-maintained path crosses through yet another stock-fence gate. Lyrical notes of Cannell Creek's winding descent waft lightly from the canyon below. Manzanita mix with the buck brush, then live oak and mountain mahogany join the ranks. Yerba santa's sticky leaves and funnel-like, pale blue blossoms add to the vegetative montage of color and texture. The path, reinforced with rocks around a culvert, crosses over a ravine, zigzags southeast up a ridge, then leaves it to traverse on northeast-facing slopes. A fork of the creek slides over slabs in a bowl far below while above you, the saddle, your point of departure from the trail, comes into view. A half mile after two small switchbacks, the trail reaches the divide at the aforementioned saddle (5260/3.0) over a branch of the Kern Canyon Fault, the contact between eastern granitic and western metamorphic rock.

Here you leave Cannell Trail for a climb of Harley Mountain and a look at Harley Mine relics. To reach these points of interest, take the ***use trail*** that climbs steeply southwest above the saddle. Turn right when you reach the crest of the ridge and note this turn as it is easy to miss on your return trip. Now heading west, you stay to the left of the ridge knobs on an easy 0.2 mile walk. Harley Mountain looms directly ahead, and up it you climb on the steep path toward the yellowish tailings (rock debris from the mine). Continue above this first gouge and tailings to another digging, then above that to a derelict chimney. Built of native rocks, this chimney is all that remains of the mine's buildings.

From the chimney, climb south less than 0.1 mile to the mountain's summit (5778/ 0.6). The register is found in a can under a few rocks. After a surfeit of spectacular views of Kernville and the lake area, return to the chimney, then find the old trail twisting down the west side through bluffs. Shortly you find tramway terminal ruins (5440/0.3) near the lower mine shaft.

Here, just as at Mineral King and Havilah, gold-bearing quartz crystallized in metamorphic heat and pressure. There deposits so galvanized finder Charles Harley that between 1876 and 1882 he tried to turn the mountain inside out grubbing for the mineral. To help in this venture, he hired Andrew S. Hallidie, who designed the famed cable car system for San Francisco. To Hallidie's specifications, a cable loop 3.0 miles long was strung from the mine to a riverside mill. Attached to the cable were buckets which, when laden with ore, sped down to the mill. But the mine could not pay for its upkeep, so when the cable broke under the strain and killed workers, the claim was relinquished.

(If you are a competent pathfinder you can descend on the Old Mule Trail from here, then hike back to your car—see T38.)

Kernville and Lake Isabella from Mule Trail

T40   Southwest Corner Kern Plateau Backpack

Besides a journey through plant zones from chaparral to lodgepole pine, this trip offers views of yawning canyons and of starkly beautiful Lake Isabella. You visit an historic Forest Service guard station at the apex of a lush meadow, wander along whispering creeks and observe a severely burned forest's slow recovery.

Distance   23.4 miles, shuttle trip
Steep Ascents   0.2 mile
Elevation Gain   5280 feet
Skills   Intermediate route finding
Seasons   Spring, summer, fall (can be hot)
Maps   USGS 7.5 min *Kernville, Cannell Pk*
Trailheads   33 & 15. This trip requires two cars. See the last of car tour T8. Drive north on county **Fay Ranch Road** (0.0/0.0) off Highway 178 in Weldon. Park the first car along the side of the road where you do not obstruct passage for ranch business at **TH15** (5.6/5.6), the end of the trip. The trail on which you return is 0.1 mile ahead next to the concrete-slab crossing of Fay Creek. Then see car tour T37. Drive the second car to the beginning of the trip at **TH33**. This is 22.2 miles from the first car.
Description   The beginning of this trip is described in T39.

Eastbound Trail 33E32 Log

T39	Sierra Way	2790	0.0
	stock-fence gate	3025	0.4
	trail jct	3520	1.1
	saddle	5260	3.0

If you spent the afternoon exploring Harley Mine, you may need a campsite and water. You can descend southeast from the saddle to seasonal Tunnel Spring, 0.4 mile down-canyon. A few camping possibilities exist from here to the next trail junction, then none after that until Pine Flat.

After leaving the saddle, Cannell Trail ascends toward the east and climbs the ridge-line. Split Mountain with a wedge of sky riven into its crown rears prominently to the west. Shortly leaving the ridgetop, the path drops abruptly to a "Trail" sign marking a junction (5600/0.8) with overgrown Potato Patch Trail 33E49, a longer route to Tunnel Spring. This trail, 33E49, originally from old Kernville, was one in a system of trails that pro-

vided the only access to the western Kern Plateau before the logging roads were built. Its lower section along Caldwell Creek was closed because of residential property. Cannell Trail replaced it.

From here to the plateau, the trail maintains the same moderate grade. As you progress, spectacular views of Lake Isabella draw attention; upslope talus with cave-like gaps does, too. Sometimes flowers saturate the trailside slopes with color.

Telephone poles with old glass insulators brought a line from Kernville to the Cannell Meadow Station and then on to the other stations on the plateau. Radio transmitters replaced the telephones. You cross under the wire six times. You soon graduate from buck brush to live oak, then white fir and Jeffrey pine, later lodgepole pine. After your path swings around a cupped hollow and past a stock-fence gate, you enter Pine Flat (7300/2.8).

The lower tip of Pine Flat is visually pleasing with its boulders and woods, but as you progress, signs of logging activity become abundant. Roads crisscross and over-lay the trail, which takes you to a cul-de-sac that doubles as a Fire Safe Area for camping (7212/0.4). An exposed wooden box-like structure with a toilet seat squats immodestly near some fire rings. Now you can choose among three routes: you can shortcut your journey 6.4 miles by taking Pine Flat Trail 34E18 east to Little Cannell Meadow; you can continue on a longer loop by road to the guard station; or you can take the most interesting but challenging route pursuing Cannell Trail.

—   —   —   —   —

On the shortcut route, stroll northeast up **SNF Road 24S12**, then turn right (south) at the 4-way junction (7350/0.4). Curve east on this logging road which reduces to trail size,

Pine Flat Trail 34E18, then you easily ascend to the saddle. Climbers of Cannell Point depart south from here—see T70. After passing through the stock-fence gate (7580/0.9), you descend steeply to the junction of Little Cannell Trail 34E16 (6960/0.6) where you turn right. Find this point in the description and proceed on the rest of your journey.

— — — — —

To continue on the longer loop, take the road to the guard station. Here, too, you walk northeast up *SNF Road 24S12* to the 4-way junction (7350/0.4) where your road bends north and eventually arrives at a 3-way junction (7524/2.7), then you fork left on *SNF Road 24S56* to the station (7510/0.7).

— — — — —

If you chose to continue along the Cannell Trail, here closed to motorcycles, you become more attentive to pathfinding. A "Trail" sign and a metal blaze point your way northwest on a spur road. After 0.1 mile, cross Cannell Creek and immediately leave the road to follow the trail next to the creek, first through ubiquitous sagebrush, then through a wild rose garden. Soon you are high above the slim creek; amazingly, it made a deep gorge in the sandy yet bouldery canyon. You venture precariously close to the

brim of the gorge before the trail descends a bit to cross Cannell Creek (7280/0.7). You then step across a downed telephone line. Bluebells decorate a pocket meadow in this scenic miniature canyon, which opens to the southern tip of lush, green Cannell Meadow.

Now after 1.5 miles from the Pine Flat cul-de-sac, the trail disappears. Look for clues to your route: diamond-shaped metal blazes, tree blazes, hanging orange ribbons. If the Cannell Trail becomes too obscure beyond the canyon, you can easily find and hike on SNF Road 24S12, which parallels the meadow to the east then northeast.

Ahead of you sits a rock island with a three-stacked "boulderman"; beyond the stack hangs a route-guiding ribbon. Also, next to SNF Road 24S12 to the right you find a metal blaze; just beyond sprawls an old campsite with a snag tagged *Wildlife tree— This tree saved for wildlife food and shelter* (7445/1.0). This was probably near the junction where the old Pine Flat Trail met the Cannell Trail before the road was built. Until your trail is restored, follow the orange ribbons indicating the way, but stay off the fragile meadow if possible. Just under a mile later, you may see one of the old signs on a broken stump indicating *Kernville 18*;

Harley Mountain above Kernville

another sign of yore on a nearby fir says *Cut-off trail*. Take the left route past jeep tracks and follow orange ribbons or very old blazes around fingers of meadow, over open spaces and through logged areas, always heading generally north-northwest. You come out very near the guard building or by a north segment of Cannell Trail on the **road** (7550/1.7), and turn left to the station (7520/0.2). A sign on the door states maps, information and campfire permits can be obtained here—a notice left from the days when this was a summer ranger's headquarters.

After leaving the station, walk east then southeast along **SNF Road 24S56**, which overlays the path of the old trail to Long Meadow. Stroll past a north continuation of the Cannell Trail (7550/0.2) and onto **SNF Road 24S12** (7524/0.5), the south extension of which ends in Pine Flat. In a mile you reach the road's summit. In spring when you descend past roadside thickets of deer brush, clusters of white flowers hang from the tips of their pliant branches; and past bushes of manzanita, panicles of pale pink cover their stiff, reddish boughs. You soon reach Long Meadow where you leave the road just before Fay Creek's culvert to hike south along **Little Cannell Trail 34E16** (7640/2.0). This trail, though obscure at times, is not difficult to follow.

You continue west of Fay Creek through an aisle of dense lodgepole pines, then cross to the east bank and descend on a path among boulders before returning to the west bank. The slender creek, channeled in its narrow canyon, swells imperceptibly from springs that nourish side meadows, then abruptly turns away from your path. A seep crosses the trail and drops in a pencil-slim, 5-foot fall, undermining the trail. You top two rounded east-west ridges then descend alongside a seasonal streamlet into the vale of Little Cannell Meadow at a 4WD road—a continuation of Cherry Hill Road, SNF Road 22S12 (6980/1.8).

Traveling south, the trail passes a discarded packer's campsite, then follows the fence around the west side of the meadow to a junction with Pine Flat Trail 34E18 (6960/

0.2), the shortcut route from Pine Flat. Shortly after, the path drops where a stock driveway (6780/0.5) crosses the meadow. Your trail does not cross the meadow but briefly joins the driveway to climb southeast up a ridgelet. Little Cannell Trail then forks left at an easily missed junction (6800/0.2) where the driveway, the wider path, descends Fay Canyon. The stock driveway meets your trail in the foothills miles below: it is extremely steep.

Head east across open, dry country and descend to briefly join a road (6680/0.3) overlapping the trail. The road was built to serve the logging of timber burned in the 1987 Fay Fire. Leave the road after it crosses the creek draining Little Cannell Meadow, where to the right, metal trail blazes indicate your path (6660/0.1).

Again head east on the path, now through patches of burn on slopes generously strewn in spring with lupines and gilias. In minutes you drop to cross Fay Creek (6620/0.3) amid blackened Jeffrey pines and unburned willows that crowd its banks. Small trout dart in the shadows of the brush. Leaving the creek to fall steeply on its way to the South Fork Kern River, you make your way on a trail which overlaps a closed road, which in turn overlapped the original trail. Soon you fork onto the Cane Meadow Road (6640/0.4), also constructed in 1987 for fire salvage timber. Walking east on the road, you notice that some trees are completely burned; some burned oaks are stump sprouting; yet other trees are untouched. You pass a spring-fed rill that meanders through an upslope minuscule meadow and ducks under the road just before you pass Fay Creek Trail 34E19 to True Meadow (6560/0.5) and Bartolas Trail 34E20 (6560/0.1) to Bartolas Country. You have now arrived at Cane Meadow.

The aftermath of lightning caused Fay Fire is striking in Cane Meadow. Jet-black skeletal trees cast vertical lines and diagonal shadows across grassy Cane Meadow. A forest of sticks covers the hillsides. But the fire did not damage the blue-eyed grass, a six petaled, ⅔ inch flower at the tip of grass-like foliage, which are still abundant in the meadow; nor did it burn the thorny wild roses, which still guard the spring that issues from beneath large boulders. Nosegays of miner's lettuce now dot the scorched soil around the meadow where there are open areas for camping.

Turning south, then southeast on *Cane Meadow Trail 34E24*, you skirt the meadow and, until the trail has been redefined, follow flag markers through the grasses, over the churned terrain and for a very short time on road. When you are south of the meadow, watch for a tree blaze next to a path across the stream: here leave the road and cross the stream. Follow the old well-build trail south; its down-slope side secured by rock retaining walls. Completely out of the burn for a while, you descend on six switchbacks, which ease the steepness of the path, and view the spread of South Fork Valley below.

In time, you curve by an outcrop of granite and a sometimes fence and again enter the burn. At this level, Fay Canyon to the right was not burned, but the adjacent canyon to the left was. Spring wildflowers abound on the charred ground as you descend through plant zones, sometimes zigzagging, and pass a couple of very burned "Trail" signs. Below, the scorched foothills contrast with the vivid green pasture of Quarter Circle Five Ranch. You head for the gate of a stock fence that crosses your route; it is also the boundary of Sequoia National Forest. Then once again next to Fay Creek, a companion on much of the later segment of the plateau adventure, you trudge down to the county road (4080/4.2) and hike to your shuttle car.

T41   Forebay Aerobic Day Hike

Residents of the Kernville area hike up this Edison road as a routine exercise. It is ideal because its nearly constant 11.5% grade allows you to choose and maintain your best pace for aerobic conditioning. Campers will find it a great warm up.

Distance   3.0 miles, round trip
Steep Ascents   None
Elevation Gain   790 feet
Skills   Easy route finding; easy hiking
Seasons   All year
Map   USGS 7.5 min *Kernville*
Trailhead   34. See car tour T37.
Description   You take the Edison *dirt road* (2710/0.0) north, which curves and switchbacks up the rounded, furrowed foothills, dwarfed by canyon peaks. Viewing this scenery clockwise as you ascend, you see: Piute Mountains to the south; Split Mountain, Bull Run Canyon, unnamed prominences and Baker Point, whose lookout tower sometimes catches a glint of sunshine, across the river to the west; the jagged, saurian spine of Yellow Jacket Peak on this side of the canyon to the north. Along the way you witness the minute by minute shadowing of crags and ravines as the sun arcs, watch the clouds build or dissolve as weather fronts move through, observe the subtle changes as the seasons march by.

The last and steepest switchback points you southeast for the final elevation gain and your cool-down stroll along the exposed aqueduct to the forebay (3500/1.5), the terminus of the aqueduct.

The system of conduit and flume comprising the aqueduct has a capacity to carry 640 cubic feet of water per second. The generators can supply a maximum of 36 megawatts of electricity, more than twice the energy needed by Kern River Valley. The path of a tramway used to hoist material up the ridge north of the penstocks is still visible. A few of the tramway rails now support a collection fence along the last 0.2 mile of road.

T42   Yellow Jacket Climb

Yellow Jacket, a prominent, elongated mountain east of Kern River, rises abruptly above Headquarters, Camp 3 and Hospital Flat campgrounds. The tans, reds and ambers of its deep furrows and sharp ridges catch the setting sun in an ever-changing kaleidoscope of color and pattern. Unnamed on maps, its light travel justifies the spirit of adventure felt by the relatively few who climb its steep slopes.

Distance   3.6 miles, round trip
Steep Ascents   0.9 mile
Elevation Gain   2550 feet
Skills   Easy route finding; Class 2 climbing
Seasons   Fall, winter, spring
Map   USGS 7.5 min *Kernville* Yellow Jacket Peak is 35°49'27"N, 118°26'18"W
Trailhead   35. See car tour T37. From MTN 99, turn acutely south on **SCE dirt Road** (0.0/0.0), pass two standing chimneys, a cattle guard and several lesser roads while traveling up Cannell Creek Canyon to a fork (1.0/1.0). Drive ahead on the upper road, which turns north on a U curve into a tributary canyon. **TH35** is at the base of the next U curve (0.8/1.8).
Description   A few digger pines offer token shade on this trek up Yellow Jacket—it can be hot. Although the Edison aqueduct tunnels through the heart of the mountain, carrying Kern River water to the penstocks south of you, you must carry your own supply. From the trailhead (3500/0.0), climb steeply on a **cross-country** route north-northwest up a ravine left of the main canyon and left of a jutting, massive rock formation.

Leaving the ravine, continue on an ascending, diagonal northwest traverse, high on the west slopes of the north-trending canyon. Steadily gaining elevation, aim to cross above the gullies where heavy brush and large boulders would make for more difficult hiking. At times you tread on grassy slopes, but more often you climb on decomposed granitic soils or across loose slides of metamorphic rock chunks.

Your immediate goal is the northernmost peak opposite the saddle at the head of this wide canyon. At length you reach and walk along the ridgecrest to that peak, the second highest point on Yellow Jacket. You curve west around the point, staying about 30 feet below its summit. Yellow Jacket's craggy west face drops precipitously, but it is not difficult to pick your way among its boulders to regain the ridgeline and climb 0.3 mile northwest to the summit (6047/1.8)

The prize for all this effort is the extended view of the Kern River and its watershed country. This view includes the village of Kernville straddling the river and the waters of Lake Isabella stretching to the south.

T43   Day Hike to Salmon Creek in Kern River Canyon

A nook on an oak-shaded terrace by a glimmering band of Salmon Creek is the destination of this short trip. This idyllic setting entices you to a family breakfast or picnic lunch. The trip is recommended for year-round, but if you choose to go in summer, avoid the sizzling summer sun in the canyon by making an early start.

Distance   3.0 miles, round trip
Steep Ascents   0.2 mile
Elevation Gain   810 feet
Skills   Easy route finding; easy-moderate hiking
Seasons   All year (can be hot)

Map   USGS 7.5 min *Fairview*
Trailhead   36. See car tour T37.
Description   From the hilltop campsite (3650/0.0), walk briefly east up a prospector's **road,** then turn right onto **South Rincon M'Cyclepath 33E23** (3675/0.1),

just short of the prospector's pit. You soon turn east to ascend brush-covered, south-facing slopes of an unnamed canyon.

Somewhat higher in the canyon, the trail zigzags up a ridge and then enters the Kern Canyon fault zone, where it dips through a gully, then curves north, among scattered live oaks and pinyon pines. The course leads over a low saddle (4460/1.0) and then continues along rolling terrain in spotty shade. Occasional spring displays of Indian pink spread under an oak tree here an there along the wayside. This plant is easily recognized by its bright red, three-cleft, five-petaled ray flowers; its leaves grow oppositely on the stem.

Soon oaks extend their boughs over several medium campsites on terraces. The terrace overlooking Salmon Creek, the destination of this trip (4380/0.4), has a large fire ring along with benches and a counter

Yellow Jacket north of Kernville

assembled from lumber left after Salmon Creek bridge was constructed. You can view distant Salmon Falls after a hike on the trail of around 0.3 mile north of this terrace.

T44   South Rincon Trail Day Hike

This route follows the line of ancient Kern Canyon Fault, and passes near Packsaddle Cave en route. Spring wildflowers grow in dazzlingly varicolored displays along the trail. Salmon Creek Falls, the highest falls in the Southern Sierra, is seen from the best vantage point, albeit still at some distance.

Distance   6.8 miles, shuttle trip
Steep Ascents   1.1 mile
Elevation Gain   2770 feet
Skills   Easy route finding; moderate-strenuous hiking
Seasons   Fall, winter, spring
Map   USGS 7.5 min *Fairview*
Trailheads   36 & 56. This trip requires two cars. See the end of car tour T52. Turn south on the *spur road* off Sherman Pass Road (0.0/0.0), descend to Rincon Camp (0.5/0.5). Leave the first car here at **TH56** for the end of the trip. Then see car tour T37. Drive the second car to the beginning of the trip off MTN 99 at **TH36**. This is 10.1 miles from the first car.
Description   The beginning of this trip is described in T43.

Northbound 33E23 Log

T43 hilltop campsite	3650	0.0
Rincon M'cyclepath	3675	0.1
saddle	4460	1.0
Salmon Creek	4380	0.4

Now Rincon Trail 33E23 crosses the alder-lined creek on a bridge not recommended for horses. The trail switchbacks up a south-facing slope. Then the gradient eases and the path proceeds north-northwest past chaparral portals through which, in the high eastern distance, Salmon Creek Falls can be seen. During the snowmelt of an average or better snowpack, the upper falls resembles Yosemite's Nevada Falls, the lower its Vernal Falls. There was once a trail to the base of the falls, but now, unless you are willing to bushwhack, these portals offer the best view. As you progress, the ascent steepens to the highest of the four prominent saddles on this trip (5540/1.2). On a clear winter day, you can see some peaks of the distant High Sierra mantled in snow.

Upon leaving the saddle, the path descends steeply, undulates past Packsaddle Creek and its canyon, ascends a tad, then turns west where it meets Packsaddle Trail 33E34 (4480/1.7) of T45. Packsaddle Cave is located 0.2 mile west; your route turns briefly east at the junction. After a few yards, the gulch turns north. Your trail follows it and crosses yet another saddle (4980/0.4), then dips across the Brin Canyon watershed, crosses the last saddle and eventually descends moderately, first west of a ravine, then east of it. The saddles on the Rincon Trail, low points along the ridges, are the result of deformation caused by ancient seismic activity.

After trailside slopes level out, you trace a wavering course across a boulder- and forest-flat to a ford of Brush Creek. Here at unimproved Rincon Camp is a Fire Safe Area with many large campsites sheltered by huge willows and digger pine trees. After the creek ford, you pass unmaintained Brush Creek Trail, no longer recognized as part of the Forest Service trail system, then arrive at your shuttle car (4310/2.0).

T45   Packsaddle Cave Day Hike

Packsaddle Cave is no virgin. Long ago vandals violated her by destroying all the stalactites and stalagmites within sight. It is still impressive, well worth a visit.

Distance   4.8 miles, round trip
Steep Ascents   0.2 mile
Elevation Gain   1315 feet
Skills   Easy route finding; moderate hiking
Seasons   Fall, winter, spring
Map   USGS 7.5 min *Fairview*
Trailhead   37. See car tour T37.
Description   After crossing the highway from the parking lot, climb 200 yards up a *jeep road* (3555/0.0), then branch right onto *Packsaddle Trail 33E34.* A moderate to steep incline leads up from the junction through a corridor of chaparral composed mostly of buck brush: a common ceanothus on dry slopes of the Southern Sierra. In spring, its rigid, dense branches support small clusters of white flowers whose strong, sweet perfume pervades the air.

Along the crunchy, metamorphic-rock trail, you find the westward view marred by rust tailings spilling from the Fairview Mine. After you gain more elevation, your view west catches the checkerboard-mantled Greenhorn Mountains: the lighter spots shorn of all trees by loggers—called "clear cutting."

Soon cross high on the right side of a saddle, then descend to cross another (4460/1.3). Beyond the second saddle, you lose 310 feet in elevation before fording Packsaddle Creek (4130/0.5). Passing one small campsite here, you return to the creek's south side at another small campsite. Next climb above cascades, then boulder-hop the stream one last time. You shortly pass an oak-shaded medium campsite, then you veer northeast on the rough, cobbled tread to briefly rise in a ravine. Just before reaching a junction with the South Rincon Trail, turn sharply northwest onto a *lateral* (4500/0.6) to Packsaddle Cave, a scant hundred yards up the slope.

T46   Indian Wells Valley Car Tour on Highways 14 & 395: Highway 178 to Nine Mile Canyon Road
(With Directions to Trailheads 39-44)

This short tour travels along the foothills that front the progressively higher and steeper Sierra, and skirts above the desert of Indian Wells Valley with its distant communities. Deep in the valley's interior, the growth of Ridgecrest reflects the increased activity at China Lake Naval Weapons Center. The Center, a think tank and experimental laboratory, operates somewhat independent of the vagaries of the military budget, giving Ridgecrest a modicum of stability.

Distance   16.9 miles, one way

Steep Ascents   None

Elevation Gain   150 feet

Skills   Easy route finding; paved highway

Seasons   All year

Maps   Kern and Tulare counties maps

Tourhead   7. The junction of Highway 14 and Highway 178 West is **TH7**. This is 41.2 miles north of Mojave and 2.7 miles south of Highway 178 East. This short tour joins car tours T1 (Highway 14 south) and T8 (Highway 178 West) with T100 (Highway 395 north) and T52 (Nine Mile Canyon west).

Description   To your left as you leave Highway 178 West junction (3186/0.0/0.0) and travel north on *State Highway 14,* scan the west foothills for a glimpse of the ancient creosote rings described in T25, then glance east to Indian Wells Valley, which held a shallow lake 20,000 years ago. You soon meet eastbound State Highway 178 East (2.7/2.7) where travelers depart for the desert towns or for **TH39** of side trip T47, Trona Pinnacles. You quickly pass the Homestead Cafe, then the Indian Wells Restaurant, fronting the silhouette of Mount Jenkins. The restaurant is hedged with trees and shrubs watered by the wells that gave the valley its name. After a brief ascent of a ridge, those seeking **THs 40–42** of Ts 48–50, to Five Fingers, Jenkins and Owens climbs make a cautious left turn onto a dirt road (2.3/5.0) just below the crest; the rest of you stay on Highway 14.

For you turning left on this washboard *dirt road,* high-clearance, 4WD cars are recommended, but with care, conventional cars can usually make it. From the junction with Highway 14 (0.0/0.0) drive northwest up Indian Wells Canyon, cross both aqueducts and arrive at the empty rock and mortar square receptacle of Powers Well (2.6/2.6). This is **TH40** for T48, Five Fingers Climb. Beyond the well (check the mileage), quickly turn right at a fork (0.1/2.7), continue upcanyon left of the main wash, ignore spur roads. At another fork (2.5/5.1) turn right, immediately dip through a wash. Curve right through another wash 2.0 miles later. Drive around a slight ridge on the narrow road to a west ascending, rutted jeep road (2.3/7.4), which is **TH41** for T49, Mount Jenkins Climb. Continue on to Indian Wells wash by a campsite at **TH42** for T50, Owens Peak Climb (1.1/8.5).

On the Highway 14 tour, the road descends from the ridge to the bifurcated junction of U.S. Highway 395, the terminus of State Highway 14 (2465/1.8/6.8) and the lowest point of this trip. Continuing north, now on *Highway 395,* the route passes Brady's, a busy gas station and novelty minimart, then the crumbling shell of Green Acres, once a favorite stop for truck drivers. An unpaved road to your left leads up Grapevine Canyon to the sheer exposed granite of Owens Peak massif. Rock climbers use this road to gain access to Class 3–5+ routes up that precipitous east ridge. Shortly the highway crosses an intersection (5.6/12.4) with unpaved Sand Canyon Road to the left, which leads to **TH43** for T51, Boulder Peak. Paved Brown Road extends east opposite Sand Canyon Road. Near this junction geologists discovered bedrock east of the Sierra Nevada Fault lies 6500 feet below, buried in sand, gravel and cobbles.

Soon your route enters Inyo County (1.5/13.9) passing Pearsonville, a ramshackle community that caters to car needs and boasts of its High Desert Speedway. But Pearsonville boasts mostly of being the *Hubcap Capital of the World,* as a sign boldly claims. Resident "Hubcap Lucy" has

a collection of over 81,000 hubcaps, which she sells, trades, buys or makes into hubcap clocks.

Then you reach signed *Nine Mile Canyon Road,* the extension of Sherman Pass/ Kennedy Meadows Road **TH44** (2575/3.0/ 16.9). Here you turn west for the Kern Plateau car tour T52 or continue north to Lone Pine on car tour T100.

Outer-planet landscape

T47   Trona Pinnacles Side Trip

If you are a science fiction buff, the Trona Pinnacles at this 19,600-acre National Natural Landmark may look familiar. Their eerie, outer-planet landscape has been the setting for many films.

Distance   Negligible
Steep Ascents   None
Elevation Gain   Negligible
Skills   Easy route finding; easy hiking
Seasons   All year (can be hot)
Map   San Bernardino County road map

Trailhead   39. See car tour T46. From Highway 14, turn east on *Highway 178* (0.0/0.0). Stay on Highway 178 through Ridgecrest, pass Trona Road to Red Mountain (24.4/24.4), then turn right on a wide, *unpaved road* (7.3/31.7), signed *Lestle Salt*

Co. office; highway sign indicates *End 178.* Drive south toward the visible pinnacles. Take the road to the right at a fork (0.5/32.2). Cross the railroad tracks (0.8/33.0), then parallel the tracks until you drive down a dip and turn left to reach the parking lot (3.8/36.8) at **TH39**. Several roads crisscross the pinnacles area.

Description   From the parking lot, a 1/2 mile trail takes you around a large tufa tower, or you may wish to wander on your own. Over 500 spires rake the sky, many of these sun-dried towers reach 50 feet high or more. Trona Pinnacles are unequaled in North America.

These exotic looking land forms are a product of the glacial periods when this area was covered by ancient Lake Searles, a link in a chain of lakes that received water from the Sierra Nevada mountains. The towers are composed of a sedimentary material called tufa, a calcium carbonate in the form of calcite and aragonite. The carbonates in the ancient lake combined with calcium from lake bottom springs that bubbled up along a fault. This material built up around the springs, first as tubes, finally as towers that reached the surface of the lake—no higher. When the lake dried up the tufa pinnacles remained. Lesser tufa pinnacles are in the process of formation at Mono Lake roughly 190 air miles north.

T48   Five Fingers (Aquila) Climb

A dramatic flourish of sheer, barren rock rises along the southeast ridge which extends from Owens Peak to Five Fingers. Hikers capable of pathless route finding and Class 3 rock scrambling will find the highest finger a challenging climb. Unencumbered views of Indian Wells Valley and beyond add to the excitement of reaching the summit.

Distance   2.2 miles, round trip
Steep Ascents   0.8 mile
Elevation Gain   1725 feet
Skills   Intermediate route finding; Class 3 climbing
Seasons   Fall, winter, spring
Map   USGS 7.5 min *Owens Pk*
Trailhead   40. See car tour T46.
Description   Beginning at Powers Well (3450/0.0), your ***cross-country*** route leads north across the road and the wash. Leaving the easy traverse (3600/0.3) before you reach a slight ridge with jutting boulders on its upper reaches, your route climbs north up the steep (38% grade) scree-covered slopes. This effort is sometimes called a "ballbearing scramble." With each step you sink into the deep scree; best to zigzag up the fall line where a faint use trail has developed. Your immediate destination is an obvious notch between the farthest, highest crag northwest in this group and the crag to its right.

With a deserved sense of accomplishment, you reach the notch's saddle between the fourth and fifth fingers (5020/0.7). Cross over the ridgeline and drop to contour left around this impressive granodiorite spire, weathered to a light tan. Geologists note that the basement rock of these five fingers is known for its abundant small mafic inclusions and scattered hornblende.

To locate the chute with the least amount of Class 3 climbing, pass two narrow ravines on the spire, then, still contouring, pull yourself up and over a low ridge of boulders. Above you a small cairn indicates that you

Plane wreck on Mount Jenkins

have found the desired chute. Climb this southwest-trending passage, then turn left to gain the summit (5174/0.1).

On the summit of the fifth finger, you view the crags from east to west. The thumb is downslope and offset from the main group, as you might expect. The China Lake Mountain Rescue Group has pioneered routes up all these crags. The late Carl Heller reported that the thumb is a Class 3 ascent, the index finger Class 4, the middle one Class 5, and the ring finger—the next one southeast of yours—is also Class 5. This peak is sometimes called "Aguila," Latin for eagle, the pinnacles resembling tips of eagle wings.

T49   Mount Jenkins Climb from Indian Wells Canyon

The juxtaposed peaks of high, pointed Owens and massive, jagged Jenkins are easily identified from the desert communities and from peaks as far north as Mount Whitney. The climb to Mount Jenkins' summit, although difficult enough to be challenging, falls within the scope of most peakbaggers' ability. Of special interest to botanists, a rare plant on the slopes you climb, Lomatium shevockii, was first identified in 1984.

Distance   2.8 miles, round trip
Steep Ascents   1.0 mile
Elevation Gain   2545 feet
Skills   Intermediate route finding; Class 2 climbing
Seasons   Spring, fall
Map   USGS 7.5 min *Owens Pk* (Mount Jenkins, unnamed on map, is 35°42'32"N, 117°59'30"W.)
Trailhead   41. See car tour T46.
Description   From Indian Wells Canyon Road (5380/0.0), follow the wide, hard-packed, deeply-rutted *OHV road* west along a minor ridge where it soon meets an OHV road (5760/0.2) from the north. On the road you curve south around a gulch. Leave the road just after the gulch (5880/0.1) to climb *cross-country* directly west up the side of Mount Jenkins. Slipping slightly backward with each step in the soft soil and weaving among pinyon pines, you climb up the steep slopes on a route left of the jutting outcrops. Continuing steeply, you arrive at the PCT

(6950/0.4), which rounds the east side of Mount Jenkins. Major ridges from the southeast and northeast merge to form one prominent ridge, which you ascend west-southwest on a ducked *use trail,* again left of the ridgeline outcrops.

Care must be taken to protect *Lomatium shevockii* if seen. This 2–5 inch, herbaceous perennial with oval, pinnately-clefted leaves and umbels of tiny purple blooms grows along contact zones of metaphoric and granitic rock. First observed on Owens Peak, it was later seen on a southeast slope of this mountain, above the PCT.

The steepness abates for a short stretch and again resumes to the jagged crest rocks. Ducks placed by climbers lead you up some Class 2 hoists between the rugged, sky-piercing rocks, to a west side approach of the summit (7921/0.7) with its panoramic views and a plaque commemorating J. C. Jenkins (see Ts 26 & 27).

Mount Jenkins from Indian Wells Valley

T50   Owens Peak Climb from Indian Wells Canyon

Owens Peak is a counterpart of Olancha Peak: just as Olancha Peak stands pre-eminent on the northern crest of the Southern Sierra, Owens Peak commands a wider, more dramatic view than any of its peers on the southern crest.

Distance   3.6 miles, round trip
Steep Ascents   1.0 mile
Elevation Gain   2815 feet
Skills   Intermediate route finding: Class 2 climbing
Seasons   Spring, fall
Map   USGS 7.5 min *Owens Pk*
Trailhead   42. See car tour T46.
Description   From the campsite near the wash (5640/0.0) in Indian Wells Canyon, you begin with an amble west along an extended piece of rugged *road* to a *use trail* (5700/0.1) that commences on the right of the road, marked by large ducks. The route throughout the trip is marked at strategic points by ducks. Buck brush, fremontia and golden oak with cascades of grape vines narrow the trail space as you wend your way west-northwest. Golden oaks growing along canyons often reach a height of 60 feet. Its leaves are both smooth edged and toothed and have a faint yellow fuzz on the underside. But the easiest way to identify this oak is by its acorn, which is as wide as it is long and sits on a narrow cup resembling a turban.

Your path, while staying near the south bank of the creek bed, soon passes a duck: this one you ignore. The creek usually flows from the first fall storms until the last snow-banks high on the peaks have vanished. Springtime wildflowers paint nearby slopes with broad splashes of scarlet, orange, yellow, and indigo. The trail crosses a ravine and zigzags up to an opening in the brush and a confluence of canyons (6200/0.7). A climb west would take you to the Jenkins/Owens saddle and the PCT.

You curve north and climb along the creek bed, then over loose rocks and dirt in a steepening grade. Next, following ducks, you clamber over boulders up a huge slide, and engage in some brief rock climbing over exposed slabs alongside ramparts of granite. Then you continue steeply zigzagging north-

northwest through a band of forest to the summit (8453/1.0).

Although no trees restrict the comprehensive views from the top, several dwarf maple trees grow on the northwest slope and an unusual mix of limber, Jeffrey, pinyon and sugar pines, white firs and Sierra juniper survive together on the east slopes. Dozens of cliffs and spires loom along Owens east ridge extension—a rock climber's dream. Some of the most technically challenging routes in the Southern Sierra confront the equipped and proficient climber there. This ridge has been a local "playground" for the China Lake Mountain Rescue Group for over 30 years. They have identified over 75 routes with difficulty ranging from easy Class 4 to 5.10+.

If you are combining a climb of Mount Jenkins with this trip, descend as you came to a level slightly above the PCT seen across the canyon. Leave the ducked trail in the rock slide for a southwest cross-country traverse around the wooded slopes and over lesser rock slides of Owens Peak to the Owens/Jenkins saddle, ½ mile away. Stay high enough on the traverse to avoid the heavier brush down slope. Upon reaching the saddle, proceed southeast along the PCT 2.5 miles to a prominent east-northeast ridge where several ducks by the trail indicate the best place to begin your climb of Mount Jenkins. The climb and the return to Indian Wells Road are described in T49. Your car is 1.3 miles northwest of your exit on the road.

T51   Boulder Peak Climb

This peak's rounded summit sits on the crest of a ridge extending southeast from Sawtooth Peak. The summit offers wide ranging views of Indian Wells Valley with distant Naval Weapons Center and Ridgecrest. Although interesting in its own right, an ascent of this mountain provides superb conditioning for more ambitious climbs. Written in the register on top is "This peak is a coarse-ground topophyritic hornblende diorite to gabbro. Sand Canyon is fine ground quartz moziosito." Agree?

Distance   2.6 miles, round trip
Steep Ascents   1.0 mile
Elevation Gain   2765 feet
Skills   Easy route finding; Class 2 climbing
Seasons   Fall, winter, spring
Map   USGS 7.5 min *Ninemile Cyn*
Trailhead   43. See car tour T46. From Highway 395, turn west into Sand Canyon, opposite paved Brown Road. The washboard *dirt road* (0.0/0.0) heads west, over a cattleguard, rears up over one aqueduct and dips beneath the other (2.5/2.5). Cottonwoods flutter over campsites here near Sand Canyon Creek, and foundations remain where operations of famed Western author Zane Grey's favorite packers, Ken and Chester Wortley, were housed back in 1921.

The road gets increasingly rough beyond here—proceed at your car's capability and check your odometer. Dip through a wash and over another cattleguard while you round a ridge from Boulder Peak. Turn right at the next junction (1.0/3.5) and drive up a boulder-strewn road to a ravine (0.5/4.0) at **TH43**.

Directions   To begin your ***cross-country*** hike, cross the ravine (3520/0.0) emanating from Boulder Peak, hike just above it and curve up the south-facing slopes east of the crease. The grade abruptly steepens: pick your way carefully to avoid crossing creases over steep slabs or unsecured rocks. Running amid brush up loose granite grit, you find the course relentless as it takes you up to the southeast end of the rounded summit, then northwest to the apex of Boulder Peak (6283/1.3). Once on top, there is plenty of space to relax, with views of Spanish Needle, supreme in the west, and of dark basalt lava streaks on Indian Wells Valley in the northeast.

T52   Kern Plateau Car & Bicycle Tour
(With Directions to Trailheads 45–56)

People traveling in the arid Mojave Desert and the bouldery Kern River Valley are often surprised at how quickly they encounter cool, dense forests on the Kern Plateau. This trip across the center of the plateau from the desert to the river acquaints you with the high country environs and offers a palette of scenic diversity.

Distance   68.5 miles, one way
Steep Ascents   None (Long, hard grades for bicyclists)
Elevation Gain   5635 feet
Skills   Easy route finding; paved road
Seasons   Spring, summer, fall (snow not removed)
Map   Tulare County road map
Tourhead   44. From Highway 395, turn west onto Nine Mile Canyon Road (Kennedy Meadows/Sherman Pass Road). This is 16.9 miles north of Highway 178 West. The tour departs from the abutment of car tours T46 & T100.

Description   Commencing west on paved ***Nine Mile Canyon Road*** from the T junction (2527/0.0/0.0), your road quickly crosses the second LA aqueduct buried under Nine Mile Canyon's alluvial apron, then passes the above-ground pipe of the original aqueduct. The ascent steepens as the road winds along barren, precipitous canyon slopes. A section of this Inyo County road was first paved in 1989. At the crest of the canyon, your route leaves BLM's California Desert Conservation Area and crosses into Tulare County, at which point the road's name changes to *Kennedy Meadows Road, J41* (6260/10.2/10.2).

The brief, welcoming shade of pinyon pines that greets you here gives way as your route pierces Chimney Meadow, shaggy with sagebrush and rabbitbrush, and arrives at BLM's Chimney Peak Fire Station. Employees are present from 9:00–6:00 daily, and gladly lend assistance if needed. About 80 yards later you pass the first of two dirt roads (0.6/10.8) to BLM's Chimney Peak Recreation Area; the first road is a shortcut to Highway 178. Both roads serve as the northernmost loop of car tour T28.

At length you top a broad saddle and enter Big Pine Meadow. Soon to the left, you pass a defunct stone and masonry drinking fountain. Until the late 1980s its constant flow of cool water quelled the thirst of many passersby. As you travel northwest, the meadows on both sides of you, collectively called Kennedy Meadows, are mostly overrun with brush. A long time local resident recalled that much of this area was covered with thick grass until a cloudburst in 1947 gashed a ravine that lowered the groundwater level. Sagebrush then invaded the drier meadows. Others say that sagebrush replaced the grass as a result of overgrazing.

Hub of community

In this vast, lightly populated, remote country, a sign boldly claims *World Famous Beef Jerky and BBQ* available at Grumpy Bears. Can the less assuming eatery close by accommodate the overflow crowd, you may wonder. Moving on, you arrive at the right road fork (13.4/24.2) to **TH45**, Kennedy Meadows Campground, one of the five Forest Service no-fee campgrounds on the southern Kern Plateau that have all the necessary amenities except trash pick up. Those not seeking the campground, take the left fork.

To reach the campground for trips T75–T77 on the PCT, take the paved *right fork* (0.0/0.0), pass several spur roads, some leading west to Fire Safe Areas, and enter the campground's loop road (2.6/2.6). **TH45** is at the north end of the camp.

At the crotch of the fork stand the Kennedy Meadows General Store and gas pumps, the hub of the community. The store doubles on Saturday nights as the local theater. It is also an important stop for long-distance PCT hikers who send themselves food packages in care of the store.

Homesteaders began settling in the Kennedy Meadows basin in 1918, induced to stay all year by the mild winters the locale enjoys. A road superseded their access trail in 1935; most of it was first paved in 1974. Growth hereabouts was slow until the late 1980s, when a miniboom of real estate activity led to increased building.

Ahead, the road enters Sequoia National Forest (0.8/25.0), where it assumes a third name and code: *Sherman Pass Road, SNF Road 22S05,* which it keeps for the rest of this journey. Next, your route passes the PCT and immediately crosses the South Fork Kern River. Ascending west after the bridge, the route threads a corridor between Dome Land Wilderness to the left and South Sierra Wilderness to the right, and passes a road gate (3.3/28.3), which effectively stops westbound traffic in winter. (See the section on winter sports in Part 1.) The road steepens as you approach, then cross, a broad saddle, then turn north to pass the rock-quarry road (2.5/30.8) to Bitter Creek Trail 34E03, part of T77. In times past, the meadow to the left, Rodeo Flat, hosted local cowboys who gathered to display their skills and compete with one another. Now seasonal wildflowers vie for attention. A Fire Safe Area abuts the flats, and Jeffrey pines replace pinyon pines as the dominant tree on the plateau. The road (1.2/32.0) to **TH46,** Hooker Trail 35E05, branches left just beyond Rodeo Flat. The plateau tour continues straight ahead.

Volunteer clean-up project

Those seeking the path to Hooker Meadow, turn northeast on dirt *SNF Road 21S29* (0.0/0.0). Follow its wide S curve past spur roads, campsites and a cattle pen and chute. Continue past the "Trail" sign of Jackass Creek M'cyclepath 35E13 (1.6/1.6). Drive up the rough road to a cul-de-sac (0.3/1.9) at **TH46** of T78 and midsection of T77.

Beyond the roads to Hooker and Jackass trails, and the culvert giving passage to Fish Creek, you arrive at a junction (0.7/32.7) flanked by the Fish Creek Campground road, and a dirt road to the north, which rock climbers take to reach Class 3–5 routes on Fish Creek Rock. After passing Troy Meadow Campground (1.7/34.4) and its overflow Fire Safe Area, watch for **TH47** of T79, Pack Station Trail 35E07, off the short right-hand road (0.9/35.3) at the pack station's former location. A few minutes later, passing Troy Meadow and its sinuous Fish Creek, you arrive at a 4-way junction and **TH48** (8030/1.6/36.9).

Your road, SNF Road 22S05, turns left. Blackrock Road, SNF Road 21S03, described in car tour T80, is to the right. It passes the Forest Service's Blackrock Work Center and Information Station in 0.1 mile and ends at **TH76,** an overnight campground and an entrance to Golden Trout Wilderness. The road west of the 4-way junction leads to **TH49** and Beach Meadows, a uniquely suitable place for equestrians. If not seeking Blackrock Road or Beach Meadows, your route turns south.

To reach Beach Meadows, descend on oiled *Beach Meadows Road, SNF Road 21S02,* (0.0/0.0) past numerous spur roads. Turn left onto *SNF Road 21S19* (3.9/3.9) signed *Public and Administrative Pasture.* (Beach Meadows Road continues to Lion Meadows.) Your road switchbacks and forks (0.5/4.4). Take the right fork, *SNF Road 21S11,* past a Fire Safe Area to Beach Meadows (0.2/4.6) at **TH49.** There is ample space for horse trailers. Trails recommended for riding radiate from here, although some are shared with motorcyclists as well as hikers. Trips T91 & T92 begin here also.

After leaving the 4-way junction you wind among trees to cross a ridgecrest, then descend by broad curves to a junction (5.9/42.8) with the access road to Bald Mountain Lookout, T53. The road climbs 1.7 miles to a road gate at **TH50.** The Lookout and Botanical Area warrant a side trip.

On the descending road past the lookout opportunity, fleeting views to the south of Dome Land Wilderness and distant Owens Peak and Mount Jenkins flash by, and you quickly arrive at the turn-off for **TH51** of T54, Woodpecker Trail 34E08 (1.5/44.3), an extensive trail through the center of Dome Land Wilderness. Rattlesnake Creek M'cyclepath 34E07, sections of which are hiked on trips in this book, descends the canyon north of this trailhead. In 1.6 miles farther on the road, you pass Dark Canyon Trail 34E11, which drops to Woodpecker Meadow in Dome Land Wilderness, part of T54. More fleeting views, these of the Kaweah Peaks Ridge in the High Sierra, precede your arrival at a junction (3.1/47.4) with SNF Road 22S41, which leads past Bonita Meadows to **TH52** of T93, Lookout and Schaeffer mountains climb. A pipe in your road cut a few yards beyond the junction issues year-round, refreshing spring water.

Lodgepole pines curtail views of Paloma and Curliss meadows, but not of a granite bluff soon seen to the north, its face tricked out in faded streaks of orange and black, a treat on this stretch of highway. Several logging roads and motorcycle paths peel from the road, among them Trout Creek M'cyclepath 33E28 of T94 (3.0/50.4). Your route rounds the headwaters of Trout Creek where leaves of quaking aspen quiver, one of the few such groves on the plateau. Then the road crests the Sirretta-Sherman peaks ridge at Sherman Pass, where the viewpoint parking lot and **TH53** (9140/2.7/53.1) are located, the highest elevation on this tour. Vistas here include Olancha Peak and the Mount Whitney group. Three trails branch nearby: to the north, Sherman Pass M'cyclepath 34E09 of T94 &T60, parallels the highway; across the road, Sherman Peak Trail 33E35 of T95 & T94, ascends the slope; to the south, Cannell M'cyclepath 33E32, of T60, drops along Durrwood Fault and its meadows (as does the paved logging road 0.9 mile ahead).

When you leave the crest, you also leave the forest of red fir and western white pine to enter another plant zone: a mix of black oaks, incense cedars, Jeffrey pines and white firs. You descend via long-legged switchbacks to a curve around the Bush Creek bowl where, across the canyon, Spirit Rock, a large, thimble-shaped monolith, comes into view. Spires and cliffs appear far upslope to your right on a flank of Sherman Peak, examples of sediments exposed to partial or total metamorphosis and then partially broken up and engulfed by molten granite.

You next descend past a recess housing

Alder Creek, negotiate a collection of switchbacks and arrive at a junction (5880/9.4/62.5) with paved Cherry Hill Road, coded SNF Road 22S12, at **TH54.** Travelers taking car tours T55 & T66, turn left here. An assortment of trips from T56 to T74 originate at trailheads **TH57–TH71,** served by this road. The gate next to Sherman Pass Road remains open in winter until the section of highway from which you came is covered by a snowpack. Cherry Hill Road is always closed in winter.

As you leave the Kern Plateau, Jeffrey pines give way to digger and pinyon pines that poke through the roadside chaparral; then only shrubs cover the slopes as you enter a fault zone traversed by the Rincon Trail 33E23 of T96–T98. The parking lot next to a cow chute accommodates cars at **TH55** (3.1/65.6). Glancing across the canyon, you see snippets of the South Rincon Trail, and a series of saddles bridging the straight canyon of Kern Canyon Fault. The fault passes under this parking lot and continues north.

Amid buck brush, mountain mahogany and fremontia, your route proceeds past a dirt road to the left (1.2/66.8) that drops to **TH56,** at unimproved Rincon Camp By Brush Creek for T44's shuttle car. A Forest Service helispot is perched on a flat adjacent to the Rincon Road. This last leg of your descent presents views of thready cascades of granite-slab cradled Brush Creek and a great bending link of the Kern River. You reach TC Road MTN 99 at the end of your plateau journey (3780/1.7/68.5). This is also the terminus of car tour T37.

Spirit Rock

T53   Day Hike to Bald Mountain Lookout & Botanical Area

The unimpeded views from the top of Bald Mountain led the government to erect a fire lookout tower there in 1955. On this trip you can enjoy the panoramic plateau views from the tower, rivaled only by those from Kern Peak to the north, and you can explore the unique Bald Mountain Botanical Area surrounding the tower.

Distance   0.6 mile, round trip
Steep Ascents   None
Elevation Gain   155 feet
Skills   Easy route finding; easy hiking
Seasons   Spring, summer, fall
Map   USGS 7.5 min *Bonita Mdws*
Trailhead   50. See car tour T52.
Description   Your brief walk begins where a padlocked gate across the road bars further progress by car. To the right of the gate (9230/0.0), within the botanical area, a path parallels the road to the tower. It immediately leads through a forest of Jeffrey pine, red fir and limber pine, an unusual congregation of three species that are commonly separated by elevation. The 440-acre botanical site here is a metasedimentary island in a sea of granite. This rich soil, uplifted ocean bottom mud, shells and sand, supports abundant diverse plant life—over 100 species.

The path leads up a brief moderate grade in forest cover, to flatten out in shrub cover. This cover yields to the Bald Mountain potentilla growing here and no where else. This modest, woody shrub of the rose family is separated by over 100 miles from its nearest, somewhat similar relative, which grows only on limestone peaks of the White Mountains. How each came to evolve where it did is the kind of enigma that you find so often here in the Southern Sierra, the kind of question that inspires fascination with this land.

You soon join the road, which ends at the lookout steps (9382/0.3). Climb up to the catwalk 40 feet above the ground. From the 200 square-foot room, the fire-control technician on duty overlooks, as do you, 1000 square miles of Dome Land, South Sierra and Golden Trout wildernesses, and lands beyond to Mount Whitney.

T54   North Dome Land's Woodpecker Meadow Backpack

This journey's ingress and egress follow sylvan canyons with delicate streams. The streams exit near Woodpecker Meadow, a refreshing contrast to the surrounding brush, then slip into boisterous Trout Creek with its inviting fishing ponds and bathing pools. Solitude usually prevails in this lightly visited northwest corner of Dome Land Wilderness.

Distance   9.5 miles, loop trip
Steep Ascents   0.2 mile
Elevation Gain   2010 feet
Skills   Easy route finding
Seasons   Spring, summer, fall (can be hot)
Maps   USGS 7.5 min *Bonita Mdws, Sirretta Pk*
Trailhead   51. See car tour T52.

Description   This jaunt begins on ***Woodpecker Trail 34E08*** at the junction (8300/0.0) of Sherman Pass Road. The descending route parallels the highway, offering outstanding views of Dome Land Wilderness against a backdrop of Owens Peak and Mount Jenkins silhouetted on the distant Sierra crest. Quite soon the trail enters an extension of Dome Land Wilderness created by the California Wilderness Act of 1984.

You descend southeast on a moderate grade in a Jeffrey pine forest and brush past bush lupine and sagebrush. To the northeast, Bald Mountain lookout tower glistens in the sunlight. As the path nears the canyon crease, you step gingerly through a muddy seep, the first of several en route which have water even in the driest years. This spring nourishes the huge willows in the crease, which you cross, but supplies very little surface water. Soon black oak amalgamates with the forest; you stay close to the creek bed on southwest-facing slopes. Then the grade eases, as the creek swings away to join Dark Canyon Creek.

You emerge from the canyon, note the occurrence of pinyon pine indicating drier climes, and suddenly turn left at a sometimes obscure junction (6820/2.8) with an 0.3-mile path to Dark Canyon Trail. You soon cross a gulch, leave conifer cover, and wind southward, your path now hedged by buck brush ceanothus. This dense brush clothed the slopes in the wake of the 1947 Woodpecker Fire, preventing the former pinyon and Jeffrey pine forest from reestablishing itself. While in the brush, you arrive at a junction with a former road, now *Rockhouse Basin Trail 35E16* (6690/0.6), where you turn right.

Your road/trail west traverses sunny, rolling terrain, dips through a trickle, then crosses the combined flow from Dark Canyon and the canyon you descended. Beyond, the trail becomes flanked on the south by Woodpecker Meadow and on the north by a jumble of boulders concealing a tree-shaded campsite. A spring emerges from between boulders, but its water is well-guarded by nettles that sting, and wild roses that scratch. In the summer it is sullied by cows. The junction (6610/0.5) of Dark Canyon Trail 34E11 is immediately west of this campsite.

The view from the campsite reveals narrow, grassy Woodpecker Meadow sloping to Trout Creek. The broader view of the granites of Dome Land is obscured somewhat by trees. If you wish a creekside campsite, con-

Kern Plateau from Bald Mountain

tinue west on Sirretta Trail 34E12 (the continuation of Rockhouse Basin Trail). A sunny campsite with a fizzy bathing pool is about a half mile ahead—watch for its path. Beyond the spur path and a climb over a ridgelet, you will find shaded campsites along Trout Creek and, after a ford, along Little Trout Creek, around a mile from this junction.

To begin the return leg of this loop, hike north on *Dark Canyon Trail 34E11.* Hiking in a 3-5-foot maze of ceanothus, you top a hill after 210 yards. Then on canyon slopes roughly 50 feet up from Dark Canyon Creek, you enter conifer shade and remain in forest for the rest of the hike. After a ford of the creek above slick rocks, you encounter a junction (6810/0.7) with the connector path from Woodpecker Trail. Turn left to ascend west along the willow-choked creek on a path strewn with chips of platy metamorphics. You pass two tributaries as you follow the canyon, which eventually makes a wide curve north. Brownish-pink bluffs on the canyon's far side remain from a basalt flow that occurred in the Tertiary period, at least 4 million years ago. The bluffs were buried in debris and then exposed by erosion. On a nearly level stretch, near a reliable trickle of water, pass a large campsite to your right, then stroll past tall brush in a northernmost lobe of the Woodpecker Burn. You reenter the woods, then dip through the Dark Canyon creek bed, now dry. Keep close to this bed as you wind past dark gulches where wild roses lurk, then pass through a stock-fence gate.

Shortly after the fence, you abruptly turn right, head east to cross the dry crease now on a section of trail realigned in the 1980s, not shown on the topo map. The trail turns at a switchback, then traverses back, crosses the

dry bed again and passes the abandoned zigzag trail just before turning north to level off on a broad, flat saddle. Soon you reach several campsites and a junction (8410/3.4) with a logging road. Dark Canyon Trail 34E11 continues on to Sherman Pass Road. You leave the trail to turn right onto the *logging road.*

The road leads east, then north, for 0.4 mile, then climbs southeast to a saddle. It then curves north, descends and follows a canyon northeast. After crossing the tip of a ridge, the road descends to your waiting car (8300/1.5).

T55   Big Meadow Car & All-Terrain Bike Tour
(With Directions to Trailheads 57-62)

This trip takes you to the southern Kern Plateau with its cool, green forests, cascading creeks, expansive meadows and many shady places to camp or picnic. It circles 920-acre Big Meadow, one of the most botanically diverse meadows in the entire Sierra.

Distance   30.5 miles, semiloop trip
Steep Ascents   None
Elevation Gain   2000 feet
Skills   Easy route finding; unpaved roads
Seasons   Spring, summer, fall (no snow removal)
Map   Tulare County road map
Tourhead   54. From Sherman Pass Road, SNF Road 22S05, turn south on Cherry Hill Road, SNF Road 22S12, just west of the road gate, **TH54.** This tourhead is 62.4 miles west of Highway 395 and 6.0 miles east of TC Road MTN 99. It departs from car tour T52.
Description   Make a sharp turn off Sherman Pass Road (5880/0.0/0.0) and travel generally south on winding, paved *Cherry Hill Road, SNF Road 22S12.* A pleasing mix of black oak, incense cedar, Jeffrey pine and white fir shade the slopes. This road was built to service the first commercial logging on the Kern Plateau: the 1956 Salmon Creek Sale. You quickly pass a Fire Safe Area for camping. More hidden campsites, usually occupied on weekends, can be found in shaded nooks along Alder and Brush creeks,

which you cross on narrow bridges. After you cross Poison Meadow Creek the pavement ceases. For a while you travel over a thin veneer of oil-based asphalt, chuckholed and patchy. The rest of the route is over graded dirt roads.

Poison Meadow, then SNF Road 23S14 (7.6/7.6) to Brush Creek Overlook, are to your left. The bladed logging Overlook Road ascends gradually through the woods, passing secluded campsites before it forks in 2.6 miles. The right fork goes 0.6 mile to Snake Spring; the left fork, in 0.4 mile, to a campsite and an interesting 8069-foot overlook of the large Brush Creek Basin. Your road, however, SNF Road 22S12, bends southeast, skirts west of namesake Cherry Hill and arrives at a junction with Horse Meadow Road (1.5/9.1) where those seeking **TH57** turn right; the rest continue on Cherry Hill Road.

Horse Meadow Road (0.0/0.0) descends to Horse Meadow Campground (1.3/1.3), where 41 nicely separated, tree-shaded units, some next to Salmon Creek, are available at no charge. The camp provides the usual amenities, but you must take out your trash. This is **TH57** for T56–T58.

On Cherry Hill Road, pass Deadwood Road, SNF Road 23S09, one of many spur logging roads. Some of these roads have Fire Safe Areas and hideaway campsites; others wind endlessly through logged areas. Virtually every forest on the southern Kern Plateau has been selectively logged; still much beauty remains. In minutes you arrive at SNF Road 23S08 (0.5/9.6). Hikers wishing to shorten their Salmon Creek hike by 1.9 miles, one way, can drive the length of this road 3.9 miles west to a cul-de-sac where the trail briefly overlaps the road, passing a Fire Safe Area and other campsites by the creek and a private community of trailers.

You, on the other hand, steer straight ahead on 22S12 until you come to the next fork of importance (1.9/11.5). Those whose destination is the southern tip of the plateau will save mileage by progressing straight ahead, around the west side of Big Meadow. You turn left on **SNF Road 23S07** to the east side of the meadow.

Climb immediately on SNF Road 23S07, bump along its rocky surface, then pass to your right, the entry to a Fire Safe Area next to Salmon Creek; and to your left, the entry to creekside campsites and **TH58** to T59–T61, Sirretta, 34E12, and Cannell, 33E32 trails (0.7/12.2). Rounding a north bend with vignettes of Big Meadow, you journey over Salmon Creek past the unobtrusive green buildings of Big Meadow Cow Camp to the left and its cow chute to the right. This cow camp, rebuilt in 1980 after the original log cabin burned, is probably the most comfortable in the Sierra; it boasts a hot shower and a flush toilet for its ranch hands. for a short time the buildings served as a guest ranch for cross-country skiers, but fickle snow conditions around Big Meadow ended that use.

Beyond, you arrive at the first of three trailheads. **TH59,** Manter Trail 34E14 for T62 (0.7/12.9), is the northernmost entry

Lower Brush Creek

from here into Dome Land Wilderness, which borders the mountain rim to the east. **TH60,** South Manter Trail 34E37 (1.6/14.5) for T63, by the cattle pen, the easier of the two Manter trails into the wilderness, comes next. Both trails offer creekside beauty. In another minute is **TH61** for T64 & T65, Big Meadow Trail 34E15 (0.1/14.6), which crosses the south tip of the wilderness and goes on to Taylor Meadow.

Beyond the trailhead, you travel through

some clear cut areas that were replanted in early 1987 and seem to be thriving despite the drought years that followed. Turning and winding you eventually pass Camp Andrew Brown, a church camp, then rejoin *Cherry Hill Road, SNF Road 22S12* (7880/2.8/ 17.4) at **TH62**. You can take car tour T66 here to explore the southernmost tip of the Kern Plateau; this trip goes north, straight ahead to complete the circle around Big Meadow.

Along this stretch the 920-acre meadow spreads velvet in the setting of its guardian mountains, the jewel in a crown of Southern Sierra meadows. One fifth of all native species in the state grow here; over 400 cataloged plant species and variations of species have been identified. The meadow was formed by silted-in sag ponds on the active dip-slip Durrwood Fault. A swarm of small earthquakes in 1983–1984 were centered here in this tranquil country. In 1988, with the assistance of The Trust for Public Land, a non-profit conservation group, the Forest Service acquired this meadow from the A. Brown family, who wish the meadow to remain unchanged. Therefore, it will still be used for grazing, but it will not be flooded over and rimmed with condominiums.

You continue north past Salmon Creek's meadow exit and another Fire Safe Area, then meet the junction (1.6/19.0) where you earlier branched to the east. This completes your meadow circle. You retrace your route to Sherman Pass Road (5880/11.5/30.5).

T56   Deadwood & Cannell Trails Day Hike

This trip's slick-rock pools, tree-shaded nooks, creekside paths, broad meadow vistas and challenging elevation gains await hikers looking for a scenic outing and an interesting workout.

Distance   7.8 miles, loop trip
Steep Ascents   0.2 mile
Elevation Gain   1390 feet
Skills   Easy–moderate route finding; moderate–strenuous hiking; not recommended for equestrians
Seasons   Spring, summer, fall
Map   USGS 7.5 min *Sirretta Pk*
Trailhead   57. See car tour T55.
Description   Begin this trip on the camp entry road at the north tip of Horse Meadow Campground next to a concrete dip containing an unnamed stream. On *Deadwood Trail 34E13* (7380/0.0), here edged by rocks, you gently ascend northeast along the stream's left bank. Very quickly, you find yourself walking over exfoliated granite near child-sized bathing pools. Soon you pass a tenacious juniper tree, leave the slabs temporarily, then return to them before entering the forest of Jeffrey pines and white firs. You pass alongside collapsed debris of a shack or lean-to, cross the creek's streamlets amid a variety of flowers sprinkled like confetti and climb up and over Cherry Hill Road (7680/ 0.7). (The trail to this point does not appear on the topo map.)

Beyond the road, the cobbled trail takes you along the right bank, then to a stepping-stone crossing of the little creek. The path threads through a brief grassy patch where a stream from the canyon east of Cherry Hill arrives, then through a sunny stretch to cross Deadwood Road (7795/0.3). The trail parallels the road, climbs up a broad ridge, then turns right to cross a stream rushing down from Deadwood Meadow, which this route bypasses. Leaving the stream and its canyon, the path leads east over gentle terrain to the next canyon and creek.

Soon you ford this creek and the tree-shaded trail steepens as you climb northeast above the canyon crease on a narrow nose— exposed granite stretches along the canyon wall opposite this ridge. Miniature sloping meadows appear on your climb across seeps and springs of cool and shady well-watered slopes. To your left the creek chortles over cascades, but where the path's grade eases, the creek ceases and you cross its dry bed twice. Walking east now, you hike through a grassy flat that must have been a meadow but now supports a forest of lodgepole pines. The path disappears from time to time, but blazes and ducks or route-lining logs guide you on. While in the woods, this trail ends at a junction with a segment of Cannell Trail (8770/ 1.5). Some may wish to return the way they came for a 5-mile round trip. Continuing on the loop trip, you turn right onto *Cannell Trail 33E32.*

Ambling south through dense forest, you gain a saddle on Sirretta Peak's west flank and begin to descend a fairly steep canyon. In time you cross fledgling Salmon Creek, pad through seeps from above trail springs and meet the south end of Sirretta Trail 34E12 (7949/1.8). Next you gently descend through the emerald vale nourished by Salmon Creek and its tributaries to hike on a spur dirt road, then cross Big Meadow Loop Road, SNF Road 23S07, (7820/0.5).

Descend past a Fire Safe Area as you continue on the dirt road, which overlapped a piece of the Cannell Trail. You hike past high brush on the northwest hem of Big Meadow, with views ahead of Cannell Peak rising above meadow pasture. Eventually, at a Fire Safe Area, you approach the huge culvert through which Salmon Creek crosses under Cherry Hill Road, SNF Road 22S12 (7740/ 0.8).

Beyond the culvert, now on a *use trail,* enter a narrow canyon in which you soon climb over boulders on the creek's right side, then follow its descent generally northwest to cross a spur road near a Fire Safe Area (7540/0.7). Still on the right side of the meandering creek, where the canyon opens to include side canyons, you pick your way carefully over slabs which are sometimes slick. Salmon Creek slides over these smooth granites and forms into inviting pools. Cross to the left bank, follow the creek, now demurely hiding under willows, then under a coniferous forest, then you hike across SNF Road 23S08 (7380/1.2).

Returning to the stream's right bank, the path passes yet another Fire Safe Area, winds among seasonal water-loving wildflowers to end at Horse Meadow Campground (7340/ 0.3), completing the loop trip.

T57 Meadow to Meadow Salmon Creek Day Hike

High in a north canyon between Sirretta Peak and Dome Land Wilderness, trickles from seeps and springs combine to form the headwaters of Salmon Creek. From the canyon, the little creek makes a U turn through the north tip of Big Meadow before flowing over slick rocks and entering Horse Meadow. There the meandering creek acquires direction and heads west eventually to tumble off the Kern Plateau and join the waters of Kern River. This trip explores a wandering, cascading segment of the creek as it flows from Big Meadow to Horse Meadow.

Distance 4.4 miles, round trip
Steep Ascents None
Elevation Gain 400 feet
Skills Easy route finding; easy hiking; not recommended for equestrians
Seasons Spring, summer, fall
Map USGS 7.5 min *Sirretta Pk*
Trailhead 57. See car tour T55.
Description From the south tip of Horse Meadow Campground's main loop, find the *use trail* (7340/0.0) that soon parallels the creek. Walking east along the left bank, you follow the curves of the sun-spangled stream through lush, flowered meadows. Tall crimson columbines nod here and there on the well-watered terrain. They are easy to recognize by their crown of five, hollow, pointed vivid orange-red petals with yellow stamens that hang like a delicate tassel. Pass a Fire Safe Area to your left and quickly cross spur road SNF Road 23S08 (7380/0.3) and Salmon Creek.

You find the use trail on the creek's right bank now, pass a campsite and gently ascend into forest. After a sudden right turn you climb a sunny, bouldery path above the willow-hidden creek. When the path disappears, follow the creek as it slides over slabs, some with bathing pools so enticing you must at least pause to dangle your feet in the cool water.

Continue upstream along the left bank where the canyon opens to receive a neighboring canyon with its creek. To your right a massive granite spall creates a checkerboard effect on one side, a fan effect on the other. You soon cross another spur road (7540/1.2) and another Fire Safe Area; your route continues on the creek's left bank. Ahead, the canyon narrows and appears to threaten difficult climbing, but you climb easily over boulders then back to creekside when possible. Passing a campsite, you arrive at Salmon Creek's massive culvert under Cherry Hill Road, through which you can see distant cows grazing on Big Meadow. Now your route takes you up and over the road and down to Big Meadow (7740/0.7). Here some may have a car waiting in the Fire Safe Area

Granite spalling

by the meadow; otherwise, return the way you came.

T58   Salmon Creek Day Hike
With Excursion N: Fishermen's Trail

Abundant wildflowers, peaceful recesses, fishing ponds and smooth-rock bathing pools await you on this hike. Those who persevere to the end of the trail view a snippet of Greenhorn Mountains framed by the V-shaped slot, through which Salmon Creek plunges off the plateau. Only those skilled in technical rock climbing can pass the slot to see dramatic Salmon Creek Falls.

Distance   9.0 miles, round trip
Steep Ascents   0.2 mile
Elevation Gain   955 feet
Skills   Easy route finding; moderate hiking; not recommended for equestrians
Seasons   Spring, summer, fall
Maps   USGS 7.5 min *Sirretta Pk* (0.1 mile) *Fairview*
Trailhead   57. See car tour T55.
Description   From the northeast side of Horse Meadow, 0.1 mile down a spur road

west of the campground road, *Salmon Creek Trail 33E36* (7315/0.0) leads northwest as it winds among lodgepole pines around the edge of Horse Meadow. It first follows the meadow access road, then crosses the grassy flows from an upslope spring, and progresses along the meadow's north fringe to a junction with a fishermen's trail (7280/0.6). The fishermen's trail continues straight ahead, which some hikers may wish to explore. The Salmon Creek Trail turns sharply left where it crosses Salmon Creek on a large log, and on this trail you skip the following excursion description.

Excursion N: Fishermen's Trail

This path often becomes dim and sometimes vanishes altogether while it follows the tumbling creek to a second junction with the Salmon Creek Trail. Refreshing bathing pools and shady nooks where Gilbert trout hide (but certainly not salmon), appear within the first mile.

Distance   4.4 miles round trip
Steep Ascents   0.2 mile
Elevation Gain   740 feet
Skills   Intermediate route finding; moderate-strenuous hiking
Map   USGS 7.5 min *Fairview*
Description   Beyond the log-crossing junction (7280/0.0), the rough, bouldery *fishermen's trail* heads west along the creek. Almost immediately it crosses granite slabs peeled like layers from an onion. It helps to have shoe soles that grip the surface when hiking on this type of rock. Where loose granitic sand thinly covers the surface, walk extra carefully: this scree acts like ball bearings underfoot.

Your trail dips then ascends a minor ridge before it returns to the creek. Soon the path nears a creekside campsite with a large, built-up fire ring. Those who wish to can cross the creek easily here and climb up the opposite bank about 30 feet to the Salmon Creek Trail. Continuing west, the fishermen's trail again encounters granite sheeting on which you make your way carefully along slabs, then down to a series of stair-stepping cascades with various sized pools—a wonderful place to picnic and bathe. Across the creek, fractured granite splashed with orange lichen enhances the beauty of the little canyon as the trail winds beyond the pools through manzanita and sagebrush, then among scattered trees.

Shortly you hike past a spring-watered grassy patch, notice a campsite and step across a side creek. Then you climb among

boulders, passing left of one outcrop whose face is vertically striped, and another with black "columns" before approaching the creek again. Continue to climb over steep ridges and near the stream, sometimes on use paths, sometimes cross-country, until you reach Salmon Creek Trail (6820/2.2) near its lower creek crossing.

*   *   *   *   *

After crossing the creek on the log at the beginning of the fishermen's trail, Salmon Creek Trail 33E36 skirts the west side of Horse Meadow for 0.1 mile then quickly curves right into the woods. The trail descends to cross a side creek sprinkled with leopard lilies, and continues just above Salmon Creek where you can see a section of the fishermen's trail below. Then the route crosses the second of seven side creeks on this route, all tucked in lush canyons where the path sometimes disappears in tall grass and high lupines, and descends toward Salmon Creek again. A steady climb takes you to the cul-de-sac of SNF Road 23SO8 (7180/1.3). (You can drive to this point to begin the hike here. See car tour T55.)

Still walking west, now among Kern ceanothus, you top the second of three ridgelet crossings, then descend on a some-

A Salmon Creek pool

times soggy slope where hip-high lupine impinge on the trail. The deep blues of monkshood and giant larkspur add colorful accents that enhance the slope's viridescence. After rounding a fourth ridge under boughs of white fir, lodgepole and Jeffrey pines, zigzag down a steep slope, then cross Salmon Creek through a parting of willows and creekside dogwood (6820/1.2). The fishermen's cross-country route joins you here.

You now gently descend between dry, south-facing slopes and the more vegetated creekside where you spot a couple of campsites. After an easy stroll, ascend to the end of the trail on a bouldery ridge (6760/1.4), where you see the Greenhorn Mountains peek through the brink over which the creek abruptly leaves the Kern Plateau. You can descend to Salmon Creek pools below by following a ducked path across steep friction slabs just before reaching the top of this ridge. About 0.1 mile west of the pools you reach the brink of Salmon Creek Falls. At one time there was a trail from the Kern River to the bottom of the falls, but at present the best view of them, especially in the spring, is from the South Rincon Trail, T44.

T59   Twisselmann Botanical Area Day Hike
With Excursion O: Sirretta Peak

The Twisselmann Botanical Area features the southernmost grove of foxtail pines in California and one of the few slopes known where limber, lodgepole, western white, Jeffrey and foxtail pines grow together. The trip is further enhanced by views of the Big Meadow area.

Distance   7.8 miles, round trip
Steep Ascents   None
Elevation Gain   2130 feet
Skills   Intermediate route finding; moderate-strenuous hiking
Seasons   Spring, summer, fall
Map   USGS 7.5 min *Sirretta Pk*
Trailhead   58. See car tour T55.
Description   From the end of the parking area at the north tip of Big Meadow, hike north on **Cannell Trail 33E32** (7830/0.0), immediately cross a tributary of Salmon Creek, then quickly dip to cross the main stream on logs. Next you walk north through a gem of a meadow ringed with trees, then across another tributary. You quickly reach a forked junction (7940/0.4) where this trail continues left and your route **Sirretta Trail 34E12,** forks right.

Now your path ascends moderately up a side ravine; then enters Salmon Creek Canyon. In ½ mile from the trail junction, the route follows a 1980s realignment of the trail, which ascends along the east side of the canyon. You can see the abandoned trail below alongside of the diminishing creek. The route passes a couple creases where bracken ferns reside, rarely seen hereabouts. As the path gains elevation, red firs replace lodgepole pines, then foxtail pines replace red firs. Foxtail pines grow in gravelly soil just below timberline, usually with very few understory plants. Their short, five-clustered needles densely surround their branches, which resemble a fox's tail. This tree survives the extreme weather of a high country where competing trees cannot exist.

Springs and the meadowy headwaters of Salmon Creek disappear behind you and views of Big Meadow far below and Sirretta Peak high to the west capture your attention as you steadily climb the switchbacks toward the pass. Those who wish to climb Sirretta Peak follow the use trail (9480/2.5), which branches to the left, 0.3 mile before the pass. The rest continue to the pass and skip the following excursion description.

Excursion O: Sirretta Peak

Sirretta Peak anchors the south end of a prominent northwest–southeast hydrographic divide, Sherman Peak the north. Views from both peaks are praiseworthy; but Sherman Peak's easily accessible summit was chosen for a radio relay tower, while Sirretta Peak, with its pulpit of sky-reaching granite, became the setting for a wedding.

Distance   1.4 miles, round trip
Steep Ascents   0.2 mile
Elevation Gain   500 feet
Skills   Intermediate route finding; Class 2 climbing
Description   On the well-ducked ***use trail*** (9480/0.0), you climb north almost to the saddle, then zigzag steeply west for 240 vertical feet to the plateau. Once on the tableland, stroll southwest, first on the left side of the ridge, then the right, to the boulders on the end of the plateau. Climb an ascending slant on the north side of these boulders, pass near a snag amidst the rocks, then climb over the boulders eastward to the summit (9977/0.7).

*   *   *   *   *

On Sirretta Trail 34E12, past the excursion's use trail, a short stint takes you to the pass (9580/0.3). To reach the slope with the unusual mix of pines, cross the pass, leave the realigned path and locate the tree blazes indicating the old trail, which is shown on the topo maps. Follow the blazes northeast to a gently tilted plateau. Here you leave the old trail to turn northwest about 500 yards to a wide canyon (9200/0.7) that slopes down

Foxtail pine

past Sirretta Meadows. The mix of trees found here was first described by John Thomas Howell, past Curator of Botany at the California Academy of Sciences. He claimed these foxtails among the finest found anywhere. This large area was named to honor Ernest Twisselmann, a rancher turned botanist who identified and cataloged much of the flora in Kern County.

T60   Big Meadow-Sherman Pass Loop Backpack

On this journey you experience the contrast between a pristine forest and one altered by heavy logging. The first leg of the hike explores a foxtail pine grove and a dense, virgin woods laced with springs and streams. On the return route, you hike through a red fir forest interspersed with large stumps of old growth trees. You observe evolutionary changes along the Durrwood Fault as well.

Distance   22.5 miles, loop trip
Steep Ascents   0.2 mile

Elevation Gain   4560 feet
Skills   Easy route finding

Seasons   Spring, summer, fall
Maps   USGS 7.5 min *Sirretta Pk, Bonita Mdws*
Trailhead   58. See car tour T55.
Description   The beginning of this trip is described in T59.

Northbound 33E32 Log

T59 parking area	7830	0.0
Sirretta Tr 34E12	7940	0.4

Northeastbound 34E12 Log

Cannell TR 33E32	7940	0.0
Sirretta Pk use tr	9480	2.5
Sirretta Pass	9580	0.3

Beyond the pass you continue on re-aligned trail through a stock-fence gate, descend southeast among foxtail pines framing vignettes of Olancha Peak, then turn sharply northeast to follow a gully. After a switchback you curve around the meadow headwaters of Little Trout Creek. Large campsites sit at each end of the meadow. At the meadow's foot you hike on old trail (8970/1.3). Now on a long descent, follow the ridge between Little Trout Creek and Snow Creek, alternating between zigzags down the crest and traverses down the southeast-facing slopes. You level out along often dry Snow Creek, pass a few seeps and springs, and cross Little Trout Creek (7020/3.4). Beyond more springs, one of which you ford on a causeway, you meet a forked junction with *Trout Creek Trail 33E28* (6990/0.1), which you take.

Motorcycles are forbidden on this section of the trail. It proceeds generally northwest, skirts a small campsite, jumps a bog-lined gully and then at a stock-fence gate enters the enchanted canyon of Machine Creek. Why this winsome little brook has such an unnatural name is a mystery. The path dips to ford this brook seven times in the next ½ mile; some of these fords have boulders and logs for dry crossings. The brook is decorated with plants and flowers, including creek dogwoods and demurely bowing tiger lilies: a tall flower easily recognized by its yellowish-orange, purple-spotted petals.

Beyond all the fords, still hiking along Machine Creek on the north side of the canyon, pass a creekside campsite, several

springs, and enter a densely wooded flat. You then leave the creek to climb a moderate-to-steep incline to a saddle (8060/2.1). After an easy descent, ford, then stroll parallel to a Trout Creek branch. You soon step across another branch of the creek descending from the west, and pass camping possibilities. Continuing north 0.1 mile, you cross to the creek's east bank. A rough-hewn sign posted on a tree indicates that "Busch Camp" is 16 miles east!? Immediately after the sign, return to the west bank and shortly ford Trout Creek (7700/0.8) at a stepping-stone crossing.

Bearing northwest to follow Trout Creek, you pass a campsite and reach fenced Boone Meadow, where a state's snow gauge is read from aerial photographs. Some large, tree-shaded campsites lie west of the meadow. Proceeding now up-canyon, you reach the first of several junctions (7880/1.2): Boone Meadow Trail 34E10 forks right; you fork left continuing on your trail, 33E28, northwest.

Judging by the tread, this section of Trout Creek Trail, open to motorcyclists, receives heavy use. You immediately cross a branch of Trout Creek, then ramble along the main stem of the creek past several campsites, through a long stretch of selectively logged country. In the narrow canyon you cross a spring's flow then meet another junction (8245/1.4). Leave Trout Creek M'cyclepath, turn left and cross Trout Creek on *Sherman Pass M'cyclepath 34E09*. When reading the many signs at these junctions, keep in mind that you are heading for Sherman Pass and Durrwood Meadows, not Sherman Peak. The trail at this point is very near paved Sherman Pass Road. Now you intersect another junction (8250/0.1) where you turn left, south on 34E09, to cross a creek branch and the meadow.

A gentle up and down across loggers' treads takes you to another creek crossing, through another meadow, then up again to cross a logging road. Now you begin an earnest ascent downslope from the paved road, then turn to meet it just north of the viewpoint loop at Sherman Pass (9140/1.7) where this trail ends—a good place for a rest break. While here, notice the western white pines; a tree not seen often in the Southern Sierra. Its bluish-green needles in clusters of 5s or 4s have a whitish tinge; its thin cones are 6–8 inches long.

Begin your return trip on the western side of the many-peaked ridge, which stretches from Sherman Peak to Sirretta Peak; the incoming hike was on the eastern side. From the view loop, walk several steps south along the highway past the end of the Sherman Peak Trail to *Cannell M'cyclepath 33E32* (9110/ 0.1), on which you turn left. The Cannell Trail is segmented now, but at one time it was continuous from here to Kernville. In the 1970s, it was part of the temporary route for the PCT.

The southbound trail follows the Durrwood Fault, which must have been quite active to have influenced the formation of so many saddles and sag ponds (now silted-in meadows). The fault zone stretches beyond the terminus of this trip to include Big Meadow and Upper and Lower Dry Lakes. This fault, still active, produced a series of small quakes in the late 1980s. The trail immediately crosses through a stock-fence gate, drops to Durrwood Meadows which, along with Round and Mosquito meadows, all former sag ponds, forms the headwaters of Brush Creek. Your route enters an intensely logged, extensive red fir forest. The girth of the numerous reddish stumps gives a hint of their former splendor. You become more appreciative of efforts by environmentalists to include into Dome Land Wilderness protection, the pristine forests of Snow, Machine and Trout creeks drainage, through which you hiked.

Until logging in the area is complete, it is impractical to mention here crossing or overlapping logging roads. The Forest Service makes an effort to keep the route marked. After passing Durrwood Meadows, the trail ascends slightly to a saddle crossed by a paved spur road (8940/0.9) that descends from Sherman Pass Road and parallels your trail. The path, squeezed between the paved road and fenced meadow, crosses a spring's trickle, ascends slightly above Round

Red fir stump

Meadow and a campsite, nears the spur road again, and descends a grassy, spring-watered canyon. The trail crosses tips of Mosquito Meadow then reaches the paved road's cul-de-sac (8920/2.2) and a Fire Safe Area.

The trail resumes across the cul-de-sac, and on it you pass a campsite and a flower-hedged creek, then climb to a saddle (9390/ 0.8), the highest point on the return route. You next descend among sloping, corn-flowered meadows and their springs, and arrive at a flat where faint Deadwood Trail abuts yours (8770/1.0). After a broad saddle, begin a lengthy descent on a dusty, rocky path down a fairly steep canyon. Sirretta Peak's granite prominence briefly appears to the northeast. Eventually you ford Salmon Creek, which has a campsite above its north bank, cross springs, then meet a forked junction (7949/1.8) with Sirretta Trail. Now having completed this trip's loop, retrace your incoming steps to the starting point (7830/0.4).

T61   North Dome Land Backpack

While much of the High Sierra remains under snow, Dome Land Wilderness and its adjacent high ridges are accessible and at their most beautiful. This journey samples a variety of its scenery in both de jure and de facto wilderness: chaparral to grassy meadows, arid flats to creeks, and spires and obelisks to foxtail pines.

Distance   22.3 miles, loop trip
Steep Ascents   0.3 mile
Elevation Gain   4810 feet
Skills   Easy route finding
Seasons   Spring, summer, fall (can be hot)
Map   USGS 7.5 min *Sirretta Pk*
Trailhead   58. See car tour T55.
Description   From the parking area at the north tip of Big Meadow (7830/0.0), return to **SNF Road 23S07,** turn left, and hike along the road around the northern end of Big Meadow and then south. Along the way, under forest shade, you cross culverts for Salmon Creek and a pair of its tributaries, then walk down slope from the buildings of Big Meadow Cow Camp to the next trailhead, **Manter Trail 34E14** (7810/0.8), which you take. (You can drive a shuttle car here.)

The trail briefly parallels the road, then turns southeast at the register box and bulletin board. The wide path climbs moderately up an east-trending canyon amid scattered bushes. Look for Kern ceanothus: this bush, with its holly-shaped leaves and clusters of small purple pom-poms, common on the plateau and along the Little Kern River is rarely found elsewhere, according to James R. Shevock, USFS botanist. Soon the path tops the divide and enters Dome Land Wilderness (8320/0.8).

Your trail now descends rather gently, passing through a stand of Jeffrey pines where occasional sunbeams spotlight trailside penstemon. It crosses the creek's moist channel, then rapidly loses 400 feet of elevation while passing wooded terraces and seeps from springs, which contribute enough to create the small, lively Manter Creek tributary to your right. Where the grade eases, the path passes a few large brookside campsites shaded by white fir, sugar pine and chinquapin. Solitary bits of color enhance the visual serenity: wild rose blossoms in spring, black oak leaves in fall. The trail crosses a boggy tributary and immediately after passes a forked junction with Cabin Spur Trail 34E37A (7250/1.7), a right fork lateral to South Manter Trail. The green buildings beyond the fork comprise the old A. Brown Cow Camp. Although now owned by the Forest Service, they are still used by ranch hands. Your trail then swings northeast, passes an entrance trail to a public pasture, takes you over tiny meadow fingers and ends at the junction with **Woodpecker Trail 34E08** (7180/1.0), on which you turn left.

You now climb north on a gravely, sandy tread over a hill, passing a sign remaining at the former Manter/Woodpecker trails junction, cross an often dry stream bed from the west, and hike by three successive wooded flats with camping potential. Next cross a north–south creek channel, here usually dry but as you follow its right bank, puddles from a creek-bed spring appear. Ascending in the creek's cobbly crease, then on its left side, you soon meet Dome Land Trail 35E10 from the northeast, which crosses the wash at a forked junction (7680/1.5). You continue north, leave the creek-bed ravine and arrive at the first of three saddles, passing en route an assortment of granodiorite nubbins, fins and skull-featured cliffs. Proceed northeast, cross Tibbets Creek watershed, the second saddle and then the third (8090/1.3).

Now begin a protracted, sometimes steep, descent northeast on your wide trail—a stock driveway. A lengthy granite ridge defines the canyon's southeast side; in time, a domed slope appears on the northeast side with tiny forks of Trout Creek flanking it. You cross one fork downstream from a row of potholes. There is usually a trickle of water here, though with all the green scum coating its pools, it does not look potable except to a fearless vegetarian.

The path traverses slabs then passes through a stock-fence gate, crosses an often dry second fork, and passes an obscure lateral to a creekside campsite. Now the trail veers away from the stream, descends moderately for a mile, then crosses a willow-hedged, muddy trickle of another Trout Creek tributary. Still shaded by Jeffrey pines, your path continues north. Bald Mountain and its lookout tower rise ahead; Bakeoven Pass, where a granite/basalt contact shows clearly, is northeast. Shrubs replace trees and the trail passes an obscure junction where directional signs indicate a long gone branch to Smith Meadow. (The Forest Service has agreed to leave old signs as part of Southern Sierra memorabilia, as long as they do not mislead.) The path drops to cross Trout Creek, a dependable source of water (6340/3.7).

Across the creek a small grove of Jeffrey pines invites you to linger or camp, but salt licks are dumped here and most of the area is covered with cow droppings (nicknamed "meadow muffins" and "cow pies"—a weak attempt to treat them with humor). You pass more old signs with a plethora of headings pertaining to a long-vanished segment of Trout Trail, then enter the area of the 1947 Woodpecker Fire, now treeless and densely brushed-in. Wind generally northwest through an aisle of this dense brush to a junction with **Rockhouse Basin Trail 35E16** (6690/0.8), on which you turn left. When Dome Land Wilderness was enlarged in 1984, OHV roads, of which this was one, were either closed or converted to trails. Woodpecker Trail continues north to Sherman Pass Road.

Hedged by high ceanothus, you ramble southwest over rolling terrain, then a seep, then step across Dark Canyon Creek. In 0.1 mile beyond Dark Creek, you arrive at a packer's campsite in boulders and trees on the north tip of grassy Woodpecker Meadow. The trees and grass provide a respite from the brush of the Woodpecker Burn. A spring spouts forth here among the boulders, but a pipe which made it accessible is either gone or covered with bushes and stinging nettles.

Found near water, nettles are tall plants with finely toothed leaves that grow opposite on a stem; its tiny flowers cluster in the axilla of the leaves. The plant's stinging hairs inject the irritant, formic acid. Just a few yards west of the camp is northbound Dark Canyon Trail 34E11 (6610/0.5), where this trail ends.

Your trail, now **Sirretta Trail 34E12**, still a converted road, leads west; a side trail branches off to a creekside campsite and a jacuzzi bathing hole. Your route dips across a neighboring gulch and runs briefly upslope. The road suddenly turns south to end at the creek; you continue west on a path to gain 120 vertical feet in 300 yards, cresting a minor ridge. After a brief descent, the path levels out near several shaded campsites along Trout Creek. After the first frosts, the deciduous trees that crowd the creek bank here appear as if sporting a bold golden sash.

Big Meadow from Sirretta Trail

Soon past a boulder-hop ford of Trout Creek (6730/1.2), you leave Dome Land Wilderness. Environmentalists advocate including the roadless canyon, this sylvan area laced with streams which you are about to enter, in the Wilderness. The ridge line south from Sherman Pass to Sirretta Peak would make a natural boundary.

Beyond the Wilderness border, you pass a stock gate and then stroll along the west canyonside of Little Trout Creek up an occasionally rocky, gentle-to-moderate grade. Here a wide line of willows, interspersed with scattered campsites of all sizes, cordons off the creek from the trail. Jeffrey pines and firs supplant sagebrush and buck brush as the countryside takes on a well-watered look. You ford Machine Creek and proceed straight ahead, south, through an acute-angle junction (6990/1.0) with Trout Creek Trail 33E28.

In this secluded valley, you walk above or through meadowy springs, crossing one on a short causeway, then curve to a stepping-stone ford of Little Trout Creek, just 0.1 mile from the last junction. After a 30 yard creekside amble, leave Little Trout Creek to parallel Snow Creek above seeps and springs that disappear into its often dry channel. Soon you begin a stiff pull up the ridge between Trout Creek and Snow Creek, fortunately under continuous forest cover. You wind up a moderate grade, then switchback to reach the ridgecrest. Alternate three times between zigzagging on the crest and edging across east facing slopes. When the path edges east from the crest for the fourth time, you reach a flying-buttress viewpoint, a good place to rest. Bald Mountain appears to the north with Olancha Peak peeking over its top;

Crag and Finger peaks are east of it with Kaweah Peaks Ridge to its northwest.

The trail crosses the ridge and traverses its west slope; here you approach the Sierra's southernmost foxtail pines and catch cameos of distant High Sierra peaks. Just short of a ford of Little Trout Creek near the foot of a winsome meadow and a large campsite (8970/3.5), the route shifts to a lengthy section of trail that was constructed in the 1980s to replace steep segments of the former trail. The new path, under shade of lodgepole pines, curves next to the eastside of a meadow generously endowed with cornflowers at its apex. A campsite awaits nearby. The trail climbs past one gully, approaches another, then switchbacks to return up the first gully's northwest side. Another switchback leads to a long ascending traverse which reaches Sirretta Pass (9580/1.3).

Whereas the old trail zigzagged down the ravine below the pass, you switchback beyond the pass sentinels to the southeast, then the northwest. Here a use trail (9480/0.3) leads to Sirretta Peak. See T59. After a few more switchbacks you reach the east side of the canyon, where you stay, occasionally hiking on pieces of the former path. You cross a stream from a spring and advance near Salmon Creek's meadowy headwaters before crossing another spring's effluent. Big Meadow, with Cannell Peak as its backdrop, spreads out to the south; trailside foxtail pines give way to lodgepole pines, then to Jeffrey pines and white firs. Upon turning south onto **Cannell Trail 33E32** (7940/2.5), you reach gentle terrain then stroll through a velvety dell where your path dips to cross Salmon Creek and its branches before you arrive at your car (7830/0.4).

Stegosaurus Fin

T62   Middle Dome Land Wilderness Backpack
With Excursion P: Stegosaurus Fin

This slice from the center of Dome Land Wilderness touches upon the essence of the land: a river, streams, forests and meadows in addition to the various forms upright granodiorite attain. Photographers who set up their tripods to record the many modes of exposed stone along with the tranquil, remote scenes of the wilderness interior, number among those interested in this demanding trip.

Distance   29.6 miles, semiloop trip
Steep Ascents   0.4 mile
Elevation Gain   5010 feet
Skills   Easy to intermediate route finding; not recommended for equestrians
Seasons   Spring, summer, fall (can be hot)
Maps   USGS 7.5 min *Sirretta Pk, Rockhouse Basin*
Trailhead   59. See car tour T55.
Description   (For continuity, the four main Dome Land hikes begin at the Big Meadow west entrance. However, for this trip the Chimney Peak Recreation Area east entrance has several advantages: it is 6.6 miles shorter; it breaks up the often hot Rockhouse Basin leg of the journey; and it is usually accessible when the west entrance is closed due to snow. To begin at the east entrance, **TH31**, see car tour T28 and locate the Rockhouse Basin Trail description in the text.)

If traveling during snowmelt, you may need a rope belay to cross the South Fork Kern River. The Manter Trail, the beginning of this trip, is described in T61.

Eastbound 34E14 Log

T61	SNF Rd 23S07	7810	0.0
	Wilderness border	8320	0.8
	Cabin Spur Tr	7250	1.7
	Woodpecker Tr	7180	1.0

Now strolling south on **Woodpecker Trail 34E08**, in the forest alongside the northernmost stretch of Manter Meadow, you soon pass the campsite of the part-time Dome Land ranger. You ascend a ridgelet and drop steeply to a trail junction (7020/0.8) on the north side of Manter Creek. Several campsites line the creek along the south bank. To the west, velvety Manter Meadow spreads before you.

Turn east and follow **Manter Creek Trail**

35E12 along the north bank. You soon cross a small ridge, then follow rolling terrain, mostly on corrugated south-facing slopes. Cross the creek and return quickly to the north bank again as you slowly lose elevation. Small campsites precede your arrival at Little Manter Meadow (6780/1.3). A *Trail not recommended for stock* sign is posted here. To avoid damaging the meadow, ignore the directional sign also posted, find the metal blazes to the left in the woods and circle above the springs around to the east side of the meadow. If you have difficulty finding the trail here, look for a conical juniper tree. To its right find a metal-blazed Jeffrey pine; equal distance again to the right of the pine is the trail.

Your granular path stays next to boulders high above the gorge of grassy Manter Creek. The trail passes through wild rose patches, crosses a tributary, passes campsites and enters a sagebrush flat. Here you part company with the creek (last water until South Fork), which plunges south to the river. Your path begins a 1.2 miles ascent east up a ravine, crosses over a low ridge to a larger ravine and tops out on a saddle (7340/2.0) amid drought-adapted brush. While the route of T36 bifurcates south to White Dome and north to Rockhouse Peak, your route heads straight ahead, east.

A protracted, steep descent now demands complete attention, and you soon understand why stock is not recommended on this trail. The path sometimes descends in ravines; at other times ravines resemble the path, so glance ahead to ascertain the trail's direction. Live oak and black oak offer some relief from the sun. Where the gradient eases, a new section of trail takes you northeast, then east around Rockhouse Meadow, a private inholding. (At this writing the section is only marked.) It then joins the road northeast of the property on which your route continues, then crosses the South Fork Kern River (5540/2.7).

The California Wilderness Act of 1984 added 32,000 acres to Dome Land Wilderness, including this Rockhouse Basin leg of our trip. Once across the river you resume on the road, which is also Manter Creek Trail 35E12, and hike past a right spur to the river. Only vehicles associated with the private property are allowed to use the road; other motorized vehicles are banned from the wilderness. In 1.3 mile from the river an unmarked closed road dips into a gully and heads north to connect with Rockhouse Basin Trail. This short cut saves 0.4 mile. Continuing on the Manter Trail, you reach a fork (5755/1.5). Chimney Peak Recreation Area parking lot, **TH31**, the east access to this trip, is 0.2 mile farther.

Turn west onto ***Rockhouse Basin Trail 35E16,*** then north as you leave the pinyon forest and enter the sagebrush basin where occasional Jeffrey pines shade your otherwise sunny stroll. The constant, dominant hum of cicadas (or their relatives) may be joined by the warning rattle of a snake or two. The view to the northwest includes distant, elongated Bald Mountain, on which you may spot the only lookout tower remaining on the Kern Plateau.

The trail nears the willow-lined South Fork Kern River by a campsite, then veers northeast, crosses a creek that usually flows until late summer, and reaches a posted sign (5772/2.0) indicating a ½ mile spur trail east to the PCT. The PCT parallels your trail north for a mile until you turn west where a deep northeast-facing canyon divides massive ridges on the other side of the river. The route curves past an unmarked road dubbed "Horton Trail" and proceeds to a forked junction (5670/1.4). Rockhouse Trail continues right, but you take the left fork, ***Dome Land Trail 35E10,*** still a road, to a river crossing near a campsite, immediately south of the confluence of Trout Creek (5640/0.3).

Here, drink lots of water and fill your containers: some of the creeks and springs ahead have water but are not reliable year-round sources. Now on the west side of the river, you climb on the road, which eventually becomes a path, above Trout Creek to the right and shortly pass a large blank sign near an empty register box. Beyond, you climb moderately-to-steeply southwest up a ridge past a Dome Land Wilderness sign remaining at the original wilderness border (6040/0.6). In time you cross over a brush-clad toe of a ridge and pass through a stock-fence gate to enter a conifer forest. While you ramble along on an easy, undulating path, tidbits of Tibbets Creek glisten to the left. The creek is a misspelled memorial to a man by turns butcher, poacher and the state's first game warden for the Southern Sierra, Charley Tibbetts.

The path crosses over a granite slab, then passes a campsite nestled by a boulder and shaded by a large mountain juniper. Immediately after, the former trail dipped to ford Tibbets Creek, but you stay to the right of the creek where in a half mile you reach a sandy, gently sloping flat. Flash floods in 1984 sent torrents down the usually placid stream, cutting a wide, deep channel and taking with the debris, a section of the former trail. North of the sandy flat, those with wonderful imaginations see Stegosaurus Fin, the Dome Land resident dinosaur. Skilled rock climbers see a welcome challenge (6455/2.3). If this climb is not in your plans, skip the following excursion description.

Excursion P: Stegosaurus Fin

Few climb this dinosaur deep within the wilderness interior, but those who do are greeted with panoramic Dome Land views.

Distance   3.4 miles, round trip
Steep Ascents   0.3 mile
Elevation Gain   1185 feet
Skills   Intermediate route finding; Class 4 climbing (Class 5 pitches optional)
Map   USGS 7.5 min *Rockhouse Basin*
Stegosaurus Fin is 35°56′16″N, 118°12′16″W

Description Caching your packs near the flat where you stopped on the trail (6455/0.0), you climb *cross-country* ¼ mile up a ravine trending north-northeast, then bear northwest for nearly ¼ mile, then cross a wooded flat. With the fin now directly north of you, you enter and climb a ravine, which soon veers northeast, then top an east–west divide. Now you traverse around to scramble up the Class 3 north face to the summit block. You climb this block by way of an exposed ledge leading to an east arête, which you climb to the summit (7640/1.7).

John W. Robinson, who provided the details for this account, recommends a 40-foot rappel off the summit block's north face for the initial descent. Thereafter, return as you came to the trail.

*   *   *   *   *

Beyond the cross-country exit, the trail flares away from the creek, returns, passes above a flat with a grove of young trees and a campsite ankle deep in cow meadow muffins near the confluence of the creek's forks, and flares away again. It returns to cross the north fork of Tibbets Creek, climbs 400 feet over a ridge southwest of the creek, then dips through a grassy wood to cross the stream once again.

At this point your path follows ravines and criss-crosses the fork's bed, which sometimes contains trickles of water. Now the trail enters a wonderland of immense granitic formations that dwarf you—and even smaller anomalies such as the "teed-up" boulder to your left as you approach a saddle (7660/4.6). Massive "Bart," a favorite spire among rock climbers, looms to the right of the saddle. Beyond, the path descends over mushy creeks below "Bart," leads through a stockfence gate, then over the crease containing the south fork of Tibbets Creek, and again ascends to another saddle (7845/1.1). From here the nearby upright cliffs and granodiorite blocks appear as frontier-fort palisades. After the saddle the path descends to cross a creek bed at an acute angle junction (7680/0.5) with *Woodpecker Trail 34E08,* which you take.

Tramping south on 34E08, you stay in the crease of a canyon, pass wooded flats, climb over the rim of Manter Meadow bowl and descend another 0.1 mile to the junction (7180/1.5) with *Manter Trail 34E14,* completing your loop. Here turn right and retrace your incoming route west (7810/3.5).

Teed-up boulder

T63   Dome Land's Manter Meadow Backpack
With Excursions Q–S: Granites of Dome Land, Manter Creek, and Church Dome/Black Mountain Saddle

An emerald expanse in spring, a topaz spread in fall: Manter Meadow is a halcyon retreat in an otherwise rugged and challenging land. Several day hikes originate from points around the meadow; most backpack trips in this wilderness include the meadow; and rock climbers pass it on their way to pinnacles, spires, obelisks and domes scattered about the interior.

Distance   9.2 miles, semiloop trip
Steep Ascents   None
Elevation Gain   1140 feet
Skills   Easy route finding
Seasons   Spring, summer, fall
Maps   USGS 7.5 min *Cannell Pk, Sirretta Pk*
Trailhead   60. See car tour T55.
Description   From the trailhead at the southeast corner of Big Meadow, your trip begins east on ***South Manter Trail 34E37*** (7820/0.0). The cattle pen and chute to the right attest that the trail also serves as a stock driveway, which accounts for its extra width. You approach and then ascend the short, bouldery, dry gulch to the watershed divide and border of Dome Land Wilderness (7960/0.3). Descending moderately in a lodgepole pine forest, you encounter the first trail junction (7900/0.2). Connector Trail 34E15A leads 0.2 mile south to the Big Meadow Trail for those who wish to climb Taylor Dome and go on to Taylor Meadow.

Beyond the junction, you cross the headwaters of a Manter Creek tributary, then recross it. Here you may spot a tree blaze to the right belonging to the abandoned former connector trail. The gentle descent steepens as you hike along the tributary sheathed in willows and thickets of reddish-stemmed creek dogwood. This variety of dogwood is adorned in spring with clusters of tiny white flowers, unlike the large single flowers usually associated with dogwood.

Shortly you come to the next junction (7190/1.9) where you leave South Manter Trail, which forks right at the signs. You will return on it to this junction. Continue straight ahead on ***Cabin Spur Trail 34E37A:*** a path

connecting the two Manter trails.

The connector trail heads north for 0.6 mile among Jeffrey pines on nearly level terrain. When it nears the meadow, the trees part, and your first picture-postcard view of Manter Meadow and some of the surrounding mountains appears. Then as the path curves northwest, it descends slightly just above a gushing spring and a secluded campsite, crosses another tributary of Manter Creek, part of which is diverted to supply water for the cow cabins, and meets a junction with ***Manter Trail 34E14,*** on which you turn right (7250/1.2).

In another 0.1 mile east, you pass the obscure former spur trail and Manter Cow Camp. Along with the Manter Meadow inholding, these buildings were bought by the Forest Service in 1976 after the former owner, the A. Brown Company, threatened to have the surrounding trees logged. Long before this government action, the meadow and nearby creek were named for Mantor (misspelled as "Manter"), a local pioneer sheepman and homesteader. Cowboys working the grazing allotment still use the camp.

Northeast of the cabin, the path nears the meadow, dotted with 2–4 foot bigelow sneezeweeds, recognized by their laid back, notched, yellow petals surrounding a brownish tuff-like center. How this flower got its common name is open to conjecture. Your route passes a campsite, another boggy seep, and a junction with the public pasture spur trail to the right. Soon after, your trail ends at the Woodpecker Trail 34E08 junction (7180/1.0). Backpackers, climbers and equestrians pass through this junction to the northern and middle wilderness interiors. The following optional excursion introduces you to those interiors.

Excursion Q: Granites of Dome Land

This easy hike takes you to the domes, obelisks, spires and monoliths that rake the sky in an area called Dome Land before this name was used for the wilderness.

Distance   6.2 miles, round trip
Steep Ascents   None
Elevation Gain   1050 feet
Skills   Easy route finding; easy–moderate hiking
Map   USGS 7.5 min *Sirretta Pk*
Description   Dome Land bound hikers turn left onto ***Woodpecker Trail 34E08,*** leaving the Manter Trail junction (7180/0.0) at Manter Meadow's northeast corner. You first climb north over the rim that encircles Manter Meadow. Cross an often dry stream bed, climb wooded flats like broadly-spaced steps, then ascend the wash of a narrow bouldery canyon, down which a trickle is fed by a spring tucked in the canyon's crease.

Cross to the left side of the creek, and soon recross it at the easily missed forked junction of ***Dome Land Trail 35E10*** (7680/1.5) angling in from the northeast, on which you hike.

Some see fanciful creatures and castles in the nearby massive walls of granite that soar above the pines; rock climbers see handholds, toeholds, chutes and ledges, and mentally chart a possible route. You scramble to a saddle (7845/0.5), then descend to cross the channel of Tibbets Creek, then seeps and springs. Ascending below a scattering of glistening white rock, you arrive at another saddle (7660/1.1), a gateway between towering granodiorite monoliths and spires: to the left a rock climber's dream named "Bart." Be sure to walk ahead where, to the right just beyond the saddle, completely dwarfed by the surrounding rock, stands a solitary, granite, giant teed-up "golf ball." The trail eventually descends into Rockhouse Basin; this excursion ends here.

*   *   *   *   *

Beyond this meadow looping trip's first side excursion, you turn right on ***Wood-***

Manter Meadow

pecker Trail 34E08 where you walk south through the forest and pass the unmarked, idyllic campsite of the Dome Land summer ranger, dubbed "Newman Camp" and "Mae's Meadow." You then climb a small ridge and descend steeply to a junction with Manter Creek Trail 35E12 (7020/0.8) on the creek's north bank. Several campsites line both sides of the creek. Here at Manter Meadow's lowest point and most encompassing view, waters from all the tributaries and springs in the Manter basin combine to become Manter Creek. The lengthy trail east crosses the middle of the wilderness, the South Fork Kern River in Rockhouse Basin, and ends at Chimney Peak Recreation Area. The following excursion explores the beauty of Manter Creek country along part of that trail for those who are interested. The rest continue around the meadow and skip the excursion description.

Excursion R: Manter Creek

This short adventure follows Manter Creek through a wet meadow to its tumbling exit from the high country.

Distance   3.8 miles, round trip
Steep Ascents   None
Elevation Gain   410 feet
Skills   Easy route finding; easy hiking
Map   USGS 7.5 min *Sirretta Pk*
Description   An east turn off Woodpecker Trail onto **Manter Creek Trail 35E12** (7020/0.0) at the low center edge of Manter Meadow takes you along the north bank of Manter Creek. Find the sometimes obscure trail as it winds in the forest of Jeffrey and lodgepole pines, then over a low ridge. The undulating path stays mostly on south-facing slopes, but slips over to cross a ravine and rivulet speckled with seasonal wildflowers, among them the wild geranium, whose five rose-pink to white petals display dark radiating veins. The 1–2 foot high plant has wide leaves with many points and divisions. Soon the route crosses Manter Creek then returns to the north bank where it arrives at Little Manter Meadow, nourished by several north-

side springs. Do not follow the trail into the center of the meadow; find your way around the north side to avoid damaging this fragile environment. The trail picks up east of the meadow to the right of a Jeffrey pine, which is to the right of a conical juniper.

Beyond the meadow, the trail continues east between boulders and the grassy trough of the creek, crosses a tributary and enters a sagebrush flat (6730/1.9), a half mile from the little meadow and at the end of this adventure. The path ascends the ravine ahead, but the creek turns southward to tumble down a rugged canyon where it eventually commingles with the waters of South Fork Kern River. At the foot of this wild canyon, next to the creek, is what little remains of Coogan's cabin, built in the 1920s for the child actor.

*   *   *   *   *

Beyond the second excursion, the Woodpecker Trail parts the meadow grass and crosses the curving creek. It continues south bordering the meadow's broad east side, then leaves for a short stint into the woods where it meets the South Manter Trail (7140/0.5). Here hikers can depart to see Church Dome and Black Mountain or continue on the loop trail.

Excursion S: Church Dome/Black Mountain Saddle

Barely 2.0 miles apart, spired, granitic Church Dome and flat-topped, basaltic Black Mountain present strikingly dissimilar profiles. This journey takes hikers to view both.

Distance   4.0 miles, round trip
Steep Ascents   0.1 mile
Elevation Gain   695 feet
Skills   Easy route finding; easy–moderate hiking
Map   USGS 7.5 min *Cannell Pk*
Description   Continue on **Woodpecker Trail 34E08** through the South Manter Trail junction (7140/0.0) at the southeast corner of Manter Meadow. On a wooded flat here, you begin a gentle ascent as the path curves southeast. You cross a ravine and soon leave the

shade to hike among manzanita on a broad, sunny ridge. After crossing the second ravine you ascend steeply, occasionally on loose scree, then hike over a granite shoulder. With engrossing views of Church Dome's bare pinnacles to the right and Black Mountain's forested butte to the left, you soon regain the forest and arrive at the saddle notch (7833/ 2.0) between Church and other unnamed granite promontories. The exposed rock of Church Dome awaits ascents by technically skilled rock climbers; Black Mountain welcomes the average pathfinder. For description of the Black Mountain climb, see T74.

Volunteers clearing Cabin Spur Trail

      *   *   *   *   *

Continuing the meadow romp, leave the Woodpecker Trail at the junction and turn right on *South Manter Trail 34E37,* where after 0.1 mile of woods, you skirt the southern lobe of Manter Meadow. You gently ascend west near the fence and pad through occa-

sional soggy patches below springs to round the top of the lobe. Wind through a stand of Jeffrey pines and white firs, cross a tributary and reach the junction with Cabin Spur Trail, on which you ventured many miles ago (7190/0.9). Turn left to retrace your incoming steps west (7820/2.4).

T64   Taylor Dome Climb

The towering, sculptured rocks of Taylor Dome present an exciting climb. The final ascent may be left to the skilled, but everyone can enjoy the Dome Land Wilderness views from the foot of the summit block.

Distance   4.0 miles, round trip
Steep Ascents   0.2 mile
Elevation Gain   1155 feet
Skills   Intermediate route finding; Class 2–3 climbing (Class 4–5 pitches optional)
Seasons   Spring, summer, fall
Map   USGS 7.5 min *Cannell Pk* Taylor Dome is 35°51′23″N,118°18′6″W
Trailhead   61. See car tour T55.
Description   Your route begins southeast of Big Meadow on *Big Meadow Trail 34E15* (7830/0.0) next to the road, continues up a ravine past scattered blazed Jeffrey pines, then ascends a brief moderate grade where the ravine turns away. After topping a blocky, spiry north–south ridge at a saddle (7990/ 0.3), the path enters the South Fork Kern River watershed and Dome Land Wilderness.

Now you descend a short moderate slope of decomposing granite, reach a vale of red

fir, and just before the trail turns south, pass a junction with Connector Trail 34E15A (7900/0.3), a 0.2 mile path to South Manter Trail. You then turn south to follow alongside a sometimes dry creek. After 0.3 mile, cross the creek and climb southeast for another 0.2 mile. Now watch for a sharp turn south and look for "Trail" signs to guide you. Another climb puts you atop a boulder-heaped east–west ridgecrest (8115/0.6), the southern boundary of Dome Land Wilderness.

Leave the trail at the ridgecrest on a *cross-country* route; skirt the bouldery crest by ascending east across north-facing slopes. Cross the crest in 0.2 mile, pass south of a peak, then return to climb diagonally up north-facing slopes. Curve southeast around the ridge through a wooded swale, then ascend steeply up to a barren, gritty flat. The sheer face of Taylor Dome, with many fine technical climbing routes, appears.

Here you turn east to climb to a bench between the summit block and a southern gendarme, a feature of nearly equal elevation. Much of Dome Land Wilderness spreads out before you. Proceed northeast on the narrow ledge and up the cracks to attain the summit (8802/0.8).

T65   South Dome Land Backpack

Taylor and Church domes guard southern entrances to Dome Land Wilderness. Highly photogenic and emblematic of their locale, they can entice the rock climber in all of us. Church Dome is exclusive: its easiest route is Class 5. But most hikers can climb Taylor Dome, just as viewful and inspiring. This trip leads you past the domes and past scenic Taylor and Manter meadows.

Distance   11.7 miles, loop trip
Steep Ascents   None
Elevation Gain   2090 feet
Skills   Easy route finding
Seasons   Spring, summer, fall
Map   USGS 7.5 min *Cannell Pk*
Trailhead 61.   See car tour T55.
Description   The beginning of this trip is described in T64.

Southeastbound 34E15 Log

T64	SNF Rd 23S07	7830	0.0
	Wilderness border	7990	0.3
	Connector Tr	7900	0.3
	Taylor Dome Climb	8115	0.6

Leaving the wilderness, your path descends moderately then drops steeply across east-facing slopes with awesome Taylor Dome to your left. Soon the grade becomes gentler as you approach and cross a branch of Taylor Creek. Your path follows the creek, which appears, gleaming, from a sheath of willow and wild rose, only to plunge under cover again. The path too is crowded by the growth of vigorous plants. The canyon makes two abrupt right-angle turns east. The trail emerges from it, leaving its cloak of Jeffrey pines and black oak. To the right, smooth granite sluiceboxes flushed by the creek offer good sites for sunbathing.

Your path crosses a logger's road (7120/ 2.3) and reenters forest. If you want to camp, turn south on this road and hike 0.1 mile to reach SNF Road 24S32 at the west end of Taylor Meadow. A Fire Safe Area near a spring is located opposite the stock pen, and other campsites are scattered through the woods. This is also an entry point for those taking this segment in reverse. See car tour T66 for **TH68.**

After crossing the road, still on Big Meadow Trail 34E15, you continue along the north side of the Taylor Creek branch you have been following, then pass a tributary streamlet and promptly ford the creek. A scramble up the south bank leads to a junction (7070/0.2) with Upper Dry Lake Trail 34E17. Past the junction, you walk along the south side of Taylor Creek on a meadowy path swamped by water from Upper Dry Lake. Pass a gate and a utility shack, then immediately recross the creek. This area, Taylor Meadow, was purchased by the Forest Service in 1990.

Find the path to the right of the corral and stroll southeast past the picturesque cow camp located across the creek. Ford another tributary stream and in 0.1 mile, look for an abrupt change of direction to your left at an obscure, unmarked junction (6960/0.7) of the plateau's old trail grid. *Woodpecker Trail 34E08,* which you take northeast, once connected with a path south of True Meadow; the trail you just left led to a path in Bartolas Country. Plans are to reestablish these missing links. Leave Taylor Creek to follow the fence to your left for a short time. You see an occasional tree blaze as you tromp through open country of sagebrush and a scattering of trees; then you cross the cul-de-sac of SNF Road 24S13 (7076/0.6).

Now, next to a logging road, ascend a rocky, dusty path up a moderate grade, still heading northeast, into oak tree domain. You may have to hunt for your path through logged areas and across logging roads. You descend somewhat and the first views of Church Dome appear. (Church Dome has the profile of books shelved with their bindings topside.) Cross a sometimes dry, willow-lined brook; a short scramble north takes you to the Dome Land boundary sign. Here climbers of Black Mountain depart to the right, see T74. Church Dome climbers soon depart cross-country to the left. You zigzag up to a saddle (7833/1.3) between Church Dome and other rock prominences, and through a stock-fence gate.

North of the saddle where views of spacious Dome Land unfold, a moderate descent on granite grit leads past a conifer grove fronting flat-topped Black Mountain to the east, and onto a bare granite shoulder from which Olancha Peak can be seen to the north. Now the path descends a steep slope of loose scree, levels between two gullies, then contours northwest. Dense manzanita and welcome pockets of forest hedge the path. Reentering the woods, you arrive at a junction (7140/2.0) with *South Manter Trail 34E37,* on which you turn left. The lengthy

Woodpecker Trail continues through the Dome Lands to Sherman Pass Road. West on 34E37, you skirt the southeast side of the southern lobe of Manter Meadow, round its sometimes soggy upper tip, cross a Manter Creek tributary and pass through a stock-fence gate at a junction (7190/0.9) with Cabin Spur Trail 34E37A.

Here your route, a stock driveway which doubles as a trail, turns southwest. The grade steepens and climbs amid slopes of snow bush and manzanita near a tributary adorned with creek dogwood, willow and currant. The path crosses the tributary twice before meeting Connector Trail 34E15A (7900/1.9), the other end of which you passed on the Big Meadow Trail. In lodgepole pine forest now, the route ascends a brief moderate grade to top a bouldery watershed divide (7960/0.2), where Dome Land Wilderness ends. Ahead, a short, steep descent west into a dry gulch, and then an easy stroll along its wooded, widening floor, past a stock pen, leads you to the junction (7820/0.3) with *SNF Road 23S07.* A brief stroll south on the road returns you to the starting point of this trip (7830/0.1).

Taylor Dome

T66   Southernmost Kern Plateau Car & All-Terrain Bike Tour

(With Directions to Trailheads 63–71)

This remote, quiet, gentle country with meadows, streams, forests and peaks receives few visitors. However, the lightning caused Fay Fire of 1987 disrupted the tranquility temporarily and impaired the beauty, but only at the south edge of the plateau.

Distance   20.5 miles, semiloop trip
Steep Ascents   None
Elevation Gain   1970 feet
Skills   Easy route finding; unpaved roads
Seasons   Spring, summer, fall
Map   Tulare County road map
Tourhead   62. From Sherman Pass Road, turn south on *Cherry Hill Road, SNF Road 22S12* (0.0/0.0). This is 62.4 miles west of the junction of Nine Mile Canyon Road and Highway 395 and 6.0 miles east of TC Road MTN 99, next to the Kern River. Drive to the southwest corner of Big Meadow at the south junction (13.1/13.1) with SNF Road 23S07, **TH62**, which curves east of Big Meadow. This tour is an extension of car tour T55.
Description   Your tour on *Cherry Hill Road, SNF Road 22S12* (7880/0.0/0.0), south of Big Meadow, ascends south past several roadside springs to a saddle where Cannell Peak hikers of T67 begin their climb at **TH63** (8340/1.3/1.3), on the right side of the road. In less than a minute, also on the right side, the road passes **TH64** of T68 for the middle section of Cannell Trail 33E32 (0.5/1.8), which takes those who prefer to travel by foot or hoof to the old guard station. The road rounds conifer-clad slopes high above Long Meadow to a spur, SNF Road 24S30 (2.2/4.0), which forks left to take the curious 0.8 mile to Upper Dry Lake. This lake and Lower Dry Lake are sag ponds on the Durrwood fault zone. Both were once much larger and deeper, but are silting in and will one day be meadows.

Traveling east of spring verdant, autumn tawny, Long Meadow, you meet the road to the Cannell Meadow Guard Station, SNF Road 24S12, (0.7/4.7). Here you turn left, but the old station deserves a side trip. It was built in 1905 as one in a series of buildings on the Kern Plateau for Forest Rangers on patrol; it now serves fire fighters and maintenance crews.

This side trip is the first of five diversions to special points and trailheads within this tour. You have the option of taking the trips or skipping the bracketed side trip information and continuing on the tour.

To reach **TH65** and the old station, drive straight ahead on *SNF Road 24S12* (0.0/0.0), round the south tip of Long Meadow, cross the creek's culvert, arrive at **TH65** of T69, left of the road, Little Cannell Trail 34E16 (0.2/0.2). Next, travel up and over a saddle to a junction (2.1/2.3). The station is straight ahead on *SNF Road 24S56* (0.7/3.0).

After your left turn at the junction with the road to Cannell Meadow, still on SNF Road 22S12 heading east, you soon travel next to shallow Lower Dry Lake (1.3/6.0) to the right. The lake and its campsite are hidden among the trees and easily missed. At the next road junction (1.7/7.7), you turn left onto *SNF Road 24S13* and head for Bartolas Country.

If you seek **TH66** & **TH67**, continue south on *Cherry Hill Road, SNF Road 22S12* (0.0/0.0), which swings around True Meadow and arrives at shuttle car **TH66** for T72, Fay Creek Trail 34E19 (0.6/0.6), to your left. Driving on, now into patchy Fay Burn, you pass possible campsites along Fay Creek near the sign and on to the cul-de-sac where it ends above Little Cannell Meadow and **TH67** for T70, Cannell Point climb (2.4/3.0).

Proceeding east now on SNF Road 24S13, you begin to see the devastation the Fay Fire caused. The shrubs were reduced to ashes and the trees to black silhouettes. Many of the salvageable burned trees have been logged, so the area has been scorched by the fire and churned by the loggers. But bushes are pushing up, black oaks are stump sprouting, and maybe conifers will return to this southern tip, although the area is drier than when many germinated in the more favorable pluvial periods around a century ago. Next you ascend slightly to pass a junction with a left spur, SNF Road 24S32, to Taylor Meadow (0.9/8.6).

Hikers looking for **TH68** and others wishing a campsite, turn north on **SNF Road 24S32** (0.0/0.0) to Taylor Meadow, where a Fire Safe Area and a spring are west of the meadow. Other campsites are scattered through the woods by Taylor Creek. Access to the Big Meadow Trail and **TH68** for T71, Upper Dry Lake Trail 34E17, begins north of the Fire Safe Area (2.1/2.1).

Still traveling east on SNF Road 24S13, pass a road to the left on which you will later return, then continue on to pass the right fork of SNF Road 24S14 (0.6/9.2).

Hikers seeking **TH69 & TH70,** and tour travelers who want to explore the southernmost tip of the plateau, turn right on *SNF Road 24S14* (0.0/0.0), drive south to **TH69** for T72, Bartoles Trail 34E20 (2.4/2.4). Continue to a road gate for **TH70**, T73, Bartoles Viewpoint (0.3/2.7). If the gate is

open you can drive to the end of the road near the viewpoint and Dome Land Wilderness boundary (3.7/6.4). (Leave a note so you will not be locked in.)

Circle around hidden Rattlesnake Meadow, no doubt named for local inhabitants. This meadow, True, Long and Big meadows were purchased in 1988 by the Forest Service from the A. Brown family. Soon, after a half circle and passing an even growth Jeffrey pine patch, probably an area where seedlings were planted, you come to another junction (7030/1.2/10.4). Your road, SNF Road 24S13, reaches north to **TH71**, a Dome Land Wilderness entrance. The car tour loops west on *SNF Road 24S33* to finish the circle around the meadow.

SNF Road 24S13 (0.0/0.0) to **TH71** and the wilderness trail passes a Fire Safe Area next to Taylor Creek (0.6/0.6), a remote and attractive campsite. Beyond, it reaches a cul-de-sac and **TH71** (1.4/2.0) where rock climbers hike Woodpecker Trail 34E08 to Church Dome; and Black Mountain aspirants of T74 begin.

Finishing the loop of Rattlesnake Meadow, you turn right on *SNF Road 24S13* at the junction you passed earlier (1.2/11.6), which completes your exploration of the southernmost Kern Plateau. Now return the way you came: turn right in 1.2 miles, turn right again in 3.0 miles more, then head generally north to Big Meadow (7880/8.9/20.5), where this trip began; then on to Sherman Pass Road.

Taylor Creek at Fire Safe Area

T67   Cannell Peak Climb

Adventuresome hikers with little time to sample the southern Kern Plateau's delights will find abundant views of the area, especially of Big Meadow, in this climb of Cannell Peak.

Distance   2.4 miles, round trip
Steep Ascents   0.4 miles
Elevation Gain   1130 feet
Skills   Intermediate route finding; Class 1 climbing
Seasons   Spring, summer, fall
Map   USGS 7.5 min *Cannell Pk*
Trailhead   63. See car tour T66.
Description   You start southeast of Cannell Peak from the highest point on Cherry Hill Road, SNF Road 22S12 (8340/0.0). Climb *cross-country,* west, up the steep ridge opposite the road summit, staying to the left of the outcrops. Remain on the ridge as it curves southwest, then hike on a sweeping traverse curving northwest to a superior ridge eminating from Cannell Peak. Turn up that fairly steep ridge, pass a campsite and arrive at the top of rounded Cannell Peak (9470/1.2). The register can is tucked in the side of a cairn.

Big Meadow, at the northeast base of this peak, lives up to its name. East of the meadow, you can pick out Taylor and Church domes arranged in relief against Owens Peak and Mount Jenkins among other peaks on the distant Sierra crest. The west slopes of Cannell Peak, the Corral Creek drainage, plummet amid broken cliffs in the 6000-foot-deep Kern River Canyon. On this peak you may find a deteriorating ladder leaning against a red fir. This tree was used as a fire lookout by SNF employees who camped nearby—or so the story goes.

T68   Day Hike to Cannell Meadow Guard Station

The historic station, located at Cannell Meadow, was built to house the summer headquarters of the Cannell Meadow Ranger District, Sequoia National Forest. This scenic trip also explores the headwater country of Cannell Creek.

Distance   4.2 miles, round trip
Steep Ascents   0.1 mile
Elevation Gain   1125 feet
Skills   Easy route finding; moderate hiking
Seasons   Spring, summer, fall
Map   USGS 7.5 min *Cannell Pk*
Trailhead   64. See car tour T66.
Description   From the west side of Cherry Hill Road, SNF Road 22S12 (8217/0.0), **Cannell Trail 33E32** starts through disturbed ground, then becomes trail width as it ascends south across slopes sprinkled with snow bush, chinquapin and manzanita. A smattering of Jeffrey pines and white firs has survived logging; numerous trees remain around Buck Meadow, seen across the road to the east. Your route soon tops a saddle (8430/0.6).

This well-built, rock-reinforced trail climbs the Kern Plateau from the southwest side near Kernville and extends to Sherman Pass. It was once a National Recreation Trail, but because it was segmented by logging roads only the first 8.5 miles now qualify. The late poet/environmentalist Ardis Walker recalled that he and his wife Gayle used to ride horseback on this trail and other uninterrupted trails the length and width of the Kern Plateau, trout fishing at every campsite.

From the saddle, the trail descends west, crosses a road, steepens to a moderate grade as it turns southwest, and, subsequently, crosses the wide, cobbly bed of little Cannell Creek. Near a stately incense cedar, a trickling spring and the sedges it waters, stands a post. Next to the post on the ground, a broken sign directs passersby to the *Cut-off*

Trail. This vintage sign, like others remaining, recalls the past trail system, a nostalgic piece of Kern Plateau memorabilia. A few tree blazes still mark the old cut-off trail, which is no longer discernible. Now your path runs west and ends at **SNF Road 24S56** (7550/1.2).

Continuing west, now on the road, you soon fork left onto a driveway which quickly leads to Cannell Meadow Guard Station (7520/0.3). Used by maintenance personnel and firefighting crews, the station has a commanding view of 360-acre Cannell Meadow. The roof has been replaced and a couple of sheds added to the one room cabin built of hand-hewn Jeffrey pine logs. The rest of the exterior remains as it was constructed in 1905. The Forest Service has proposed the nomination of Cannell cabin for recognition in the National Register of Historic Places.

Cannell Meadow Guard Station

Cannell Meadow, purchased in 1878 by rancher Thomas Cannell, remains with his descendants. The local district of Sequoia National Forest, in Kernville for many years, retains the name it adopted nearly a century ago while governing from this forested site, the apex of velvety green Cannell Meadow.

T69   Fay Creek Day Hike

This gentle trip suitable for the entire family, visits several inviting pine-shaded picnic sites near a melodious creek on the southernmost section of the plateau.

Distance   3.6 miles, round trip
Steep Ascents   None
Elevation Gain   680 feet
Skills   Easy route finding; easy hiking
Seasons   Spring, summer, fall
Map   USGS 7.5 min *Cannell Pk*
Trailhead   65. See car tour T66.
Description   The trail of this journey served as part of a temporary route for the PCT. For that short time, hikers from all over the USA and some from foreign countries sampled the pleasing environs of Fay Creek. You commence on this trail, ***Little Cannell Trail 34E16*** (7640/0.0), across the road from the south tip of Long Meadow, with an amble in a pine woods on the west side of Fay Creek. When the canyon narrows, you cross the little creek. Beginning its journey near the highest summit on Cherry Hill Road, Fay Creek meanders south through Long Meadow, winds among willows on the south tip of the plateau, then tumbles down the slopes to disappear in the sandy soil north of South Fork Kern River.

After descending a half mile on a sometimes bouldery path, you again cross the slender creek, then walk among side meadows with a medley of seasonal wildflowers nourished by several springs. A seep crosses the path and drops into a pocket it eroded, further undermining top soil and tread. Leaving the brook where it abruptly turns east, you top a pair of rounded ridges and descend among manzanita and other chaparral near a seasonal streamlet to the valley of Little Cannell Meadow and onto an OHV extension of Cherry Hill Road (6980/1.8).

The often dry northern edge of the meadow offers a quiet place to rest before your return trip. The flow of numerous springs waters the ground within the southern fenced area, which resembles more a grassy vale than a meadow. If time permits, some may wish to hike further, see T40 of which this hike is a middle part, or climb nearby Cannell Point, see T70.

T70 Cannell Point Climb

Climbers in search of sculpted granite, photographers stalking unusual views of Lake Isabella and geomorphologists seeking an overview of the southwest tip of the Kern Plateau and the Kern River Valley will find this trip ideal.

Distance   3.4 miles, round trip
Steep Ascents   0.8 mile
Elevation Gain   1535 feet
Skills   Easy route finding; Class 2 climbing
Seasons   Spring, summer, fall
Map   USGS 7.5 min *Cannell Pk*
Trailhead   67. See car tour T66.
Description   To cross to the other side of the narrow canyon between you and the mountain, leave the cul-de-sac of SNF Road 22S12 (6830/0.0) to descend west on the *road* beyond the parking area. Leave the road at the first dip, about 90 yards from the cul-de-sac, to walk *cross-country* along a gully down to the willow-hedged stream that drains Little Cannell Meadow. A short amble west along the dense willow's edge brings you to a bush-free crossing of the creek (6780/0.1). The trail you seek, **Little Cannell Trail 34E16,** is a bit obscure here. Turn right, ascend between the manzanita bushes, and soon pick up a clear tread.

The trail leads northwest between mountain slopes and meadow vale to **Pine Flat Trail 34E18,** on which you turn left (6960/ 0.5). The trail's grade becomes steep immediately and remains so for two thirds of the way. The path shaded by a forest of pine, oak and fir runs west along a gully then crosses it 0.3 mile past the junction. In time the steepness moderates, and it crosses a saddle through a stock-fence gate (7580/0.6).

From here you climb **cross-country** steeply southward along a rising ridgeline; keep the multifaceted outcrops to your left. Finally you cross over a gap near the summit block to approach it from the east side. Follow ducks up a chute and along the top ridge to the climax of Cannell Point (8314/ 0.5), with its encompassing views of the tip of the Kern Plateau and the Kern River Valley below.

T71 Day Hike to Upper Dry Lake

This trip penetrates a granite canyon to reach a sag pond on the active Durrwood Fault. This reedy haven of bullfrogs and bears often dries up in fall, earning the epithet "Upper Dry Lake."

Distance   2.6 miles, round trip
Steep Ascents   None
Elevation Gain   730 feet
Skills   Easy route finding; easy hiking
Seasons   Spring, summer, fall
Map   USGS 7.5 min *Cannell Pk*
Trailhead   68. See car tour T66.
Description   This is a good early morning hike for campers at Taylor Meadow or on the southernmost plateau. The trip begins in the canyon immediately north of the Fire Safe Area across the road from the cattle pen at the west tip of Taylor Meadow. **Upper Dry Lake Trail 34E17** (7100/0.0) leads west over wide tractor tread which narrows to trail width at the north bank of a Taylor Creek tributary. Soon an exfoliating granitic dome squeezes your path between it and the creek. Spiny branchlets of snow brush impinging on the trail, can scratch bare legs. This small-leafed ceanothus with its springtime clusters of fragrant white flowers, is low and flattish, as if depressed by snow.

The trail steepens, crosses the creek (usually dry here), passes shreddy-barked junipers and passes a make-shift dam, and suddenly it arrives at the cul-de-sac of SNF Road 24S30 (7830/1.3) on the southeast side of meadowy Upper Dry Lake. An archaeologist doing field work here reported seeing a black bear bathe each morning—fastidious are the Southern Sierra bears!!

T72   Southern Kern Plateau, Fay Burn Day Hike

Lightning storms raced over the mountains of California in the summer of 1987, touching off massive fires throughout the state. These storms carried no moisture to douse the lightning strikes, and many of the forests throughout the state were burned. This educational field trip takes you to view the pattern of regrowth at Cane Meadow, the heart of one of the burns.

Distance   4.1 miles, shuttle trip
Steep Ascents   None
Elevation Gain   915 feet
Skills   Intermediate route finding; moderate hiking
Seasons   Spring, summer, fall
Map   USGS 7.5 min *Cannell Pk*
Trailheads   69 & 66. This trip requires two cars. See car tour T66. Leave the first car at **TH66,** the end of the trip. Drive the second car to the beginning of the trip at **TH69.** This is 4.5 miles from the first car.
Description   Your trip begins on a trail which, before logging roads, continued north to connect with a web of trails all across the Kern Plateau to the High Sierra. This remaining section, ***Bartolas Trail 34E20,*** (6910/0.0), a seldom maintained piece, leads west from SNF Road 24S14 along the north side of Bartolas Creek. The trail passes the wide, gravelly wash of the creek with its willow clumps—a wash that seems extensive for such a slender stream—and gently ascends through a burned and logged parcel past a few remaining trees that occasionally bear the old trail blazes. Your route soon turns north up a gully in which a granite outcrop with an inward slanted surface occurs to the left. This slanted surface reveals barely visible Indian pictographs; around and over the pictures appear someone's graffiti. This destruction is why guidebook authors adhere to a tacit rule: never direct readers to Indian artifacts.

Shortly you turn west again and hike on. A road overlaps your trail for about 50 feet; then you continue hiking on a path between the road and the creek. Many burned trees have been removed. You ford the creek twice,

cross the road next to a culvert, ford the creek thrice more, and again cross the road. Lastly you step across the grassy creek bed where geraniums flourish. Frenchman Bartolas probably grazed his sheep along here roughly a century ago. You easily obtain a saddle (7140/1.5), curve north, then west, to reach the rim of Bartolas Country.

The path descends steeply with distant views of Cannell Point directly across the Fay Creek drainage and near views of abundant seasonal lupines and gilias. It then drops to the north side of a heavily logged ridge, and turns southwest to wind among saplings planted by volunteers from the Ridgecrest Oasis Garden Club. From graffiti to little trees, you have witnessed the worst and best of public contributions.

Spread before you are the lush grasses and sedges of Cane Meadow, a spring that nourished man long before the Europeans arrived, and a dead, black forest, partially logged. Broad flats west of the meadow offer camping opportunities for you who wish to spend more time exploring the effects of the extremely hot fire (6560/0.8).

The blaze began north of the community of Weldon in lower Fay Canyon. It consumed the vegetation over the foothills, then spread up a small canyon east of Fay's main drainage, where it joined another blaze. In seven days it lapped over the southern edge of the Kern Plateau and ravaged the forests here; skipped about to ignite flames reaching Little Cannell Meadow to the west, Forest Service roads to the north and threatened Dome Land Wilderness to the east: 13,260 acres in all.

For the return leg of your trip, walk north on the *logging road* to find *Fay Creek Trail 34E19* (6560/0.1) after crossing a gully where early season spring water flows. The trail parallels the road, turns north to cross another road, then follows first one, then another spring-fed creek, crossing a low ridge in between and passing several springs and small meadows along the way. In time the

trail leaves the last willows. The topo shows a trail junction here, but tractor tread has removed the trail.

For the next 0.3 miles, you ascend a moderate-to-steep grade east of a dry ravine, then arrive on nearly level ground where you make a beeline for the Forest Service road and your shuttle car (7242/1.7).

T73   Day Hike to Bartolas Viewpoint

An easy walk on a great sloping forested flat takes you to a viewpoint on the southernmost tip of the Kern Plateau. From this point the land falls away dramatically, offering spectacular views of the South Fork Valley. For those skilled in climbing, 7256-foot Bartolas spire sits invitingly on a ledge just below the viewpoint.

Distance   7.8 miles, round trip
Steep Ascents   None
Elevation Gain   450 feet
Skills   Easy route finding; easy hiking
Seasons   Spring, summer, fall
Maps   USGS 7.5 min *Cannell Pk, Weldon*
Trailhead   70. See car tour T66.
Description   From the gate crossing *SNF Road 24S14,* (6910/0.0), you walk southeast down the long road. If the gate is open you can drive to the viewpoint knoll. Because this country has ongoing logging, new and old spur roads peel from your route.

Your road follows the contour of the land, winding but staying fairly level. Then it turns southwest to climb slightly, curve around a

broad canyon and arrive at a junction of sorts (7060/2.4). The road turns sharply right here, climbs south, then again levels off. (The lesser fork at the right turn ends 0.2 mile at a saddle.) You stay on the dirt road until it reaches its southernmost point (7180/1.3). It turns northeast and ends 350 yards later.

Now your *cross-country* route leads up the knoll ahead to its south point (7240/0.2), which is the unmarked viewpoint, barely inside Dome Land Wilderness. The granite feature directly south with the USGS control name of Bartolas 7256, first appeared on the 1972 USGS 7.5 minute topographic map. Because it is named, you investigate it and are justly rewarded with grand views.

White Dome from Black Mountain

T74   Dome Land Day Hike to Church Dome
With Excursion T: Black Mountain

This route is the quickest and easiest way to reach Church Dome and Black Mountain. Those skilled in technical rock climbing will find the ascents of Church Dome's granite spires challenging; others will enjoy the nontechnical climb of Black Mountain. For nearby campers, this mini trip offers views of Church Dome en route and northern vistas of Dome Land Wilderness at trip's end.

Distance   2.6 miles, round trip
Steep Ascents   0.2 mile
Elevation Gain   760 feet
Skills   Easy route finding; easy-moderate hiking
Seasons   Spring, summer, fall
Map   USGS 7.5 min *Cannell Pk*
Trailhead   71. See car tour T66.
Description   Your hike begins on the southern section of the Kern Plateau at the cul-de-sac of SNF Road 24S13. Your trail, *Woodpecker Trail 34E08,* (7076/0.0), runs the length of Dome Land Wilderness and beyond—from Taylor Meadow to Sherman Pass Road, approximately 16.0 miles. All of the trail is described in this book, segmented into several loop trips. Your sometimes rocky, sometimes dusty trail ascends moderately northeast, shaded by oaks and pines, and occasionally overrun by wayside chaparral and seasonal wildflowers. You may have to look for the path after loggers disrupt and fragment it. At present writing, your trail crosses only a pair of logging roads on this short trip—you may find more.

In time you gain your first views of Church Dome and its gothic spires, framed by Jeffrey pines. Next you jog a bit to cross a willow-lined, often-dry stream; after a short scramble north you reach a Dome Land Wilderness sign. Those planning to climb Black Mountain leave the trail shortly after this point (see Excursion below) (7760/1.2). Technical climbers of the Church Dome spires take a cross-country route, bearing leftward toward the spires; leave this trail here or further on, depending on the ascent chosen. For nonclimbers, excellent northward views of spacious Dome Land Wilderness await you after you zigzag to the trail's

summit (7833/0.1).

Excursion T: Black Mountain

Hikers will find this tabular basaltic mountain interesting to climb; those schooled in geology will have a field day identifying volcanic rocks.

Distance   3.6 miles, round trip
Steep Ascents   0.1 mile
Elevation Gain   980 feet
Skills   Intermediate route finding; Class 2 climbing
Maps   USGS 7.5 min *Cannell Pk, White Dome*
Description   Climbers of Black Mountain, which is not visible at this point, leave the trail between the Dome Land boundary sign and the trail zigzags south of Church Dome saddle, to hike *cross-country* (7760/0.0) east-northeast on an ascending traverse. Your immediate goal is to climb onto the ridge that descends southeast from the saddle and the spires. An easy climb takes you just east of those spires, then onto the ridgetop, and just west of the much smaller outcrop down the slope. Here your view northeast of Black Mountain's south end may be obscured by trees; even when seen it does not look tabular. The view east-southeast of a table mountain beckons: do not climb the wrong mountain. Descend the gentle slope on the ridgecrest using Spire 7665, near the foot of the ridgecrest, as your landmark. Before reaching that granitic projection, descend northeast to cross the saddle (7420/1.0) leading to Black Mountain.

Beyond the saddle you climb easily over granite slabs, locate the black basalt and make your way among manzanita, live oak, pinyon and Jeffrey pines to that flow. Although the rocks look loose, they are in fact quite stable and easy to climb. Take the time to find one of the several good chutes to climb up and over the rim. Once on top locate the register can in a small cairn (7860/0.8).

Across the canyon to the northeast, rests White Dome; in the canyon, unseen, plummets Manter Creek; beyond Dome Land Wilderness to the east, peaks outline the Sierra crest.

A USGS analysis of Black Mountain rocks showed alkali olivine basalt with a Miocene age of 12.3 million years. Other similar basalts from the Kern Plateau volcanic field yielded ages of 3.6 million years, suggesting, according to the report, two separate periods of volcanism in the same region.

Church Dome, north from Woodpecker Trail

Section 3
Nine Mile Canyon/Kennedy Meadows/ Sherman Pass Road to Horseshoe Meadow Road and Golden Trout Wilderness North Border

South Fork Kern River at Strawberry Meadows

T75   PCT   Backpack in South Sierra Wilderness: Kennedy Meadows to Olancha Pass

With Excursion U: Deer Mountain

This journey through open forest and meadows takes you gently to the higher elevations of the Sierra. A country once buzzing with motorcycles, now it is wilderness filled with the sounds of silence and spacious solitude.

Distance   22.7 miles, shuttle trip
Steep Ascents   None
Elevation Gain   3870 feet
Skills   Easy route finding
Seasons   Spring, summer, fall
Maps   USGS 7.5 min *Crag Pk, Long Cyn, Monache Mtn, Haiwee Pass* (PCT sections built in the late 1980s are not on the maps.)
Trailheads   45 & 79. This trip requires two cars. See car tour T100. Leave the first car at **TH79**, the end of the trip at Sage Flat. Then see car tour T52. Drive the second car to the beginning of the trip at **TH45**, Kennedy Meadows Campground. This is 65.6 miles from your first car.
Description   This hike begins on the ***PCT*** at the north end of Kennedy Meadows Campground (6150/0.0). Your route follows the old Clover Meadow Trail, which is shaded by pinyon and juniper trees, then by Jeffrey pines along the river. It dips into a side canyon, passes through a stock-fence gate, enters South Sierra Wilderness, then approaches the river and winds to a forked junction (6240/1.1).

Here the PCT leaves the Clover Meadow Trail, which continues to a river crossing— extremely dangerous during snowmelt. The old path west of the river is used as a stock driveway. Your route, the right fork, leads to a sturdy, yet scenic, steel-girded wooden bridge built in 1984 (6300/0.8).

Beyond the bridge, the trail climbs north of a knoll, passes a campsite perched above the river, then continues over gravelly terrain past a closed connecting piece of trail to the old, deeply-rutted route. Sections of the unmaintained Clover Meadow Trail occasionally cross or coincide with the present trail. Soon your path gains the slopes of a craggy 7412-foot mountain whose soils nur-

ture an occasional prickly-pear cactus. The prominent yellow-orange blossoms of this spiny plant turn pink-to-rose as they mature. The path switchbacks once to reach a saddle, then makes a weaving traverse above the rumble of the South Fork Kern River, heard but not seen in its canyon to the east, before it dips to cross Crag Creek (6810/2.0). Yellow monkey flowers with two-lobed upper lips and three-lobed lower lips luxuriate near the banks of this creek, along with an occasional yellow cinquefoil, whose green sepals reach above the flower's petals. There are places to camp here and upstream along the old trail, all of which, however, are within 100 feet of the water—easily damaged areas the Forest Service wishes to protect.

After a short hike beyond the crossing, you abruptly face the skeletal remains of trees burned in the 1980 Clover Meadow blaze. Started by a PCT hiker's campfire that was set too close to tree branches and improperly extinguished, the wind-whipped fire engulfed 5000 acres before it was contained. Buck brush ceanothus, rabbit brush and associated xeric plants have replaced the forest; the pines are not regenerating. The stark grays and blacks of the burn contrast sharply with the creek's riparian expanse and the plush greens of Clover Meadow. You pass campsites in an unburned pocket of trees and, 1.8 miles into the burn, again reach the welcome shade of forest.

The path meets the usually dry eastern branch of Crag Creek at the junction (7560/2.5) of Clover Meadow Trail (stock driveway). In 0.1 mile the trail passes right of a campsite established in 1936, according to a concrete slab. The old trail was probably built by the Civilian Conservation Corps, which was active from 1933 to 1942, during

Black silhouettes 10 years after burn

the Depression. As the path climbs up the narrowing, boulder-strewn slot, a spring appears in the creek's channel. Its flow waters a lush growth of willows and wild roses most of the year. The grade abates amid brush and ends at a saddle with campsites and a T junction (8060/1.1) with Haiwee Trail 37E01, which follows an ancient Indian path east to the river and on through Haiwee Pass to Owens Valley. Hikers on T76 return to this point on a section of this trail.

Beyond the saddle, the PCT drops gently to Beck Meadow, a sagebrush finger of Monache Meadow. A spacious view of Monache Meadow, the largest meadow in the Sierra, includes distant Mount Whitney peering over the plateau peaks. Your route veers north from the junction (7953.0/4) of northwest-leading Beck Meadow Trail 35E15, where hikers on T77 depart, then from grooves of an old road. Jeeps first penetrated Monache Meadow in 1949, but long before that, horse-drawn buckboards left their parallel treads.

In 0.6 mile your path leaves a former section of the PCT, left to revert to nature, and turns north-northeast toward Olancha Peak beyond the lower northern slopes of nearby Deer Mountain. After crossing a seep, the

path climbs above Beck Meadow and through a gully where below, a spring's water is piped into a cow trough; the trail then passes through another stock-fence gate. To the north, Mount Langley, framed by Brown and Olancha mountains, comes into view. Its rounded backside resembles Mount Whitney's with which it is often confused. After 0.7 mile from the gate, the trail tops out on Deer Mountain's northern ridge (8390/2.2) near a dry campsite. Here you may climb Deer Mountain or skip the following description to continue on the PCT.

Excursion U: Deer Mountain

This mountain treats you to an encompassing view of the southern Kern Plateau, after you climb on forested slopes to its summit.

Distance   4.0 miles, round trip
Steep Ascents   0.2 mile
Elevation Gain   1030 feet
Skills   Intermediate route finding; Class 2 climbing
Maps   USGS 7.5 min *Monache Mtn, Haiwee Pass*
Description   Probably the least taxing route to the summit departs from the highest point on the PCT (8390/0.0) as it crests the flat north ridge of Deer Mountain, 0.2 mile before the trail reaches a switchback on the north side. To avoid most of the mountain mahogany tangles, start your **cross-country** trek south-southeast slightly to the left of the ridge. After a slight rise, dip onto a forested flat where you begin a wide curve southeast near the ridge as it becomes better defined. Continually gain elevation and slant left of the peak ahead, which is not the highest point on Deer Mountain.

Still hiking southeast, you arrive at a plateau where off to the right a jumble of boulders barely rises above the Jeffrey pine forest. Weave through manzanita toward that jumble, but again, stay left of it. Two more peaks come into view after you round this stack of rocks. Your goal is the easternmost of the two. An easy boulder scramble takes you to the summit (9418/2.0).

From west to east, Crag, Finger, Smith and Jackass peaks, then Monache, Brown, Olancha and Round mountains guard vast Monache Meadow in the foreground. Upon your return, if you descend too far to the west, you eventually reach the PCT, but if too far to the northeast, you miss the trail altogether.

*   *   *   *   *

From the ridge you briefly head southeast to a switchback, then north to drop out of the forest, and cross a retired jeep road that bisects a low, broad ridge (7940/1.0). Head northeast along the ridge, then drop to an arched 1986 vintage bridge over South Fork Kern River (7820/0.4). Interestingly, the steel in this bridge was treated to resemble an old, rusted structure, rendering it less conspicuous. The bridge spans shallow water except during snowmelt when long distance PCT hikers pass this way, then it is an important safety factor. Here you leave Sequoia National Forest and enter Inyo National Forest, but still remain in South Sierra Wilderness. An ideal campsite is sheltered by trees on the slope south of the river; exposed sites sprawl along the north bank.

Beyond the bridge, the PCT briefly overlaps a jeep road, then passes the southeast-heading Deer Mountain Trail (incorrectly signed Wildrose Trail) (7840/0.1). Before the wilderness was established, which forbade them, this path vibrated with motorcycles. Deer Mountain circle hikers on T76 leave the PCT here to hike on the Deer Mountain Trail. Next the PCT crosses a once heavily used northbound jeep road, then, trail size now, easily climbs northwest above the meadow while jogging laterally around washes and ridgelets, a feat it does well and often to stay within its required grade of 15% or less. (You can usually identify sections of PCT that overlay old trails, as then it plunges into washes and climbs over ridgelets.) In time the trail mounts a low ridge (8050/1.2) and heads north, leaves open slopes sparsely dotted with chartreuse lichen-painted boulders and enters forested Cow Canyon. Midway up this canyon the PCT resumes on old trail, which it left in Beck Meadow, and

immediately crosses Cow Creek (8260/1.3) near a cluster of campsites.

The trail soon crosses the creek, but quickly returns and ascends a canyon where Kern ceanothus debuts. The path merges briefly with a stock driveway, crosses over the creek and back, and rejoins the multiple twining path of the driveway for a short stint. Where the creek turns east, almost one mile after the last junction, the PCT continues north and quickly reaches a trickle from a spring just above. After a short, winding ascent it joins the *Olancha Pass Trail* (8920/1.2). Vegetation coils about the spring immediately south of this junction.

Your route on the conjoined trail runs eastward, now on a gentle ascent around the head of Cow Canyon. Along the way it passes disturbed terrain on the canyon side created by stock drives, and then crosses Cow Creek again just 250 yards prior to the next trail junction (9090/0.5), where the PCT departs north. Hikers who choose to continue on the PCT, turn left here. See T106. Your route continues on the Olancha Pass Trail, which slants southeast, passes a lateral to the PCT (9220/0.4), then curves around the head of Summit Meadow. In 0.3 mile from the lateral, a packer's camp and corral, jocosely signed *Jawbone Inn and Resort,* sits to the left of the trail. A shortcut to the PCT originates here. Skirting Summit Meadow on a gentle incline, your route reaches Olancha Pass and a junction (9220/1.4) with the southbound Honey Bee Trail where you join the homebound route of T102.

Eastbound Olancha Pass Trail Log

T102	Honeybee Tr	9220	0.0
	stock driveway	8600	1.0
	stock driveway branch	6760	2.6
	trail divide	5960	1.0
	3-way road branch	5790	0.5

PCT & bridge, Monache Meadow

T76   Deer Mountain Circle Backpack

This loop trip in the South Sierra Wilderness explores a National Scenic Trail, a National Wild and Scenic River, an ancient Indian trail, and offers a climb of Deer Mountain with views of the largest meadow in the Sierra.

Distance   26.8 miles, semiloop trip
Steep Ascents   0.2 mile
Elevation Gain   3740 feet
Skills   Easy route finding; not recommended for equestrians
Seasons   Summer, fall
Maps   USGS 7.5 min *Crag Pk, Monache Mtn, Haiwee Pass*
Trailhead   45. See car tour T52.
Description   Bring a sturdy walking stick and an old pair of jogging shoes to use for the many river fords on this trip. The beginning of this journey is described in T75.

Northbound PCT Log

T75	Kennedy Mdws		
	Campground	6150	0.0
	trail fork	6240	1.1
	S.F. Kern River bridge	6300	0.8
	Crag Creek	6810	2.0
	Haiwee Tr	8060	3.6
	Beck Meadow Tr	7953	0.4
	Deer Mountain Ex	8390	2.2
	jeep rd	7940	1.0
	bridge #2	7820	0.4

This remote country would have been completely changed if money had been allocated to the State Division of Highways in 1965 for the planned trans-Sierra extension of Highway 190. The state highway would have bisected Monache Meadow, followed the east side of the South Fork Kern River, then exited via Haiwee Pass. The plan was shelved, and 19 years later this section was designated wilderness; in 1987 the South Fork Kern River was included in the National Wild and Scenic Rivers System.

On this loop you find no suitable route next to the water on the Deer Mountain side that would eliminate crossing the river. The Deer Mountain Trail crosses it 13 times in 2.4 miles, although some of the fords can be bypassed by climbing over bouldered ridges to the next piece of trail. It is dangerous to cross this river during snowmelt runoff as the normally placid creek-size South Fork becomes a torrent of fast-moving, turbulent water. Autumn is the ideal time for this trip, for it is then that the willows unfurl a ribbon of gold along the banks of the sinuous river, and the fords are an easy splash through the quiet water. Several camping possibilities exist along the banks.

After you cross the bridge turn right on ***Deer Mountain Trail 35E14*** (here signed *Wildrose Trail*) and hike southeast. Rambling along the dusty, shadeless trail, formally a m'cyclepath, the thought of splashing through the water seems appealing. In 0.9 mile you come to the first crossing, then in 0.1 miles cross back again, startling teeming schools of trout in the process. After walking along a wide, gravelly stretch by a canyon for 440 yards, you again ford and return in another 0.1 mile. Between the fifth and sixth fords, when you walk a brief 45 yards on the Deer Mountain side, watch for a beaver dam. Now you pass the yawning canyon of usually dry Summit Creek and one of the many abandoned jeep roads, and then make seven crossings, which, except between the eleventh and twelfth, are equidistant from one another.

After the thirteenth crossing—the last—your path forks (7740/3.3) on the west side of the water: you take the right fork. If not alert, now by habit you may head back on the lower path for another ford of the South Fork! The river is the boundary between Inyo and Sequoia national forests; your course is again on the Sequoia side where it will stay for the rest of the journey.

Hike directly south, ascending on the sunny slopes of Deer Mountain to a broad, prominent saddle (7900/0.6), which in autumn is clothed in blooms of rabbitbrush, adding to the panoply of golds. Next you descend gently along a ridge pass an obscure path to the left, and continue to the trail's end on Dutch John Flat at a forked junction with the Haiwee Trail (7630/0.7). This trail leads to a few oak-shaded campsites next to the river.

Now on *Haiwee Trail 37E01* your route on this ancient Indian path turns right to ascend a gulch west for 0.3 mile before crossing its usually dry creek. The trail ahead is in disrepair, sections may soon be relocated. After crossing the gulch, the trail, marked by sparse metal tree blazes, heads southeast on a nearly level plain, then curves southwest and climbs over blowdowns to a saddle between an extended south ridge of Deer Mountain and Point 8118. The destruction you see around you was caused by the Clover Meadow Burn observed earlier on this trip.

Upon reaching the saddle (7975/1.0) you turn right to zigzag up the ridge, west, then

northwest. Topping it amid granodiorite protrusions, you then descend to a broad valley where you skirt a gently inclined meadow, now among unburned trees. In time you pass through a stock-fence gate at a cow camp and pass through a second gate into a corral, then out, still walking along the meadow with craggy Deer Mountain to your right. (A realignment of the trail will probably be in the forest to the left of the meadow and corral.) After this effortless stroll to an elevation of 8620 feet, you make a bouldery, often steep descent to the *PCT* (8060/2.2) at the saddle junction you met earlier on your journey. (For information on the PCT and the Wild and Scenic river, see Chapter 1.) Here you turn left and retrace your steps southwest to the trip's beginning (6150/7.5).

Jim Jenkins portaging mileage wheel, Monache Meadow

T77   South Sierra Wilderness Backpack
With Excursion V: Crag Peak

This adventure mostly within the borders of the southernmost hinterland of South Sierra Wilderness, imparts the essence of this land set aside from man's encroachment: sagebrush, aspens, sand, meadows, seeps, river, flats, mountains. It also offers the option of a challenging peak climb en route. You can experience this trip as it is described or trimmed to fit a more confined schedule.

Distance   27.5 miles, loop trip
Steep Ascents   0.2 mile
Elevation Gain   2410 feet
Skills   Intermediate route finding
Seasons   Spring, summer, fall
Maps   USGS 7.5 min *Crag Pk, Long Cyn, Monache Mtn*
Trailhead   45. See car tour T52. (For shuttle trip, leave a car at **TH46**.)
Description   The beginning of this trip is described in T75.

Northbound PCT Log

T75	Kennedy Meadows		
	Campground	6150	0.0
	trail jct	6240	1.1
	S.F. Kern River bridge	6300	0.8
	Crag Creek	6810	2.0
	Haiwee Tr	8060	3.6
	Beck Meadow Tr	7953	0.4

After the junction at Beck Meadow, your route leaves the PCT on the left fork, ***Beck Meadow Trail 35E15,*** northwest. The path climbs gently through the brush of Beck Meadow to curve around the terminus of a ridge at the foot of Crag Peak. After an easy descent into a finger of Beck, the trail leads over a rock and wire causeway to the center of the finger meadow where the route turns abruptly right. The odd abruptness marks the former junction with a long vanished section of the Albanita Trail.

Barely over 0.1 mile north from that turn, you leave the Beck Meadow Trail at another sharp turn, this time left on ***Lost Meadow Trail 35E04*** (7875/0.8), which is sometimes obscure at this point. Cross west through brush to a lone blazed lodgepole just right of a brief canyon. You zigzag up in a deep, narrow groove; the route becomes increasingly discernible with numerous tree blazes. The grade eases a bit; you climb over a low ridge, then descend along the creek that drains Lost Meadow. You soon find Lost Meadow (8310/1.1), which spreads northwest and south. (If you take a side trip across the grass to the south edge of the northwest meadow arm, you will find a rock-lined spring near a stone fireplace at a camp once known as "Waterhole 3." It was whimsically named by cowhands or packers after a 1967 film that spoofed Westerns.)

Cross the creek to the east side of the linear meadow and hike south. Take any of the trails, but stay close to the pines until the meadow parts around an island of trees and boulders. Here you leave the pines at a blazed tree to cross to the west side of the island and walk across meadow toward the woods at its south end, heading a little left of the center. Your goal is a huge lodgepole which sports a sign *Lost Meadow* and a blaze. On well-defined trail you ascend on a gentle-to-moderate grade to top a broad saddle with an abandoned lateral to the Albanita Trail. Soon, having dropped a little, you arrive at Albanita Meadow close to where its drainage, a branch of Lost Creek, turns south. This is the origin of ***Albanita Trail 35E06*** (8620/2.0), on which you turn right. From here you can climb Crag Peak or skip the excursion and continue around Albanita Meadow.

Excursion V: Crag Peak

This breathtaking summit climb has a breathtaking, premier view of Monache Meadow and surrounding and distant peaks.

Distance   6.0 miles, round trip
Steep Ascents   0.6 mile
Elevation Gain   1185 feet
Skills   Intermediate route finding; Class 2–3 climbing (Class 4 & 5 pitches optional)
Map   USGS 7.5 min *Crag Pk*
Description   From the junction (8620/0.0), you follow Lost Creek *cross-country.* It turns southeast through a neck of woods to an extension of Albanita Meadow. Stay next to the creek until it reaches a confluence with a usually dry branch from a broad north gully (8460/0.6). Here you cross the creek and head southeast over a low saddle. If you are lucky you will find remnants of the old Albanita Trail to hike on, otherwise continue cross-country to the north edge of long, narrow Corral Meadow. Cross the meadow and ascend southeast to a saddle, gaining no more than 150 feet. Contour northeast, outflanking a Finger Rock ridge, to reach the prominent saddle between Finger Rock and Crag Peak (8580/1.4).

Now you climb steeply up west-facing slopes bristling with mountain mahogany, first east up a draw, then gradually northeast to a peak. Ascending from the east side, top the summit (9455/0.7) of this peak, named on the maps and the destination of this excursion. But according to the 7.5 minute topographic map, this is not the highest peak on the mountain. The Class 3+ granite fin on the ridge to the north is the true Crag Peak— of interest to the very skilled climber only.

To reach the fin, in 0.3 mile, you bushwhack to its base, skirt the fissured east face, where Class 4 and 5 routes may be found, then turn to ascend talus west, quickly gaining an arête north of the summit. Monache Meadow sprawls to the north, as seen from here. Below you—nearly straight below, several hundred feet down the west face—a talus slope ends at the wall. The arête directly to the south becomes an extremely hazardous knife edge, which you straddle and inch along to the other side before scrambling up the 9500-foot summit. To the west beckons Finger Rock offering its difficult, technical routes.

*   *   *   *   *

Hike northwest on well-defined but unmarked **Albanita Trail 35E06,** among lodgepole pines that edge the meadow. Then cross a north extension of Albanita Meadow, curve west to arrive at an acute junction with **Hooker Meadow Trail 35E05** (8700/0.7), on which you turn left. Heading directly south, you pass fenced Aqua Bonita Spring, a tree posted *Albanita Meadow* sign and enter the woods. Ignore the blaze on a tree at the

Beck and Monache meadows from Crag Peak

edge of the meadow: it marks an alternate route skirting Albanita Meadow. Your trail is vague for several yards, but you soon see sawed blowdowns, defining the path. After a brief walk over a gravelly flat, you descend to Hooker Meadow. The lodgepole pines that dominate the forest scheme give way to dense stands of quaking aspens; the finest stands of aspens on the Kern Plateau.

Make your way up one of the paths between the brook and the west edge of the meadow. Soon to the right you see a stately grove of aspens where a cowpoke's campsite is overgrown with aspen seedlings. Next you meet a tipsy directional sign (8320/1.9) on a mound of rocks, which signals a change of direction. Beyond the sign you curve south-southwest into the woods—look for blazes. Cross another stretch of meadow and return to the woods, where you exit from South Sierra Wilderness (8300/0.7).

Beyond the border, the trail briefly plunges down a steep slope, crosses a branch of Jackass Creek, then turns south to follow the creek on its west bank, past a stock-fence gate. It soon fords the creek and in less than 0.2 mile, just prior to a prominent east-bank cow path and flat with camping possibilities, it returns to the west side. (When the brook is running very full, you may need to make a few extra crossings.) Next the trail overlaps a retired logging road and exits across the stream bed at the Hooker Road cul-de-sac (7480/1.8). Those who chose the shorter 16.9 mile route end their journey here.

Beyond the cul-de-sac, you walk along Hooker Road, **SNF Road 21S29,** as it winds past scattered campsites, spur roads and a cattle pen with its chute, to a left turn on **Sherman Pass Road** (7470/1.9). Walk a short distance southeast on the highway, past Rodeo Flat, which has a Fire Safe Area for camping, to turn left on the paved road to Bitter Creek Trail (7310/1.2). This road leads to a quarry but is now used by highway maintenance crews. You pass a corral, then in 0.1 mile, spot your trail slanting eastward up the slope.

Ascend hoof-stippled **Bitter Creek Trail 34E03** (7350/0.2), which is used as a stock

driveway in July and September, then zigzag until you cross a low ridge where pines coalesce. The pines are joined by black oaks and junipers as you hike along gently rolling hills and over an open sandy patch. Soon you walk next to an area named *Tussack Bench,* where springs nourish tussock grass, a pleasant relief from xeric brush. For the next 1.5 miles you descend along the creek, discontinuously lined with willows, crossing it frequently. While on the north side, note a soda spring seep at a tell-tale iron-stained ring.

Leaving the creek, your path ascends moderately southeast, crosses a low, rounded ridge and descends among pinyon pines and rabbit brush, which in fall color the slopes gold. The path nears the highway almost to its shoulder, then leaves it, descends next to a fence just south of the South Sierra Wilderness border, and arrives at South Fork Kern River (5990/4.5).

After a refreshing pause at the river, walk to the highway, cross the river on the bridge and stroll less than 0.1 mile to a left turn onto the **PCT** (6020/0.4). Hike north on sandy turf among high-desert flora that include orange, silvery-leafed apricot mallows; long, narrow, lobed-leafed, yellow blazing stars; and very tiny dot-flowered sand mats. You undulate through washes and cross several dirt roads that head west to sunny riverside campsites, fishing and swimming holes. Occasional junipers, then pinyons, offer bits of shade as you pass fences first on your right and then on your left, and pass through two gates. While enticing murmurs of the river increase, you reach and then round above the melodic South Fork. Gradually you approach the north end of vast, sagebrush-covered Kennedy Meadows, embraced by the gentle peaks of the semi-arid side of the Kern Plateau. Soon the river curves by the campground access road, forcing you to cross the road (6080/1.8) and proceed along higher ground for a short time before you recross it at the campground (6120/0.4). Next bisect Kennedy Meadows Campground to your car at the end of your circle journey (6150/0.2).

T78   Aspens of Hooker Meadow Day Hike

This trek leads to the finest, most stately groves of quaking aspen trees on the Kern Plateau. Beautiful in all seasons, quaking aspens reign majestically in autumn when their leaves become a palette of golden yellows.

Distance   5.8 miles, round trip
Steep Ascents   None
Elevation Gain   860 feet
Skills   Easy route finding; easy hiking
Seasons   Spring, summer, fall
Map   USGS 7.5 min *Crag Pk*
Trailhead   46. See car tour T52.
Description   This short jaunt overlaps a section of T77, but in reverse. Your trek begins at the cul-de-sac of the stockmen's road (7480/0.0) off Sherman Pass Road, on **Hooker Trail 35E05.** Heading northeast, the route crosses a branch of Jackass Creek and follows it in its narrow canyon, first on trail, then on a retired logging road, past creek-bed springs and shaded by a conifer forest. During snowmelt the path crosses the creek a few extra times, otherwise it stays on the west bank until it fords the creek near bushy willows. At this ford note the cow path along the creek's east side; the cow path is sometimes mistaken for your return route. The trail soon returns to the west bank, passes through a stock-fence gate, then turns in an easterly direction to traverse a meadow vale. Here it passes above a spring's gouge at the head of this creek.

Leaving the branch of Jackass Creek, you ascend east on moderate-to-steep wooded slopes to enter South Sierra Wilderness at its western border (8300/1.8). Then leave the woods to cross a finger of Hooker Meadow and return to the trees before again emerging onto the grassland of Hooker Meadow. Hooker, a 19th century settler, legally took this plot of land for himself on a claim that it was only a swamp, which was probably true. An old directional sign (8320/0.7) sits askew in a pile of rocks, an important landmark for your return trip. Now you turn north to follow the meadow fringe, and in a short time, you see the flutter of aspen leaves in the groves around the meadow. The stately stand to your left (8340/0.4) conceals a long aban-

doned cowpoke's camp, overgrown by numerous aspen seedlings.

Aspen trees line the north end of Hooker Meadow, as well. These smooth, greenish-white barked trees have toothed leaves—round at the base, pointed at the tip—that attach to their branches by exceedingly thin, flat stems (petioles), so that the leaves quiver in the slightest breeze. In spring they are a bright yellow-green, and in autumn turn a mellow golden yellow, best when viewed in the backlight of a low sun. Spread your ground cover and linger while the greens and golds of the leaves, the blue of the sky and the white of the drifting clouds weave you into their tapestry.

Aspens

T79   Fish Creek Day Hike

Fish Creek meanders through a medley of meadows, forests and boulder canyons, then makes a rush to the South Fork Kern River. This easy hike fords the winding creek 25 times—assuring wet feet for all. You can take this trip as described or leave your shuttle car at a half way point.

Distance   7.8 miles, shuttle trip
Steep Ascents   None
Elevation Gain   1240 feet
Skills   Easy route finding; easy hiking
Seasons   Spring, summer, fall
Maps   USGS 7.5 min *Crag Pk, Bonita Mdws (briefly), Monache Mtn (briefly), Casa Vieja Mdws*
Trailhead   47 & 76. This trip requires two cars. See car tour T80. Leave the first car at **TH76,** the end of the trip at the Blackrock Campground. Then see car tour T52. Drive the second car to the beginning of the trip at **TH47.** This is 9.7 miles from the first car. For the shorter trip see car tour T80, Monache Jeep Road.
Description   From the short spur road alongside Troy Meadow, off Sherman Pass Road, next to the former location of Kennedy Meadows Pack Station, *Pack Station Trail 35E07* (7740/0.0) takes you directly north-west, while Fish Creek wanders about to your right. The trail momentarily leaves the sedges and grasses to run over sandy slopes and ravines with ubiquitous lupines. Freshets funneled off the road cause not only these ravines but dump silt into the creek as well, destroying valuable trout-spawning beds. Add cattle and people to the scene and the toll is great on the fishery. In an effort to catch the silt and halt the creek's erosion, volunteers from Trout Unlimited placed filter traps, log guards and rocks along a portion of its bed and banks.

The path veers north, passing an old sign at the east end of Beach Ridge Stock Trail 34E21 (7760/0.7). It then leaves verdant Troy Meadow to enter a lodgepole pine forest, where several large campsites lie near a sometimes dry tributary, then fords sinuous Fish Creek eight times in 0.6 mile. In the following 0.2 mile your trail crosses meadow terrain, returns to forest and enters a little canyon beside the willow-jacketed creek. After two more fords of the creek and beyond a campsite in a grove to the right, the trail passes a junction (7825/1.4) with an abandoned eastbound lateral.

Now your trail, renamed *Fish Creek Trail 34E33,* continues north, ascending and sometimes undulating. It enters a stock-fence gate, fords the creek twice, passes a campsite, fords thrice more, then breaks into the lengthy glade of Smith Meadow. On occasion, you can observe the path's own contribution to the silting of Fish Creek; stay on the path to prevent damage to surrounding meadows.

Your trail traverses mid-meadow with views of Smith Mountain to the east, crosses Fish Creek again, then passes a pocket of trees before reentering woods. Ascending somewhat, it soon passes a road to Smith Meadows Cow Camp then dips to ford a tributary bringing its seasonal contribution to Fish Creek from the west. Shortly to the right of the trail sits the rusted hulk of a pickup; above the clunker Grainite Knob looms distant to the meadow plain. Albanita M'cycle-path 35E06 (8070/2.7) briefly coincides with your path until it reaches an east-west dirt road where it leaves it. Beyond the road, your northbound flora-encroached path is sandwiched between SNF Road 20S37 and the creek. The path crosses the paved road (8140/0.3) near a *sharp curve* road sign. For the short version of the trip, which is 5.1 miles to this point, retrieve your shuttle car here.

Now the path, renamed *Smith Meadow Trail 34E06,* immediately enters into the high grasses and multiple mix of wildflowers north of the road. Cattle seem to miss tromping and chewing some meadow pockets here and the flowers bloom profusely well into mid-summer. A few tree blazes show the way first to the more open area, then to a crossing of Fish Creek 0.4 mile from the road. Look for the wildflower monkshood along the next section of creek. Monkshood like larkspur, is blue, grows tall and has broad multi-lobed, toothed leaves; but it has a "hood" and no "spur," and is infrequently seen on the Southern Sierra's east side.

You soon enter a tight canyon with granite rock slides, known locally as Rocky Canyon, and hop the creek three more times to encounter a logging road (8540/0.9) next to a large campsite. Do not cross the makeshift log bridge: walk north on the road for 50 yards, then pickup the trail through meadow. Cross Fish Creek, now often dry, four times before leaving the meadow gardens. Nearing the end of your trip, now in forest heavily logged to the wilderness border, you cross Black Rock Mountain M'cyclepath 34E26, a trail built to loop motorcycles away from wilderness. Cross the creek bed and several logging roads, turn left near the entry of Golden Trout Wilderness (8980/1.7) and walk southwest to Blackrock over-night camping facilities and corrals, and your shuttle car (8960/0.1).

T80 Blackrock Car & Bicycle Tour on the Kern Plateau
(With Directions to Trailheads 72–76)

The ribbon of pavement on which this tour travels, curves through a flower-speckled, selectively-logged forest to the edge of Golden Trout Wilderness and a walk-in campground for hikers and equestrians.

Distance   8.1 miles, one way
Steep Ascents   None
Elevation Gain   930 feet
Skills   Easy route finding; paved road
Seasons   Spring, summer, fall
Map   Tulare County road map
Tourhead   48. From Sherman Pass Road at a 4-way junction, turn north onto Blackrock Road, SNF Road 21S03, at **TH48.** This is 36.9 miles west of Highway 395 where Sherman Pass Road is called Nine Mile Canyon Road and 31.6 miles east of MTN 99 Road, next to the Kern River. Blackrock Road departs from car tour T52.
Description   From the 4-way junction (8030/0.0/0.0), you head north on paved **Blackrock Road, SNF Road 21S03,** and immediately arrive at Sequoia National Forest Blackrock Work Center and Information Station (0.1/0.1). See Chapter 4 for services and hours. Riding up a gentle incline past clumps of snow bush and manzanita, and through a coniferous woodland, you pass spur roads and cross over two culverts for ephemeral branches of Fish Creek to reach the fork of paved Monache Jeep Road, SNF Road 21S36 (3.4/3.5). Here you can take a scenic side tour, which leads to **TH72 & TH73** for peak climbs, or skip the following description and continue on Blackrock Road.

Those taking this side trip, turn right on **SNF Road 21S36 Monache Jeep Road** (0.0/0.0), descend on slopes high above Smith Meadows with vignettes through forest to the east of Smith Mountain. Next, cross Fish Creek and the half-way point of T79 next to the creek (1.6/1.6). Curve around the northern lobe of Powell Meadow where there are campsites and piped spring water from a water tank, then continue on to a junction (2.0/3.6) where the road to Monache Meadow loses its pavement and forks left. Brief sections of that 4WD dirt road are very rough.

Beyond the fork, still on paved **SNF Road 21S36,** pass Granite/Broder Trail 35E02, cross a meadow, then pass to the right of prominent Granite Knob, and, immediately afterwards, your road forks left (1.5/5.1). Park on the right side of the dirt road alongside a driveway to a meadowside campsite at **TH72** (0.1/5.2) for T81, Granite Knob Climb. Continue on the same road to the cul-de-sac (0.5/5.7) for Jackass and Smith mountain climbs at **TH73**. The logging road goes beyond the cul-de-sac, and, if open and in good condition, you can drive on it to the saddle to start T82 & T83 from there.

On Blackrock Road, head generally north, where to your right, bits of Smith Meadows can be seen snuggled against the flanks of Smith Mountain and Granite Knob. Smith Mountain and Smith Meadows were named for a family who, generations later, still owns Smith Meadows and continues to graze cattle hereabouts. In the fragrant pine and fir forest, you approach a left road fork (2.2/5.7). Those seeking Osa Meadows and **TH74** and **TH75** of T84–T86 turn here. Everyone else skip the following description and continue north.

To reach Osa Meadows, another jewel in Kern Plateau's brooch, turn left on *SNF Road 20S25* (0.0/0.0), a maintained dirt road. Then descend northwest past numerous spur roads and trail crossings to a Fire Safe Area in the pines at **TH74** (3.0/3.0), east of Osa Meadows for T84 and T85. For the Manzanita Knob Hike, T86, stay on the same road, ascend to a switchback, then curve north to a saddle where the road ends in a cul-de-sac at **TH75** (0.9/3.9) and the Golden Trout Wilderness border.

On Blackrock Road, curve to the east while crossing over the culvert of a seasonal brook that flows southeast to Fish Creek. Buttercups and cinquefoils nod in a meadow to the northwest, bisected by the brook. Within minutes you curve around a ridge, and then straighten out on a north-trending track. One mile beyond the Osa Meadows junction, you pass SNF Road 21S03J, which leads to Kennedy Meadows Pack Station.

The road soon dips a little while approaching the base of Fish Creek's gully, passing Blackrock Mountain Trail, built for motorcyclists in the late 1980s to replace trails closed to them by wilderness legislation. Then quickly arrive at road's end (8960/2.4/8.1) **TH76** and an overnight campground built in 1987 for Golden Trout Wilderness adventurers. For equestrians, there are eight flats with grills, each with a corral, on the east side; and for hikers, there are eight flats with grills on the west side. Ample parking exists on both sides except on holidays when streams of parked cars line the road. Trips T87–T90 in Golden Trout Wilderness begin here.

Shadows

T81   Granite Knob Climb

The south end of this curtain of granite appears to have resisted the elements more than the rest of the knob, which has talus flanks. The final ascents of this knob and its neighbors, Jackass Peak and Smith Mountain, challenge you and reward you with views of the central Kern Plateau.

Distance   1.6 miles, round trip
Steep Ascents   0.1 mile
Elevation Gain   640 feet
Skills   Intermediate route finding; Class 2 climbing
Seasons   Spring, summer, fall
Map   USGS 7.5 min *Monache Mtn*
Trailhead   72. See car tour T80.
Description   Two routes ascend a gentle ravine through the forest southeast of Granite Knob. You can follow pieces of an abandoned logging road which begins at the road fork; or you can zigzag among the trees following the first gulch crossed via a culvert

after the road fork. Leaving SNF Road 21S36 (8420/0.0) on a *cross-country* hike, ascend the ravine northeast toward the saddle between Granite Knob and Peak 9021. After 0.5 mile, before reaching the saddle, veer left to climb west up the steep flank of the knob. Heavy growth of Kern ceanothus, manzanita, chinquapin and snow brush among the boulders slows your progress as you pick your way to the north summit block. Here you ascend one of the fractured granite chutes that lead to the top of Granite Knob (9060/0.8), which offers views of its plateau domain.

T82   Jackass Peak Climb

In addition to the satisfaction of achieving this mountain's short but demanding final ascent, you attain views of the Southern Sierra's largest meadow, Monache Meadow, and tallest mountain, Olancha Peak, and close-at-hand landscapes of South Sierra Wilderness.

Distance   2.0 miles, round trip
Steep Ascents   0.1 mile
Elevation Gain   750 feet
Skills   Intermediate route finding; Class 2– 3 climbing
Seasons   Spring, summer, fall
Map   USGS 7.5 min *Monache Mtn*
Trailhead   73. See car tour T80.
Description   Hike southeast on the logging *road* extending beyond the cul-de-sac of SNF Road 21S36 (8540/0.0). In minutes it rounds a bend; your unmarked, abandoned *trail* (8570/0.2), which looks more like a drainage crease than a path, crosses the road at a culvert. Turn left onto it and continue generally southeast. Curve around a minimeadow and oozing spring, then climb over a low, rounded ridge. Before this trail was closed, weekend motorcyclists used it as a speedway. You may still taste their dust as

you approach a junction (8780/0.4). Turn left here on *Jackass Peak M'cyclepath 35E03.* (If you missed the abandoned trail at the beginning, stay on the road until you reach a saddle and Albanita M'cyclepath 35E06, then turn left on it to the Jackass Peak junction.)

After a brief walk north on 35E03, before it begins to descend, leave it (8820/0.1) to climb east, *cross-country,* up the gentle, then steep slopes of Jackass Peak. You ascend through Kern ceanothus, then chinquapin bushes and boulders, and upon approaching the summit block, turn for a brief run south to outflank the summit's sheer granite walls. Climb over talus, spiraling first east and then north up a chute to the summit (9287/0.3).

T83   Smith Mountain Climb

Located in the center of the Kern Plateau, this mountain offers unobstructed views in all directions of the plateau and beyond. Even if you do not climb the final ascent, an easy hike to the base of the summit block reveals impressive views.

Distance   2.8 miles, round trip
Steep Ascents   0.1 mile
Elevation Gain   995 feet
Skills   Intermediate route finding, Class 2 climbing
Seasons   Spring, summer, fall
Map   USGS 7.5 min *Monache Mtn*
Trailhead   73. See car tour T80.
Description   This trip, along with the Jackass Peak climb, begins southeast at the *road* extension beyond the cul-de-sac of SNF Road 21S36 (8540/0.0). Continue on the road past the abandoned trail where Jackass Peak climbers turn left (8570/0.2), and hike up an easy grade to a broad saddle. Here you turn right on *Albanita M'cyclepath 35E06* (8700/0.4), for a few minutes' walk southwest to the prominent ridge extending northeast from Smith Mountain summit. Leaving the trail (8720/0.1), you climb *cross-country* up the ridge among red firs and western white pines. In a short while you confront an impressive granite monolith, which you pass to its left to reach a broad, manzanita-patched saddle. Continue south, climb to the left of the next outcrop, a pile of boulders, then, from the east side, make the

final ascent up the view-commanding summit block (9533/0.7).

Granite monolith, Smith Mountain

T84   Osa & Beach Meadows Loop Day Hike

This easy though lengthy hike makes an ideal day trip from a campsite at Osa or Beach meadows. It skirts three velvety meadows circled by pines and follows a tranquil brook.

Distance   9.8 miles, loop trip
Steep Ascents   0.1 mile
Elevation Gain   1095 feet
Skills   Easy route finding; easy–moderate hiking
Seasons   Spring, summer, fall
Map   USGS 7.5 min *Casa Vieja Mdws*
Trailhead   74. See car tour T80. (If you begin this trip from Beach Meadows, see car

tour T52 for **TH49**.)
Description   This journey begins on *Little Horse M'cyclepath 34E02* (8520/0.0), across an Osa Creek tributary above the meadow's southeast lobe by the road on which you arrived. Heading in a westerly direction, your path arcs alongside the meadow, passes a campsite, travels alongside of an often dry tributary, then crosses it.

Next the path climbs a gentle grade southwest, nears a logging road and passes one of its spurs on a saddle (8540/0.9).

Ahead lies a bowl shorn of its trees by a burn and subsequent salvage cut—an eerie scene. There is no tree regrowth in the basin, but the planted seedlings on the surrounding slopes have weathered well. Trod through the bowl and again cross a spur road (8500/0.9), then follow near it over a low saddle. Descending south on an easy grade, you travel on or next to a logging road. Here and there are natural groves of numerous lodgepole and red fir seedlings reaching for sunlight; the sunlight that amply bathes Little Horse Meadows. In the meadow, a tree blaze indicates that the old trail crossed the dense grasses some years back. A trench containing Little Horse Meadows' stream, bisecting the meadow, has numerous rock and screen weirs along its path. These were built to catch sediment, thereby reducing the depth of the trench in hopes of spreading and keeping the water throughout the meadow.

After hiking along the fringe of Little Horse Meadows, you stroll over two low ridges, the second with impressive boulders,

then descend south into drier climes, crossing another spur road and the Beach Meadows Road to Lion Meadows (7740/ 2.9). Now heading north between Beach Meadows Road and Beach Creek, you meet the Beach Trail (7770/0.1), on which you will continue north after visiting Beach Meadows.

Turning right onto **Beach M'cyclepath 34E01,** dip to cross Beach Creek, ascend slightly to meet the end of Bonita Flat Trail 34E04 (7770/0.1) from the south, curve to the terminus of Albanita M'cyclepath 35E06 (7770/0.1) from the northwest and descend to privately owned Beach Meadows (7730/ 0.1). Another in a string of early century guard stations used by rangers on patrol, the Beach Meadows cabin sits like a patriach at the head of his meadow. It is still used by the Forest Service. These stations may one day be recognized in the National Register of Historic Places.

Returning on the loop hike, **Beach M'cyclepath 34E01** leads you pass the Little Horse Trail junction (7730/0.3), were you are joined by backpackers on T85. The route travels north sandwiched between the road to Lion Meadows and Beach Creek, then

A-tramplin' & a-chewin' along Beach Creek

crosses that road (7825/0.3) near an immense culvert, built to accommodate this slender creek during its greatest snowmelt swell. The trail continues a constant gentle-to-moderate ascent up the narrow canyon of Beach Creek, graced by abundant wildflowers and grassy banks. The way is shaded by white firs and Jeffrey pines, later by lodgepole pines, then red firs; all hanging their lacy needle awnings over the path.

Your trail crosses the creek from Little Horse Meadows where it joins Beach Creek, then makes several crossings of Beach Creek and meanders into a meadowy patch. Here the trail crosses the meadow's drainage over

a rock and wire fortification, levels where trees lie asunder, and again crosses a rock and wire causeway.

Soon you walk around the head of a meadow, Beach Creek's origin, and ascend rather steeply to cross the spur road to Little Horse Meadows (8725/3.2). A descent ensues over trucked-in sand, which quickly gives way to the loose, dusty dirt so common on motorcycle paths. After a brief climb over a ridgelet, you join the Osa Meadows Road (8628/0.7) for a short way, leave it, then cross it again where Osa Meadows and Little Horse Trail (8520/0.2) come into view at the end of your adventure.

T85   Jordan Hot Springs-Kern Flat Backpack

This expansive loop trip travels through both Golden Trout Wilderness and multi-use Forest Service land. The route skirts a medley of grassy meadows, follows numerous brooks, and passes an historic hot springs while descending the Kern Plateau slopes. The trail wanders along an extensive stretch of raucous North Fork Kern River, then climbs back to the ruffling meadows of the plateau. The plant zones vary, the scenery changes dramatically and the pleasure received equals the abundant energy expended.

Distance   28.8 miles, loop trip
Steep Ascents   0.6 miles
Elevation Gain   4385 feet
Skills   Easy-intermediate route finding
Seasons   Spring, summer, fall (Wilderness permit required)
Maps   USGS 7.5 min *Casa Vieja Mdws, Hockett Pk (briefly), Bonita Mdws*
Trailhead   74. See car tour T80.
Description   South of the campsites in the Fire Safe Area at Osa Meadows, your trail, *Beach Trail 34E01* (8510/0.0), climbs an easy grade east near the left bank of Osa Creek. In 0.1 mile your route passes an abandoned southbound path, then meets southbound Blackrock Mountain M'cyclepath 34E26 (8600/0.3), a trail built in the late 1980s to loop motorcycles away from the wilderness.

Your trail, the left fork, 34E01, curves around a glade with flourishes of corn lilies, passes over an intermittent creek on a log causeway, fords Osa Creek, and almost immediately intersects a logging road. This

road, reactivated in the late 1980s, has many new spurs to accommodate the ongoing logging that reaches to the edge of the wilderness. Zigzagging among huge red fir stumps, the trail again crosses a road, then tops a broad saddle and enters Golden Trout Wilderness and Inyo National Forest (9115/1.3). The differences between wilderness and multiuse land use is strickingly apparent.

Your route now descends on the *Casa Vieja Trail*—the same trail with a new name. Soon it levels around a meadow and passes a large campsite. Thereafter its descent increases beside another ephemeral brook, levels and passes a campsite to the left just before joining the path from Blackrock Gap (8335/1.3). The junction is indicated by a small sign; the trail disappears here in the hard pack. Now at Casa Vieja Meadows the route joins T87.

Northbound Blackrock Trail Log

T87 Casa Vieja Tr	8335	0.0
Jordan Hot Springs/		
River Spring trs	8300	0.1

Westbound Jordan Hot Springs Trail Log

Blackrock/River

Spring trs	8300	0.0
Hot Springs lateral	6370	3.0

You can visit the springs and wander about on any of the paths; however, the main trail arcs around the north edge of the Jordan Hot Springs area. From the Hot Springs lateral to the cabins, you turn sharply right to pass behind Shorty's cabin. Next cross Ninemile Creek after which you turn abruptly northwest, ford Redrock Creek, then meet the Indian Head Trail (6600/0.5), where you join the route of T89.

Westbound Jordan Hot Springs Trail Log

T89	Indian Head Tr	6600	0.0
	Sidehill Mdw Tr	6060	2.3
	Hells Hole Tr	5430	1.3

From the junction with Hells Hole Trail, *Lion Trail 33E21*, the left fork, gently ascends southwest among mature incense cedars to a broad saddle. You can recognize incense cedars by their fragrant wood, the shreddy texture of their bark, and their fondlike sprays of flat needles, pointed at the tips. These trees are sometimes mistaken for redwoods, none of which grow east of Kern River. Signs here incorrectly identify the division between Inyo and Sequoia national forests (the correct border, according to the topo map, is 0.1 mile north of the junction). The trail descends sharply near a crease, then switchbacks south to an unmarked junction with a 0.4 mile path up-river to Painter Camp (5260/0.3) (See T89 for its history).

You tramp south, inland from the constant hum of the Kern River, and with only snippets of it to view. In a little over a half mile, ford the shaded branchlets of the creek from Manzanita Canyon, briefly zigzag down to step across a sliver of another creek, then climb over a saddle. South of the saddle's ridge, near a campsite and away from your path, stacked boulders create a bit of a tunnel, beyond which your trail nears the river. Along the banks, often opposite granite cliffs across the river, a succession of coarse sand flats offer good campsites.

Another brief ascent passes a path (5040/2.2) to a footbridge: the third bridge span-

ning the North Fork Kern River south from its headwaters at the Kings-Kern Divide. After a step-across ford of Grouse Canyon's creek and a climb over a ridgelet, you find the ruins of a crashed aircraft, 0.3 mile from the footbridge junction. The seven cylinder rotary engine, cockpit and other parts are scattered on either side of the trail. The craft was heading for an airstrip that was in place on grassy Kern Flat across the river.

The trail winds alongside the river, then over a sandy plain with numerous downed trees. It dips and climbs, passes riverside campsites, at length crosses Osa Creek (5010/2.3), then arrives at a juntion with Sacratone Flat Trail 33E19 (4995/0.1). At this point your route, Lion Trail 33E21, coincides with that of T92, then with T84 where you will find the descriptions for the rest of your odyssey.

Southeastbound 33E21 Log

T92	Sacratone Flat Tr		
	33E19	4995	0.0
	Soda Creek	5390	1.2
	first road crossing	7760	4.2
	third road crossing	8150	0.7
	forth road crossing	8070	0.5
	Bonita Flat Tr 34E04	7760	1.4
	Beach Tr 34E01	7770	0.9
	Beach Mdws	7730	0.2

Northbound 34E01 Log

T84	Beach Mdws	7730	0.0
	Little Horse M'cyc		
	34E02	7730	0.3
	road to Lion Mdws	7825	0.3
	road to Little Horse		
	Mdws	8725	3.2
	Osa Mdws Rd	8628	0.7
	Osa Mdws	8520	0.2

Plane wreckage

T86   Manzanita Knob Day Hike

This easy outing for a family offers a leisurely hike to isolated Manzanita Knob with sights of distant, massive mountains contrasted to close-at-hand delicate tree seedlings.

Distance   3.0 miles, round trip
Steep Ascents   None
Elevation Gain   505 feet
Skills   Easy route finding; easy hiking
Seasons   Spring, summer, fall
Map   USGS 7.5 min *Casa Vieja Mdws*
Trailhead   75. See car tour T80.
Description   The route to the summit of Manzanita Knob follows retired roads on a north-trending ridge within Inyo National Forest and Golden Trout Wilderness. To begin, pass the barrier at the north end of the cul-de-sac (8820/0.0), enter the wilderness and walk generally north on the retired logging **road** along the eastern slopes of the ridge. The logged forest is struggling to reestablish itself: the fragile seedlings on the roadbed are slowly erasing man's use. The desire for an easily identifiable border between wilderness and multiuse land resulted in the unusual inclusion of this logged area into wilderness.

Soon Kern Peak appears to the north, with the bald crown of Indian Head next to Redrock Meadow below it; then "Miss" Olancha debuts to the east. In just over a half mile, you descend on a right fork. Continue straight ahead where another road forks left. Both left forks lead to cul-de-sacs. Then you turn left around a fallen tree, climb to the ridgecrest and travel north along the crest. Here you venture off the road momentarily to scan the west for views of The Needles, the Western Divide, Kern River Canyon and beyond to Farewell Gap and the Little Kern drainage. You soon reach the pile of boulders among manzanita bushes that is the summit of aptly-named Manzanita Knob (9121/1.5). If you wish to sign the register tablet, you will find it in a jar under stacked rocks. The views of Kern Peak and Indian Head from here are framed by boughs of red firs and western white pines.

North Fork Kern near Osa Creek

T87   Jordan Hot Springs Backpack

An abundance of wildflowers scattered along a chortling creek and in the emerald meadows that gently slope from the hot springs and former resort, add to the beauty of this trip's historical route and destination.

Distance   10.6 miles, round trip
Steep Ascents   None
Elevation Gain   2640 feet
Skills   Easy route finding
Seasons   Spring, summer, fall (Wilderness permit required)
Map   USGS 7.5 min *Casa Vieja Mdws*
Trailhead   76. See car tour T80.
Description   From the north end of the parking lot at the terminus of Blackrock Road (8920/0.0), the wide *path* commences northeast, meets the end of Smith Meadow Trail 34E06 (8980/0.1), then enters Golden Trout Wilderness and Inyo National Forest at Blackrock Gap.

Beyond the gap, the ***Blackrock Trail*** descends gently amid the pleasant ambiance of lodgepole pines and stately red firs past what local packers called "Linnie's Meadow." On a short causeway, it fords the meadow's often dry stream and resumes its descent near it. In time the trail passes a west side meadow, swings northwest, again across the stream, then along the wooded hem of vast, vivid, spring-green Casa Vieja Meadows. This expanse of grass is untouched by sagebrush, the bane of so many Southern Sierra meadows. The meadow's vibrant health may be partially due to the log weirs emplaced in the late 1940s along Ninemile Creek, which spread water through the grassland.

With a string of campsites and a log cabin used by snow surveyors to the left and the meadow with its fence to the right, you pass the T junction (8335/2.0) of Casa Vieja Trail. Its path southwest is undefined here: only a tree-posted *Osa Meadows* sign indicates the trail junction where T85 joins your route. In minutes you ford Ninemile Creek and turn left (8300/0.1) onto ***Jordan Hot Springs Trail*** at its junction with River Spring Trail.

This trail, Jordan Hot Springs and Jordan Peak commemorate John Jordan, who in 1861 received permission to build a toll road

across the Sierra to link the rich gold and silver mines of Owens Valley to San Joaquin Valley. The Jordan Hot Springs Trail of today is on or close to a segment of that trans-Sierran trail blazed by John and his sons. The actual blaze was a tree slash 8 inches wide and 14 inches long. In 1862, John Jordan lost his life attempting to raft across the swollen Kern River. He had filed the trail's readiness for pack stock with Inyo County and was returning to notify the Tulare County Supervisors. The blazed route received occasional use, but interest in it as a toll road diminished after the road from San Joaquin Valley to Owens Valley via Walker Pass opened in 1864.

Jordan Hot Springs Trail veers northwest on a gentle grade quickly replaced by a knee-shocking descent; the jolting relieved by two pairs of short switchbacks. Indian paintbrush, mountain bluebells, shooting stars—at least a dozen other wildflowers—and the melodious creek closely flank the trail. After a ford of cobbly Ninemile Creek, the descending trail passes above a winsome campsite, then opposite a talus slope of broken granite and down two more sets of switchbacks to a second ford.

The path, soon muddied by springs, one of which pours from a mossy boulder nook, passes a small flat above Long Canyon Creek suitable for camping and drops to cross that creek above its confluence with Ninemile Creek. A log jam aids your ford. The trail turns west alongside alder-shaded Ninemile Creek, passes another campsite and again fords the creek, this time where it curves north against a ridge. Conifers continue to shelter the trail as its grade and that of the nearby slopes becomes gentle. Your route leaves the Jordan Hot Springs Trail at a junction (6370/3.0) with a lateral to the former resort. The lateral takes you under a welcoming wood-framed entry and over a meadow to the resort grounds (6400/0.1).

Concessionaires have leased this land from the Forest Service and have operated the resort—a lodge/restaurant, several cabins and enclosed hot tubs—with few nods to modern technology since the days the Jordan route was blazed. When Golden Trout Wilderness was established by Congress in 1978, Jordan Hot Springs was included. Following the policy of the Wilderness Act, the Forest Service closed the resort when the lease expired in November, 1990. The cabins, several of which have been declared historically significant, are privately owned.

Plans for the area include creating an open, more natural hot pool where the present bath houses stand.

The Jordan Hot Springs Trail continues right at the junction with the lateral. It passes behind Shorty's cabin, crosses Ninemile Creek and curves around the Jordan Hot Springs area where there are several campsites concealed within the edge of the forest north of the meadow. Shorty, a prolific cabin builder in the late 1800s, built well-constructed huts, but people of large frame felt unwelcomed as the doorways were designed for Shorty's five-foot stature.

Old bath houses, Jordan Hot Springs

T88   Redrock Meadows Backpack
With Excursion W: Indian Head

Indian Head, the copper-toned monolith, reaches above an evergreen forest to cast its presence at the foot of creek-laced Redrock Meadows. The route to this ideal retreat passes intriguing River Spring.

Distance   17.2 miles, round trip
Steep Ascents   None
Elevation Gain   1140 feet
Skills   Easy route finding
Seasons   Spring, summer, fall (Wilderness permit required)

Maps   USGS 7.5 min *Casa Vieja Mdws, Kern Pk*
Trailhead   76. See car tour T80.
Description   The beginning of this trip is described in T87.

Northbound Blackrock Trail Log

T87	parking lot	8920	0.0
	Smith Meadow Tr	8980	0.1
	Casa Vieja Tr	8335	2.0
	Jordan Hot Springs/		
	River Spring trs	8300	0.1

Northeast of Jordan Hot Springs junction, your trail, now *River Spring Trail,* immediately passes a large campsite with log benches tucked in the fringe of the forest and a junction (8330/0.1) with the eastbound Jordan Trail, a segment of the trans-Sierra route blazed over 100 years ago. If funds permit, a summer ranger headquarters in the vintage cabin 0.2 mile east on the Jordan Trail.

Slowly gaining elevation, your path stays just inside the lodgepole woods from a panhandle of the meadow, tops a low saddle, and in 1.7 miles crosses Lost Trout Creek on a log causeway. Several large campsites are snuggled among the boulders and trees nearby; other camping possibilities are plentiful along this route. Beyond several broad saddles, your trail dips to cross the first of two eastbound forks of Long Canyon Trail (8480/2.4) and fords Long Canyon Creek. After skirting a meadow to the east, the trail passes the second of the two forks to Long Canyon (8640/0.4).

Now your undulating northwestbound trail passes Beer Keg Meadow, crosses the lesser and main branches of Long Stringer with their hanging meadows and corn lilies, the plump stemmed, ever-present meadow plants that resemble cornstalks. The shoots of this plant are poisonous to livestock if ingested. They have learned to avoid it. This selective grazing may explain the plant's abundance, perhaps at the expense of more appetizing cattle tidbits. In 0.7 mile after the stringer, the trail reaches River Spring (8635/2.1). Here a spring bursts so boisterously from beneath the trail that it looks as if it is exiting from a culvert.

Passing less dramatic springs, you shortly get your first glimpse of rust-colored Indian Head, named for the Indian Head penny. After you ford the east branch of Redrock Creek, an even more striking view of the monolith appears, with vividly colorful lower Redrock Meadows in the foreground. Ideal campsites abound between the forks of the creek and around the two roofless cabins built in 1916: the first as a cow camp, the second, a hunter's cabin. The trail junction here at the first cabin (8650/1.4) is the cog of many trips: hikers on T89 continue straight ahead onto Indian Head Trail, those on T115 arrive from the Cold Meadows Trail, while others on T90 turn east onto the Templeton Trail. This meadow is the destination of this trip. Experienced climbers may wish to try the following excursion.

Excursion W: Indian Head

This metamorphic monolith, the color of a tarnished penny, is miles distant from other rocks of its kind. The Head presents many challenging technical routes for rock climbers.

Distance   1.7 miles, round trip
Steep Ascents   0.1 mile
Elevation Gain   350 feet
Skills   Easy route finding; Class 3 climbing (Class 4 & 5 routes optional)
Map   USGS 7.5 min *Kern Pk*
Description   The route is straight ahead from the junction (8650/0.0), now on *Indian Head Trail.* You hike west of the first cabin, ford the next branch of Redrock Creek and continue left where the Cold Meadows Trail (8670/0.1) forks right. You then head west to ford another fork of the creek, cross a meadow to the trees at your left and climb to a saddle at the nape of Indian Head (8860/0.6). Here you leave the path to contour *cross-country* to a chinquapin-choked chute on the south face, then turn north. The route inclines steeply, first up through the brush and then through a talus-bound tunnel. Soon, upon reaching the crest, you turn east and in just a few steps top the summit (9000/0.15).

T89   Three Waterfalls Backpack

With three spectacular waterfalls, Casa Vieja and Redrock meadows, Jordan Hot Springs and the Kern River, this trip in the Golden Trout Wilderness ranks among the most attractive outings in the eastern Southern Sierra.

Distance   30.2 miles, semiloop trip
Steep Ascents   0.4 mile
Elevation Gain   5170 feet
Skills   Easy route finding
Seasons   Spring, summer, fall (Wilderness permit required)
Maps   USGS 7.5 min *Casa Vieja Mdws, Kern Pk*
Trailhead   76. See car tour T80.
Description   The beginning of this trip is described in T87 & T88.

Northbound Blackrock Trail Log

T87 parking lot	8920	0.0
Smith Meadow Tr	8980	0.1
Casa Vieja Tr	8335	2.0
Jordan Hot Springs/ River Spring trs	8300	0.1

Northbound River Spring Trail Log

T88 Jordan Hot Springs/ Blackrock trs	8300	0.0
Jordan Tr	8330	0.1
1st fork of Long Canyon Tr	8480	2.4
2nd fork of Long Canyon Tr	8640	0.4
River Spring	8635	2.1
Templeton/ Indian Head trs	8650	1.4

Westbound Indian Head Trail Log

Ex W Templeton/ River Spring trs	8650	0.0
Cold Mdws Tr	8670	0.1
Indian Head saddle	8860	0.6

Beyond Indian Head saddle, the path plunges down the canyon slopes to the creek on wide switchbacks. Near the tumbling creek, leaves of aspens, a tree uncommon on the Kern Plateau, flutter in the slightest breeze. The trail crosses to the east bank of the creek; in ½ mile it returns to the west bank, then crosses a side brooklet adorned with mountain bluebells. The sound of the 30-foot waterfall fills the air long before it comes into view. An ensuing pair of switch-backs drops the trail to a creekside campsite and a use trail back to the churning, cascading falls.

In less than a mile beyond the falls, you leave the splender of the creek and its can-yon, and eventually meet and take *Jordan Hot Springs Trail* (6600/3.6), which here arcs around the meadowland of Jordan Hot Springs. Many campsites dot the slopes and numerous paths lead to the historic site. (See T87.)

To continue, find your trail on the north side of Ninemile Creek, climb a bluff and stay high above the stream while heading west. In time you pass a northbound trail to Sidehill Meadow (6060/2.3), then zigzag widely on a descent toward a Ninemile Creek ford where alders curtain the banks near a campsite.

Across the creek, the path curves south, then west around the fenced, privately owned cabins and meadow at Soda Flat, then passes through a stock-fence gate, and drops moder-ately via switchbacks. In 0.3 mile beyond the switchbacks, it meets an often obscure but important junction with Lion Trail 33E21 (5430/1.3). Here your route forks right on *Hells Hole Trail,* north of Peak 5637, passes through a stock-fence gate, and in less than 0.2 mile recrosses Ninemile Creek and reenters Inyo National Forest. (If you do not cross the creek and instead begin a series of tight zigzags down a moderate slope, you have missed the junction and have joined T85's route southwest to Kern Flats.)

The path rises a tad and descends west from the ford, and in around 0.1 mile nears the howling 80-foot falls where Ninemile Creek plummets into the depth of a shadowy granite chasm. The path descends out of earshot of this spell-binding treasure, and branches northwest where a lateral (5210/ 0.5) splits off toward Painter Camp near the Ninemile Creek/Kern River confluence. These cabins, which were built by J. A.

Painter in the first decades of the 1900s, have been declared a state historical monument and are in the process of being restored. Painter had his own saw mill on site while building the structures. He also constructed a rock flume with a waterwheel to power a generator that supplied electricity for the camp. Since Painter's death, several generations of a Porterville family (not related to Painter) have leased the camp from the Forest Service. The lease has expired and campers are allowed to use the open facilities and its corral—with care.

Beyond the camp lateral, your route climbs steeply via numerous zigzags to top a promontory with car- and cabin-size boulders (5640/0.4). This ascent may be too steep for some horses. The trail levels, then begins a northwest descent. Just before returning to the river, a short lateral (5360/0.2) leads to the slabs overlooking the only recognized "falls" along the length of the Kern River. The crashing water, really a magnified cascade, billows against granite slabs and sprays in dazzling, prismatic colors.

The path from the falls to the Cedars of Hells Hole Camp undulates gently over and down riverside terraces offering tempting campsites, but the most desirable campsite lies just ahead at Hells Hole, at the end of the trail (5420/1.1). This idyllic campsite, the antithesis of its "Hells Hole" name, is located on a large flat area shaded by alders and incense cedars in a hide-away nook next to the rumbling river, a small sandy beach, a backdrop slope of lacy ferns, and a refreshing stream. You may have to share it: occasionally packers bring parties of fishermen here.

When homeward bound, return to Jordan Hot Springs and the Indian Head Trail junction (6600/5.8) the way you came, then continue on Jordan Hot Springs Trail past Shorty's cabin southeast of the meadow, to the Hot Springs lateral (6370/0.5). Beyond the lateral, you pass through a stock-fence gate, climb up along Ninemile Creek, which you cross in 0.6 mile; then in another 0.8 mile, you ford Long Canyon Creek. Ford Ninemile Creek twice more on a moderate-to-steep ascent relieved occasionally by sets of short switchbacks, pass a few campsites, then reach a junction (8300/3.0) with ***Blackrock Trail***. Here, you again retrace your incoming route to the end of this hike (8960/2.2).

Falls on Ninemile Creek

T90   Kern Peak via Redrock Meadows Backpack

Kern Peak, one of the tallest on the Kern Plateau, rises 11,510 feet. This trip through scenic Golden Trout Wilderness, approaches the peak from its south side, which is forested and relatively smooth, in provocative contrast to its bare, precipitous east and northwest faces.

Distance   30.2 miles, semiloop trip
Steep Ascents   0.1 mile
Elevation Gain   5510 feet
Skills   Intermediate route finding; Class 2 climbing
Seasons   Spring, summer, fall (Wilderness permit required)
Maps   USGS 7.5 min *Casa Vieja Mdws, Kern Pk, Templeton Mtn, Monache Mtn*
Trailhead   76. See car tour T80.
Description   The beginning of this trip is described in T87 & T88.

Northbound Blackrock Trail Log

T87	parking lot	8920	0.0
	Smith Mdw Tr	8980	0.1
	Casa Vieja Tr	8335	2.0
	Jordan Hot Springs/		
	River Spring trs	8300	0.1

Northbound River Spring Trail Log

T88	Jordan Hot Springs/		
	Blackrock trs	8300	0.0
	Jordan Tr	8330	0.1
	1st fork of Long		
	Canyon Tr	8480	2.4
	2nd fork of Long		
	Canyon Tr	8640	0.4
	River Spring	8635	2.1
	Templeton/		
	Indian Head trs	8650	1.4

Your route on the ***Templeton Trail*** turns east (right) by the south side of a roofless cabin, passing several campsites sprawled on the flats beneath the needled boughs of the pine forest. The trail immediately angles off to the right before it reaches a second roofless cabin, then takes you east along the meadow's edge. The trail enters a dense stand of lodgepole pines, traverses a grassy meadow's length north-northeast to a blazed tree where it reenters forest, then crosses a spring-fed branch of Redrock Creek, 0.9 mile beyond the River Spring Trail junction. This is the last dependable source of water until

Templeton Cow Camp. Now your path climbs up a steepening ridge and at length reaches a broad, forested saddle (10,260/ 2.6) astride the crest of the Toowa Range.

Stash your packs on this saddle, which provides vast room for dry camping, then turn northwest, ***cross-country,*** to climb Kern Peak. The ascent is gentle-to-moderate the first ½ mile whereupon you reach a lengthy ridge plateau. When you see Kern Peak through a forest gap: turn sharply left; mark this point for the return trip; and note the Toowa range configuration southeast of the saddle.

Strolling west now, your route soon takes you over a talus rise, then levels again while curving southward, where it reaches the boulder moraine of Kern's east-facing, glacial-carved cirque. A cliff to your left curtails the cirque, most of which lies to your right. The route ascends steeply 200 feet up the bouldered headwall to the crest where the cirque and cliff meet. Beyond this obstacle, the route easily climbs the crest north-northwest to Kern Peak, offering increasingly expansive views that climax at the summit (11,510/2.1). A platform and a toppled shingled roof are among the remains of a lookout that once capped this marvelous peak.

To continue your trip, return to the saddle (10,260/2.1) where you left your pack, turn left onto the ***Templeton Trail*** and descend northeast on a zigzagging path, which runs across east-facing slopes toward, then onto, an incipient ridge. On this slight ridge at an easily missed point, 0.6 mile from the saddle, you turn briefly south, drop off the ridge, then skirt a ravine that declines northeast from the saddle. The descent eases at a glade, and a short time after that you pass the compound comprising Templeton Cow Camp. Just beyond the camp are two easily missed junctions: a blazed but unmapped cut-off to the Ramshaw Trail forks left opposite the grassy fenced meadow; a second cut-off trail continues ahead where the Templeton Trail forks left, 18 feet before the fence turns an oblique angle. You take the second *cut-off* trail (8800/2.1), compacted by cow camp users. The little used Templeton Trail from here to the 3-posted junction in sagebrushy Templeton Meadow is vague. The cut-off path follows the fence west then into a side meadow, crossing often dry Strawberry Creek. Here the five-finger leafed, yellow, five-petal flowered slender cinquefoils bloom vigorously in spring.

Near Templeton Mountain, no signs remain of an airstrip once frequented by light planes, bold but dwarfed against the hulking mass of the conical mountain. You soon join the **Ramshaw Trail** (8660/0.7). Now walking directly southeast toward the distant bulk of 12,123-foot Olancha Peak, the highest peak on the pleateau, watch for the junction with **Long Canyon Trail** (8615/0.5), which you find on the inside edge of a dense stand of lodgepoles. Traveling south now on Long Canyon Trail, past old campsites hidden among the trees, you ford a spring-fed brook, then cross slender Fat Cow Meadow. After a brief 80-foot climb to a low saddle and junction (8740/1.0), you continue on your trail to the right; Bakeoven Trail descends straight ahead.

Your shaded path climbs a gentle grade soon by the upper tip of Schaeffer Meadow, then crosses both its creek, and in 0.9 mile later, Schaeffer Stringer, which, although spring-fed, is often dry by early summer. Beyond the stringer, the trail climbs moderately to a Toowa Range saddle (9460/2.0), where western white pines join the forest, and fleshy, red, plump snow plants, up to 18 inches in height, poke through the soil. This plant does not make its own chlorophyll, but lives on decayed organic matter—one of nature's sanitary agents. Although considered rare, this protected plant is frequently seen in the Southern Sierra.

You descend on a route that is mostly downhill from now to Casa Vieja Meadows.

This path was one in a system of trails used for the first temporary PCT; a PCT shield remains on the lodgepole to the right. Suddenly out of the forest, you walk across a gritty, inhospitable plain once dubbed "Dancha Desert," where few plants survive. You may find spunky mat lupines, a few grass tuffs and pussy paws. The white-pink flower balls of pussy paws spread out symmetrically from a basal rosette of spoon-shaped leaves. Leaving that desolation behind, evening primroses appear and Clarks Nutcrackers caw at you from their perches on foxtail pine branches. You quickly approach the upper reaches of the grassy meadows of Long Canyon, then ford a spring-fed tributary to Long Canyon Creek.

Across the narrow meadow, hidden among the trees, sits an auxiliary lodge for guests of long defunct Monache Meadow Lodge. You pass to the right of fence poles marking the boundary of this private property and curve to meet its entry path. Here on a two-foot post a "Trail" sign directs northbound hikers around the private area (8880/2.0).

Cross a bog and pass to the right of a tree with a large slash of a sheepherder's carving: a cross on top, letters in the slash and a saw-toothed lower border. You drop to the meadow's edge then fork right on the upper path easing away from the meadow. In a short time Long Canyon Trail splits with paths on either side of Long Canyon Creek: both head west to River Spring Trail. You cross the creek at the northwest corner of Long Canyon

Remains of lookout tower, Kern Peak

Meadow by a post with signs (8580/1.1) and hike south now on *Lost Trout Trail*.

Curve to the right of another private sector with a log house (under construction at this writing) to a signed pole just inside the meadow's western edge and cut along the expanse to walk next to the woods. Now you follow one of the multiple paths to join a jeep road, on which you ascend to a low saddle (8760/0.6). The road climbs over a ridge to Big Dry Meadow, turns at a junction then returns to your trail, but you leave the road at the saddle, locate the trail to the right and de-

scend southwest across a small meadow, then on to cross Dry Meadow and its Lost Trout Creek. Look for the poles with "Trail" signs at the entrance and exit of the meadow.

Follow the defined trail through the woods, where it meets a junction (8700/1.6) with the jeep road from Big Dry Meadow. A short descent takes you to the Jordan Trail junction (8430/0.5), then down to the USFS cabin, Casa Vieja Meadows and west across the meadow to *River Spring Trail* (8330/0.4), where you finish your loop. Now retrace your incoming route to your car (8920/2.3).

T91   Bonita Burn Backpack

This unusual nature hike encompasses flora and fauna in a new ecosystem: regrowth after the 1977 lightning-caused Bonita Fire. Not all of the area surrounding this loop was burned—you can enjoy grassy meadows and glens, streams and forested flats and wide open views of the large Rattlesnake Creek drainage bowl.

Distance   11.7 miles, loop trip
Steep Ascents   0.2 mile
Elevation Gain   1885 feet
Skills   Easy route finding
Seasons   Spring, summer, fall
Maps   USGS 7.5 min *Casa Vieja Mdws, Bonita Mdws*
Trailhead   49. See car tour T52.
Description   This hike begins to the west of the buildings at Beach Meadows. There has been some restructuring of the trail system here to exclude motorcycles from Beach Meadows in favor of horse travel. Hiking west along the fence on *Beach Trail 34E01* (7730/0.0), you immediately meet a junction with the west end of Albanita M'cyclepath 35E06, where you turn left (7770/0.1). Quickly, 34E01 forks right (7770/0.1), but you continue through the fork on *Bonita Flat Trail 34E04* to veer southwest around the head of Beach Meadows. The trail passes two closed branches of Little Horse M'cyclepath flanking Beach Creek, which you cross. An orange and black metal sign posted directly to the north, high upon a lodgepole pine, guides snow surveyors. This is one of several meadows where the Forest Service conducts

winter surveys to determine the amount of snow and its water content.

Stay on your trail as two paths fork left, then walk by a "Trail" sign on a post in the center of a barren, sandy slope. Cross a Beach Meadows access road and skirt northwest around a meadow lobe, past a closed trail, following helpful "Trail" signs. Turning southwest you meet Lion Trail 33E21 (7760/0.9). Still on 34E04, you are suddenly out of the mature pine and fir forest and into the exposed northern fringe of the Bonita Burn. The seedlings you see were planted by the Forest Service after burned trees were removed. Two tenths of a mile after a cabin access road, you encounter a helpful landmark in a maze of paths, a sign post with two "Trail" signs on it. Here you turn 90° right and hike southwest into forest. In less than another 0.2 mile, you cross a logger's road (7740/0.7).

Now gaining appreciable elevation for the first time on this hike, your route tops a ridge where manzanita has returned, but not the scattered pines that once dotted the slopes. The trail descends gently then plummets: the steep grade relieved by a long switchback constructed in the 1980s. After another switchback the trail leads to an incense cedar- and pine-sheltered campsite alongside a branch of Beach Creek, and 200 yards later, it crosses the creek (6900/1.4). Below the crossing a colony of cone flowers flourishes on the moist banks. These large, yellow-petaled flowers have unusual protruding, conical, brown-to-purple centers. The deep gashes on the fire-burned slopes, hereabout, were caused by the lack of ground cover and the slopes inability to retain moisture. The resulting runoff carries soil to the flowers but silts the creek.

Near the confluence of Beach Creek and the tributary by which you have descended, you see a flat crisscrossed with logs surrounded by burned snags. In 1980 you could find a cabin's foundation here and a rock-lined grave marked by a make-shift cross—now silted over or washed away. In about ½ mile from the confluence, ford alder-lined Beach Creek (6400/1.1). Even in fall, enough water flows here to sound a throaty lisp. Continue west on the south bank, beneath boughs of incense cedars, to pass through a stock-fence gate. You quickly recross Beach Creek near a packer's campsite spread on the north bank. Now saunter across Bonita Flat, where a forest thrives despite evidence of burn on the trunks of some trees. Gradually turning southwest, you dip into Lion Creek's wild rose gully and several other gullies before reaching a junction with *Rattlesnake M'cyclepath 33E22* (6125/1.2), where Bonita Flat Trail ends and travelers on T92 turn right.

You, however, turn left on 33E22 to boulder hop Beach Creek near a large campsite. After a gentle ½ mile ascent southeast along Rattlesnake Creek, you leave tree cover to climb amid a regrowth of black oaks. A pair of switchbacks, which do not appear on the topo map, carries you above the creek on a long traverse were drought-tolerant pinyon pines join the vegetation. Descend gradually to follow the curve of a broad, grassy canyon, again in woods, then climb over a ridge densely covered with Kern ceanothus. Descending again, you near a

branch of Rattlesnake Creek, and reach an obscure junction with *Bear Trap Trail 34E23* (6600/2.4), marked by an upslope, tree-posted "Trail" sign. Take the left fork, 34E23, northeast. If you cross the creek, you missed the junction.

The well-blazed trail climbs within sight of the Rattlesnake Creek branch for 1.5 miles, passing through brush regrowth before it enters a pocket of unburned trees. A steep ascent up an exposed ridge ends at a logging road and a saddle (7820/2.2). Here again the Forest Service planted seedlings after the burned trees were salvaged for timber. Beyond the saddle, the trail descends to join *Beach Trail 34E01* (7740/0.2).

Out of the burned area now, hike north catching vignettes of vast Beach Meadows, and pass the old Beach Trail and a packer's campsite. Walk past a road to a meadow cabin, hop over a spring's outlet stream and continue beyond a junction (7720/0.5) with Beach Ridge Horse Trail 34E21. Then you cross the meadow near a snow survey gage and a pair of signs and reenter forest. In a short time you reach the historic Beach Meadows cabins where the loop trip and exploration of the Bonita Burn ends (7730/0.9).

Cone flowers

T92　Kern River/Osa Creek Confluence Backpack

This rigorous trip enters a stretch of the North Fork Kern River in Golden Trout Wilderness that can only be reached by foot or hoof. The route follows creeks with hidden campsites, touches meadows and passes through two major burns.

Distance　22.2 miles, semiloop trip
Steep Ascents　0.6 mile
Elevation Gain　4220 feet
Skills　Easy-intermediate route finding
Seasons　Spring, summer, fall (Wilderness permit required)
Maps　USGS 7.5 min *Casa Vieja Mdws, Bonita Mdws, Durrwood Crk, Hockett Pk (briefly)*
Trailhead　49. See car tour T52.
Description　The beginning of this trip is described in T91.

Westbound 34E01 Log

T91　parking lot	7730	0.0
Albanita M'cyc 35E06	7770	0.1
Bonita Flat Tr 34E04	7770	0.1

Southwestbound 34E04 Log

Beach Mdws Tr 34E01	7770	0.0
Lion Tr 33E21	7760	0.9
logger's road	7740	0.7
Beach Cr branch crossing	6900	1.4
Beach Cr crossing #1	6400	1.1
Rattlesnake M'cyc 33E22	6125	1.2

Turn west on ***Rattlesnake M'cyclepath 33E22,*** the only motorcycle trail used on this trip, and follow it through a boulder-strewn flood plain, then under shade of unburned Jeffrey pines and incense cedars past a campsite. You will find several camping opportunities along this length of Rattlesnake Creek.

Within the next 0.7 mile, the trail and the creek intertwine, and you come to the first of its six crossings. The second and third can be avoided by a short, simple scramble along the southwest bank, but the following three require a boulder hop, a wade or a log crossing. Beyond the last ford you edge inland to hike on open, dry, brushy slopes, then, suddenly, on a patchwork of grassy slopes where numerous springs surface. The next patch of grass spreads below the trail, while above, sits a broken-down hut. Soon, to the

left and below, boulders surround flats, and the creek slides over slick slabs into refreshing alder-lined pools. This setting offers the best campsites along the way.

Moving on, you cross a junction (5380/3.3) with long abandoned Old Sheep Driveway, which climbs steeply up the ridge, ending north of Stony Meadow. You continue on 33E22, dip across two large dry washes, then reach a junction (5200/1.0) where you take the right fork onto ***Sacratone Flat Trail 33E19.***

Money has been allocated to reroute this trail; however, at this time the steep, eroded path heads north up a narrow canyon, past a couple of springs (one with a nearby cattle trough) to a saddle (5900/1.3). After passing through a stock-fence gate, it drops steeply, still among brush and open forest, which pinyon pines have joined, to broad, grassy Sacratone Flat. Profuse cedar seedlings decorate the entry here into the Golden Trout Wilderness (5550/0.5). After a slight

Beach Meadows, snow survey pole

climb the trail drops steeply, switches northeast and back, then crosses Soda Creek (5020/0.8). North of the creek, a flat of crisscrossed downed trees confronts you, the result of the 1975 Flat Fire started by a campfire. Near this devastation, the Sacratone Trail ends, and *Lion Trail 33E21* (4995/0.3) leads you to the Kern River/Osa Creek confluence (4960/0.2) and several campsites, the destination of this trip. The Lion Trail follows the river north to Jordan Hot Springs Trail near Ninemile Creek. Osa in Spanish means "female bear," and some mighty big bears have been seen in this area. Be sure to hang your food properly.

Your return begins at the Lion/Sacratone Flat trails junction (4995/0.2) where T85 joins the route. Although the trail has been improved, you still have a taxing 3000 foot-elevation gain to reach the plateau. You may wish to camp near the Soda Creek crossing, then beat the heat with an early start the next morning.

Progressing southeast on *Lion Trail 33E21,* you again hike through the destruction caused by the Flat Fire, which burned both sides of Kern Canyon, then, left of Soda Creek, climb up a gentle-to-moderate, sometimes steep ascent. Springs to the right of the path precede your ford of the creek above its confluence with a stream from Lion Meadow. Attractive, tree-shaded camping possibilities along the cascading creek occur from these springs to Soda Creek crossing (5390/1.2). Now hiking on a section of trail built in the 1980s (the new alignment is not shown on the topo map), you leave Golden Trout Wilderness, ascend southeast high above Soda Creek's south branch and stroll in a brushy area burned in the 1977 Bonita Fire. At length a fortified switchback returns you around the nose of Point 7489, where you join the former trail. You curve around a crease, abruptly turn left to cross a ridge and soon meet the extension of the road from Beach Meadows (7760/4.2).

Flat of downed trees

The path resumes across the road—the first of eight road crossings and the first of five that cross the road from Beach Meadows—and follows below the road's curve above Lion Meadows for 0.4 mile, where it again crosses the road to climb south of a spring and its well-watered flora. Of these, senecio's flat-topped, terminal, yellow clusters reach nearly 5 feet. The path parallels the road past a road gate and a cul-de-sac, formally the end of the road, then crosses it (8150/0.7).

Still on Lion Trail 33E21, climb east to a saddle, then descend among slopes of lupine to cross the road for the fourth time (8070/0.5). Next, climb around a ridgelet, cross the same road for the last time, cross three spur roads through logged burn and finally descend, still east-southeast, to meet the junction (7760/1.4) with *Bonita Flat Trail 34E04.* Now you turn left to retrace your steps to Beach Meadows (7730/1.1).

T93   Lookout & Schaeffer Mountains Climb

Schaeffer and Lookout mountains, both on one extended ridge, make easy trophies for peakbaggers climbing scenic heights in the Southern Sierra.

Distance   4.8 miles, round trip
Steep Ascents   0.3 mile
Elevation Gain   1605 feet
Skills   Intermediate route finding; Class 2 climbing
Seasons   Spring, summer, fall
Maps   USGS 7.5 min *Bonita Mdws, Durrwood Crk*
Trailhead   52. See car tour T52. Turn north on *SNF Road 22S41* (0.0/0.0), pass a Fire Safe Area at Bonita Meadow. (The old Forest Service patrol cabin is somewhat obscure across the grassy plain.) Turn left at the junction (2.3/2.3) with SNF Road 21S57. Continue on SNF Road 22S41 until T junction (1.5/3.8). Turn right onto *SNF Road 21S46.* Stay on this road to its cul-de-sac (0.8/4.6) at **TH52,** to the right of Danner Meadow.
Description   From the cul-de-sac (8820/ 0.0), step over the road barrier to follow the *road* for 0.2 mile around the head of cattleman-commemorating Danner Meadow, a private inholding amid public land. Locate the ducked *use trail* that climbs west up the moderate-to-steep slope. If you do not see it, ascend cross-country to the south (left) of a small ravine. In 0.4 mile the grade momentarily eases as you reach a south ridge. Now bend northwest, your direction for the rest of the hike, to follow this major ridge. The boulder and chinquapin summit of unpertentious Lookout Mountain (9722/0.8)

is soon reached and worth a pause. Despite scattered pines, the gunsight of Farewell Gap is visible on the distant northwest horizon and Sherman Peak rises directly south. When chinquapin appears in the Southern Sierra, it indicates an elevation of at least 8000 feet. This evergreen bush with yellowish gray-green leaves and spiny burs that house bitter tasting, though edible nuts, grows under open forest on dry, rocky slopes.

Descending along the ridge on a *cross-country* route sometimes marked by ducks, you dodge to the right of ridgeline outcrops and boulder hills often mistaken for Schaeffer's peak, to reach a saddle (9180/ 1.1). Next you scramble up and over a prominent jumble of boulders also mistaken for the peak, then, 0.1 mile beyond, gain the modest summit of Schaeffer Mountain (9340/0.5). You can record your ascent by signing the register in a can located in an obvious man-made cairn. As with most of Southern Sierra place names, this one belonged to a stockman, a sheepherder of the 19th century. (Coincidentally, "shepherd" in German is "Schäfer.") The sprawling mountain's impressively sheer and convoluted west face is 0.4 mile north of the summit. There emerald Stony Meadow nestles near the foot of its talus, and you have great views of The Needles, Dome Rock and Kern River Canyon.

T94   Durrwood Creek to Sherman Peak Backpack

A relaxed stroll under a canopy of pine boughs, through pockets of quaking aspens, alongside brooks and meadows, marks the initial leg of this journey. A summit visit to one of the highest mountains on the southern Kern Plateau, caps the return trip.

Distance   14.2 miles, loop trip
Steep Ascents   0.3 mile
Elevation Gain   2865 feet
Skills   Easy route finding; Class 1 climbing
Seasons   Spring, summer, fall
Maps   USGS 7.5 min *Sirretta Pk, Bonita Mdws, Durrwood Cr*
Trailhead   53. See car tour T52.
Description   The music of this trip can best be heard on weekdays when motorcyclists are few, or during Stage II fire restrictions when they are forbidden on trails. This trek commences on **Sherman Pass M'cyclepath 34E09,** a few steps north of the viewpoint parking lot off the paved road (9140/0.0). You descend from the highway moderately-to-steeply through a forest of red fir and western white pine, cross a logger's road and its spur, then step over a miniscule Trout Creek tributary draining a minor meadow. After rambling over a low ridge, cross another branch of the creek at a junction (8250/1.7), where you turn sharply right. In minutes you cross Trout Creek itself at a junction (8245/0.1) with **Trout Creek M'cyclepath 33E28,** which you take northwest, this time making a sharp turn left. Ascending on the dusty trail to the right of the creek, you quickly meet Sherman Pass Road (8300/0.2).

North of the road, shaded by lodgepole pines, your path ascends easily along Trout Creek, its banks flecked with corn lilies and lupines. You may notice tree blazes near remnants of trail which cross a meadow. The old route was redesigned to reduce damage to the delicate grasses and now stays to the right of the creek and meadow. Your path traverses a bit of another meadow and fords a side creek over a culvert, then shortly turns left to dip into the usually dry upper reaches of Trout Creek. A dense lodgepole forest crowds your path, and aspen trees make a shimmering debut. Your trail then crosses a dirt road, ascends a modest grade, levels in a glade, then climbs moderately to arrive at a watershed divide with a traversing logging road (8780/1.5).

A short descent, still northwest, brings you to Corral Meadow where a pitched, corrugated roof covers an open structured cow camp, and a sign prohibits pasturing horses. Traveling near the fence beyond the cow camp, you shortly saunter over a causeway protecting an aspen-fringed lobe of the meadow. In the center of Corral Meadow, a silvery, sinuous creek begins its journey to the North Fork Kern River, and you hike along in the woods near it, sometimes walking over additional lobes, cattle cropped like mowed lawn. You soon confront another sign, this one yellow and black nailed to a lodgepole. It shouts *Attention!* then assures you of six months in prison and or $250.00 fine if you harm survey markers! Regaining composure, you eventually join **Schaeffer M'cyclepth 33E24** (8510/1.1) at the north tip of Corral Meadow, near camping possibilities.

Now on 33E24, continue to follow the Corral Meadow branch of Durrwood Creek. You cross a sometimes dry tributary next to which Schaeffer Trail arrived, and pass above a couple of springs. Turning southwest, a long descent leads you to a junction with North Meadow Pass 33E27 (8110/1.2), at the confluence of Durrwood Creek and the Corral Meadow branch. You will return to this junction with its few small creekside campsites. You continue to descend on 33E24, now along Durrwood Creek. Historian Bob Powers notes that this misspelled place-name records the fleeting presence of Billy Durwood, foreman of the A. Brown Ranch in 1879.

The path remains well-defined even through grassy stretches. Listen to the lulling rush of the wind in the pines and the dulcet tones of the creek as you watch for a sprinkling of aspen trees to your right by a gully. They mark the turnoff to your destination campsite. Cross the gully, then leave the trail (7860/1.2), which goes northward crossing a sagebrush flat as it proceeds to Stony Meadow. You follow the stream bed southwest, *cross-country,* to Durrwood Creek, which you ford on a loosely laid log bridge. You now arrive at once signed, *Scotch Whiskey Camp,* established sometime before 1939, according to the oldest date found near a fire ring. A stone and mortar stove, a flat rock counter and several log stumps make this a comfortable camp. The fall camper, however, may hope the resident bear has dinner elsewhere, for in autumn the camp's surrounding current bushes produce red ripe berries, one of bruin's favorite foods. Before breaking camp, hike along the creek for 0.2 mile to view the aspen-clad bowl where Durrwood Creek plunges off the plateau.

On the homeward leg, return to *North Meadow Pass M'cyclepath 33E27* junction (8110/1.2). Now on 33E27, you step across the Corral Meadow tributary then boulder hop Durrwood Creek, after which you turn right and head southwest up the canyon of another tributary. Hike first on the creek's left side, then the right where the trail steepens, leave the creek, swing around a pint-sized meadow, pass several campsites

and ascend to a ridge top. A 4×4 road drops southeast of this ridge to the watershed divide above Corral Meadow where you crossed it earlier. Your route, however, turns right (look for a tree blaze), ascends south on trail then joins the 4×4 to a saddle with campsites and a 4-way road junction (9055/1.8): your road/trail; two roads from the southeast; and one heading up the flank of Sherman Peak onto which you turn left. Ascend southeast on the *4WD road* past a pair of switchbacks, curve east to another road fork (9415/0.8). Again take the left fork to continue your ascent to Sherman Peak (9909/0.9).

This peak once had a fire lookout. Now a radio relay with assorted antennae tops the peak. After signing the register tablet to be found in a can, scan the horizon for extensive views in all directions.

For the last of your journey, return to the road, walk east past two hairpin curves to a trail (9820/0.2) marked by a duck. Here you take *Sherman Peak Trail 33E35* down eight zigzags to old signs on a post (9490/0.5) standing lonely on a saddle. With its message no longer legible and the cross trail it marked no longer apparent, it still serves as a landmark for peak climbers. Beyond the post, you easily climb a knoll, drop to its southwest side, cross to the northeast side of two peaks, and southwest of another one, then descend to the paved road and your waiting car (9140/1.8).

T95   Sherman Peak Day Hike

The whole family can enjoy the hike to the summit of this mountain. At 9900 feet, it qualifies as a major peak, but the ascent is gradual or helped by switchbacks. The views you will capture atop include Split Mountain, Dome Rock, and the High Sierra, aloof and supreme.

Distance   5.0 miles, round trip
Steep Ascents   None
Elevation Gain   1170 feet
Skills   Easy route finding; easy hiking; Class 1 climbing
Seasons   Spring, summer, fall
Maps   USGS 7.5 min *Sirretta, Bonita Mdws (0.1 mile), Durrwood Cr*

Trailhead   53. See car tour T52.
Description   Your outing begins across the highway from the viewpoint loop at Sherman Pass (9140/0.0). *Sherman Peak Trail 33E35* gently undulates, first west, then mostly on a northwest course through a forest of red firs, foxtails and western white pines. It takes you left of a peak, then right of several,

then left of the last intervening peak, crossing wide flats in between. This gentle terrain lends itself wonderfully to cross-country skiing; however, it is earmarked as a possible site for an alpine ski development.

Sherman Peak is hidden from view until you return to the west side of the elongated ridge on which you have been climbing since the start. The radio relay tower and various antennae on top identify your destination. On the last broad saddle, you pass a post with a couple of weathered, old signs, hardly legible, but remain as part of the plateau's nostalgic past (9490/1.8).

Eight zigzags lead up a moderate grade to the north side of the peak where you meet a **4×4 road** (9820/0.5), on which you ascend via two hairpin curves amid sunlit chinquapin to the top. Stroll past the relay outpost and lookout ruins to the highest jumble of rocks, the summit of Sherman Peak (9909/0.2).

Weathered signs

T96   Backpack to the Forks of the Kern via the Kern Canyon Fault

This trek follows a straightaway, roller coaster segment of the Kern Canyon Fault. Along the way you can bathe in refreshing pools formed by cascading Durrwood Creek, fish at the confluence of Little Kern and North Fork Kern rivers in the Golden Trout Wilderness, and, if you have a trained eye, observe rock deformations of the fault zone. This hike is especially accommodating to groups seeking commodious campsites and a challenging but manageable route.

Distance   22.6 miles, round trip
Steep Ascents   0.5 mile
Elevation Gain   4765 feet
Skills   Easy route finding
Seasons   Fall, winter, spring (Wilderness permit required)
Maps   USGS 7.5 min *Fairview, Durrwood Crk, Hockett Pk (briefly)*
Trailhead   55. See car tour T52.
Description   From the parking lot (4840/0.0) off Sherman Pass Road, you commence north along the short earthen **road** next to a cattle pen, then pass through a stock-fence gate where the road joins **North Rincon M'cyclepath 33E23** (4890/0.1), which began at the paved highway. Shortly after

crossing through a road gate, the path, also a stock driveway, ascends a moderate grade that is rockiest where it winds among steep-gouged ravines from the east. To the west, exposed bands of limestone are visible until the trail tops the first saddle (5500/1.0) of this trip. The saddles along the length of this trail were formed by the grinding and subsequent decomposition of the ridges by the movement of the ancient fault, which runs in a straight north-south line from Kings-Kern Divide to Lake Isabella. Some geologists extend it to Arvin in the San Joaquin Valley, including Breckenridge and White Wolf faults. From this saddle you can see The Needles to the north-northwest, and with binoculars, you can identify the Lookout tower on the westernmost needle. (See this book's companion volume for The Needles trip.)

Descending from the saddle, the trail passes a spring supplying water to a plastic tub used as a cattle trough. Soon chaparral gives way to a mixed forest of oaks, firs and pines as the trail crosses a steep east-facing slope, then switchbacks before arriving at the boulder-strewn meeting of several canyons. At this juncture your trail passes Kern River Trail 33E30 (4700/1.3), and those on T97 leave to descend the west canyon. The creek, dry here, usually picks up at least a trickle, but, with the exception of Durrwood Creek, most streams in this area are seasonal. Numerous campsites occur all along this route; only a few are mentioned. You can find private and isolated sites in the canyon to the south of this junction.

Your trail, 33E23, soon crosses a second and third saddle (5260/1.5), dips to ford an alder-lined brook and passes, just above the brook, an obscure junction with a trail to long defunct Durrwood Camp. With the help of your map, the unmaintained 2.4 mile-trail is not difficult to follow after you differentiate the beginning of the trail from cow paths. It offers a magnificent view from a saddle en route of Peppermint Creek gliding down its granite channel. The disheveled 1920s buildings on a terraced flat, a one-time favorite hideaway serviced by pack trains, sit amid pines and precipitous canyon walls near a crook of the Kern River.

On the Rincon Trail, your obvious north-trending path crosses a low saddle then fords another stream. Just up the slope it reaches the fifth in this series of saddles (5340/1.0). Passing another spring, the now descending trail arrives at a forked junction with a shortcut to Cedar Canyon Trail (5160/0.3). Travelers on T98 may choose to take this

Durrwood Creek

route, which is fairly easy to follow (look for tree blazes) and saves 0.6 mile. Your trail is the lower fork, the Rincon, which soon arrives at a large oak-shaded flat, 6.0 miles from the beginning of the trip. Here several large campsites spread near the brink of Durrwood Creek, a good first day destination for groups who need ample room for camping. Immediately your trail drops to cross year-round Durrwood Creek, which slides over slabs and falls into pools—you can hardly resist doing likewise.

Refreshed, climb steeply out of the colorful gorge and walk 90 yards to the junction with Cedar Canyon Trail 33E26 (5069/0.8), where those on T98 seeking Stony Meadow leave the Rincon Trail. You continue north. Far to the west you can see Dome Rock as well as The Needles fronting Slate Mountain, both favorites of rock climbers. Barely discernible on the west ridge are caps of basalt separated from the rest of the Little Kern Basalt Flow by a gorge over 1000 feet deep, cut by the Kern River in the last 3.5 million years. Eventually you pass another bathtub trough next to cow trampled springs, and cross cobbly washes as you continue on an easy, long ascent to the last saddle (5740/3.2) and highest point on your trip.

After crossing the saddle, the trail leaves chaparral with its interior live, black and white oaks to swoop down, sometimes steeply, in an elongated canyon shaded with cedars, white firs and Jeffrey pines. The path descends amid pungent kit-kit-dizze, a low growing evergreen plant with fern-like leaves. Kit-kit-dizze is the Miwok Indian name for this plant, which was used to make medicinal tea. It is also referred to as "Mountain Misery" because its sticky gum soils clothing.

After crossing the canyon's creek eight times, you enter Golden Trout Wilderness and skirt close to the precipitous riverbank brink of the Kern, then arrive at a split in the trail. Descend here to the spacious sandy flat at the Forks of the Kern (4700/2.1), the destination of your trip.

T97   North Rincon and River Day Hike

A hike through semi-arid terrain along the most obvious fault in the Sierra Nevada, a descent through a narrow canyon of mixed metamorphic rock above a cascading stream and a stroll by the banks of one of the most scenic segments of the wildly attractive Kern River await takers of this trip.

Distance   7.4 miles, shuttle trip
Steep Ascents   0.1 mile
Elevation Gain   660 feet
Skills   Easy route finding; moderate hiking; not recommended for equestrians
Seasons   Fall, winter, spring
Maps   USGS 7.5 min *Fairview, Durrwood*
Trailheads   55 & 38. This trip requires two cars. See the last of car tour T37. Leave the first car at **TH38,** next to Johnsondale Bridge, for the end of the trip. Then see the last of car tour T52. Drive the second car to the beginning of the trip at **TH55.** This is 3.1 miles from the first car.
Description   The beginning of this trip is described in T96.

Northbound 33E23 M'cyclepath Log

T96 parking lot	4840	0.0
saddle #1	5500	1.1
Kern River Trail 33E30	4700	1.3

Your route leaves the North Rincon Trail, turns left on **Kern River Trail 33E30,** which soon drops west near the creek. The trail is obscure here; your route follows the stream. Look for the mine in the canyon's north slope, and make your way to it over friction slabs, which may be icy. Here you will find a 30-foot tunnel whose entrance is sheltered by a hip-high wall of stacked rocks.

Beyond the mine you stay high on a narrow ledge blasted out of marble and other resistant metamorphics, high above the steep-sided, handsome gorge. Looking back at the head of the canyon, you see the stream's long, lacy apronlike falls and a high limestone/marble fin that looms to the south. Shade comes quite early to the base of that falls.

As you progress down-canyon, you pass boulders colored a dull red. Not due to a rare lichen or an unusual mineral deposit, the origin of this unusual color stems from a pilot's miss drop of fire retardant material. Below, the stream glides from pool to pool on a bed of slick granite, and you descend out of the canyon at a campsite where the River Trail makes a 90° left turn (4040/0.8).

Heading south along the Kern River, the path crosses the creek and disappears in a field of boulders. The trail resumes after the boulderfield. Several good campsites nestle next to the river here and for the remainder of the hike.

In spring and early summer from the Forks of the Kern and next to your route, bobbing rafters swiftly descend one of the most beautiful and demanding sections of whitewater commercially run in California. You, however, trod along propelled by your own power, equally enveloped in the beauty that surrounds you. Across the river, horizontal bands of recrystalized limestone run in granite slabs, and, half way through this last leg of your journey, the slender ribbon of Dry Meadow Creek tumbles and curls into the Kern River. On this 4.0-mile stretch of river you are sure to see fly-fishermen casting for wild trout.

Too soon, you stroll over chunks of metamorphic rock as you approach the foot of the metal staircase next to the two Johnsondale bridges. Climb the 58 stairs and cross the foot bridge to your awaiting shuttle car (3820/4.2). (There are plans to enlarge the parking and create a path from the road to the River Trail.)

Bobbing rafters

T98   Forks of the Kern Backpack via Stony Meadow

Combine Kern Canyon Fault's deformation, Durrwood Creek's cerulean pools, Stony Meadow's lichen painted backdrop, Forks of the Kern's racing waters and you have a varied trip with much appeal. But with taxing elevation gains and some demanding pathfinding, you will earn each treasured moment.

Distance   29.1 miles, semiloop trip
Steep Ascents   1.0 mile
Elevation Gain   7155 feet
Skills   Intermediate route finding
Seasons   Spring, summer, fall (can be hot)
(Wilderness permit required)
Maps   USGS 7.5 min *Fairview, Durrwood Cr, Hockett Pk*
Trailhead   55. See car tour T52.
Description   The beginning of this trip is described in T96.

Northbound 33E23 Log

T96	parking lot	4840 0.0
	saddle #1	5500 1.1
	Kern River Tr 33E30	4700 1.3
	saddle #3	5260 1.5
	saddle #5	5340 1.0
	Cedar Cyn cutoff	5160 0.3
	Cedar Cyn Tr 33E26	5069 0.8

Turning right and ascending east on **Cedar Canyon Trail 33E26,** you soon walk near the fence of a signed *Special use pasture—Not for public use.* The barbed wires travel up granite slabs while the trail passes below them near a spring. When the fence returns, follow it around two right-angle corners, then curve southeast on a cobbly path above another spring, and approach Durrwood Creek near enough to hear its rumble where the unmarked cutoff (5400/0.7) joins your path.

East of the junction, your trail, now a wide swath, reaches the first of seven switchbacks and zigzags on a slope stippled with cow tracks. The steadily ascending, exposed path reveals expanding, inspiring views to the west of Slate Mountain, The Needles, Farewell Gap and the Great Western Divide. Mountain mahogany lines the trail on both sides. This woody brush with small wedge-shaped leaves clustered near branch tips turns silvery when clad in its corkscrew, feathered plumes. The trail crosses a nose while passing through

a stock-fence gate, and afterward makes a lengthy traverse of southeast-facing slopes. Then it curves around a gulch and shortly dips to ford year-round Cedar Canyon brook.

The path resumes its up-canyon course on a long traverse southeast of the brook. Soon it enters the welcome shade of numerous incense cedars and other conifers, crosses many seeps on a well-watered slope, passes a small campsite and leads to another step-across ford of the Cedar Canyon brook. Next the path makes a zigzagging climb up a ridgelet between two forks of the brook, passing camping possibilities en route. Curving southeast, the route, guided by a "Trail" sign where the terrain levels, again crosses the brook then meets **Schaeffer M'cyclepath 33E24** (7800/3.7), on which you turn left.

The Schaeffer Trail north of the junction was deleted years ago from SNF system of trails. The Forest Service has a plan for this area: first it will subject this pristine forest to the logger's saw; then it will reestablish the Schaeffer Trail to loop motorcycles away from the wilderness area. Until the trail is redefined, hiking along it requires attentive pathfinding.

In 0.2 mile north from the junction, the trail reaches tiny, secluded Stony Meadow, ringed with trees, snuggled near the chartreuse and rufous lichen splashed shards of Schaeffer Mountain. The trail crosses the meadow which has tree blazes at both sides, a large campsite on its southern edge, and, midway, the effervescent headwaters of Cedar Canyon brook. North of the meadow the route weaves among pines, passes a campsite, curves to round Cedar Canyon, then turns right, northeast to climb beside the dry, steep crease of the canyon and top the watershed divide (8150/0.9).

From here to the Rattlesnake Trail, your course follows north-trending ridges high above Rattesnake Creek bowl to the east. The path descends northeast across the divide, but quickly curves north to follow the tree blazes below the crest to a junction with long abandoned, east-descending Old Sheep Drive (7960/0.3), one of the few identifiable sheep trails of the many that once crisscrossed the Southern Sierra from the late 1800s to early 1900s.

The trail continues straight ahead, north-northwest, traversing steep slopes—sometimes the blazes are infrequent, sometimes the cycle tread skirts below them. In 0.7 mile, the route bends west to continue along the main ridge nearing a saddle, then diagonals downslope north until it turns right, north-northeast, atop a brief, nearly flat side ridge, about a half mile beyond the saddle. Leaving the main ridge here, the route follows this major side ridge down the crest through a small burn, then narrows into aisles through

the brush which often impinges on the trail. After what may seem a long time of intense pathfinding for you, the trail passes the ridge's Point 6737 by slanting down east-facing slopes before returning to the ridge's crest and down to an obscure 3-way junction with *Rattlesnake Trail 33E22* (6000/3.3) where Schaeffer Trail 33E24 ends. Here your route descends north on 33E22, then northwest. If you are suddenly hiking east, you missed the junction.

With views to the north of Hockett Peak and the intervening Flatiron, you descend beside a gulch, cross its slabby bed and enter Golden Trout Wilderness. Then follow ducks over an open flat, an isolated outlier of the Little Kern Basalt Flow. When the path becomes obvious, you hike northwest along a gulch, and switchback westward 11 times, first down a ridge and then down west-facing slopes. The shimmering Kern River seems

Along North Fork Kern River

near-at-hand, and the Forks of the Kern can be seen to the west. At length you leave the brush, enter an oak woods and cross a usually stagnant trickle of water. You then stroll west between the tumbling river and the steep slopes over hummocky gravels, past boulder bars, among alders and through conifer stands. Soon you notice a platform next to the gaging station on the north bank. It was here that a cable spanned the Kern carrying a "flat car" in which a person sat as he pulled himself, hand over hand, to cross the river—now part of Kern River memorabilia.

Beyond the site and a campsite, the path undulates then forks. The upper path skirts high above a sandy flat; the right fork descends to the Forks of the Kern, where the spacious flat provides numerous campsites. The Little Kern River convenes with the North Fork beyond this flood plain. On the north bank in September 1975, a campfire fanned by wind roared out of control; it became known as the Flat Fire. Within hours flames had jumped the Kern River upstream and also spread up-canyon through Kern Flat to Hockett Peak Creek. The dense brush burned with such heat that in many locations the roots of all plants were killed.

After crossing the flat, you climb onto the *North Rincon Trail 33E23* (4720/3.0), round the steep, eroding south bank of the Kern, leave Golden Trout Wilderness and enter a tributary canyon which follows the Kern Canyon Fault. A long, sometimes steep climb south ensues as you crisscross the canyon's creek, mostly under welcome shade, eventually reaching the saddle (5740/2.0).

South of the saddle you leave the forest and enter chaparral country, but oak trees offer shade from time to time. In autumn the black oaks among them are jeweled with gold to rust leaves; in spring with reddish leaf buds. The leaves are sharply lobed and toothed. Leaves of white oaks, in contrast— yellow to brown in fall, green in spring—have rounded lobes and edges—white oak acorns are long and conical. Rambling south, you pass a cow trough mounted on stilts next to a spring. To the west, you can see through the canyon portals The Needles and Dome Rock; then, to the east, the rim of granite where Durrwood Creek plummets off the plateau. In time you reach the junction with Cedar Canyon Trail 33E26 (5069/3.2) where you left the Rincon Trail 23.1 miles back in your travels. Now retrace your steps to the parking lot (4840/6.0).

T99   North Fork Kern River Day Hike

The ever-changing Kern River crashes through the canyon during snowmelt, then diminishes as summer progresses, exposing water-smoothed boulders and granite-lined corridors. In fall, its quiet waters reflect the golds of graceful willows and cotton-woods. In any season, those who walk along this trail witness this river's grandeur and applaud its inclusion in the National Wild and Scenic Rivers System. Those who fly-fish along this stretch applaud the wild trout program introduced in 1990, as well.

Distance   8.4 miles, round trip
Steep Ascents   None
Elevation Gain   240 feet
Skills   Easy route finding; easy hiking; not recommended for equestrians
Seasons   All year
Maps   USGS 7.5 min *Fairview, Durrwood Cr*
Trailhead   38. See car tour T37.
Description   To find the trail from the parking lot (3820/0.0), cross Kern River on the old bridge, then descend the 58 metal steps next to the bridge to the riverside. This bridge replaced one yanked off its moorings by a flood in December 1966. It, in turn, was replaced for vehicle travel in 1983, but was left standing for foot travel. The steps and steep bank essentially eliminate horse and motorcycle use on the trail; however, there are plans to carve a ramp from the road to the trail.

You proceed north from the bridge

(3770/0.1) on *Kern River Trail 33E30,* and ascend on chips of metamorphic rock up a gentle-to-moderate grade over riverside bluffs, then descend to interspersed riverside terraces. Across the river a mine's adit appears through its framework and surrounding foliage; and on your side appear unwelcomed trailside clumps of poison oak. Around 2.0 miles from the bridge you see across the river, a canyon mouth of slabs so smooth as to seem caressed by debouching Dry Meadow Creek.

The trail ahead crosses ledges carved from steeply inclined slabs, passes a huge boulder-cave housing a small campsite, and proceeds on wide terraces, each with inviting campsites. Predominant among the trees offering year-long shade on the river trail are large,

mature interior live oaks. You can identify this abundant oak by its acorn, slender and deeply set in its cup. Other aspects of its morphology vary frustratingly; the 1–2 inch-long leaf can have a rounded or tapered tip; and the margins can be smooth or toothed.

Soon you pass another boulder-sheltered campsite. Looking now across the river, near the canyon's rim you can see columnar jointed lava similar to, but less spectacular than that found far to the north at Devils Postpile. These columns are remnants of the Little Kern Basalt Flow. Suddenly you reach a boulder-hopping segment after which the trail resumes to head east, up-canyon. Since the trail leaves the river, you, on a riverside stroll, turn around to retrace your steps (4040/4.1).

T100   West Rim Owens Valley Car Tour on Highway 395: Nine Mile Canyon Road to Lone Pine
(With Directions to Trailheads 77–83)

The Sierra Nevada Mountains to the west, peering over foothills or sweeping up from alluvial fans and bajadas, rise 8000 feet from the valley floor at the beginning of this tour and increase in elevation to the 14,000-foot, sky-piercing Mount Whitney group at the end. The lower Coso Range to the east forms a backdrop to sheer, basaltic ridges and the solitary Red Hill volcanic cone. High desert valleys confined between the mountains contain tranquil lakes, alkali dry beds, verdant cultivated fields and small, isolated towns, some with cafes and gas stations.

Distance   54.6 miles, one way
Steep Ascents   None
Elevation Gain   1160 feet
Skills   Easy route finding; paved road
Seasons   All year
Map   Inyo County road map
Tourhead   44. The junction of Highway 395 and Nine Mile Canyon (which becomes Kennedy Meadows Road, then Sherman Pass Road) is **TH44.** It is 10.1 miles north of Highway 14's terminus. This tour departs from the juxtaposed car tours of T46, south, and T52, west.
Description   Leaving the Nine Mile Canyon junction (2575/0.0/0.0) on *U.S. Highway 395,* gently ascending the end of Indian Wells Valley, your straightaway route directs

you generally north along the geologically fascinating Sierra Nevada fault zone. During seismic activity, the valleys on the east side drop while the mountains on the west side rise. Beyond the basaltic ridge to your left lies a portion of the restricted testing ground of China Lake Naval Weapons Center, a complex the size of Delaware. Among the many weapons developed at this research center is the highly acclaimed sidewinder missile: still considered an effective weapon although 35 years old in 1991.

You soon reach the narrowest point in your tour where the 1923 vintage Little Lake Hotel (7.0/7.0) still welcomes guests. This hotel, once a popular stopover for travelers when it took two days to reach Owens Valley

Little Lake Hotel

from Los Angeles, served as home to the early employees at the Weapons Center. Here demure, spring-fed Little Lake, nestled at the foot of volcanic flows, brims with rippling water. The fence-enclosed lake, a remnant of the prehistoric Owens River, is a *Great Basin Foundation Conservation and Research Project.*

Now in Rose Valley, if you have time to explore Fossil Falls and the Red Hill cinder cone area, make a detour by turning right on Cinder Road (3.0/10.0) to **TH77** of T101. A highway rest stop (4.9/14.9) near a gas station, garage and snackshop is next on your travels. This rest stop, off Gill Station Road, is an oasis thought to be on the bed of one of the ancient shallow lakes formed by glacial melt.

Moving on, you can see a white swath of pumice to the east, then the stucco and rock buildings of the imaginatively named hamlet of Dunmovin to the west. "J. C." called a halt to his roaming here at the foot of the Sierra crest. His stone-and-cement marker with the dates "1909–1932" is found near the buildings next to the highway. In a mile past the second of two roads to the Haiwee power plant, you arrive at the unsigned T junction (7.6/22.5) of Haiwee Canyon Road. Hikers heading for **TH78** on T102 take this road after leaving their shuttle car at Sage Flat. The dirt road to the trailhead is signed for southbound traffic on this divided highway.

North and South Haiwee reservoirs to the

right are part of the LA aqueduct complex; the second aqueduct to LA begins here. Both lakes, a combined length of 7.0 miles, provide a natural fresh air and desert sun purification of the water before it enters a closed system. The 5700-kilowatt Haiwee Hydroelectric Power Station, built in 1927, is one of five along the system in Owens Valley. Of interest to paleontologists are the hills behind the reservoirs, which have white sedimentary rocks rich in animal fossils. With distant North Haiwee Reservoir still at your right, you arrive at paved and signed Sage Flat Road (3.9/26.4) where hikers heading for **TH79** for Ts102, 103, 105, 106 turn left, while the rest skip the following description and continue north.

Driving west on paved *Sage Flat Road* (0.0/0.0), you soon enter Inyo National Forest (3.3/3.3) where the pavement ends, but you continue on the most traveled road at all forks to arrive at a large lot, **TH79,** (2.1/5.4), with a horse corral and a white stucco building. The hiker's parking lot is 0.3 mile farther.

On Highway 395 shortly after crossing the aqueduct, skilled mountain climbers bent on scaling Olancha Peak's east face, T104 at **TH80,** turn left on unpaved, but signed *Walker Creek Road* (3.6/30.0). Next a plaque near a plaster tepee commemorates M. H. Farley who built the first mill and furnace in Owens Valley. The small town of Olancha includes a BLM fire station, motels, a service station, cafe, post office, and a quonset hut whose facade carries the name "Jot-em Down Store," nudging the memories of people who tuned in to yesteryear's radio series *Lum 'n' Abner.* Torrents of water poured down the mountain canyons here in a 1989 summer storm, crumbling the walls of the open aqueduct and inundating this small town with mud and water. The occasional huge boulders you see along your journey were carried to their present locations by debris flows such as this. You quickly reach the junction (1.6/31.6) of State Highway 190 to Death Valley, where people heading for

Darwin Falls turn east to drive to **TH81.**

Now your tour rolls through the town of Cartago, then along the west side of Owens Dry Lake. Here chemical plants recovered soda ash from the lake bed—white waste piles still remain—the pink coloration on the bed is due to algae and bacteria. This lake must have been a magnificent sight when its large expanse of water glittered in the hollow of the soaring mountains. The pre-1913 salt lake was about 30 feet deep and covered 100 square miles. During the glacial period, the lake was larger and deeper, but as the glaciers receded, the water level dropped below its outlet. Although Owens River continued to bring water to the lake, a large percentage evaporated leaving visible, successively diminishing shore lines. In 1913, the Los Angeles Department of Water and Power diverted the water of Owens River into its aqueduct system and the lake became a dry, alkaline depression. At the historical monument (9.8/41.4) ahead, to the right of the road, you can read about the charcoal kilns and spin visions of how the lake was when the Bessie Brady and the Mollie Stevens steamed across the waters burdened with wood or ore. The kilns are a mile east of the plaque. Back on your current voyage, you reach Cotton-

wood Road (1.8/43.2) where hikers turn off for **TH82** of T108 and T111. If not seeking that trailhead skip the following description and continue north.

To reach the trailhead, turn west on the thin pavement of signed *Cottonwood Road* (0.0/0.0), drive near the power plant, cross the LA aqueduct (0.2/0.2), cross Cottonwood Creek several times, pass a few creekside campsites and arrive at road's end at **TH82** (4.0/4.2). Here you can park under the shade of golden oaks.

Continuing north on Highway 395, you pass narrow Lubkin Canyon Road (7.0/50.2), a shortcut to Horseshoe Meadows Road. In 1.2 miles you reach Diaz Lake, a good place to camp or picnic, or shower after a backpack. This lake, not a part of the aqueduct system, is owned by Los Angeles and leased to Inyo County for a recreational park. It is a fault sink that was formed by the 1872 earthquake, which was estimated to be 8.0 to 8.5 on the Richter Scale. The quake produced sizable ruptures from Haiwee Reservoirs to north of Big Pine.

Beyond the lake, approaching the town of Lone Pine, is the Mount Whitney Golf Club

Charcoal kilns

where the dramatic scenery must make it hard to concentrate on the game. Right of the highway, the Visitors Center offers a wide selection of books, maps, postcards and all kinds of information. State Highway 136 to Death Valley departs north of the center. Inyo National Forest's Mount Whitney Ranger District office (4.2/54.4) for permits and information is to the right of Highway 395. Your tour ends at the junction (3733/0.2/54.6) of Whitney Portal Road, **TH83,** in "down town" Lone Pine; car tour T109 to Horseshoe Meadow begins with a left turn here.

T101   Fossil Falls Side Trip

This family outing lets you observe the dramatic results of two of nature's mightiest forces: water and volcanoes; and takes you into land inhabited in historic times by the Little Lake Shoshone Indians.

Distance   0.4 mile, round trip
Steep Ascents   None
Elevation Gain   None
Skills   Easy route finding; easy hiking
Seasons   All year (can be hot)
Map   Inyo County road map
Trailhead   77. See car tour T100. From Highway 395 north of Little Lake, turn east onto paved *Cinder Road* (0.0/0.0). Drive beyond its pavement, turn right at a fork (0.5/0.5), follow BLM *Fossil Falls* signs to **TH77** (0.6/1.1).
Description   Leave the parking lot (0.0/0.0) at the informational sign to the south and follow the *path* to the head of the 100-foot, double, dry falls (0.2/0.2); or, venture on your own. You can play among the water-smoothed lava rocks and enjoy the basics of rock climbing by using the many hand holds and foot holds.

The prehistoric Owens River flowed south through here between the Coso Mountains to the east and the Sierra Nevada Mountains to the west. The river, which connected a series of lakes, was fed by the receding Pleistocene Sierran glaciers. This south section of Owens River dried up when the glaciers disappeared. One of the series of lakes was the Red Hill playa between the cone and the falls.

Bursting on the scene around 15,000 years ago, sizzling lava from nearby volcanic eruptions flowed into the river channel and became what you see before you: lava rocks sculptured and polished by the erosional forces of the river. The pot holes were cut into

the lava by powerful whirlpools swirling with rocks and sand: vortices that fixed onto small holes and scoured them into the larger cups that exist today. The little holes in the lava rocks strewn about you were made by gas bubbles caught in the molten material as it

Fossil Falls

cooled. The red cinder cone to the north resulted from molten material ejected from a vent in the earth's crust. The ejacta quickly cooled forming porous rock known as scoria.

It is believed that people lived here along the river and lake. In historic times, the Little Lake Shoshone Indians were living here when the first explorers ventured through. These Native Americans roamed far to harvest nuts, gather seeds and hunt animals. Look for the smooth concave rocks, called metates, on which they processed food; and obsidian chips, arrowheads and other stone age tools they chiseled. The Indians found the obsidian in the Coso Range northeast. Remember, it is unlawful to remove or disturb the artifacts, including the obsidian chips.

For more information, the BLM office in Ridgecrest has informative free pamphlets about this area.

T102   East Rim South Sierra Wilderness Backpack
With Excursion X: Round Mountain

Because this trip begins and ends in desert-facing canyons, you can enjoy it early and late season when many other mountain approaches are blocked by snow. You are treated to views of Rose and Owens valleys from the deep canyons of Haiwee and Olancha passes, both former Indian routes, and vistas west through the open country of the middle Kern Plateau.

Distance   17.0 miles, shuttle trip
Steep Ascents   None
Elevation Gain   5260 feet
Skills   Easy route finding
Seasons   Spring, summer, fall (can be hot)
Map   USGS 7.5 min *Haiwee Pass*
Trailheads   78 & 79. This trip requires two cars. See car tour T100. Leave the first car at the end of Sage Flat Road at **TH79**. Drive the second car 3.9 miles south on Highway 395 to Haiwee Canyon Road. Turn right on the dirt *road* (0.0/0.0), drive west to the parking lot just beyond the ruins of Sam Lewis Pack Station (2.6/2.6) at **TH78**, where this trip begins. This is 11.9 miles from the first car.
Description   This trailhead is the site of Sam Lewis Pack Station, at one time a thriving facility that introduced hunters and fishermen to Troy Meadow on the plateau. When the logging road to Troy was built, its trade was felled with the trees. Begin your hike on the extended *road* beyond the parking area (4940/0.0), and quickly enter Haiwee Creek Canyon alongside the creek, the only dependable source of water until Honeybee Creek or the South Fork Kern River. Confining shrubbery; itself enveloped in

summer by a suffocating shag of grapevines, narrows the road to trail width (5035/0.3), after space for a small campsite and a car turnaround. Proceeding west on the *Haiwee Trail*, your route is sometimes overrun by this vegetation during the next mile of creek hopping—eight fords in all.

You make the first ford just beyond a stock fence next to huge old cottonwoods; the next through a willow thicket; then near wild roses making the wide creek crossing prickly going for hikers wearing shorts; then back to the north bank. Now follow a rock-lined causeway of sorts, which raises you above muddy banks of the reed-choked creek. Sloshing along with wet feet through the last four crossings, you return to the north side of the creek about 0.2 mile before the confluence of a south canyon (5900/1.6).

Just beyond the branching of Haiwee Creek, on a westward course, you come upon an orangish-brown mineral spring glistening in the path. Columbines bloom as late as October beside seep springs along this stretch. After four switchbacks beneath oak boughs, you can pause or overnight at a medium campsite on a knoll, around 0.3 mile beyond the confluence.

The path continues west across a sunny slope, curving and stretching and switchbacking three times, then an extended leg northeast returns west just short of a gully. Now the trail curves part way around a headwater canyon of Haiwee Creek's north branch; beyond the next ravine it passes a small campsite asquat a shelf. Two switchbacks gain another gully, all the while affording glimpses to the east of sky-blue Lower Haiwee Reservoir some 3700 feet below. A final 13 switchbacks take you into higher altitude vegetation: manzanita, chinquapin, white fir and Jeffrey pine. The path then climbs over Haiwee Pass into South Sierra Wilderness (8180/2.8). This pass coincides with a route for an extension of State Highway 190 that was never funded, and is no longer under consideration.

Past camping prospects, you now descend west on a gentle gradient amid sunswept brush, mountain mahogany and juniper. Deer Mountain looms in the west. When you reach the Honeybee Trail T junction (7900/0.9) in a wide south-facing canyon, turn right.

Hiking north on the **Honeybee Trail,** ascend on the high side of a broad saddle, then descend to cross a side canyon, rise over a slope and drop to slender Honeybee Creek (7800/0.9). Several littered packer/hunter campsites line the creek, which is fed by up-canyon springs. If the creek is dry, the springs, your last source of water en route, may also be dry. To resupply then, truck 0.3 mile, cross-country, down-canyon to the South Fork Kern River.

The route proceeds along the right side of the creek, crosses over in 0.4 mile just beyond a spring and leaves the canyon to rise above it until it reaches a collection of seasonal seeps and springs and another untidy campsite (8380/1.5). Now the trail leaves Honeybee Creek gully with Round Mountain directly north of it, to follow the next crease left. The path climbs over a ridge where a spacious, sometimes sepia-toned canvas of Monache Meadow with its wandering South Fork Kern River spreads to the west below. Next the

path contours around a west-facing canyon to a broad saddle (8930/1.7) where climbers of Round Mountain exit. The landmarks are: unimpressive Point 9003 immediately west; a jagged outcrop just east with Round Mountain directly in back; and a lone juniper tree, like a sentry, atop the saddle next to the trail. The open country is covered with sagebrush and bitterbrush; the trail seems to be the only available place to pitch a tent. Those who do not climb Round Mountain can ignore the following description and continue north.

Excursion X: Round Mountain

Captivating views from the prominent summit and the easy cross-country route make this an attractive adventure for all. But the mountain's distance from a trailhead has limited the names on the register to a stalwart few.

Distance   1.8 miles, round trip
Steep Ascents   0.3 mile
Elevation Gain   955 feet
Skills   Easy route finding; Class 1–2 climbing
Description   Head east-northeast, *cross-country,* (8930/0.0) from the lone tree to a notch between the bouldery mass ahead, weaving around the dense low-growing

Filtering water, Honeybee Creek

brush. Beyond the outcrop, curve to approach the summit on its moderately steep, rocky, northwest slopes. Clusters of foxtail pines, a tree that grows only at high altitudes, pepper the landscape.

At the summit (9884/0.9), gaze north to the awesome east face of Olancha Peak plunging 8000 feet via cliffs, flying buttresses and convoluted canyons to the gently declining floor of Owens Valley.

*   *   *   *   *

From the lone tree saddle, you journey homeward by skirting another west-facing canyon and climbing onto and along the Sierra crest, where you head northwest, again through groves of mountain mahogany. Staying on the right side of the ridge with one notable exception, a 60-foot drop west, you reach the highest point on the trail, 9320 feet, then descend to Olancha Pass (9220/2.2), where you turn right on the *Olancha Pass Trail.*

Walk east along the stock driveway, braided with side paths, descend to cross the headwater trickle of Summit Creek, pass a cow trough and arrive at a saddle where the cow trail (8600/1.0) parts from yours and plummets down the canyon. Some astonished hikers plummet with it—watch for the signs.

Your path, the horse trail to the left, swings around the next canyon north, switchbacks then curves in to round a gully and out to round a knob. The Inyo Mountains, the chalky, mottled hues of the Coso Range, the alkali flats of dry Owens Lake and the startling blue of Haiwee Reservoir vie for attention now as the trail descends northeast, just below, then over a ridge and back to drop down the canyon wall. The trail makes several switchbacks, then meets a branch of the stock driveway (6760/2.6).

In arid country now, you pass the cow trail and head through a stock-fence gate, where you arrive at the junction of another split in the trail (5960/1.0). The equestrian trail drops south, then east 0.3 mile; the hiking trail continues north toward Walker Creek for 0.25 mile to a "Trail" sign, where it swings back to end at a 3-way branch of the dirt road (5790/0.5) near your shuttle car.

T103   Olancha Peak Backpack via the PCT

Olancha Peak, the tallest peak in the Southern Sierra, stands supreme. While its west slopes have the rounded, molded look of many Kern Plateau mountains, its east face remains chiseled and steep from the southernmost quarry of ice age glaciation in the Sierra Nevada.

Distance   22.0 miles, round trip
Steep Ascents   0.6 mile
Elevation Gain   6335 feet
Skills   Easy route finding; Class 2 climbing
Seasons   Spring, summer, fall
Maps   USGS 7.5 min *Haiwee Pass, Monache Mtn (0.2 mile), Olancha, Templeton Mtn*
Trailhead   79. See car tour T100.
Description   Two trailheads and parking lots are off Sage Flat Road: one for horses, one for hikers. Equestrians ascend the trail to the west of and behind Inyo's maintenance building located at the south end of the golden and live oak-shaded parking lot. Hikers find their fork of *Olancha Pass Trail* south of their sunny parking area where the access road branches three ways (5790/0.0). The hiker's route climbs west above the cars for 0.3 mile amid scattered pinyon pines to a sharp left turn south on Walker Stock Driveway, then turns west where it meets the equestrian trail (5960/0.5).

Now in South Sierra Wilderness, you pass through a stock-fence gate and branch right of a cow path, then traverse above a usually dry canyon. Soon the trail forks (6760/1.0): the stock driveway leads into the canyon crease, you switchback eight times up to a ridgecrest with a small campsite on the divide between the nameless canyon from which you came and Walker Creek Canyon. Shortly you encounter an orange and chartreuse lichen-splotched granite mass, dictating another switchback. Continue to climb up, sometimes via switchbacks; then you curve around the canyon, which displays impressive sharp crags on its south ridge. In time you gain a saddle (8600/2.6) where the steep stock driveway again joins you. On a wide trail now with southern views of Round Mountain, pass a cow trough, step over the snowmelt headwaters of the east Summit Creek and climb to the Olancha Pass and Honeybee Trail junction (9220/1.0).

A few steps later a duck marks a use path that heads west to Summit Meadows and on to connect a web of erosive OHV paths, unused as such since the wilderness designation. You skirt the meadow where camping possibilities exist next to the gathering waters of the westside Summit Creek. Near the head of the meadow, to the right of the path, a crude table and stove plus a corral mark the Bear Trap Meadow use trail to the PCT, but you quickly meet and bear right onto the next *lateral* to the PCT (9220/1.4). Turn north on the *PCT* (9240/0.5) when you meet it.

The trail runs across slopes of chinquapin and manzanita, fords Cow Creek and zigzags many times amid currant bushes, a favorite berry of black bears. Now leaving the forest, the PCT continues to parallel the creek, which flows amid groups of corn lilies. The open tread is sandy and often very dusty, but it still supports the colorful scarlet gilia, a cluster of red flowers with tubular necks and pointed, star-like lobes. The gradient steepens, and the trail zigs sporadically as it climbs a side canyon. Then it fords a perennial brook, which originates in the meadow springs above, where cattle and horses sometimes frolic. The trail then switchbacks near a large campsite among boulders by a foxtail pine, with an extended view of Monache Meadow, cone-shaped Monache Mountain and the sandy flood plain of South Fork Kern River.

Minutes beyond this campsite, a short path climbs off our trail to a small plateau with off-trail campsites and a corral. A verdant, watered meadow sports numerous mountain bluebells, an aptly named flower resembling tiny, hanging bells whose style extends like a clapper. Mosquitoes may make lingering in spring or early summer a bit unpleasant. The grade diminishes as the PCT moves into the shade of lodgepole and occasional foxtail pines—isolated species of the impressive foxtail pine groves ahead.

Atop a ridge, the path proceeds past a junction, obscured by a large fallen tree, with the Bear Trap Meadow use trail mentioned earlier. North of the fallen tree your path ascends gently-to-moderately, curves northwest and crosses another open slope with seasonal streamlets and seeps. The farther north the trail climbs on this slope, the more remarkable are the Southern Sierra views. Even the San Gabriel mountains, which stand above the Los Angeles basin, show faintly through the haze. In almost one mile the trail crosses a flat, forested ridge with considerable camping potential. Provocative vignettes of Olancha Peak, Mount Langley, the Kaweah Peaks Ridge and Kern Peak may be seen framed by the boughs of the forest.

Continuing to climb, the path curves around a headwaters bowl of Monache Creek and then levels off on a saddle of a ridge that juts out from the west-facing slope of Olancha Peak. This, the highest point of the trail on the side of Olancha Peak, is a good departure point for the nontechnical 1550-foot climb to the top (10,540/3.4).

You ascend northeast on a *cross-country* route among foxtail pines to timberline, aiming for the slope north of the summit, where the rounded and gentler terrain makes for an easy final ascent, but only after you have pulled up and over scores of large boulders. Unexpected among these boulders are vigorous plants of yellow columbine. Then you scale the summit (12,123/0.6). Here at the top stands a tall stack of rocks, a cairn, precariously perched on a slab that juts over the sheer eastern face. The first recorded ascent of Olancha Peak was made by James

Scott Broder in 1864.

You might pause to reflect on the fate of the Indians for whom this summit was named. Olanche and Yaulanchi were spoonerisms for Yaudanchi, a tribe of Yokuts Indians that probably traded with either the Paiutes north of Owens Lake or the Kosos south of it. The decimated Yaudanchi now reside on the Tule River Indian Reservation.

T104   Olancha Peak Climb via the Northeast Ridge

Only hikers in top physical condition and skilled in route finding should attempt this ascent, which is by far the most challenging climb in this book. The route leads cross-country from the desert to the summit, passing next to the dramatic ice-carved east face of Olancha, the Southern Sierra's tallest, most prominent peak.

Distance   10.0 miles, round trip

Steep Ascents   3.0 miles

Elevation Gain   8205 feet

Skills   Advanced route finding; Class 3 climbing (Class 4 & 5 pitches optional)

Seasons   Spring, fall

Map   USGS 7.5 min *Olancha*

Trailhead   80. See car tour T100. Turn west off Highway 395 onto unpaved, signed *Walker Creek Road* (0.0/0.0). The first mile skirts jaggedly rectilinear property boundaries. You quickly branch southwest (0.4/0.4), cross the aqueduct on a narrow bridge and fork west (0.2/0.6). Cross a railroad track, pass a spur road, turn south, later west at a junction (0.9/1.5), then northwest (0.2/1.7) to follow the powerlines. At the point where the lines and the road turn northeast in unison (3.7/5.4) pull off the road at **TH80**. (Do not descend the canyon.)

Description   Climber Dick Beach pioneered this route during the mid 1960s. From the powerline road (3920/0.0), proceed amid sagebrush west-southwest. Notice the vast number of Class 4 and 5 routes apparent on precipices that loom by the mouth of Cartago Creek Canyon to the north. A ridge caps that canyon's north-facing slopes. Your route, however, is the second ridge south from Cartago Canyon, which you ascend, entering Golden Trout Wilderness.

Progressing up steep, sandy slopes on the ridgecrest, you soon penetrate a cloak of pinyon pines, live oak and mountain juniper, yielding with elevation to a woods of white fir and Jeffrey pines, and eventually reach the first landmark: a hill (7540/1.5) on the crest. Behind the hill stretches a rolling span of ridge which, compared to the slopes it abuts, can be seen as a virtual flat. It comes as a welcome respite. At this point where an outcrop bars the ridge, leave it, contour across the southeast-facing slopes of an incipient canyon, and then climb the rock barrier. Both the canyon and the ridge you followed are soon indistinguishable from the east-facing slopes you now climb. At last the terrain becomes gentler, you top a small hill (9320/0.9) and pause to take in the extent of Owens Valley before you.

Continue up the ridge, but soon leave the crest to pass north below ridge-straddling outcrop 10,010. Thereafter you regain the crest (9920/0.6), from which the awesome east face of Olancha Peak is sporadically visible. Before the now gentle incline abates, you have the opportunity to traverse a few hundred yards to the north, where you will find several small campsites near a branch of Cartago Creek.

Climb the steepening ridgecrest, between the east face and the southernmost cirque in the Sierra, then you attain a rolling plateau reminiscent of the one atop Mount Whitney. Its relatively gentle slopes beckon you southwest to the summit (12,123/2.0), with its spectacular views.

T105   Middle Golden Trout Wilderness Backpack
With excursions Y, Z, & AA: Brown, Templeton
& Monache Mountains

The highlights of this backpack are the meadows it visits, the mountains it skirts and the river it crosses. Each meadow provides its own charm: willowy turf, velvety grass, rosy flats and sagebrush terrain. Two volcanic mountains en route present the beauty of symmetry and solitude. The South Fork Kern River demonstrates force in early season as it crashes against massive boulders; then serenity as its dwindling water gathers in placid pools.

Distance   35.0 miles, semiloop trip
Steep Ascents   0.3 mile
Elevation Gain   6150 feet
Skills   Easy route finding
Seasons   Spring, summer, fall (Wilderness permit required)
Maps   USGS 7.5 min *Haiwee Pass, Monache Mtn, Templeton Mtn*
Trailhead   79. See car tour T100.
Description   The beginning of this trip is described in T103

Westbound Olancha Pass Trail Log

T103	Sage Flat Rd	5790	0.0
	equestrian tr	5960	0.5
	stock driveway	6760	1.0
	saddle	8600	2.6
	Olancha Pass	9220	1.0
	lateral to PCT	9220	1.4

Shortly after the lateral on the Olancha Pass Trail, you meet the PCT junction north (9090/0.4). This is the east end of a PCT jog that coincides with your route for a short stint. You cross the trickle of Cow Creek, then curve around Cow Canyon to the PCT junction south (8920/0.5) where it leaves your route.

A few minutes beyond the south junction, a use path to Olivas Cow Camp splits to the left. Your trail, a stock driveway with few blazes, which frequently fragments into multiple paths, descends west among pines on a moderate grade and passes another use trail to Olivas Cow Camp near the foot of the grade. Here at the foot are large campsites—no problem finding flats for camping on this trip—a dirt road on which you will return, and a ford of Monache Creek (7990/1.9). Your route, now a road, takes you past a green gate

to one of the several cabins of Monache Cow Camp at the north tip of Monache Meadow. The June 1959 issue of *Sunset* magazine featured these cabins as the Monache Meadow Lodge: a secluded place only reached by light airplanes or pack trains. Later, when jeepers and bikers came into the area in great numbers, the lodge lost its quiet charm, went private, and has since had a series of owners. In the interest of preventing a commercial development here in Monache Meadow, the Trust for Public Land, a non-profit conservation organization, purchased the land in 1990 to hold until the Forest Service can buy it.

Beyond the cabin, you bear right at the junction (7980/0.1) and head northwest toward Brown Meadow, now on the ***Strawberry Trail***. You hike over a hill to reach Hessian Meadow, a slender strip with willows and wildflowers. Step over a spring-fed rill and cross to the meadow's west edge. You ascend through the woods on a moderate grade; the creek to your right softly clatters down its ravine like the sound of wind chimes in a gentle breeze. At length you climb a few switchbacks to reach a wide saddle and the border of Golden Trout Wilderness (9020/2.4). Here peakbaggers and view seekers turn left to climb Brown Mountain. Others continue on and skip the following description.

Excursion Y: Brown Mountain

This easy mountain trek affords beginners an opportunity to try cross-country climbing, and it gives climbers of all abilities unobstructed views of vast Monache Meadow.

Distance 1.8 miles, round trip
Steep Ascents 0.2 mile
Elevation Gain 965 feet
Skills Easy route finding; Class 1 climbing
Map USGS 7.5 min *Templeton Mtn*
Description The *cross-country* route leaves the Strawberry Trail at the wilderness border (9020/0.0) and climbs west-south-west around chinquapin and blowdowns under a canopy of mixed pines and firs. The grade is gentle to moderate, then steepens, then becomes gentle again as it nears the summit.

A few foxtail pines flourish on the rounded top where the register can with a tablet rests among easily climbed boulders (9981/0.9). One of the tablet's notations reads, "Built this monument while fighting fire in August, 1949." The fire explains the numerous blowdowns. When you descend, use Olancha Peak to the east to direct you to your trail.

*   *   *   *   *

Brown Cow Camp/Olancha Peak

A few hundred yards north of the saddle, the trail descends past several small campsites and parallels the sometimes dry Brown Meadow brook, which here flows down a slim channel. The grassy creek lining progressively widens resulting in ever larger meadows. Soon your path cuts across one of these meadows and the brook in its middle. Back in the forest, now west of the creek, the trail reaches Brown Cow Camp. Its weathered, 1914, notched-log cabin, at the fringe of pastoral Brown Meadow, reposes before the majesty of Olancha Peak—postcard perfection.

Beyond the barbed-wire fence enclosure, a use trail to Bell Camp and the PCT near Gomez Meadow, departs to your right. You continue north along the meadow, veer northwest through a neck of the woods, then abruptly drop into the canyon of the South Fork (8420/2.8). During drought years, the river barely flows in a quiet stream, but during snowmelt after a normal winter, it becomes a broiling rush as it thunders against

the boulders, shards, and cliffs of granite that contain and direct its path.

You ford the river, ascend a short, steep grade, then stroll west through rolling sagebrush terrain toward conical Templeton Mountain. Dense mats of ground-hugging dwarf monkey flowers, when in bloom, add a strawberry pink to the rose-tan sand flats of Strawberry Meadows north of you, a part of Templeton Mountain's alluvial apron. Soon you make a running leap across Strawberry Creek and in ¼ mile jump back. Next step over a side brook, which supplies all the water for down-stream Strawberry Creek after snowmelt. After the path enters the edge of a dense lodgepole pine woods, you turn acutely south at the junction of Long Canyon Trail (8615/2.2). If you are on one of the many cow paths that parallel Strawberry Creek, you may miss the signs. At this junction you may choose to take the mountain excursion or continue on and skip the following description.

Excursion Z: Templeton Mountain

As the conical shape suggests, this is a volcanic mountain, but of Tertiary andesite, not basaltic cinder, unlike the volcanic peaks to the northwest at Tunnel Meadow. You can climb Templeton Mountain from any access point. This route is the shortest and steepest (straight up) but not difficult.

Distance   1.8 miles, round trip
Steep Ascents   0.5 mile
Elevation Gain   1355 feet
Skills   Easy route finding, Class 1–2 climbing
Map   USGS 7.5 min *Templeton Mtn*
Description   At the junction (8615/0.0), you set your *cross-country* course north-northeast, then cross a length of alluvium skewered by Strawberry Creek, here often dry. As you climb, the terrain graduates from soil to pebbles to flat chunks and finally to boulders, some quite wobbly on the steep slope. It also progresses from lodgepole pines to junipers to foxtail pines on top. Pausing to look back, you discover that you and the junc-

tion you left form a direct line with bald Peak 10,009, the most eastern point on the Toowa Range.

Large, almost flat and bouldery with no outstanding outcrops describes the top of Templeton. You will have to hunt for the summit (9975/0.9) with its register can. As you walk around the perimeter, you will have a dramatic view of the many mountains and meadows that make up the Kern Plateau.

$$* \quad * \quad * \quad * \quad *$$

On *Long Canyon Trail*, you walk south through a corridor in the forest and quickly ford the year-round brook (8620/0.3) east of a cluster of old campsites. Cross a slim extension of Fat Cow Meadow, climb a little to a low saddle and a junction (8740/0.7) where you leave Long Canyon Trail, which turns right, and bear south-southeast on *Bakeoven Trail*, dropping to Schaeffer Meadow. Now you cross the west end of the meadow and the spring-fed creek, which glides down its middle. After a short trek in dense forest, you dip to cross Schaeffer Stringer and its meadow. An iron spring oozes 0.1 mile east alongside the creek. South of the meadow, the trailside slope declines steeply to the east, but you can neither see nor hear the South Fork Kern River, ensconced in this defile. Shortly you leave Golden Trout Wilderness (8820/2.0).

The path crosses several rills, gains a plateau, then descends among slender brooks and grassy meadows where it sometimes becomes obscure. Half way down the slope you come upon an aged sign (8330/2.0), *Grant Trail to Long Canyon,* on a Jeffrey pine to your left. It was a shortcut used by Monache Lodge clientele to reach the auxiliary lodge in Long Canyon. There is hardly a trace of that trail. The path soon levels out, passes to the right of a barbed-wire fence, enters a sagebrush meadow and fizzles out. The route continues ahead to an east-west *jeep road* (7940/1.2), onto which you turn left.

Walk east along the jeep road, cross the meadow stream on a makeshift log bridge and proceed over a barren, decomposed granite sand dune, past cabin access roads to a junction (7930/0.5) at the end of the dune with a road to Monache Mountain. Here Monache Mountain climbers turn right to approach the mountain, while nonclimbers continue east and pass over the following description.

Excursion AA: Monache Mountain

This mountain, like Templeton Mountain, is steep, yet easy to climb. Among the trees from its top, you view the immensity of Monache Meadow and the supremacy of Olancha Peak.

Distance   3.2 miles, round trip
Steep Ascents   0.8 mile
Elevation Gain   1480 feet
Skills   Easy route finding; Class 1 climbing
Map   USGS 7.5 min *Monache Mtn*
Description   From the junction (7930/0.0) of two jeep roads at the east end of the gritty dune, you turn right and walk south along the *road* to a gate. Straight ahead of you rises cone-shaped Monache Mountain. Now you follow a *use path* to the left along the outside of the fenced area. As you near the mountain, the sagebrush is replaced with mushy meadow grass, then in an open space between two fenced enclosures you choose the best place to ford Soda Creek (7000/0.6).

Now on a *cross-country* climb, ascend on pebbly slopes east of Forest Service cabins and corral. As the slope steepens, pines and manzanita patches congregate in greater numbers; rocks increase in size. This mountain, like Templeton Mountain, is Tertiary volcanic andesite in origin. Tertiary is a period within the Cenozoic Era; this Era ranges from 65 million years ago to current times. The mountain probably formed from earth fissures some 12 to 15 million years ago when the range was first uplifted along the Sierra Nevada Fault. Andesite is an intermediate volcanic rock. In magma form, it is not as viscous (did not contain as much silica) as rhyolite, which hardens quickly, (example: Cross Mountain), or as little as basalt, which flows freely (example: Malpais Lava). Thus this mountain obtained its cone shape but did not spill over. Temperature and dissolved gases in the magma were factors, too: high temperature and large amounts of gas increase flow and force.

Upon reaching the summit (9418/1.0) you can see Monache Meadow, the largest meadow in the Sierra Nevada. Beyond and northeast of the meadow, you can see Olancha Peak, the highest peak in the Southern Sierra. The view is most dramatic when snowmelt runoff gathers in huge, sky-blue pools on the meadow floor and snow blankets Olancha Peak.

*   *   *   *   *

Beyond the mountain turnoff, while you continue east, you pass a road to the upper reaches of the river, a camping area, and a junction with a road heading south before you reach a ford of South Fork Kern River (7860/1.0) at a wide crossing in Monache Meadow. "Monachi" or "fly people," was the name given to the local Indians by their western neighbors, the Yokuts, because their primary foodstuff and trading article was the pupae of a fly collected at Owens and Mono lakes. Monache was considered for the name of the county, which became Inyo County.

Turn left at the next junction, still on a road, and pass by the fenced compound of cabins that comprises the old Monache Meadow Lodge mentioned earlier. Quite soon you reach the campsites at Monache Creek and meet your incoming trail (7990/1.2). Now you return on the *Olancha Pass Trail* (be careful not to fork to the right soon after you begin to ascend, or you end up at Olivas Cow Camp) and make your way to Sage Flat and your starting point (5790/9.3).

PCT shield

T106   PCT Sierra Crest Backpack:
Olancha Pass to Horseshoe Meadow

This trip follows the Sierra crest over elevations ranging from 9000 to 10,500 feet. On the crest you have the inviting option of climbing three high Southern Sierra peaks. Occasional crestline windows to the east offer wondrous views of Owens Valley, while panoramic views to the west take in much of the Kern Plateau.

Distance   32.6 miles, shuttle trip
Steep Ascents   None
Elevation Gain   7000 feet
Skills   Easy route finding
Seasons   Spring, summer, fall (Wilderness permit required)
Maps   USGS 7.5 min *Haiwee Pass, Monache Mtn (0.2 mile), Olancha, Templeton Mtn, Cirque Pk*
Trailheads   79 & 88. This trip requires two cars. See car tour T109. Leave the first car at Horseshoe Meadow, **TH88,** the end of the trip. Then see car tour T100. Drive the second car to Sage Flat, **TH79,** the beginning of the trip. This is 51.0 miles from your first car.
Description   The beginning of this trip is described in T103.

Westbound Olancha Pass Trail Log

T103	Sage Flat Rd	5790	0.0
	equestrian tr	5960	0.5
	stock driveway	6760	1.0
	saddle	8600	2.6
	Olancha Pass	9220	1.0
	lateral to PCT	9220	1.4

Northbound PCT Trail Log

Olancha Pass Tr	9220	0.0
PCT	9240	0.5
Olancha Peak saddle	10,540	3.4

(PCT hikers continuing north from Kennedy Meadows on T75, turn left on the PCT off Olancha Pass Trail. Meet the PCT lateral junction at 9240 feet in 0.2 mile.)

An alternative to climbing Olancha Peak for plateau views is Point 10,600, west of the saddle and the trail. Campsites abound around the saddle.

From the saddle east of Olancha Peak and the cross-country climb to the summit, the PCT drops to Gomez Meadow on a gentle-to-moderate grade. It zigzags five times and then curves around the headwaters bowl of Monache Creek. The trail leads across a watershed divide, where it leaves South Sierra Wilderness and enters Golden Trout Wilderness. Beyond, it makes a northern descent, passing above a seasonal spring on exposed slopes with views of boulder-tipped Kern Peak across the Kern Plateau. This 11,510-foot peak counterbalances Olancha Peak; the two are among the highest points on the plateau.

Now the PCT meanders northwest, dropping in and out of forests, traversing seeps and springs that find their way to Brown Meadow and Long Stringer, and passing en route a picturesque "rabbit ears" rock outcrop. The trail gradually curves northeast, then bends southeast to cross a year-round creek (9030/3.7) with camping potential near its banks. From the creek the PCT leads north and then east on a slightly rolling course. It then bends sharply north-northwest and crosses a meadowside trail at a causeway abutment (9010/0.7). This is just west of very level Gomez Meadow.

The causeway's 35-yard length elevates the path above the sodden stringer beneath. Shooting stars seem almost airborne across the meadow. The common name of this flower is well-chosen, because its swept-back crimson/purple petals suggest flight. The PCT resumes at the north abutment and immediately crosses another meadowside path. It then curves northeast, then gradually northwest and soon skirts Big Dry Meadow. A path to the meadow leaves your trail opposite a tree-posted sign. Reminiscent of Indian lore, it says, *May the Great Spirit shine on your day in rainbow colors.*

You pass creekside campsites, then ford the step-across stream (8940/1.7) at the mouth of Death Canyon. A path immediately beyond the creek crossing takes equestrians to one in a series of corrals and camping areas built for the PCT trail crews of Inyo National Forest. Next you labor up 26 broadly spaced switchbacks on the blocky, spired ridge west of the canyon. Cross the crest of this ridge for the last time at a saddle near the Sierra crest. Foxtail pines now shade you and red, mountain pride penstemon decorate your path as you descend gently to a crestline saddle (10,390/3.7) from which the eastern slope drops precipitously to Owens Lake. This alkali flat is usually dry because Los Angeles Department of Water and Power diverted its inflow. You ascend on seven switchbacks, to attain a long, crestline prominence, reaching an elevation of 10,700 feet, with grand views of Owens Lake and the Coso and Inyo mountains east of it. Olancha and Kern peaks dominate the southern half of the horizon. At length you leave the ridgetop in a descending traverse of west-facing slopes, then curve west, and, just before leveling out near a saddle, meet a junction (10,425/1.5) where a faint, ½ mile-long lateral descends north to campsites and a corral. There is usually water from nearby springs. Below the junction, you skirt west across a saddle, then meander more or less northwest, crossing two more crest saddles. Just east of the second saddle (10,260/1.6) you find another corral, campsite and spring. About ½ mile later you cross yet another saddle.

Now you leave one cattle allotment and enter another. In fact, the whole plateau is a patchwork of these parcels: wilderness classification does not ban grazing. Most of the cattle people involved have been summering their animals in these allotments for several generations.

The PCT curves north where Sharknose Ridge juts off to the west, then skirts the west edge of wide Ash Meadow, traversing a nearly level stretch of Sierra crest. Here skilled cross-country hikers can wend their way east-northeast, 2.2 miles, to climb Muah Mountain. The PCT leaves the crest to make a brief, easy descent of west-facing slopes before passing a path (10,000/1.8) to another corral down in a ravine above Mulkey

Craggy outcrops line PCT

Meadows. Mount Langley, the southernmost 14,000-foot peak in the Sierra Nevada, sinks behind the shoulder of Trail Peak, and views of Mulkey Meadows improve as the dusty PCT descends. It bends east around a spur ridge, and then regains the Sierra crest after almost a mile on nearly level trail. Here, at a low saddle between the watersheds of Diaz Creek and Mulkey Creek, the PCT turns north (9670/1.8). At this point a cow path crosses the PCT; this is the path you take to climb Muah Mountain as described in T112.

The PCT now climbs the crest in a gentle-to-moderate grade and curves gradually northwest. After a mile it switchbacks on the crest, then leaves it for a short climb north to top a broad ridge south of Dutch Meadow. (North-to-south trekkers be alert lest you wander onto a former trail, again in use, to Mulkey Meadows. Take the left fork.) Bear northwest at a junction (9960/1.3), just below the next switchback, but if you need water, a campsite, a corral, turn right on the

0.2 mile lateral to Dutch Meadow.

The PCT climbs west switchbacks to the Sierra crest, attains a spur ridge, bends from north to west around a canyon, and then contours over to cross Mulkey Stock Driveway at Mulkey Pass (10,380/1.5). Beyond the driveway, the PCT traverses around the south side of a crestline-straddling hill to reach Trail Pass and a junction (10,500/0.8) with the Trail Pass Trail and a cross-country route to Trail Peak (see T113).

Here you leave the PCT and turn right on *Trail Pass Trail*. Weave north then switchback down the canyon, turning abruptly left where a section of trail was retired (10,080/0.6). You then make a long descending traverse along the lower slopes of Trail Peak to cross Horseshoe Meadow and its creek. Beyond, you ascend slightly to a 4-way junction (9940/1.3) and continue on, now on *Cottonwood Pass Trail* to your shuttle car at the Kern Plateau parking area and overnight campground (9940/0.2).

T107   Darwin Falls Side Trip

Darwin Falls, a 70-foot year-round cascade at the end of a narrow canyon whose vertical walls dwarf the viewer, would merit a special trip even if located in the Sierra. But this waterfall is in the desert!

Distance   1.6 miles, round trip
Steep Ascents   None
Elevation Gain   210 feet
Skills   Easy route finding; easy hiking
Seasons   All year (can be hot)
Map   Inyo County road map
Trailhead   81. See car tour T100. From Highway 395 in the town of Olancha, turn east on *Highway 190* (0.0/0.0), which winds through the desert between Coso and Inyo mountains. Turn west onto an unmarked, unpaved road (29.7/29.7), one mile before Panamint Springs. The **dirt road** curves southwest in a broad canyon to a fork (2.4/32.1). Take the right fork down into the wash and stop by a BLM gate (0.3/32.4), **TH81.**
Description   Begin in Darwin Canyon by stepping through the wide space between the

metal rails of the BLM fence (2550/0.0). There is no marked trail; you follow the stream **cross-country.** A few tamarisk shrubs appear where the canyon narrows. This graceful plant with attractive, spring-blooming plumes of pink flowers is sometimes referred to as "Salt-cedar." The non-native plant has some value as an erosion retardant, but it requires large quantities of water, an undesirable characteristic where water is so valuable. Also, tamarisks proliferate rapidly at the expense of native vegetation; its seeds are too small to be eaten by birds; and its scaley, salty leaves are unpalatable to native browsing animals. For all of these reasons, despite its beauty, removal projects have begun throughout the desert. Along the canyon to the right, a rusted pipe also taps this precious water.

In a few places you will have to scramble over greenish boulders of chlorite andesite volcanic rock. Just before you reach the foot of the falls, you contend with boulders and a willow thicket (2760/0.8). The 70-foot cascading falls bends in its narrow canyon—you see its last free fall. Desert wildlife abounds here, for this is the only water for miles around. You are asked not to contaminate it in any way.

Among other interesting sites hereabouts, is the mining town of Darwin, around 9.0 miles further up the unpaved road. It once boasted a population of 5000 people when lead, zinc, and silver were mined in the area.

T108   Timosea Peak Climb

This summit provides a viewpoint to the east of the impelling sweep of dry Owens Lake's alkali flats toward the Coso and Inyo ranges, and to the southeast down into the sheer wall depths of Cottonwood Creek Canyon. The route to the top makes a fine conditioning hike for alpine ascents.

Distance   3.0 miles, round trip
Steep Ascents   1.0 mile
Elevation Gain   3325 feet
Skills   Intermediate route finding; Class 2 climbing
Seasons   Spring, fall
Map   USGS 7.5 min *Bartlett*
Trailhead   82. See car tour T100.
Description   From the end of Cottonwood Road (5340/0.0), hike *cross-country* north-northeast into Golden Trout Wilderness past a curtain of mixed evergreen and deciduous shrubbery, to a boulderhop ford of Cotton-

wood Creek: a dangerous wade during spring runoff.

Beyond the creek, you climb steeply north on a sandy, brushy slope. You soon intercept a very slight ridge and ascend its crest amid ceanothus and mountain mohogany. Pinyon and Jeffrey pines then appear, at first scattered across the slope, soon congregating in stands. At length you meet the main ridge. You bear northwest up the crestline, and soon reach an easier gradient to attain the summit (8664/1.5).

Switchbacks on Horseshoe Meadow Road

T109   Horseshoe Meadow Car Tour
(With Directions to Trailheads 84–88)

Driving this road, although paved and wide, requires your absolute attention, but passengers are treated to breathtaking views of Owens Valley far below and jagged, granite bedrock nearby. In the high elevation setting at the end, you can picnic, explore Horseshoe Meadow, fish for golden trout, or just relax and inhale the fragrance of pine-perfumed air.

Distance   22.8 miles, one way
Steep Ascents   None
Elevation Gain   6400 feet
Skills   Easy route finding; paved roads
Seasons   Spring, summer, fall
Map   Tulare County road map
Tourhead   83. The junction of Highway 395 and Whitney Portal Road in the city of Lone Pine is **TH83**. This tour begins at the terminus of car tour T100.
Description   Proceed west from the junction on **Whitney Portal Road** (3733/0.0/ 0.0). This is the access road to renowned 14,494-foot Mount Whitney, the highest mountain in the contiguous United States. From this vantage point Mount Whitney is tucked back and north of Lone Pine Peak, which appears to be most prominent.

You immediately enter BLM's Alabama Hills Recreation Area. The land in view around you is in the process of rapid change in geological terms of time. The Sierra is rising, a process that began some 15 million years ago. The weathered, rounded, rough granitic Alabama Hills surrounding you appear geologically older than the jagged Sierra escarpment; in fact, they are the same rock and age as that of the Sierra, but were left behind when the range was uplifted. At the same time, the bedrock floor of Owens Valley lies 6000 feet or more below sea level, suggesting that it has been dropping as the Sierra and Inyo mountains rise. Just west of the canal crossing, a side road leads to view the 10- to 15-foot high north-south 1872 fault scarp: an example of this earth activity.

Driving west you see people fishing and seeking relief from the intense summer heat along the cottonwood/willow-shaded banks of Lone Pine Creek threading its way next to

the road. To the right in 2.8 miles, you pass Movie Road where many of the old Westerns were made. Astride their horses, actors such as Tom Mix, William Boyd and John Wayne rode off into the Alabama Hills. A commemorative plaque next to Movie Street was dedicated in 1990 during Lone Pine's Movie Festival by Roy Rogers, who also made films here. The Lone Pine area and especially the Alabama Hills have been favorite locations for filming all types of movies and TV series from 1920 to present days. Scenes in the Lucille Ball, Desi Arnaz comedy *The Long Long Trailer*, 1954, were filmed here. Among the TV series were: *Tales of Wells Fargo*, 1957–62; *Have Gun Will Travel*, 1957–63; *Rawhide*, 1959–66; *Bonanza*, 1959–73. Directors carefully positioned their cameras to exclude the highly recognizable Sierra crest.

Shortly after Movie Road, turn left on **Horseshoe Meadow Road** (3.1/3.1), where you make a protracted, moderate ascent south. In 1.7 miles you pass BLM's Tuttle Creek Campground road which leads to camping areas on willow-lined Tuttle Creek in less than a mile. The usual amenities of an established campground are offered without fee. As you travel along, Lubken Canyon Road comes in from the east (3.6/6.7). This narrow, paved 3.4 mile road bypasses Lone Pine and saves drivers from the south 7.7 miles.

You next pass the gate (3.1/9.8) at Carroll Creek. It remains open in winter, affording cross-country skiers access to snowline. Hazardous conditions are cited as one of the reasons this road is not plowed: namely, massive avalanches that roar down from the flanks of Wonoga Peak. Skiers eager to reach the untouched snow on the plateau and mountain slopes should keep this in mind. An alternative is a wearing hike up Cottonwood Canyon. See T111.

Horseshoe Meadow Road probably would not be built today: the prohibitive cost of blasting the granite slopes and the highly visible scarring of the Sierra escarpment would end the project before it began. The original impetus for the road came from Inyo County and the city of Los Angeles, who sought to exploit the water, power-generating and recreation potential of the upper basin. Their first attempt to build this access road was halted in 1929 when their construction equipment proved inadequate to get past the cliffs of Wonoga chute. In the 1960s, a Trail Peak ski-development proposal led to renewed efforts to finish the road. An extension was completed by 1967, but the development plans were shelved after a Forest Service reappraisal. The road became a heavily used entree into the Sierra backcoun-

try. Hazardous overflow roadside parking and crowded camping conditions needed to be addressed. In the 1980s, the road was extended farther and completely paved. The overnight camping facilities and equestrian grounds were added, the pack station was moved to the flats and the trails were rerouted to commence from the campgrounds.

Driving on, you quickly gain altitude via long-legged switchbacks, and are treated to expansive eastward views from the kind of dizzying heights you usually reach only in a low-flying aircraft—or a hang glider. Below, earthy pastel hues of Owens Valley dissolve into distant blues of Coso and Inyo mountains. You see an awesome display of chiseled bedrock granodiorite at the fourth switchback; then curve deeply into an east-trending ridge eminating from Wonoga Peak on the final short switchbacks. Ahead you enter a pinyon-juniper woodland so common on the eastern slopes. Traversing southwest you soon reach Walt's Point (9180/8.7/18.5)

Weathered Alabama Hills

Hang gliders poised for flight, Horseshoe Meadow Road

where a plaque commemorates Walter G. Millet, whose interest and labor helped spur the first extension of this road.

This ledge plays a major role for those who enjoy the sport of hang gliding. In the 1980s world distance records were set here. By the 1990s, "tandem," "out and return," "triangle" and female world distance records from this launch had not been broken elsewhere. It is a favorite launch place in spring and summer for 100-mile flights. Poised for flight, hang gliders, attached to their colorful wings like mammoth birds, peer down the canyon at a pair of ribbons whose flow pattern indicates the desired updraft for launch. At the right moment they leap into space above the precipitous canyon where Owens Dry Lake spreads 6000 vertical feet below. Earthlings cautiously peer over the edge—

You pass the paved parking spaces to the right for Little Cottonwood Creek **TH84** of T110 (0.3/18.8), then pass the point of departure for Cottonwood Canyon Trail of T111 to the left at **TH85** (1.7/20.5). (Check your mileage to locate this trailhead as it is hard to identify from the north side of the road.) Old campsites are still in use to the left, and the abandoned section of Cottonwood Lakes Trail comes into the right a second before your road curves south and you cross Cottonwood Creek. Pass a gate, beyond which you

find Mulkey Stock Driveway **TH86** of T112 & T117 (1.7/22.2), marked only by a fishing regulations sign nailed to a tree. (Inyo Forest personnel would prefer people hike to the trail via a use path found to the south of the camping area ahead where there is adequate parking.) A fork to the right takes you to the visitor's information trailer, the next fork (0.2/22.4) leads to the Cottonwood Lakes loop road and **TH87**. People seeking the Kern Plateau loop drive straight ahead and skip the following directions.

The Cottonwood Lakes loop road (0.0/ 0.0) to the right leads past the walk-in campground, then to the Cottonwood Lakes Trail, **TH87** for T110's shuttle car (0.6/0.6). The road continues to the equestrian center with corrals and campsites and on to the pack station and overflow parking.

You drive ahead on the Kern Plateau loop road to **TH88** (9940/0.4/22.8), the conjoined beginning of Trail Pass and Cottonwood Pass trails of many trips in this book. The road loops around to a hiker's walk-in campground, limited to one night at a small fee, and to a picnic area shaded by lodgepole pines. Horseshoe Meadow spreads to the south.

T110   Little Cottonwood Creek Day Hike
With Excursion BB: Wonoga Peak

*The ingress of this trip penetrates remote country where solitude is almost guaran-
teed and pathfinding skills are challenged; the egress follows one of the most popular
trails in the area. In this pleasing theater of nature's handiwork, you hike alongside
singing creeks and peaceful meadows, thread cool forests and view cameo appear-
ances of glacial carved Sierran mountains.*

Distance   7.2 miles, shuttle trip
Steep Ascents   None
Elevation Gain   1400 feet
Skills   Intermediate pathfinding skills;
moderate to strenuous hiking
Seasons   Spring, summer, fall
Maps   USGS 7.5 min *Bartlett, Cirque Pk*
Trailheads   84 & 87. This trip requires two
cars. See car tour T109. Leave the first car at
TH87, the end of the trip at the Cottonwood
Lakes loop parking lot. Drive the second car
back to **TH84** at Little Cottonwood Creek.
This is 4.2 miles from the first car.
Description   Your route, ***Little Cottonwood Trail,*** switchbacks above the paved
parking spaces on the north side of Horse-
shoe Meadow Road (9260/0.0). This trail
was built as a shortcut to private Golden
Trout Camp before the road was extended. At
the last switchback, you turn right. Here
Little Cottonwood Trail coincides with a segment of the Hockett Trail, pioneered in 1864
by John Benjamin Hockett. The original trail
spanned the Sierra from Visalia to Fort
Independence, and served the army as well as
prospectors at the Coso silver mines.
 Your path quickly enters Golden Trout
Wilderness and crosses Little Cottonwood
Creek, then ascends next to it. The valley
opens to the northeast beyond a short stretch
where the path is pinched between the
alder/Jeffrey pine/willow-bracketed creek
and exposed granodiorite rock. The trail is
met in this open section near a campsite, by a
use trail (9480/0.4) to Wonoga Peak. You
can either climb the peak or skip the excursion description and continue along the trail.

Excursion BB: Wonoga Peak

*Once you have visited Wonoga Peak, you
will want to return again, for from this little
known peak await awesome views of Owens
Valley and the High Sierra escarpment.*

Distance   1.4 miles, round trip
Steep Ascents   0.2 mile
Elevation Gain   1895 feet
Skills   Intermediate route finding; Class 2
climbing
Map   USGS 7.5 min *Bartlett*
Description   Upon leaving the Little
Cottonwood Trail (9480/0.0), your ***use trail***
ventures north up the canyon drainage, then
fades. You continue to climb ***cross-country***
near the ravine on whichever side has the
largest spaces between sagebrush clumps and
tangles of mountain mahogany. As the
canyon curves northeast, you climb among
pine trees and head for visible Wonoga Peak,
the highest granite point at the apex of the
right-angled crest. Stay to the right of the
bowl as you approach the crest, then cross
over the top.
 Beyond, you turn left on a steep climb
north, seeking grassy pockets between the
large boulders whenever possible. Just past
the peak you turn back, south, to easily
ascend to the summit (10,371/0.7). Ribbons
atop indicate wind currents for hang gliders
riding the thermals. This is one of the most
sweeping views in the Sierra of its eastern
escarpment; it is viewed from a perch 7000
feet above Owens Valley.

 *   *   *   *   *

Cross the creek at the use trail junction, ascend a switchback on the Little Cottonwood Trail, hike ½ mile northwest, then west and recross the creek before reaching a large campsite. Although a trail of sorts continues on the south bank, you hike on the north bank above a spring with its spongy grass, then along the sunny, sandy path past another campsite, over a low boulder rise to a ford of a brook. Head west on a sometimes obscure path along Little Cottonwood Creek, then along a meadow-enclosing fence.

A campsite next to another spring beyond the meadow marks the final crossing of Little Cottonwood Creek. The trail leaves the creek's canyon to climb a broad ridge northwest, then west. An abundance of ducks guides the way up to and over a wide south-extending shoulder (10,660/2.9). You can also follow the overhead telephone line. (Most of the lines on the Inyo Forest are still in use, unlike those on the Sequoia.)

While distant views of the dramatic mountains surrounding the Cottonwood Lakes Basin enrich your descent, switchbacks help you down the steep slopes to fenced Golden Trout Camp (10,200/1.0), a non-profit educational facility owned by Thacher School of Ojai, California. Each semester, Thacher closes for one week during which students and staff explore the Sierra. The camp, which is on government leased land within Golden Trout Wilderness, is available to other outdoor education and research groups. "Camp Bug Hunter" was the earthy name affixed to this site in 1916.

The route south from the camp differs on every map. The former trail on the east bank of Cottonwood Creek is badly fragmented. The Cottonwood Lakes Trail emplaced years ago on the west bank was realigned in the 1980s to reach the Cottonwood Lakes parking lot: this is the trail you seek. On a *cross-country* route, follow the private property south as best you can, then turn right to cross the meadow and the creek below the fence. You quickly meet and turn left on the heavily used **Cottonwood Lakes Trail.** You soon cross over a moraine, then meet obscure South Fork Trail (10,035/1.5) just before crossing South Fork Creek. Beyond, you ascend the slopes leaving Cottonwood Creek valley, curve southeast to pass a junction (10,120/1.2) with a trail to equestrian campsites with corrals and the pack station, and hike on past a trail to Cottonwood Pass/Trail Pass trails junction. You continue on the Cottonwood Lakes Trail to the parking lot (10,045/0.2) and your shuttle car.

T111   Cottonwood Creek Canyon Day Hike

A braided, tumbling stream, a towering, flying buttress, leaf-strewn glens and an overlay of human history await you on this trip.

Distance   5.6 miles, shuttle trip
Steep Ascents   None
Elevation Gain   None
Skills   Easy route finding; moderate hiking
Seasons   Spring, summer, fall (avoid during heavy snowmelt)
Maps   USGS 7.5 min *Cirque Pk, Bartlett*
Trailheads   85 & 82. This trip requires two cars. See car tour T100. Leave the first car at **TH82,** the end of the trip on Cottonwood Road. Then see car tour T109. Drive the second car to the beginning of the trip at **TH85.** (Although billed as a separate shuttle

trip, this adventure is better as a tag at the end of other hikes in the Horseshoe Meadow area. Then one person can drive the car down to **TH82** to pick up the hikers, thus avoiding extra trips on Horseshoe Meadow Road.)
Description   Begin south of Horseshoe Meadow Road on the *dirt road* (9327/0.0) that takes you 0.1 mile east to the site of Colonel Sherman Stevens' sawmill. Over a century ago this entrepreneur built the mill and a flume down the canyon next to the creek to satisfy the appetite of a mining town for timber. The town was Cerro Gordo, a

name which, translated from the Spanish, means "Fat Hill." It was located far across Owens Lake, high in the Inyo Mountains, atop a silver vein that was indeed fat with wealth for the miners. Because the Inyo Mountains stand in the rain shadow of the Sierra Nevada, few trees grow there. The miners needed timbers to shore up their tunnels and to shelter themselves in the winter. From the mill, where you now stand, timber raced down the flume to Owens Lake, then a vast saucer of briny water. There some of the logs were converted to charcoal at the shoreline kilns, for later shipment; the rest were freighted across the waters by steamer, en route to Cerro Gordo. By 1877 all of the mine's known resources were exhausted and the town was abandoned. The mill stopped production; its flume soon collapsed. Nearly 90 years later, a campfire gutted the mill; then vandals wantonly damaged the kilns at Owens Lake—now protected with fencing.

The piece of pipe upslope was part of a penstock that supplied water to spin the sawmill's turbine. The rusted metal pieces strewn about and the stack of slivered lumber remain. You soon pass a weathered, low-roofed notched-log cabin, the only loggers' house that survived. (The metal shack was constructed later.) As you descend *Cottonwood Canyon Trail* look for heaped flume boards.

You see Horseshoe Meadow Road climbing to the northeast, around you dry slopes of mountain mahogany give way to patches with thickets of willow, currant and wild rose that infringe on the seldom maintained trail. After a switchback, you cross the creek on a wooden bridge; the trail (8880/0.5) from Last Chance Meadow meets yours. You may puzzle over a wooden barrier placed across the path. You may also puzzle, from time to time, when the trail unravels, but apart from strands leading to the several campsites spotted along the route, they rejoin. This pattern of paths is typical of a stock driveway, which this was. Now cattle are trucked up the mountain in spring; then herded down the mountain in fall via steep Wormhole Canyon, south of here. This was also the path by which

people reached Horseshoe Meadow before the road was built. Stalwart ski mountaineers still use it to reach the pristine snowfields of the plateau. You have a comparatively easy hike on the trail, now in the shade of red fir, lodgepole and western white pine.

Cross the ephemeral creek draining Last Chance Meadow, perched far upslope: its water ices over the path during a freeze. Shortly you cross a larger stream issuing from springs above. When the trail splits again, take the high path. You traverse in open country above the creek, then switchback twice to rejoin the split section of trail and zigzag down to cross Cottonwood Creek (7780/1.5).

Except during snowmelt, the ford is not difficult. A bridge once spanned the creek 140 yards upstream from here. If you look at the trees at about a height of 40 feet, you will see that some have avalanche "burns"—bare spots where the bark has been gouged away from the cambium by the torrents that knocked the bridge off its northern abutment during the winter of 1969—a season of record snowfall. Now on the north bank, elderberry bushes thrive. Its 2–8 inch wide, flat top clusters of creamy white flowers turn to clusters of blue berries in autumn. Large creekside campsites appear under canopies of firs and oaks; you then ford Little Cottonwood Creek (7360/0.6). Minutes later, the path disappears beneath the brush at the foot of a rock slide, do not cross the creek, but push your way through the brush. You soon regain the trail as it curves around a ridge beyond the rocks. After descending on loose slope soils and gravels, with the inspiring turret of Timosea Peak looming to the east, turn right at another split in the trail and recross Cottonwood Creek on a steel-girdered bridge (6220/1.5) inscribed *Cottonwood #1/1963.*

Sometimes gnats become annoying during the last part of this hike. Clouds of adult gnats swarm near the stream and surround you as you hike by. Their larvae in streams and lakes are important food for fish. While fanning the gnats away you hardly notice the arching golden and live oak boughs around you or the olive drab, pink and gray of the various surfaces of the buttress high above you. The differing textures survive from an early engulfment and alteration of ocean- and stream-bed deposits by molten granite.

You soon pass a trailside cairn, evidently indicating the start of one of the routes up Timosea, but not the one in this book (see T108), then pass the Golden Trout Wilderness sign, hop a small creek and arrive at an opening where your car awaits (5360/1.5).

T112   Muah Mountain Backpack

Muah is a favorite of peakbaggers, both for its prominence and for its views. Horizons up to 75 miles away can be scanned from its crest. Pivoting on its top, you view first Telescope Peak, the farthest, easternmost identifiable point in the desert ranges; then, revolving clockwise, you successively discern the ramparts of Olancha Peak, Kern Peak, the Great Western Divide and Mount Langley.

Distance   12.4 miles, round trip
Steep Ascents   0.6 mile
Elevation Gain   2715 feet
Skills   Intermediate route finding; Class 2 climbing
Seasons   Spring, summer, fall (Wilderness permit required)
Maps   USGS 7.5 min *Cirque Pk, Bartlett*
Trailhead   86. See car tour T109.
Description   This hike begins on *Mulkey Stock Driveway* (9915/0.0) where Horseshoe Meadow Road bends southwest 0.1 mile before it reaches the road to the Visitor Information trailer. A fishing regulation sign nailed to the pine is the only sign at the entrance of this trail. (A use trail south of the campground is INF's preferred beginning of this trail because of ample parking there.) The trail leads through the woods to a cattle pen and chute, where the INF's preferred path comes in. Turn left along the pen, then descend on a gravelly slope into Golden Trout Wilderness.

Cross the creeks from Horseshoe Meadow and Round Valley and follow on a soft, sandy trail along the east side of the meadow to a forked junction (9870/0.9) with an abandoned segment of Trail Pass Trail. Continuing on Mulkey Stock Driveway, the left fork, you now ascend into forest, cross a seasonal creek and zigzag up any of the multiple paths created by cattle herds and drovers, to the pass (10,380/0.8), one of the easiest to cross on the Sierra crest.

Here you turn left toward Olancha Pass on the *PCT,* which seems to be the least defined path at this junction. After a barely perceptible rise, you swerve in around a canyon and out around a ridge, then traverse above a Dutch Meadow canyon. After a pair of switchbacks, you pass a *public corral* sign and a use path (9980/1.5) to meadowside campsites and the Dutch Meadow spring-fed creek.

The PCT turns abruptly southeast at the meadow path and descends on the left side of a broad ridge. A former defunct trail from Dutch Meadow to Mulkey Meadow splits off the PCT to the right side of the ridge. At length your trail levels on a low saddle between the watersheds of Mulkey and Diaz

Muah Mountain south to Olancha Peak

creeks where you leave the PCT and turn left on a cow path (9670/1.3).

The eastbound *cow path* emerges from forest, turns southeast and travels awhile along the sage-dotted margin of Diaz Creek's meadowy banks above the marshy grass. The route leaves the meadow and enters the woods where the first canyon comes in on the south. At this point look for the *use trail* marked by a duck near a possible campsite, about 100 feet west of the canyon's creek. After nearly ⅓ mile of steep canyon climbing on this path, the gradient eases. Now you look ahead for your next landmark: a steep, shal-

low gully that forks southeast into which creekside willows slightly indent. Cross the creek in a grassy clearing and resume your trek on a use path, now on the left side of the willow-choked creek, to the shallow gully.

Here your *cross-country* route turns up the gully, which flattens and disappears on Muah's steep west-facing slopes, then it reaches the ridge top of Muah Mountain. Skirting north of the outcrops astride the ridge, each appearing to be the summit, make your way to the last prominent boulder outcrop, the summit of Muah Mountain (11,016/1.7).

T113   Trail Peak Climb

Trail Peak stands near center on the northern Kern Plateau. Just about every peak and meadow in the eastern Golden Trout Wilderness can be seen from its summit, plus many of the Great Western Divide and High Sierra mountains. If you can hike and climb up a slope, you can achieve the summit of this mountain, the third highest on the Plateau. Its prominence and location make it an exciting climb even for the very skilled peakbagger.

Distance   6.0 miles, round trip
Steep Ascents   0.4 mile
Elevation Gain   1665 feet
Skills   Easy route finding; Class 2 climbing
Seasons   Spring, summer, fall
Map   USGS 7.5 min *Cirque Pk*
Trailhead   88. See car tour T109.
Description   From the top of the Kern Plateau parking lot, take the *Cottonwood Pass Trail* (9940/0.0) west into Golden Trout Wilderness to a 4-way junction (9940/0.2). The trail to Cottonwood Lakes parking lot branches north, Cottonwood Pass Trail continues west while your trail, now *Trail Pass Trail,* heads south to Horseshoe Meadow. Here you have an open view of Trail Peak, the highest mountain seen on the ridge to the south. It and its neighbor peaks on that section of the Sierra crest were intended for a vast alpine ski complex, for which Horseshoe Meadow Road was initially extended. The Forest Service withdrew its approval after viewing the submitted plans, and now the mountains are protected from develop-

ment by Golden Trout Wilderness.

On a beveled log, you ford the meadow-threading creek, cross a low, sandy ridge, enter woods, and contour southeast part way around Round Valley while steadily gaining elevation. At the junction of an unmarked, retired segment of trail (10,080/1.3), turn acutely right where, via switchbacks and zigzags, you climb south to the pass (10,500/0.6).

The PCT traverses the pass and so do you, heading west, but you leave the trail quickly to climb *cross-country* directly up the slope. Shaded by scattered foxtail pines, you climb steeply, weaving around boulders, then at length, climbing and weaving over boulders. The grade eases, then you climb southwest up the summit's gentle slope, past three stony rises and reach the summit (11,605/0.9)—elevation according to the 1988 topo—11,622 feet on the survey marker. Many of the elevations on the new provisional topographic maps differ from previous numbers. Considering advances in technology, the newer figures are probably more accurate.

Here at the top, you can look for a favorite mountain or meadow on the eastern Golden Trout Wilderness and no doubt find it. Judging by the quantity of scat left by marmots on the rocks, they, too, spend a lot of time scanning wilderness.

Marmot

T114   Horseshoe Meadow to Kern River Backpack

This journey takes you across the varied terrain of northern Golden Trout Wilderness on the Kern Plateau to a descent into the glaciated valley of the Kern River. You should plan a layover day at this superb river setting. The towering, chiseled, granite walls compare favorably with those of Yosemite Valley.

Distance   40.6 miles, semiloop trip
Steep Ascents   0.5 mile
Elevation Gain   6300 feet
Skills   Easy route finding
Seasons   Spring, summer, fall (Wilderness permit required)

Maps   USGS 7.5 min *Cirque Pk, Johnson Pk, Kern Pk, Kern Lakes*
Trailhead   88. See car tour T109.
Description   The beginning of this trip is described in T113.

Westbound Cottonwood Pass Trail Log

T113	Kern Plateau parking		
	lot	9940	0.0
	4-way jct	9940	0.2

Southeastbound Trail Pass Trail Log

	4-way jct	9940	0.0
	abandoned trail section	10,080	1.3
	Trail Pass	10,500	0.6

The PCT crosses astride the pass; on Trail Pass Trail you descend south of it on eight switchbacks, then gradually curve southwest. Portals in the foxtail forest afford a glimpse of Olancha Peak on the southern horizon; then, in the lodgepole forest, a peek at Kern Peak. You cross and then descend alongside a gurgling brook lined with willows, corn lilies and currants, but swing away from it before reaching the several large campsites along its banks. Soon you pass an extension of the Templeton Trail (9400/2.1); and, in minutes, walk through a junction (9340/0.2) with eastbound, multi-laned Mulkey Stock Driveway on the meadow floor.

Around you, narrowing margins of sagebrush that infringe Mulkey Meadows attest to over a century of grazing. You tramp west on interwoven paths across a slender south-flowing creek and thread among low sagebrush, then over a nearly denuded grit slope,

Mulkey Meadows from PCT

which every meadow of size seems to have. This grit is punctured with green gentian, a sturdy plant over a foot tall. Along its stems are compact whorls of leaves with tiny four-petaled, purple-veined, white flowers. Beyond, a finger of Bullfrog Meadow is speckled with narrow-leafed, shiny-yellow, meadow buttercups. You leave meadows temporarily, pass through a stock-fence gate and ascend among trees to top a broad, low gap (9580/2.1).

While approaching the South Fork Kern River, you may see a bluebird, robin or black-hooded junco flit about near springs and grasses. Turn left to hike south along fledgling South Fork (9280/0.8). North of the turn is a small, secluded, slope-perched campsite. The river originates in the mountains between Trail and Cottonwood passes, just over two air miles from here. The downstream trail was blasted out of the rock in places. Columbine and monkey flower nod in the granite niches, while willow and currant intermittently screen the stream whose banks host an assortment of wildflowers. An easy ford, then you descend on the river's west bank, soon passing the vague McConnel Meadow Trail (9030/0.6), which forks east. Flats across the river make good campsites.

As the canyon widens, you duck in and out of dense stands of lodgepole, then pass through a creaky-hinged stock gate and arrive at the forest edge of sagebrushy Tunnel Meadow. A 1500-foot runway near the river, a corral and small piles of rubble in the pines to your left remain of the once flourishing Tunnel Air Camp. In operation since 1946, it was ghosted by the Wilderness Act. You proceed straight ahead past a lateral (8950/1.5) leading west to the Siberian Pass Trail. Shortly after the forest pinches off the meadow, and you meet the south terminus of the Siberian Pass Trail (8930/1.0). When you leave the junction, you come upon a large dip in a ridge. This depression has a curious history.

Here Golden Trout Creek and South Fork Kern River flow on collision courses, bending sharply away at the last moment, their pattern like a crazy "X" blocked in the center by the ridge on which you stand. In the late 1800s, farmers in the South Fork Kern River Valley wanted more water for their crops than the South Fork could supply. They eyed Golden Trout Creek covetously and devised a plan to divert its water. The plan was implemented in 1886 when a tunnel was punched through this low ridge, the center of the "X," which diverted water from Golden Trout Creek into the South Fork Kern River. The tunnel served its purpose for a short while then caved in; it was replaced by an open cut, which also collapsed. A 1.5 mile ditch to divert the creek's water north of the tunnel was then dug. It, too, was plagued with problems, and when suits over water rights were filed around the turn of the century, the project was abandoned. The ditch is still apparent east of the Siberian Pass Trail, but little evidence remains of the tunnel.

You move on and pass Tunnel Guard Station, once the hub of much activity, now occasionally manned in summer. When you arrive at "Chickenfoot" junction (8900/0.3), Trail Pass Trail ends. Ramshaw Trail heads southeast, Kern Peak Trail, south (a wonderful climb of Kern Peak begins here. See T117), and *Golden Trout Trail* starts ahead—so do you.

Once out of the forest on the wide, sodden, meadowy bank of Golden Trout Creek, your route turns west. It crosses the creek at an unmarked junction (8895/0.3) with the seldom maintained Bear Meadow Trail, which begins straight ahead, south. After you wade through the water next to the fence, the sandy path returns you to the woods where it meets the next junction (8890/0.6). Hikers on T115 fork left on Volcano Trail at this point.

Continuing on Golden Trout Trail's granitic grit, you veer northwest, then catch a glimpse of the Groundhog Cinder Cone. Groundhog was the scene of the greatest activity in what geologists term the Toowa Valley trio. Although not the largest cone, lava—basalt, to be sure—burst forth from its base, filling Golden Trout Canyon to a considerable depth.

In a half mile from the last junction, you curve west; watch lest you march straight ahead on a cow path to Groundhog Meadow. Near Golden Trout Creek, now often on basaltic gravel, step over the brook draining Groundhog Meadow, cross a bouldery ridge and return to Golden Trout Creek. Here the path and the creek are pressed between granite slopes to the right and the bulging basalt flow to the left.

In this press, you arrive at the junction of the Little Whitney Trail (8480/2.7), which begins here. You cross the creek at this point, pass through a gate of the High Sierra Stock Users' fence, pass campsites and curve around the Malpais (Bad Country) basalt flow. You branch right from the junction (8390/0.4) of the Volcano Trail's west end, cross the south tip of Little Whitney Meadow and again ford Golden Trout Creek. (To avoid crossing the creek twice, you could walk ahead on Little Whitney Trail from the junction, pass through the Stock Users' gate, hike over Little Whitney Meadow to the cow

Tunnel before collapse

camp fence, leave the trail for a left turn on a use trail, ford Johnson Creek and curve west through the meadow to the right of Golden Trout Creek.)

Members of the High Sierra Stock Users Association, with the approval of the Forest Service, have fenced the meadow south of the cow camp, which allows their horses to roam and graze freely within its wide confines. This is a popular camping area for all equestrians; hikers may find the best sites taken and other sites scattered with horse biscuits instead of the usual cow muffins.

Two paths ascend into a lodgepole forest at the southwest tip of Little Whitney Meadow—take either one, they soon join. You emerge from the fence enclosure, then make a final ford of Golden Trout Creek, peaceful here before it races down its steep gorge. You ascend to cross a decomposing basalt flow, then alongside a spring-watered meadow with camping possibilities, cross it and its brook, pass a streamside campsite and arrive at Natural Bridge (7955/1.9), a tufa and basalt phenomena.

Beyond the bridge, you see that water from the first of two streams you step across is diverted into a ditch from which it seeps to moisten meadow grasses. Jeffrey pines and white firs have replaced lodgepole pines; Kern ceanothus and manzanita form the understory brush.

The trail steepens as you leave the roof of basalt flow. This lava is speculated to have filled the canyon to a depth of 600 feet around 2.5 million years ago. Some proposed that the lava flow and upward earth thrusts account for the unique species of golden trout found on the Kern Plateau: these trout originally were Kern River rainbows which were then isolated upstream by the upheavals and evolved independently of their parent stock.

Descend the steep slopes on short zig-zags, then you traverse around a canyon high above and south of the thundering cascades of Golden Trout Creek. You may be able to see the spindrift of Volcano Falls from the trail. Continuing to switchback down between the river's giant east walls, you pass

near columnar basalt, the type that makes up Devils Postpile. The canyon's U-shaped profile betrays its glacial origins. Kern Canyon glaciers advanced as far south as Hole-in-the-Ground sometime in the last three million years. They left in their wake the wide, riverside terraces below and the awesome bluffs towering overhead.

As for man's impact, much of the route you have followed on this trip coincides with the old Hockett Trail, a trans-Sierra supply route of the late 1800s. A move is afoot by history buffs to encourage the Forest Service to place *Hockett Trail* signs at significant points along its route.

After a half mile trek southwest along the sandy, manzanita-clad terrace, you descend past a lateral north to a private cabin and immediately cross the substantial steel-girder bridge (6300/2.8) spanning the Kern River. West of the river, in Sequoia National Park, you will find large, terraced campsites shaded by Jeffrey pines and serenaded by the river's tumbling water. An invitation, it seems, to linger, relax, visit the ranger station 0.3 mile up the trail or walk south to Kern Lakes (just over 2.5 miles to Little Kern Lake). Extensive trips south and west are described in this book's companion edition; trips north are included in *Sierra South,* published by Wilderness Press.

On this tour, you return to Little Whitney Meadow (8390/4.7) the way you came. Try to tackle the steep canyon ascent in the cool of the morning. Once there you have a choice of two routes to Big Whitney Meadow. The first route, the scenic creek trail, is easy to follow; it has 780 feet less elevation gain than the second route, but is 1.6 miles farther. The second, a lesser used trail, climbs through the woods southeast of Johnson Peak.

If you choose the first route, retrace your incoming steps 4.3 miles to the Siberian Pass Trail, just east of the Forest Service cabin at Tunnel Meadow, then follow T115 description from there until you join the second route at Big Whitney.

Northbound Siberian Pass Trail
T115   Trail Pass Tr   8930 0.0

Barigan Stringer Tr	9400	3.0
Little Whitney Tr	9740	2.4
Cottonwood Pass Tr	9740	0.1

— — — — —

If you choose the second, take the *use trail* to the southwest corner of the cow-camp fence (8440/0.6) on the north tip of Little Whitney Meadow, and follow the fence on the west side to the buildings. Now on *Little Whitney Trail,* you go through the gate of the Stock Users' fence and onto the left path where the trail splits. (The right path continues along the fence; neither trail enters the camp.) Now traveling northeast, you climb in forest to cross a broad pumiced ridge, ejecta from the nearby Little Whitney Cinder Cone, a dwarfed distant relative of the Groundhog and South Fork cones.

Abruptly the forest ends at Salt Lick Meadow (8700/1.2). Here you turn right, cross the soggy south tip of the meadow, jump its creeks, then enter the forest to the east on a wide path. Continuing east, you cross a wooded section, then another meadow. In this second glade, follow a path east across the grass, but turn off near the end to slant northeast across the meadow tip and enter the forest on a broad path identified by a square blaze on a tree left of the path. (If you continue straight across the meadow to the woods, you find a blaze next to a path that turns back to Little Whitney Meadow.)

In 0.1 mile after reentering the woods, you leap across Johnson Creek. Replenish your water supply here. You now head northeast up a long, moderate incline away from Johnson Creek, but in time, return to cross a usually dry incipient branch of the creek twice; then you zigzag up a steep slope to a saddle (10,280/3.4). All the while solitary Johnson Peak fills the view to your left.

You take a few descending switchbacks in forest above an expansive meadow, then cross Barigan Stringer, the Rocky Basin Lakes outlet, which is often dry late in summer. Just beyond the creek you pass a 4-way junction (10,083/0.5) with the trail to Rocky Basin. You climb over a moraine ridge, then

Little Whitney Meadow

down a long gradual descent to the *Siberian Trail* (9740/2.5), where you join the alternate route from Little Whitney Meadow. Turning north, you quickly meet the Cottonwood Pass Trail (9740/0.1).

Turn right on the *Cottonwood Pass Trail,* which heads east. You leave pine forest for a barren, gritty sand slope where pussy paws and monkey flowers stipple the tan slopes rose, and disc and ray blooms of woolly daisies dab them saffron. You then cross a sagebrush and grass meadow, ford a serpentine branch of Golden Trout Creek's headwaters midway, and ascend on a sandy slope to a stand of pines with mat lupine groundcover. This pattern of slope, meadow, creek and pines is repeated twice. En route you pass several campsites, some hidden back from the path; an obscure meadow-crossing shortcut to the Siberian Trail at the end of the pine-covered "island"; and a USGS snow survey cabin deep in the woods.

Now in forest again, beyond Big Whitney Meadow, you curve south and gear down to tackle the switchbacks (10,000/2.4). If you plan an overnight near these ascending switchbacks, the next day's climb seems much easier. Climb the first 11, then cross

Stokes Stringer, which is the outlet of Chicken Springs Lake and the drainage of Cottonwood Pass's west side. A climb on 19 more switches, all of which make an otherwise steep climb into a moderate ascent; a long traverse next to a willow, currant and grass canyon meadow; then four more switchbacks; and you arrive at a fragile alpine fell field with a festive array of wildflowers. Soon you veer northeast just several yards south of large campsites overhung by foxtail pine boughs.

Snow survey pole #251 stands in the meadow to your right. Aerial photographs are taken by the California Department of Water Resources during winter months to measure snow depths and determine the amount of spring runoff—Sierra snow is a water source of great importance in California. In a short time you cross the PCT (11,160/2.0) and a few steps later the pass. You now follow the description in the last paragraph of T116.

Eastbound Cottonwood Pass Trail Log

T116	PCT/pass	11,160	0.0
	cabin lateral	9960	2.4
	4-way jct	9940	1.2
	Kern Plateau parking lot	9940	0.2

T115   Saddles, Ridges, Passes and Kern Peak Backpack

This trip explores the serenely picturesque northwest mountains, valleys and waterways of Golden Trout Wilderness on the Kern Plateau. It involves pathfinding skills over a roller-coaster route which climbs 2860 feet to its highest, most inspiring wonder—Kern Peak.

Distance   47.8 miles, loop trip
Steep Ascents   0.1 mile
Elevation Gain   8935 feet
Skills   Intermediate route finding; Class 2 climbing
Seasons   Spring, summer, fall (Wilderness permit required)
Maps   USGS 7.5 min *Cirque Pk, Johnson Pk, Kern Pk*
Trailhead   88. See car tour T109.
Description   The beginning of this trip is

described in T113 & T114.

Westbound Cottonwood Pass Trail Log

T113	Kern Plateau parking lot	9940	0.0
	4-way jct	9940	0.2

Southeastbound Trail Pass Trail Log

	4-way jct	9940	0.0
	abandoned trail section	10,080	1.3
T114	Trail Pass/PCT	10,500	0.6
	Templeton Trail extension	9400	2.1

Mulkey Stock Driveway	9340	0.2
gap	9580	2.1
South Fork Kern River	9280	0.8
McConnel Meadow Tr	9030	0.6
Siberian Trail lateral	8950	1.5
Siberian Pass Tr	8930	1.0
Chickenfoot jct	8900	0.3
Bear Meadow Tr	8895	0.3
Volcano Tr	8890	0.6

The left fork, the *Volcano Trail,* takes you southwest through a stand of lodgepole pines over a toe of basaltic flow, then out of the forest to a right turn onto the flood plain of Golden Trout Creek. Two paths at present lead to a creek crossing. Choose the one heading west toward the saddle south of the red cinder cone known as "Groundhog." The path takes a diagonal swath through a young grove of pines and encroaching willows to cross the creek where destination signs are tacked low and easily missed on creek-side pines.

After the ford, your route skirts the bank upstream and joins a trail marked by a large blaze with an X: the stream crossing of the alternate path. The trail leaves the creek, ascends gently west, then moderately up the slope at the right of talus rubble to the saddle (9140/1.0), the least gain of your roller-coaster climbs. Superimposed on the granite knob directly to the northwest sits Ground-hog Cinder Cone. You have been walking across some of its finely-ground ejecta since crossing the creek.

Next, the trail declines southwestward via several linked zigzags to the edge of Volcano Meadow. Here, marked by blazes on infrequent, lone trees, your route crosses the sometimes soggy south end of the meadow to a 4-way junction (8705/1.0): Volcano Trail continues northwest across the meadow to eventually meet the Golden Trout Trail; Right Stringer Trail heads west, then climbs southwest into the wild country between Golden Trout Creek and Ninemile Creek—country best left undisturbed for nature's creatures; and your route, *Cold Meadow Trail,* leads south (left) from here.

Your path, unraveled into multiple treads

Trail Pass

by cattle, ascends through the forest near Left Stringer's east bank, then abruptly turns right at a "Trail" sign (8980/1.1), where it is met by Bear Meadow Trail, which looks like a cowpath as it continues up the east bank. Turning west, your route quickly fords the stringer where another blaze and X mark the crossing. It ascends moderately, then easily along the creek's fork, through a small meadow, then crosses the fork to its east side. The grade increases, then moderates as the path approaches and crosses the saddle (10,190/1.7) on the crest of the Toowa Range. (A destination sign on the saddle indicates a route to West Stringer and Kern River. It is mostly pathless to Sidehill Meadow, where it becomes a mapped trail to Jordan Hot Springs Trail.)

Your route, the Cold Meadow Trail, sheers away toward the southeast. Soon the forest thins, then the path descends and curves across west-facing manzanita-clad slopes. This descent ends just downslope from a small granite outcrop. From there the path makes a short ascent, rounds a spur ridge and contours above gooseberry bushes clumped about a spring. The contour ends at a lopped-off ridge top (9980/2.0) with views of the basin to the southeast. Cold Meadows, your next destination, is nestled against the bottom of the ridge and out of view.

The trail between this ridge top and Cold Meadows has long since disappeared, though you may find pieces of the switchbacks indicated by the Forest Service map. (The topo map trail is incorrect.) Until the trail is rebuilt, make your own switchbacks down the steep slopes east-southeast to Cold Meadows where a few campsites are located along the west rim.

Notice the topography across the meadow. Your trail picks up again at the tip of a south-trending, bouldery ridge which descends along the top third of the meadow's east edge. Cross the grassy plain with its iron-stained springs and meadow brook to that point (9200/1.7). Curve around the base of this ridge, between it and a branch of Cold Meadows Creek. In 0.3 mile turn right at a campsite to cross the branch, curve south, then cross another branch of the creek. Here you climb southwest, then turn sharply northeast to a saddle (9750/1.3) on a ridge separating Cold and Redrock meadows. A weathered sign on a trailside tree comically refers to this saddle as *Gooney Ridge*.

Still on Cold Meadows Trail, you descend generally southeast via zigzags and switchbacks, soon revealing in the basin the contrasting "putting green" of Redrock Meadows against the tarnished copper bald of Indian Head monolith. You are guided by ducks now and then where the trail becomes vague in the basin. Heading southeast, then south, you hop a branch of Red Rock Creek and converge with *Indian Head Trail* (8670/2.0), where Cold Meadows Trail ends. Then ford the middle branch of Red Rock Creek, pass right of a roofless cabin to a meeting of three trails (8650/0.1): Indian Head Trail, north, which you leave; River Spring Trail, south; *Templeton Trail,* northeast, onto which you turn. Camping is excellent here before your 2860-foot climb to Kern Peak, but flats are available for dry camping at Kern Peak saddle, also. Now find the description in T90 for your hike to Kern Peak.

Northeastbound Templeton Trail

T90	Indian Head/River		
	Spring trs	8650	0.0
	saddle	10,260	2.6
	Kern Pk	11,510	2.1

On this trip, you do not stash your back-

Kern Peak from Trail Pass Trail near Tunnel Meadow

packs as suggested in T90, but instead tote them laboriously up the headwall to the wonderous views from Kern Peak. From the peak you can pick out nearly all of the mountains and meadows of the plateau; most of the peaks of the surrounding ranges; and, on clear days, many peaks on distant ranges.

Thoughts drift and time dissolves in such a place, but when you must leave, briefly descend on the south side, then turn right to follow ducks that lead down boulders to the peak's west side. Here you find the gravelly, well-defined **Kern Peak Trail.** Follow the trail, which crosses over a minor spur to the north face, then zigzags down to timberline. You make a short traverse northeast, then descend along a north-northeast ridge to a saddle (10,500/1.4). On the saddle you curve north, then drop by switchbacks into the headwaters bowl of Kern Peak Stringer.

After fording the stringer below a meadow cuddled in the lap of an ancient cirque, you turn to follow the creek's tumbling descent down a narrow, flower-bedecked slot, first on its left bank, then its right, then back on its left again (9000/2.0). The sylvan canyon spreads at this point and the trail fades. Here the topo map shows a trail continuing along Kern Stringer to the Ramshaw Trail—what is there is a series of cow paths. Do not follow these, but leave the creek and head northwest along gently sloping country. Cross a minor crease, then ford a creek from Bear Meadow. The trail from here to the junction had disappeared, but in 1990 the old route was remarked with ducks and newly blazed trees.

On this blazed trail, you climb to an isolated grove of juniper trees and ascend near ball-bearinglike scree to a saddle (9060/1.0), south-southwest of tree-hidden Red Hill. Pass through a stock fence gate, curve around Red Hill for 0.5 mile, then head directly north to the Chickenfoot junction (8900/1.2), where you meet your incoming path and complete the first loop of your double loop trip. Retrace your steps northeast along **Trail Pass Trail,** pass the guard station and tunnel site to a forked junction (8930/0.3) where you leave your incoming route and turn onto

the **Siberian Pass Trail,** the left fork.

After the taxing, though rewarding, journey over Kern Peak, you now have an easy stroll up a narrow canyon, slowly gaining elevation, with Golden Trout Creek softly murmuring to your left. The unnatural-looking trench to the right was dug in the 1880s by Chinese laborers to divert water from Golden Trout Creek to South Fork Kern River to supply more water to South Fork Valley ranchers, 50 air miles south. The project was abandoned, but the trench is still evident. Good-sized lodgepole pines growing in its confines attest to its age. In 1.3 miles you cross the creek. You can still see the disturbed ground marking the beginning of the ditch.

Hiking north along the left bank, you pass several campsites and walk next to the creek from time to time. At length you pass the junction (9400/3.0) of Barigan Stringer Trail to Rocky Basin Lakes (not shown on the topo). You pass a spring watered patch of grass, then ford the seasonal water of Barigan Stringer, a meadow-beaded brook, the outlet of Rocky Basin Lakes. Continue north into Big Whitney Meadow, a vast mosaic landform with broad sweeps of sand, sagebrush and grass laced with numerous, winding creeks that form the headwaters of Golden Trout Creek. To the north, the crest of Siberian Outpost and the rounded shoulder of barren Cirque Peak form the backdrop.

Continuing on the gently rolling terrain, you curve east to pass the Little Whitney Trail (9740/2.4), access route to its namesake meadow and the main route to Rocky Basin Lakes. Then you quickly meet and turn right on the western terminus of **Cottonwood Pass Trail** (9740/0.1), which takes you over Cottonwood Pass, the last ascent on your trip of saddles, ridges, passes and peak.

Eastbound Cottonwood Pass Trail Log

T114	Siberian Pass Tr	9740	0.0
	1st switchback	10,000	2.4
T116	Cottonwood Pass/PCT	11,160	2.0
	cabin lateral	9960	2.4
	4-way jct	9940	1.2
	Kern Plateau parking lot	9940	0.2

T116   PCT Cottonwood Crest Backpack: Trail Pass to Cottonwood Pass

Golden snags and checkered bark of foxtail pines, and muted white, abrasive granite fragments coincide along this trip as foregrounds to background panoramas of plateau meadows, jagged-toothed High Sierra peaks, and distant horizons of desert and Southern Sierra ranges.

Distance   10.7 miles, loop trip
Steep Ascents   None
Elevation Gain   1220 feet
Skills   Easy route finding
Seasons   Spring, summer, fall (Wilderness permit required)
Map   USGS 7.5 min *Cirque Pk*
Trailhead   88. See car tour T109.
Description   The beginning of this trip is described in T113.

Westbound Cottonwood Pass Trail Log

T113 Kern Plateau parking lot	9940	0.0
4-way jct	9940	0.2

Southeastbound Trail Pass Trail Log

4-way jct	9940	0.0
abandoned trail section	10,080	1.3
Trail Pass/PCT	10,500	0.6

From the pass the *PCT* ascends gently northwest amid foxtail pines and talus, switchbacks twice and then rounds the north-facing slopes of 11,605-foot Trail Peak. Portals in the forest frame exhilarating views of Mount Langley and its precipitous ridges, and nearer views of Poison Meadow below. Your trail continues west past a path (10,740/1.3) which descends to a corral and meadowside campsites, then immediately crosses cold Corpsmen Creek. In about ⅓ mile the PCT leaves the slopes of Trail Peak to intersect the crest at a saddle (10,740/0.6), and traverses southwest along a route that offers sweeping views of Mulkey Meadows below. The path then curves northward, passing small meadows. Their seeps and springs combine to become the headwaters of South Fork Kern River, a stream that meanders through three wildernesses, gathering the

Golden Trout Creek near Big Whitney Meadow

flow of creeks on the east side of the gentle plateau, until it courses off the south end in a harsh area known as "the roughs."

Foxtail pines shade you, parting occasionally to reveal views of the Great Western Divide mountains. In time you round a watershed divide and pass through a west-facing meadow. This meadow's drainage finds its way into Golden Trout Creek where it travels west to tumble off Kern Plateau's basaltic rim into the glacial-carved trench of the North Fork Kern River—the river's main branch. After hiking over a spur-ridge saddle, you meet **Cottonwood Pass Trail** at Cottonwood Pass (11,160/2.9). A favorite place to overnight is Chicken Spring Lake, 0.6 mile

farther ahead on the PCT. Campsites abound there and on weekends, so do people using them.

Your route turns right, crosses the pass, and descends east on a rickrack of switchbacks which are divided midway by a flower-speckled, willow meadow. After the last of the switchbacks, the path gently declines through woods, crosses Cottonwood Pass's creek, passes a lateral path (9960/2.4) to a Forest Service cabin and turns left to cross another creek. A seemingly endless walk ensues north of Horseshoe Meadow. Finally the path angles up to a 4-way junction (9940/1.2), where the trail leads to the hiker's parking lot (9940/0.2).

T117   Horseshoe to Templeton Meadows Backpack
With Excursion CC: Kern Peak

Wide open Golden Trout Wilderness country unfolds in this journey. Mid-spring you discover vividly green meadows luxuriant with wildflowers and snowmelt runnels, which lace the nearby slopes as well. The proximity of Golden Trout Creek and South Fork Kern River and the superb hike up Kern Peak make this an excellent three-season outing.

Distance 32.2 miles, loop trip
Steep Ascents None
Elevation Gain 3290 feet
Skills Easy route finding
Seasons Spring, summer, fall (Wilderness permit required)
Maps USGS 7.5 min *Cirque Pk, Johnson Pk, Kern Pk, Templeton Mtn*
Trailhead 88. See car tour T109
Description The beginning of this trip is described in T119 & T118. (If you are unable to secure a permit to use Cottonwood Pass Trail, switch to Trail Pass Trail and follow the first parts of T113 & T114 to the Ramshaw Trail.)

Westbound Cottonwood Pass Trail Log

T119	Kern Plateau parking lot	9940	0.0
	4-way jct	9940	0.2
	cabin lateral	9960	1.2
T118	Cottonwood Pass/PCT	11,160	2.4
	switchback	10,000	2.0
	Siberian Pass Tr	9740	2.4

Turning left on the **Siberian Pass Trail**, your route heads south along the side of Big Whitney Meadow and immediately passes the Little Whitney Trail (9740/0.1). While your path leads above Golden Trout Creek, it crosses a side stream with campsites up-canyon, then it edges near the creek, which enters a canyon and ducks around car-size boulders by a fractured granite slope. The route next crosses mossy Barigan Stringer, the outlet creek of Rocky Basin Lakes, then passes Barigan Stringer Trail (9400/2.4) descending from the lakes.

You descend gradually, pass a few campsites, then ford the softly tumbling creek. To the east of the trail a 1.5-mile ditch remains; for its history and that of the tunnel site ahead, see T114. In a short time you reach the junction (8930/3.0) with **Trail Pass Trail** and turn right onto it.

Your west heading trail dips as it crosses

216

EXPLORING THE SOUTHERN SIERRA: EAST SIDE

the point where the tunnel collapsed. It next passes a compound in which several 1925 vintage buildings make up the Tunnel Guard Station, occupied occasionally by the summer back-country ranger. Just a few minutes' stroll beyond it brings you to a chickenfoot junction (8900/0.3). Here the Trail Pass Trail ends and gives rise to southwestbound Golden Trout Trail, southbound "middle claw" Kern Peak Trail and southeastbound Ramshaw Trail. At this point you can choose to climb the peak or skip the excursion description and turn left on the Ramshaw Trail.

Excursion CC: Kern Peak

The hike up the trail to this peak is a must for all Southern Sierra back-country explorers. The views as you climb the north face above timberline are dizzying, and, from the top, dazzling. On a clear day you can see north to the Kings-Kern Divide and south to the mountains rimming Los Angeles.

Distance   11.2 miles, round trip
Steep Ascents   0.2 mile
Elevation Gain   2610 feet
Skills   Easy route finding, Class 1–2 climbing
Map   USGS 7.5 min *Kern Pk*
Description   From the chickenfoot junction (8900/0.0), you hike south on the **Kern Peak Trail** for 0.5 mile, then ascend southeast to curve around Red Hill Cinder Cone, which you see framed by lodgepole pines to

Beaver dam, Ramshaw Meadows

your left. The first 2.0 miles of this trail disappeared years ago, but in 1990, the trees along the old trail were blazed and ducks were placed to reestablish the path. Passing through a stock-fence gate, you arrive at the "Pumiced Land" (dubbed thus by J. C. Jenkins, an incurable punster), a saddle of hard pack volcanic ejecta south of the cinder cone.

From the saddle (9060/1.2), you descend southeast next to scree into an isolated grove of junipers, then cross the creek coming down from Bear Meadow. Passing possible camp sites, you continue southeast for 0.4 mile, then curve south as you near Kern Peak Stringer and enter the stringer's narrow canyon. Here you quickly ford the creek (9000/1.0) as directed by a small arrow carved into a lodgepole pine.

Now hiking on the east bank among brambles and over logs, you cross a pair of flora-hidden creeks just prior to fording the stringer to its northwest side, 0.6 mile from the last ford. Here you ascend moderately and, in another 0.6 mile, again hop over Kern Peak Stringer, this time below a meadow-floored cirque.

Beyond, the trail ascends southeast via switchbacks out of the canyon to a broad saddle (10,500/2.0) on a spur ridge. Curving southwest, it climbs the spur, then below the crest, it traverses amid foxtail pines to tree line. The off-set roof of the summit's dismantled lookout soon becomes visible. With spectacular views on the last segment, the wide, gravelly, well-defined path zigzags among boulders on Kern Peak's north face, then climbs over a minor spur to the west of the peak where it disappears. Ducks delineate your ascending route amid boulders, to the peak's south side and up to the platform that remains on the top (11,510/1.4).

After signing the register found in a metal container by the platform, scan the horizon. You can see the sculptured Great Western Divide topped by Coyote Peak directly west; the muted reds of Kaweah Peak over barren Boreal Plateau, northwest; the haunting Mount Whitney group to the left of bouldery Langley and Cirque peaks, north; the elongated Sierra crest with Olancha Peak, east; and the montage of meadows, valleys and mountains of the surrounding Kern Plateau below.

(For a shortcut on your return trip, after the third ford of Kern Stringer, continue along cow paths on either side of the creek until you meet and turn right onto the Ramshaw Trail.)

      *   *   *   *   *

Your route on the ***Ramshaw Trail*** southeast of the chickenfoot junction drops next to South Fork Kern River past a large campsite. Then it veers away to cross slopes of pumice that decline from Red Hill Cinder Cone to the right, and leads through a stockfence gate. Beyond, it briefly descends, then levels off, emerges from the forest and commences a long stretch alongside Ramshaw Meadows on a sandy, dusty tread. Hikers from Kern Peak Excursion join the route where it crosses Kern Peak Stringer (8700/ 1.3).

Immediately to your left, the sagebrush meadow is pierced by a snow survey pole, then a section is fenced and signed *Resource Restoration Area, Closed to Grazing.* Out in the meadow just north of the fence, the South Fork Kern River balloons into a doubledammed beaver pond with a beaver den and accommodates a spring of teal.

You eventually pass a meadow-bound nubbin of granite, and from there your path continues southeast past fords of two brooks. On a few sandy slopes alongside the trail in Ramshaw Meadows, you may be privileged to see ground-hugging tufts with tiny, white star-centered, lavender flowers. They are *Abronia alpina,* the Ramshaw four-o-clock, which grow nowhere else in the world. These flowers are protected and monitored, and of course should not be picked; the trail was even rerouted to keep them from being trampled.

After awhile the trail leaves the meadow to climb amid pines south to a saddle and a stock-fence gate (8820/2.5). Beyond, at the base of this slope, the brook of Lewis Stringer glides on a glittering bed of mottled rose and russet, some of the colors of the small golden trout that dart about in it, as they do in most

every stream in the Golden Trout Wilderness. Southeast of the ford, your path leaves the woods just after an unsigned cut-off (8660/0.4) to Templeton Cow Camp departs to the south (not shown on topo maps). Your route bears southeast across Templeton Meadows, whose name remains from the time Benjamin Templeton grazed sheep here. Just after you cross a sluggish branch of Movie Stringer (named after a film was made here), look for three posts that protrude from the sagebrush: the posts mark a junction (8620/0.8) with the ***Templeton Trail,*** on which you turn acutely left.

Head north across sagebrush-covered Templeton Meadows aiming toward an island of boulder outcrops fronting distant Trail Peak. En route you again hop the branch of Movie Stringer; then, a half mile from the Ramshaw Trail junction, you intercept South Fork Kern River where it goosenecks east. The only way across this river in any season is to wade.

The trail climbs among the boulders of the outcrop, over an open plain, behind another set of rocks, through a stock-fence gate and past an adjunct of Ramshaw Meadows toward a low, forested saddle (8780/2.0). Thereafter, just inside the woods, the path skirts an extension of the meadow, then leaves the trees to cross a margin of sagebrush and dip through two often dry creeks. Your course then climbs the middle canyon of three prominent canyons. The gradient eases as the trail crosses a false saddle and contours around a drainage, then ascends again to a true saddle (9590/2.3).

Movie Stringer, Templeton Meadows

The ensuing gentle descent soon flattens and you leave the woods to arc northeast through a cattle-cropped lobe of Mulkey Meadows. Mulkey and Ramshaw were cattlemen of the late 1800s. Hike parallel to a torpid Mulkey Creek on a path that is sporadically overrun with new grass. Shortly you step across the influx of a steam from Bullfrog Meadow, then cut diagonally across Mulkey Meadow. After leaping a brook from a north canyon, you turn right at a junction (9340/2.6) onto one of the multiple tracks of **Mulkey Stock Driveway.** If you were to continue north for 0.2 mile, you would join Trail Pass Trail, a shorter route to Horseshoe Meadow by 1.9 miles.

The eastbound stock driveway route eventually reaches the influx of a brook near the mouth of its canyon. Several large campsites lie a few hundred yards upstream in the woods. Mulkey Meadows narrows ahead of you, confined by the bulk of both Trail Peak to the north and Sharknose Ridge to the south. After a lengthy traverse, which includes a climb over a sandy ridge whose slope above Mulkey Creek has sloughed to a precarious drop, your route turns northeast. The trail now climbs among trees, drops to cross a north meadow lobe and brook, returns to forest and crosses in front of Mulkey Cow

Camp, a hut built in 1923 which has two glassless windows crisscrossed by barbed wire. Passing through more meadow and forest, the trail finally turns north to climb the curves and zigzags to Mulkey Pass (10,380/3.9).

You now take one of the several paths north that twist down from the pass, veer northeast to cross an ephemeral creek, scuff along the sandy clearing of Round Valley and pass a closed leg of Trail Pass Trail (9870/0.8) that has been replaced. The dainty white, five-petaled flowers on reddish stems that grow here seem incongruous on these harsh gravels. Their common name, mouse tails, seems out of place, too, until you notice the shape of their basal leaves.

You cross the creeks draining Round Valley and Horseshoe Meadow in quick succession, leave Golden Trout Wilderness, pass a cattle pen and chute and reach paved Horseshoe Meadow Road (9915/0.9) at a wooden fish regulation sign tacked to a lodgepole pine. From here you tramp west along the pavement to Cottonwood Pass trailhead (9940/0.7). (Or you could take the use trail west of the cattle pen, wind south of the picnic and camping areas, join the Cottonwood Pass Trail and turn right to the trailhead.)

Lower Rocky Basin Lake

T118   Rocky Basin/Johnson Lakes Backpack
With Excursion DD: Johnson Peak

A captivating corner of Golden Trout Wilderness awaits those who seek these cerulean lakes, cupped in highly-fractured granite cirques. The splendor of these isolated lakes is enhanced by foxtail pines, which march to timberline.

Distance   33.9 miles, semiloop trip
Steep Ascents   None
Elevation Gain   4540 feet
Skills   Easy route finding
Seasons   Spring, summer, fall (Wilderness permit required)
Maps   USGS 7.5 min *Cirque Pk, Johnson Pk*
Trailhead   88. See car tour T109.
Description   The beginning of this trip is described in T119.
Westbound Cottonwood Pass Trail Log
T119   Kern Plateau parking

lot	9940	0.0
4-way jct	9940	0.2
cabin lateral	9960	1.2
Cottonwood Pass/PCT	11,160	2.4

Beyond the pass you hike southwest, in alpine terrain, barely losing elevation. You pass a fishing regulation sign and a snow survey tower. Then you curve west around foxtail-pine protected campsites and begin a plunge down the steep west-facing canyon, moderated by a total of 34 switchbacks and enhanced by views of Big Whitney Meadow, Johnson Peak and, across the unseen Kern trench, the Kaweahs. After several switchbacks, you traverse the north side of the bowl, then descend by a series of switchbacks to a crossing of Stokes Stringer. You continue to descend, then level out after the last group of switchbacks (10,000/2.0). You pass campsites, well back in the trees to the left, and meadow runnels. These runnels are usually not the best source of water in late spring. After hiking over a tree-shaded, boulder-scattered low ridge, you enter Big Whitney Meadow proper.

This large meadow has a forested island at its core surrounded by banks of sandy grit. In summer these banks are splashed with rosy swatches of tiny monkey flowers, often referred to as "belly flowers"—you need to be prone to inspect them. Your route crosses the gravelly banks and a meadow-draining creek, then passes a pole that indicates the terminus of a barely perceptible cut-off to Siberian Pass. Your trail skirts the north side of the island; there are camping possibilities here. The next ford, the main branch of Golden Trout Creek, supplies the best source of water en route at Big Whitney Meadow. The path continues west through the end of the Cottonwood Pass Trail (9740/2.4) on to *Siberian Pass Trail,* then forks right onto the *Little Whitney Trail* (9740/0.1).

Shortly after the junction, you find to your right, just off the Little Whitney Trail, a pine with a large slash. Upon closer inspection it resembles an old Basque carving. These turn-of-the-century carvings by lonely shepherds, once found throughout the Sierra, are rarely seen now. They usually include a Christian cross, which is lacking here.

After a few zigzags and an extended traverse on this long, gently ascending climb west, the trail crosses a crease with snowmelt runoff. Two campsites are located near the crease. Another series of zigzags and a traverse and the path crosses a ridge. Next it switchbacks down among boulders to a junction (10,083/2.5) where your route follows the *Barigan Trail* to the right. The trail climbs north, to the right of Barigan Stringer, which receives most of its water from Rocky Basin Lakes—when the lakes are low, Barigan is dry. The trail splits (10,360/1.1): equestrians cross the stringer and follow the old trail; hikers continue up the rocky path past a willow-filled tarn and around another shallow tarn. Ducks and blazes mark the ascending, boulder-strewn trail to the most eastern and largest of the aptly named Rocky Basin Lakes (10,780/1.0). Secluded campsites can be found on the northeast side of the lake and on the ledge to the west.

For a visit to the rest of the lakes, you head **cross-country** across the ledge to the south edge of the middle lake, cross the equestrian trail and continue next to the most southern of these shimmering lakes tucked in their glacial excavations.

To reach Johnson Lake, leave the most southern Rocky Basin Lake, ascend southwest up a prominent ravine; before the ravine ends turn left to cross over a bouldery ridge and scramble, still southwest, down and around a finger of the headwall. (To reach Funston Lake, beyond Golden Trout Wilderness, you scramble up to the Boreal Plateau on this headwall ridge.) You contour northwest to a drop to solitary Johnson Lake (10,640/2.0) and its campsites, another gem cuddled in an ice-scoured bowl. A climb up Johnson Peak makes a fitting climax to this trip.

Excursion DD: Johnson Peak

This peak, conical in shape but not volcanic in origin, stands like a watchman, guarding the northwest corner of the plateau's Golden Trout Wilderness, taking in panoramic views of the Boreal Plateau and the Kern Plateau.

Distance   2.6 miles, round trip
Steep Ascents   0.1 mile
Elevation Gain   735 feet
Skills   Intermediate route finding; Class 2 climbing (Class 3–4 pitches optional)
Map   USGS 7.5 min *Johnson Pk*
Description   From the south end of Johnson Lake (10,640/0.0), you contour on a **cross-country** route above the canyon that receives Johnson Lake overflow, ascending to reach the saddle (10,820/0.9) south of the lake between Johnson Peak and Peak 11,062. From the saddle climb southeast among the foxtail pines and around the boulders. Above timberline you scramble easily over boulders, then, from the north side, you ascend up the fractured rocks that cap the peak. After about 50 feet of clambering over large boulders on top, you negotiate the final stair steps to the summit of this prominent mountain (11,371/0.4). The Boreal Plateau fills the north views; Big and Little Whitney meadows enrich the east and south scenes.

*   *   *   *   *

On your homeward journey, retrace your route to the junction of the Cottonwood Pass Trail (9740/6.7). At this point you can choose to retrace your incoming route on the Cottonwood Pass Trail or explore a northern loop through the tip of Siberian Outpost, an additional 4.1 miles.

Johnson Lake and Peak

Continuing north on the lodgepole pine-shaded *Siberian Pass Trail,* you pass in 0.2 mile, a good sized campsite across the path from a meadow-edge spring. (The next reliable water is Chicken Spring Lake, 7.7 miles ahead.) After a stroll west of Big Whitney Meadow, you ascend gently to cross a ridge and pass the beginning of a faint cut-off trail to Big Whitney (9960/0.9). For several more miles you gain elevation on a gentle-to-moderate grade; switchbacks emplaced in the early 1970s ease these otherwise steep stretches to Siberian Pass (10,900/2.3). At the pass you leave Golden Trout Wilderness and Inyo National Forest for a 1.6 mile loop into Sequoia National Park.

You cross the two easternmost prongs of Siberian Outpost and their usually dry creeks—the area is appropriately named for its stark appearance—and reach a junction (11,139/0.7) with the *PCT,* onto which you turn right. Ascending eastward, you leave Sequoia National Park (11,320/0.9), reenter Golden Trout Wilderness and cross a seasonal creek. The trail becomes annoyingly sandy as it describes a horseshoe around a small cirque where a meadow and campsites replaced a shallow lake. You next descend to a ravine emanating from a saddle south of visible Cirque Peak. Just beyond the ravine, 1.9 miles from the Park border, you pass the route to ascend that summit (See T119).

Beyond, you slip over a spur ridge, and, with foxtail-framed views of Chicken Spring

Golden-mantled ground squirrel

Lake, switchback down to cross the lake's outlet stream (11,235/3.1). To view the lake in its granite cirque, leave the trail and stroll northwest to the shore. Heavily used campsites nearly ring the lake. Here your food is under attack: golden-mantled ground squirrels will snatch bits and pieces if they can before chatty Clark's Nutcrackers swoop in for a chunk or two.

Back on the PCT, you descend a short way to meet the Cottonwood Pass Trail (11,160/0.6) and return on your incoming route (9940/3.8).

T119   Chicken Spring Lake Backpack
With Excursion EE: Cirque Peak

Tucked in the hollow of a glacial-carved granite basin tempered with foxtail pines, this alpine lake attracts many campers. Although heavily used, the lake with its campsites scattered on all but the north shore, shows little abuse.

Distance   9.0 miles, round trip
Steep Ascents   None
Elevation Gain   1305 feet
Skills   Easy route finding
Seasons   Spring, summer, fall (Wilderness

permit required)
Map   USGS 7.5 min *Cirque Pk*
Trailhead   88. See car tour T109.
Description   This trip commences at the west end of the Kern Plateau parking lot

Evening primrose

(9940/0.0) on wide, gravelly *Cottonwood Pass Trail*. Along the path, travelers may see nosegays of low growing evening primroses. These showy flowers have large, yellow, heart-shaped petals. Beautiful by themselves, they are especially striking when growing with the contrasting purple of mat lupines.

You quickly enter Golden Trout Wilderness, which surrounds much of the excluded paved road. When a road (such as Horseshoe Meadow Road) penetrates a wilderness of which by law it cannot be a part, boundaries are drawn along the road's corridor—this is called "cherry stemming." You soon part company with hikers heading for Trail Pass at a 4-way junction (9940/0.2). Take the right fork.

A tree-posted sign prohibits campfires at Rocky Basin Lakes and Chicken Spring Lake. After a lengthy walk heading west near Horseshoe Meadow, you cross mushy ground on a built-up causeway, ford a creek and there pass a lateral (9960/1.2) to a meadowside cabin. Built as a stockman's line cabin around a century ago, it was refurbished and is now used by back-country rangers and snow surveyors. After a long, gentle incline beyond another creek crossing, you climb 18 switchbacks. Foxtail pines infiltrate the ranks of lodgepole pines, then you cross a wildflower-embellished meadow. Following a ladder of another 15 switchbacks you climb over Cottonwood Pass and arrive at the PCT junction (11,160/2.4).

Your route turns right onto the *PCT* to curve around the head of an alpine meadow west of the pass. The trail ascends among pines, then reaches the outlet stream of Chicken Spring Lake. Here your route turns right onto a use trail (11,235/0.6), heading north alongside the often dry stream. The tranquil lake scene (11,242/0.1) is an invitation to linger. The burned tree on the west shore which was struck by lightning in the summer of 1989 makes a myth of the long held belief that lightning strikes the tallest object in an area.

Excursion EE: Cirque Peak

Breathtaking views await those who venture up the slopes of this lofty peak. It sits on the John Muir/Golden Trout Wilderness border, thereby qualifying half the peak as the highest point in the Golden Trout Wilderness. The route stretches above timberline into tame boulder fields.

Distance   5.4 miles, round trip
Steep Ascents   0.2 mile
Elevation Gain   1665 feet
Skills   Easy route finding; Class 1–2 climbing (Class 3–5 pitches optional)
Description   Cross Chicken Spring Lake's outlet stream on the *PCT* (11,235/0.0), then switchback over a spur ridge overlooking the lake and traverse northwest among foxtail pines. You can leave the trail at any point after the peak's summit comes into view. It presents a rounded, westerly backside, drops off to the east and sits north of a crest-straddling saddle; the peak looks benign from the trail.

One easy *cross-country* route leaves the PCT (11,300/1.5) 0.1 mile before the trail dips into a ravine, which descends from the crest saddle. Climb north-northeast, then veer north toward the visible summit, weaving around boulders on a gravelly slope, then climbing over a few to reach the apex (12,900/1.2). Views from the top reveal incredible scenes in all directions, but the barren, bold mass of Mount Langley immediately north and the broad, semi-circular, ice-scooped cirque that sliced part of Cirque Peak remain the most dramatic.

Part 3
Appendix

After exploring the 1272 miles of trails and cross-country routes described in this book (equal to walking from San Diego to mid-Oregon on the coast highway); after gaining 278,730 feet in elevation (equal to 45 climbs up Mount Whitney from Whitney Portal); you have earned a refreshing dip!

Tripfinder Table

Trip Number	Activity								Season				Data						Type				
	Car	Bicycle	A-T Bike*	Day Hike	Climb	Backpack	Equestrian*	Side Trip	Winter	Spring	Summer	Fall	Distance (Miles)	Steep Assents (Miles)	Elevation Gain (Feet)	Route Finding	Climbing	Difficulty	One Way	Shuttle	Round Trip	Loop	Semi Loop
Section 1 Highway 58 to Highway 178																							
1	●								●	●	●	●	41.2	0	1100	E			●				
2						●	●			●		●	34.6	0	6600	E				●			
3								●	●	●			–	0	0	E		E					
4				●					●	●		●	3.2	0.5	1390	E	1-2				●		
Ex-A				●					●	●		●	6.8	0.7	2855	I	2				●		
5	●		●						●	●	●	●	26.4	0	5585	E			●				
6				●					●	●		●	2.2	0.6	1155	E	1-2				●		
7								●	●	●	●	●	–	0	0	E		E					
8	●	●							●	●	●	●	32.4	0	2060	E			●				
9				●			●		●	●	●	●	8.8	0	1630	E		M			●		
Ex-B				●						●	●	●	3.0	0.2	675	I	1-2				●		
10				●								●	5.6	1.5	2985	I	1				●		
11				●					●	●		●	4.8	0.6	2405	I	2				●		
12	●	●							●	●	●	●	19.7	0	2500	E			●				
13				●					●	●		●	3.4	1.4	2670	I	2-3				●		
14				●					●	●		●	5.8	1.5	3700	I	2				●		
15			●				●		●	●	●	●	7.8	0	1765	E	1	M-S			●		
16						●	●		●	●	●	●	20.6	0	2345	E				●			
17	●		●						●	●	●	●	30.7	0	4440	E							●
18				●					●	●		●	0.8	0	405	E	1				●		
19			●				●		●	●		●	5.6	0	340	E		E	●				
20						●	●		●	●	●	●	13.8	0	860	E			●				
21				●					●	●		●	4.8	0.3	1570	E	1-2				●		
22			●				●		●	●		●	8.2	0	805	E		M			●		
Ex-C				●					●	●		●	1.6	0.5	900	E	1				●		
23						●	●		●	●		●	15.4	0	1960	E				●			
24	●		●						●	●	●	●	21.1	0	2350	E							●
Section 2 Highway 178–Nine Mile Canyon/Kennnedy Meadows/Sherman Pass Road																							
25				●					●	●	●	●	0.5	0.2	420	E		M			●		
26				●			●		●	●		●	10.0	0	1535	E		M-S			●		

Trip Number	Activity								Season				Data						Type				
	Car	Bicycle	A-T Bike*	Day Hike	Climb	Backpack	Equestrian*	Side Trip	Winter	Spring	Summer	Fall	Distance (Miles)	Steep Assents (Miles)	Elevation Gain (Feet)	Route Finding	Climbing	Difficulty	One Way	Shuttle	Round Trip	Loop	Semi Loop
Ex-D					•				•	•		•	1.0	0.2	630	E	2				•		
27						•	•			•	•	•	28.3	0	4755	E				•			
Ex-E					•					•	•	•	1.2	0.4	975	I	2				•		
Ex-F					•					•	•	•	2.0	0.5	1435	I	2				•		
Ex-G					•					•	•	•	3.6	0.4	1375	I	2-3				•		
Ex-H					•					•	•	•	1.6	0.3	845	I	3				•		
Ex-I					•					•	•	•	1.0	0.2	725	E	2-3				•		
Ex-J					•					•	•	•	2.0	0.6	1710	I	2				•		
28	•		•							•	•	•	44.5	0	6280	E							•
29					•					•	•	•	3.8	1.0	2250	I	2-3				•		
Ex-K					•					•	•	•	1.6	0	655	I	2				•		
30					•					•	•	•	10.2	0.7	2525	I	3				•		
31					•					•	•	•	8.1	0.7	2415	I	2						•
32						•	•			•	•	•	23.3	0	2990	E				•			
Ex-L					•					•	•	•	1.8	0	250	E	1				•		
33			•				•			•	•	•	3.6	0	530	E		E			•		
34			•				•			•		•	4.8	0	600	E		M			•		
35			•				•			•		•	3.4	0	305	E		E			•		
36					•					•	•	•	13.0	1.3	3845	I	2-3				•		
Ex-M					•					•	•	•	2.6	0.3	1045	I	2-3				•		
37	•	•							•	•	•	•	32.8	0	1900	E			•				
38					•							•	5.2	1.6	2900	I-A	2				•		
39			•	•			•		•	•		•	10.6	0.5	3350	I		M-S			•		
40				•	•	•				•	•	•	23.4	0.2	5280	I				•			
41		•	•						•	•	•	•	3.0	0	790	E		E			•		
42						•			•	•		•	3.6	0.9	2547	E	2				•		
43		•	•				•		•	•	•	•	3.0	0.2	810	E		E-M			•		
44		•	•				•		•	•		•	6.8	1.1	2770	E		M-S		•			
45		•	•				•		•	•		•	4.8	0.2	1315	E		M			•		
46	•								•	•	•	•	16.9	0	150	E			•				
47								•	•	•	•	•	-	0	0	E		E			•		
48					•				•	•		•	2.2	0.8	1725	I	3				•		

| | Activity | | | | | | | | Season | | | | Data | | | | | | Type | | | | |
Trip Number	Car	Bicycle	A-T Bike*	Day Hike	Climb	Backpack	Equestrian*	Side Trip	Winter	Spring	Summer	Fall	Distance (Miles)	Steep Ascents (Miles)	Elevation Gain (Feet)	Route Finding	Climbing	Difficulty	One Way	Shuttle	Round Trip	Loop	Semi Loop
49				●						●		●	2.8	1.0	2545	I	2				●		
50				●						●		●	3.6	1.0	2815	I	2				●		
51				●					●	●		●	2.6	1.0	2765	E	2				●		
52	●	●								●	●	●	68.5	0	5635	E			●				
53						●				●	●	●	0.6	0	155	E		E			●		
54							●	●		●	●	●	9.5	0.2	2010	E						●	
55	●		●							●	●	●	30.5	0	2000	E							●
56				●						●	●	●	7.8	0.2	1390	E-I		M-S				●	
57				●						●	●	●	4.4	0	400	E		E			●		
58				●						●	●	●	9.0	0.2	955	E		M			●		
Ex-N				●						●	●	●	4.4	0.2	740	I		M-S			●		
59			●	●			●			●	●	●	7.8	0	2130	I		M-S			●		
Ex-O					●					●	●	●	1.4	0.2	500	I	2				●		
60						●	●			●	●	●	22.5	0.2	4560	E						●	
61						●	●			●	●	●	22.3	0.3	4810	E						●	
62							●			●	●	●	29.6	0.4	5012	E-I							●
Ex-P					●					●	●	●	3.4	0.3	1185	I	4				●		
63						●	●			●	●	●	9.2	0	1140	E							●
Ex-Q				●			●			●	●	●	6.2	0	1050	E		E-M			●		
Ex-R				●			●			●	●	●	3.8	0	410	E		E			●		
Ex-S				●			●			●	●	●	4.0	0.1	695	E		E-M			●		
64					●					●	●	●	4.0	0.2	1155	I	2-3				●		
65						●	●			●	●	●	11.7	0	2090	E						●	
66	●		●							●	●	●	20.5	0	1970	E							●
67					●						●	●	2.4	0.4	1130	I	1				●		
68			●	●			●			●	●	●	4.2	0.1	1125	E		M			●		
69			●	●			●			●	●	●	3.6	0	680	E		E			●		
70					●					●	●	●	3.4	0.8	1535	E	2				●		
71			●	●			●			●	●	●	2.6	0	730	E		E			●		
72				●			●			●	●	●	4.1	0	915	I		M		●			
73			●	●			●			●	●	●	7.8	0	450	E		E			●		
74				●			●			●	●	●	2.6	0.2	760	E		E-M			●		

Trip Number	Car	Bicycle	A-T Bike*	Day Hike	Climb	Backpack	Equestrian*	Side Trip	Winter	Spring	Summer	Fall	Distance (Miles)	Steep Assents (Miles)	Elevation Gain (Feet)	Route Finding	Climbing	Difficulty	One Way	Shuttle	Round Trip	Loop	Semi Loop
Ex-T				•						•	•	•	3.6	0.1	980	I	2				•		

Section 3 Nine Mile Canyon/Kennedy Meadows/Sherman Pass Road– Horseshoe Meadow Road

Trip Number	Car	Bicycle	A-T Bike*	Day Hike	Climb	Backpack	Equestrian*	Side Trip	Winter	Spring	Summer	Fall	Distance (Miles)	Steep Assents (Miles)	Elevation Gain (Feet)	Route Finding	Climbing	Difficulty	One Way	Shuttle	Round Trip	Loop	Semi Loop
75						•	•			•	•	•	22.7	0	3870	E						•	
Ex-U				•						•	•	•	4.0	0.2	1030	I	2				•		
76						•					•	•	26.8	0.2	3740	E							•
77						•	•			•	•	•	27.5	0.2	2410	I						•	
Ex-V				•						•	•	•	6.0	0.6	1185	I	2-3				•		
78			•				•			•	•	•	5.8	0	860	E		E			•		
79			•				•			•	•	•	7.8	0	1240	E		E		•			
80	•	•								•	•	•	8.1	0	930	E			•				
81				•						•	•	•	1.6	0.1	640	I	2				•		
82				•						•	•	•	2.0	0.1	750	I	2-3				•		
83				•						•	•	•	2.8	0.1	993	I	2				•		
84		•		•			•			•	•	•	9.8	0.1	1095	E		E-M				•	
85						•	•			•	•	•	28.8	0.6	4385	E-I						•	
86			•				•			•	•	•	3.0	0	505	E		E			•		
87						•	•			•	•	•	10.6	0	2640	E					•		
88						•	•			•	•	•	17.2	0	1140	E					•		
Ex-W				•						•	•	•	1.7	0.1	350	E	3				•		
89						•	•			•	•	•	30.2	0.4	5170	E							•
90						•	•			•	•	•	30.2	0.1	5510	I	2						•
91						•	•			•	•	•	11.7	0.2	1885	E						•	
92						•	•			•	•	•	22.2	0.6	4220	E-I							•
93							•			•	•	•	4.8	0.3	1605	I	2				•		
94		•				•	•			•	•	•	14.2	0.3	2865	E	1					•	
95		•	•				•			•	•	•	5.0	0	1170	E	1	E			•		
96						•	•		•	•		•	22.6	0.5	4765	E					•		
97				•					•	•		•	7.4	0.1	660	E		M		•			
98						•	•			•	•	•	29.1	1.0	7155	I							•
99			•						•	•	•	•	8.4	0	240	E		E			•		
100	•								•	•	•	•	54.6	0	1160	E			•				

Trip Number	Car	Bicycle	A-T Bike*	Day Hike	Climb	Backpack	Equestrian*	Side Trip	Winter	Spring	Summer	Fall	Distance (Miles)	Steep Assents (Miles)	Elevation Gain (Feet)	Route Finding	Climbing	Difficulty	One Way	Shuttle	Round Trip	Loop	Semi Loop
			Activity						Season				Data						Type				
101								•	•	•	•	•	0.4	0	0	E		E			•		
102						•	•			•	•	•	17.0	0	5260	E				•			
Ex-X				•						•	•	•	1.8	0.3	955	E	1-2				•		
103						•	•			•	•	•	22.0	0.6	6335	E	2				•		
104				•						•		•	10.0	3.0	8205	A	3				•		
105						•	•			•	•	•	35.0	0.3	6150	E							•
Ex-Y				•						•	•	•	1.8	0.2	965	E	1				•		
Ex-Z				•						•	•	•	1.8	0.5	1355	E	1-2				•		
Ex-AA				•						•	•	•	3.2	0.8	1480	E	1				•		
106						•	•			•	•	•	32.6	0	7000	E				•			
107							•	•	•	•	•	•	1.6	0	210	E		E			•		
108				•						•		•	3.0	1.0	3325	I	2				•		
109	•									•	•	•	22.8	0	6400	E			•				
110			•		•					•	•	•	7.2	0	1400	I		M-S		•			
Ex-BB				•						•	•	•	1.4	0.2	1895	I	2				•		
111			•		•					•	•	•	5.6	0	0	E		M		•			
112						•				•	•	•	12.4	0.6	2715	I	2				•		
113			•							•	•	•	6.0	0.4	1665	E	2				•		
114						•	•			•	•	•	40.6	0.5	6300	E							•
115						•				•	•	•	47.8	0.1	8935	I	2					•	
116						•	•			•	•	•	10.7	0	1220	E						•	
117						•	•			•	•	•	32.2	0	3290	E						•	
Ex-CC				•						•	•	•	11.2	0.2	2610	E	1-2				•		
118						•	•			•	•	•	33.9	0	4540	E							•
Ex-DD				•						•	•	•	2.6	0.1	735	I	2				•		
119						•	•			•	•	•	9.0	0	1305	E					•		
Ex-EE				•						•	•	•	5.4	0.2	1665	E	1-2				•		

*Car tours, day hikes and backpack trips are indicated that can double for all-terrain bicycle and/or equestrian use.

Ex-optional excursion of prior trip

E-Easy; I-Intermediate; A-Advanced; M-Moderate; S-Strenuous

Glossary

ACEC Designated Area of Critical Environmental Concern under the Bureau of Land Management's *California Desert Conservation Area Plan* of 1980

Aerie Nest of a bird of prey built in a high place

Alluvial fan Fan-shaped deposit of sediment formed when a stream's slope is abruptly reduced

Alluvium Sediment deposited by a stream or flash flood

Apiary Place where bees are kept for their honey

Arête Sharp, narrow crest of a mountain ridge, or a knifelike ridge separating two adjacent glaciated valleys

Bajada Apron of sediment along a mountain front created by connecting alluvial fans

Bedrock Solid rock underlying gravel, sand, etc.

Belay Secure a person or thing by rope

Blaze Bark scraped from a tree trunk to mark a trail. Also a diamond-shaped metal plate nailed to a tree

Blowdown Tree toppled by wind

BLM Bureau of Land Management

Cairn Large stack of rocks to mark a summit, junction or point of interest

Cirque Excavation made by glacial erosion

Cow path Path developed by repeated cattle use

Cross-country Across country without a trail

DFG Department of Fish and Game

Dry camp Campsite with no nearby water source

Duck Low stack of several rocks to mark a trail

Duff Decaying organic matter on forest floors

Escarpment Steep slope or cliff usually formed by faulting

Fault Fracture in rock strata caused by earthquake movement

Fire Safe Area Camp area where use of stoves and campfires are allowed during fire restriction stages

Glen Narrow, secluded valley

Granite Overall word for rock that solidified beneath the earth's surface and has varying amounts of minerals

INF Inyo National Forest

Massif Large block of earth

M'cyclepath Motorcycle trail open to all users

Meadow muffins Cattle excrement

Metamorphic rock Rock formed by alterations of preexisting rock

Multi-use Term used by agencies to designate areas open to many uses

Nose Projecting end of a hill or ridge

OHV Off-highway vehicle

Packer's campsite Ample campsite sometimes with crude tables, stools, and grill

Pass Passage between two mountains

PCT Pacific Crest National Scenic Trail which stretches from Mexico to Canada

Peakbagger Person who climbs peaks

Pluton Large body of rock formed beneath the earth's surface

Prospect Place where a mineral deposit was sought

Quail Guzzler Structure constructed to collect water for animals

Riparian Flora, usually trees, lining watercourse

Round trip Trip to a destination and back the same way

Saddle Low horizontal section on a ridge between two higher points

Scarp See escarpment

SCE Southern California Edison

Scissors junction Forks at a junction that spread like the blades of a scissors

Semiloop trip Loop with a repeated section

Scree Sheet of coarse, loose, decomposed granular debris on mountain slopes

Shuttle car Car left at the end of a one-way trip

Shuttle trip One way

Sierra crest High ridges and peaks forming the eastern edge of the Sierra Nevada Mountains

Snag Upright, dead tree

SNF Sequoia National Forest
Stock driveway Path used to drive cattle to and from cattle allotments
Stringer Watercourse synonymous with creek, stream, etc.
Swale Low area of land, sometimes marshy
Switchback Sharp-angled curve reversing direction of a trail on a steep slope
Tailings Rock debris left at a mine site
Talus Accumulation of rock debris at the base of a cliff
Tarn Small lake, usually one that fills a cirque
Topographic map Detailed map indicating elevations by contour lines
Trail biscuit Horse excrement

Traverse Cross the land usually at a slight angle
Trending Term used in this book as slopes decreasing in elevation toward a direction or canyons narrowing in width toward a direction
Use trail Nonconstructed trail developed by repeated use
USFS United States Forest Service
USGS United States Geological Survey
xeric Dry desertlike conditions
Xerophyte Plant adapted to very dry climate
Zigzag Short, wide curve in a trail on a slope, usually in a series.

Bibliography
Biology

Behler, John L., and F. Wayne King. 1979. *The Audubon Society Field Guide to North American Reptiles and Amphibians*. New York: Knopf, 743p.

Brown, Vinson, and George Lawrence. 1965. *The Californian Wildlife Region: Its Common Wild Animals and Plants*, Second Revised Edition. Healdsburg: Naturegraph Publishers, 129p.

Dodge, Natt N. 1963. *100 Desert Wildflowers*. Globe: Southwest Parks and Monuments Association, 58p.

Drummond, Roger. 1990. *Ticks and What You Can Do About Them*. Berkeley: Wilderness Press, 65p.

Fisk, Leonard O. 1969. *Golden Trout of the High Sierra*. Sacramento: California Department of Fish and Game, 15p.

Jaeger, Edmund C. 1969. *Desert Wild Flowers*, revised edition. Stanford: Stanford University Press, 322p.

Keator, Glenn, and Valerie R. Winemiller. 1980. *Sierra Flower Finder*. Berkeley: Nature Study Guild, 126p.

Klauber, Laurence M. 1972. *Rattlesnakes, Their Habits, Life Histories, and Influence on Mankind*, Second Edition. Berkeley: University of California Press, 1536p.

Mirov, Nicholas T., and Jean Hasbrouck. 1976. *The Story of Pines*. Bloomington: Indiana University Press, 148p.

Munz, Philip A. 1963. *California Mountain Wildflowers*. Berkeley: University of California Press, 122p.

Niehaus, Theodore F. 1974. *Sierra Wildflowers: Mt. Lassen to Kern Canyon*. Berkeley: University of California Press, 223p.

Russo, Ron, and Pam Olhausen. 1987. *Mammal Finder*. Berkeley: Nature Study Guild. 94p.

Ryser, Fred A. Jr. 1985. *Birds of the Great Basin, A Natural History*. Reno: University of Nevada, 604p.

Storer, Tracy I., and Robert L. Usinger. 1963. *Sierra Nevada Natural History*. Berkeley: University of California Press, 374p.

Sudworth, George B. 1967. *Forest Trees of the Pacific Slope.* New York: Dover (1908 reprint with new Foreword and Table of Changes in Nomenclature), 455p.

Thomas, John Hunter, and Dennis R. Parnell. 1974. *Native Shrubs of the Sierra Nevada,* California Natural History Guides:34. Berkeley: University of California Press, 127p.

Twisselmann, Ernest C. 1967. *A Flora of Kern County, California.* San Francisco: The University of San Francisco, 395p.

Udvardy, Miklos D. F. 1977. *The Audubon Society Field Guide to North American Birds: Western Region.* New York: Knopf, 855p.

Verner, Jared, and Allan S. Boss, et al. 1980. *California Wildlife and Their Habitats: Western Sierra Nevada,* General Technical Report PSW-37. Berkeley: Pacific Southwest Forest and Range Experiment Station, Forest Service, U.S. Department of Agriculture, 439p.

Wade, Dale A., and Jon K. Hooper. 1980. *California Rattlesnakes,* leaflet 2996. Berkeley: University of California, 7p.

Watts, May Theilgaard, and Tom Watts. 1974. *Desert Tree Finder.* Berkeley: Nature Study Guild. 61p.

Watts, Tom. 1973. *Pacific Coast Tree Finder.* Berkeley: Nature Study Guild, 62p.

Weeden, Norman R. 1986. *A Sierra Nevada Flora.* Berkeley: Wilderness Press, 406p.

Geology

Bergquist, J. R., and A. M. Nitkiewicz with geochronology by R. M. Tosdal. 1982. *Geologic Map of the Dome Land Wilderness and Contiguous Roadless Areas, Kern & Tulare Counties, California,* Miscellaneous Field Studies, Map MF 1395-A. Reston: U.S. Geological Survey, Map and text.

Collins, Lorence G. March, 1989. "Origin of the Isabella Pluton and Its Enclaves, Kern County, California." *California Geology,* 53–59pp.

Milliken, Mark. 1990. *Geology Field Trip to Mono/Owens Valleys Guidebook.* Bakersfield: U.S. Bureau of Land Management, 32p.

Ross, Donald C. 1986. *Basement Rock Correlations Across the White Wolf-Breckenridge-Southern Kern Canyon Fault Zone, Southern Sierra Nevada, California,* U.S. Geological Survey Bulletin 1651. Washington: U.S. Government Printing Office, 25p.

Ross, Donald C. 1987. *Generalized Geologic Map of the Basement Rocks of the Southern Sierra Nevada, California,* Open-File Report 87-276 (preliminary report). Menlo Park: U.S. Geological Survey, Department of the Interior, 28p.

Ross, Donald C. 1989. *Air Photo Lineaments, Southern Sierra Nevada, California,* Open-File Report 89-365 (preliminary report). Menlo Park: U.S. Geological Survey, Department of Interior, 23p.

Ross, Donald C. 1989. *The Metamorphic and Plutonic Rocks of the Southernmost Sierra Nevada, California, and Their Tectonic Framework,* U.S. Geological Survey Professional Paper 1381. Washington: U.S. Government Printing Office, 159p.

Samsel, Howard S. 1962. *Geology of the Southeast Quarter of the Cross Mountain Quadrangle, Kern County, California.* San Francisco: California Division of Mines and Geology. Map and text.

Schaffer, Jeffrey P., et al. 1989. *The Pacific Crest Trail, Volume 1: California.* Berkeley: Wilderness Press, 474p.

Sharp, Robert P. 1976. *Southern California, K/H Geology Field Guide Series.* Kerndall/Hunt Publishing Cmpany, 191p.

Tarbuck, Edward J., and Frederick K. Lutgens. 1984. *The Earth: An Introduction to Physical Geology,* Second Edition. Columbus: Merrill Publishing Company, 591p.

Troxel, Bennie W., and Paul K. Morton. 1962. *Mines and Mineral Resources of Kern County California,* County Report 1. San Francisco: California Division of Mines and Geology, 370p.

Whistler, David P. 1990. *Field Guide to the Geology of Red Rock Canyon and the Southern El Paso Mountains, Mojave Desert, California.* Los Angeles: Natural History Museum of Los Angeles County, 15p.

Wilkerson, Gregg, et al. 1990. *Kern Canyon Geology-Archaeology Field Trip Overview.* Bakersfield: U.S. Bureau of Land Management publication, 19p.

History

Austin, Mary. 1986. *The Land of Little Rain,* 6th printing. Original 1903. Albuquerque: University of New Mexico Press, 171p.

Barras, Judy. 1984. *Their Places Shall Know Them No More.* Bakersfield: Sierra Printers, Inc., 91p.

Brown, Henry M. August, 1984. "The Tunnel" *Los Tulares: Quarterly Bulletin of the Tulare County Historical Society.* 1–4pp.

Browning, Peter. 1986. *Place Names of the Sierra Nevada.* Berkeley: Wilderness Press, 253p.

Jenkins, J. C., and John W. Robinson. 1979. *Kern Peak-Olancha, High Sierra Hiking Guide #13.* Berkeley: Wilderness Press, 90p. (out of print)

Powers, Bob. 1971. *South Fork Country.* Los Angeles: Westernlore Press, 123p.

Powers, Bob. 1974. *North Fork Country.* Tucson: Westernlore Press, 159p.

Powers, Bob. 1981. *Indian Country of the Tubatulabal.* Tucson: Westernlore Press, 103p.

Walker, Ardis M. 1973. *Golden Trout and The Kern Water Shed.* Bakersfield: The Kern Plateau Association, 8p.

Wortley, Ken. 1987. *Historic Land of the Rio Bravo.* Kern River Valley: reprinted from the Sierra Rainbow.

Index